DILBERT
TURNS 30

Recent DILBERT® Books from Andrews McMeel Publishing

Cubicles That Make You Envy the Dead

Dilbert Gets Re-accommodated

I'm No Scientist, But I Think Feng Shui Is Part of the Answer

Optimism Sounds Exhausting

Go Add Value Someplace Else

I Sense a Coldness to Your Mentoring

Your New Job Title Is "Accomplice"

I Can't Remember If We're Cheap or Smart

Teamwork Means You Can't Pick the Side that's Right

How's That Underling Thing Working Out for You?

Your Accomplishments Are Suspiciously Hard to Verify

Problem Identified and You're Probably Not Part of the Solution

I'm Tempted to Stop Acting Randomly

14 Years of Loyal Service in a Fabric-Covered Box

Freedom's Just Another Word for People Finding Out You're Useless

Dilbert 2.0: 20 Years of Dilbert

This Is the Part Where You Pretend to Add Value

DILBERT

TURNS 30

DILBERT
BY SCOTT ADAMS
dilbert.com

Andrews McMeel
PUBLISHING®

INTRODUCTION

Can you believe *Dilbert* launched in newspapers thirty years ago??? A lot has changed since then. For example, in the early days of the *Dilbert* comic, readers complained that it was poorly drawn. Their criticisms made me feel sad. Now, after three decades of perfecting my artistic skills, I'm proud to say *Dilbert* is still poorly drawn, but at least it made me rich, and that takes a lot of the sting out of the insults. I call that progress.

A few years ago, I started drawing Dilbert without his iconic necktie. Now he only wears casual clothes at work. And Wally stopped bringing his own coffee mug to the office. Now he usually sports a Starbucks-looking disposable cup. As the world evolves, so too does the *Dilbert* universe. No longer are the engineers in Dilbert's office afraid of downsizing. They know engineers are in high demand, although that could change by the time you get around to reading this introduction.

One thing that hasn't changed, at least not enough, is the ubiquity of cubicles. Lots of workplaces have tried open office plans, and that has some advantages, but I hear complaints about the distractions and lack of privacy. I have mocked cubicles for thirty years straight, and it seems the cubicles won. But I'll keep after them. I'm not a quitter.

Another big change in the world is that my readers were human beings when the comic strip launched in 1989. Now most of you are cyborgs—part human and part smartphone. In the early days of the comic, the *Dilbert* characters had no smartphones, because obviously they had not yet been invented. Once smartphones became ubiquitous, I started including them in the strip, even when they were not part of the joke. Today, if I draw a scene in which someone enters a room, the other people in the room are likely to be looking at their laptops or phones. If you are like the *Dilbert* cast, and you are using technology to augment what your brain and body can do, you're definitely a cyborg, and a sexy one. I'm confident of that, because peer-reviewed scientific studies have proven that *Dilbert* readers are smarter and sexier than the average. I'll include a link to that study unless I forget.

What was I talking about?

S.Adams

Scott Adams

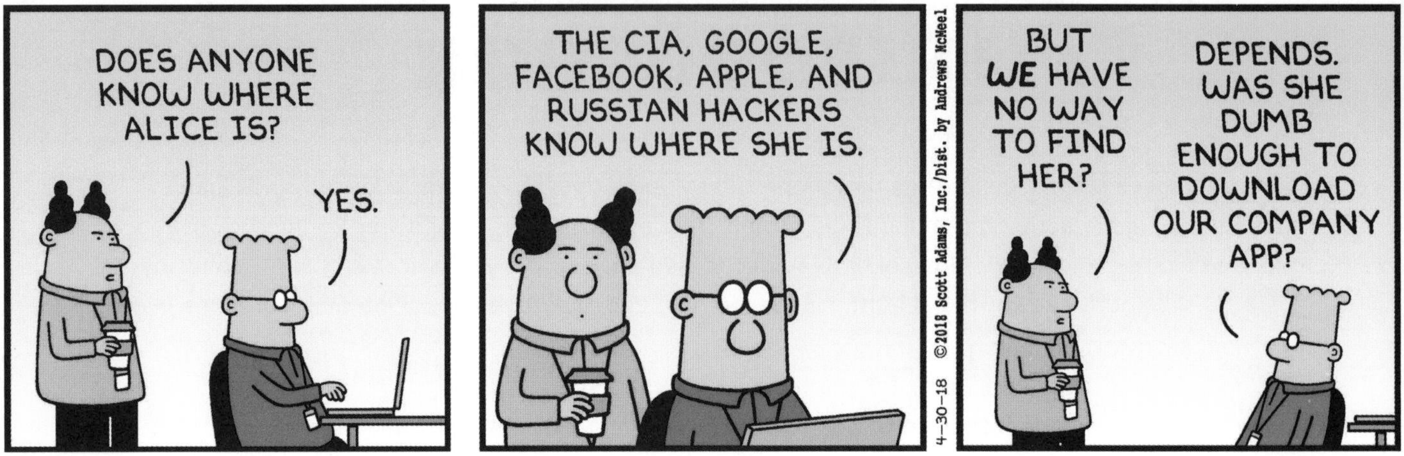
DOES ANYONE KNOW WHERE ALICE IS?
YES.
THE CIA, GOOGLE, FACEBOOK, APPLE, AND RUSSIAN HACKERS KNOW WHERE SHE IS.
4-30-18 ©2018 Scott Adams, Inc./Dist. by Andrews McMeel
BUT ***WE*** HAVE NO WAY TO FIND HER?
DEPENDS. WAS SHE DUMB ENOUGH TO DOWNLOAD OUR COMPANY APP?

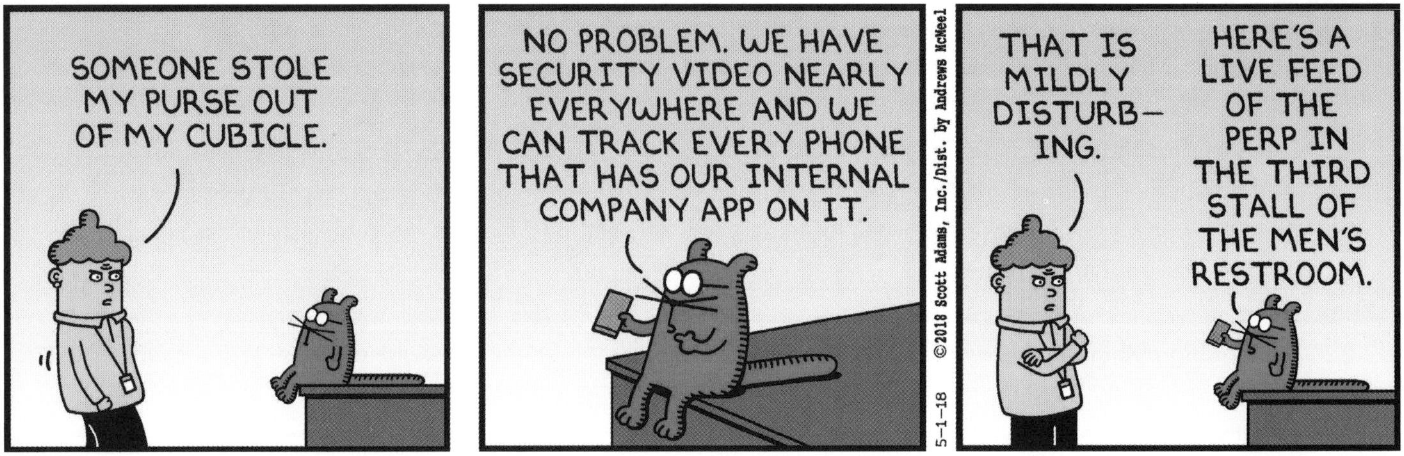
SOMEONE STOLE MY PURSE OUT OF MY CUBICLE.
NO PROBLEM. WE HAVE SECURITY VIDEO NEARLY EVERYWHERE AND WE CAN TRACK EVERY PHONE THAT HAS OUR INTERNAL COMPANY APP ON IT.
5-1-18 ©2018 Scott Adams, Inc./Dist. by Andrews McMeel
THAT IS MILDLY DISTURB-ING.
HERE'S A LIVE FEED OF THE PERP IN THE THIRD STALL OF THE MEN'S RESTROOM.

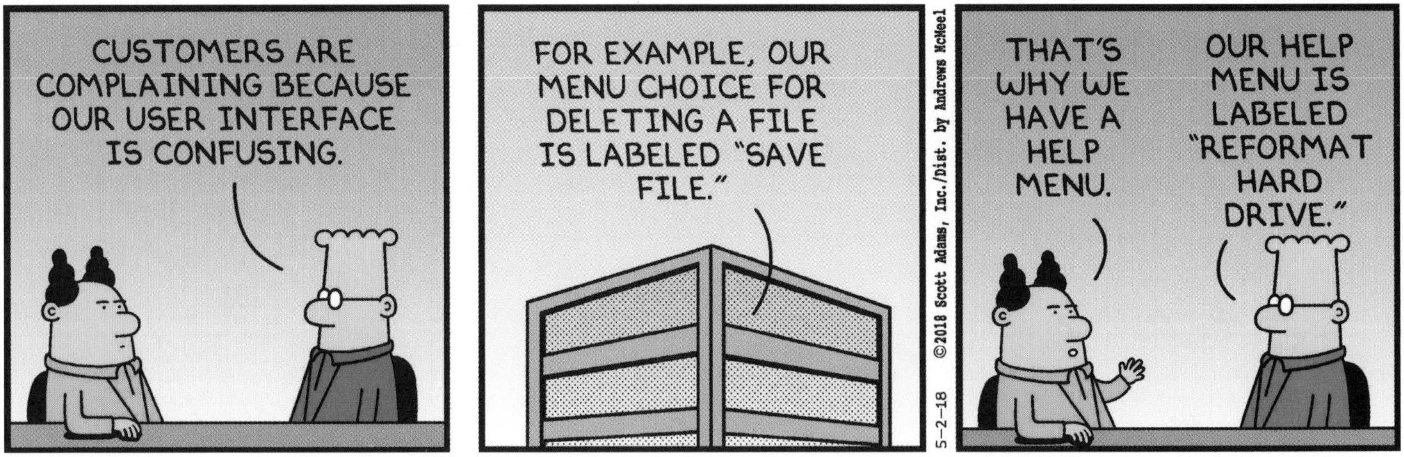
CUSTOMERS ARE COMPLAINING BECAUSE OUR USER INTERFACE IS CONFUSING.
FOR EXAMPLE, OUR MENU CHOICE FOR DELETING A FILE IS LABELED "SAVE FILE."
5-2-18 ©2018 Scott Adams, Inc./Dist. by Andrews McMeel
THAT'S WHY WE HAVE A HELP MENU.
OUR HELP MENU IS LABELED "REFORMAT HARD DRIVE."

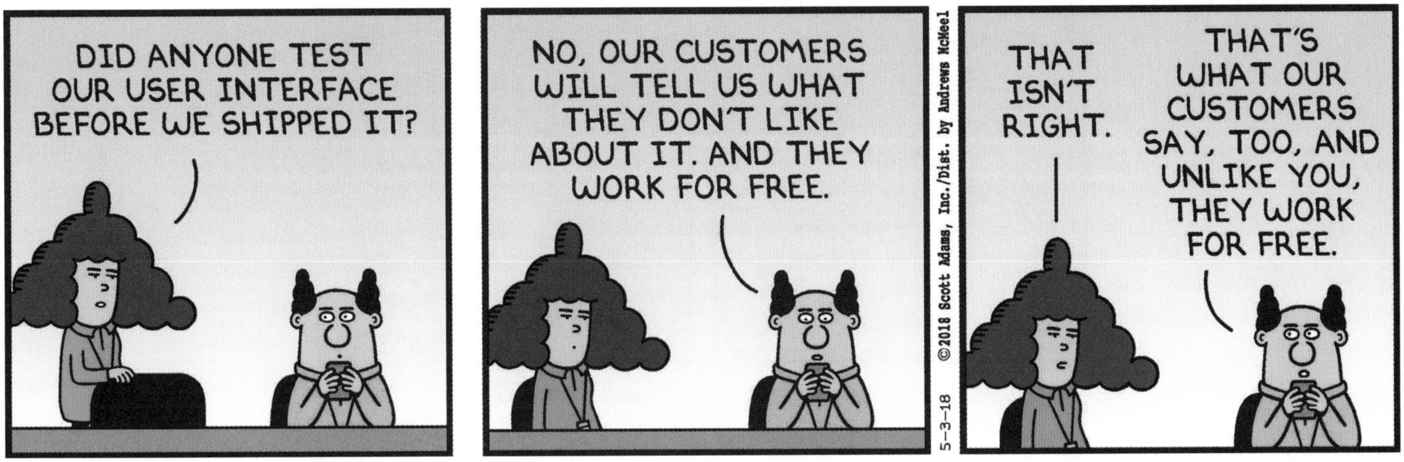
DID ANYONE TEST OUR USER INTERFACE BEFORE WE SHIPPED IT?
NO, OUR CUSTOMERS WILL TELL US WHAT THEY DON'T LIKE ABOUT IT. AND THEY WORK FOR FREE.
THAT ISN'T RIGHT.
THAT'S WHAT OUR CUSTOMERS SAY, TOO, AND UNLIKE YOU, THEY WORK FOR FREE.
5-3-18 ©2018 Scott Adams, Inc./Dist. by Andrews McMeel

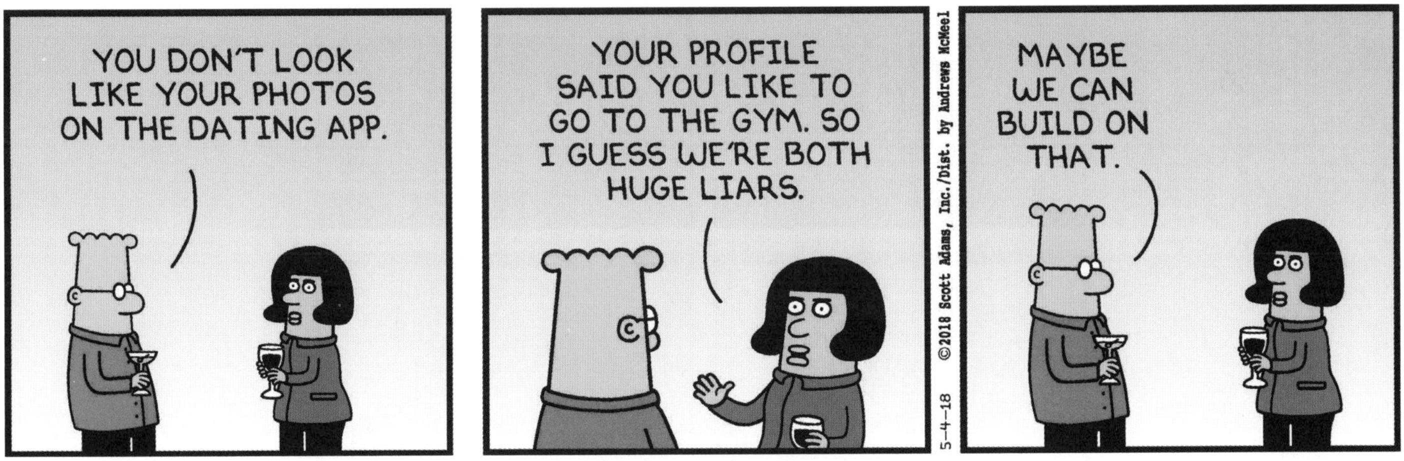
YOU DON'T LOOK LIKE YOUR PHOTOS ON THE DATING APP.
YOUR PROFILE SAID YOU LIKE TO GO TO THE GYM. SO I GUESS WE'RE BOTH HUGE LIARS.
MAYBE WE CAN BUILD ON THAT.
5-4-18 ©2018 Scott Adams, Inc./Dist. by Andrews McMeel

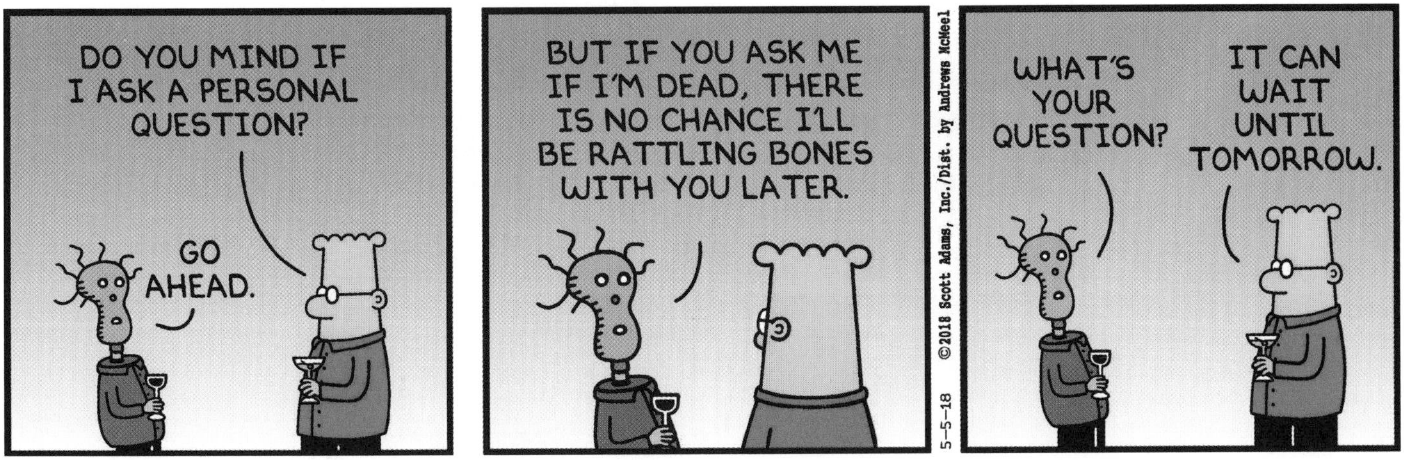
DO YOU MIND IF I ASK A PERSONAL QUESTION?
GO AHEAD.
BUT IF YOU ASK ME IF I'M DEAD, THERE IS NO CHANCE I'LL BE RATTLING BONES WITH YOU LATER.
WHAT'S YOUR QUESTION?
IT CAN WAIT UNTIL TOMORROW.
5-5-18 ©2018 Scott Adams, Inc./Dist. by Andrews McMeel

WOULD YOU LIKE TO BUY AN INSURANCE POLICY TO PROTECT AGAINST A HUMOROUS DEATH?
WHY WOULD I NEED IT?
WELL, LET'S SAY YOU'RE AT THE ZOO AND YOU DROP YOUR SUNGLASSES INTO THE LION PIT.
© 2018 Scott Adams, Inc./Dist. by Andrews McMeel
YOU LOWER YOURSELF INTO THE PIT TO GET THE SUNGLASSES, BUT THE LIONS GET TO YOU FIRST.
YOU DON'T WANT THE HEADLINES TO READ "POINTY-HAIRED IDIOT MAULED TO DEATH BY THE KING OF THE JUNGLE."
SO INSTEAD, THE MOMENT YOU DIE, MY AGENTS RUSH IN TO CREATE A NARRATIVE FOR THE MEDIA.
IN THIS CASE, WE MIGHT SPIN THE STORY AS "LOCAL MAN TEACHES ZOO HOW TO REDUCE FOOD COSTS."
5-6-18
ARE THE POLICIES AFFORD-ABLE?
YES, IF YOU WAIVE COVERAGE FOR MASCOT-RELATED DEATHS.

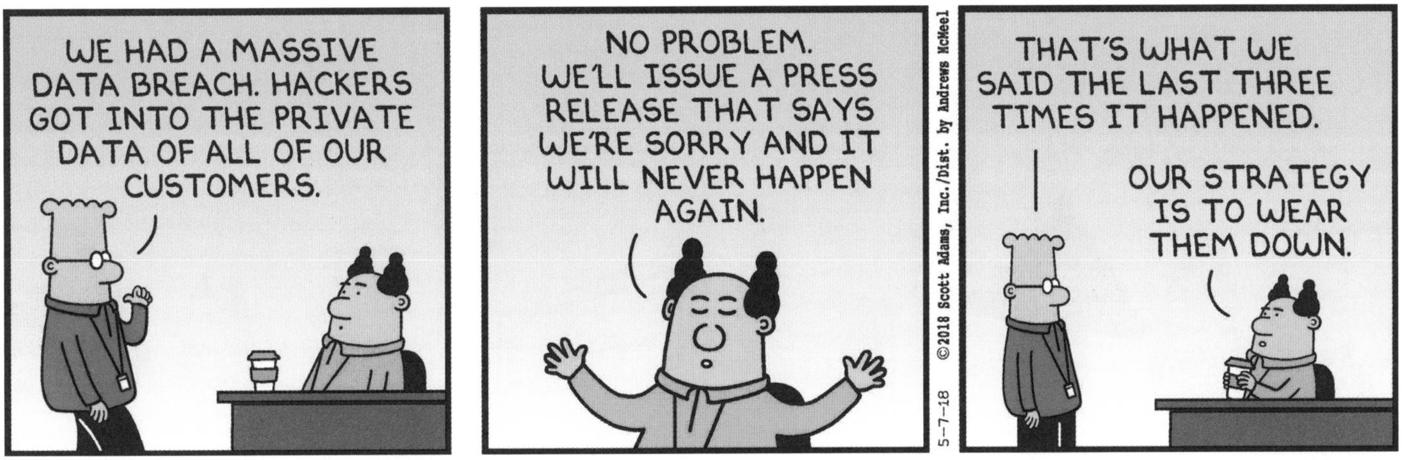
WE HAD A MASSIVE DATA BREACH. HACKERS GOT INTO THE PRIVATE DATA OF ALL OF OUR CUSTOMERS.
NO PROBLEM. WE'LL ISSUE A PRESS RELEASE THAT SAYS WE'RE SORRY AND IT WILL NEVER HAPPEN AGAIN.
5-7-18 ©2018 Scott Adams, Inc./Dist. by Andrews McMeel
THAT'S WHAT WE SAID THE LAST THREE TIMES IT HAPPENED.
OUR STRATEGY IS TO WEAR THEM DOWN.

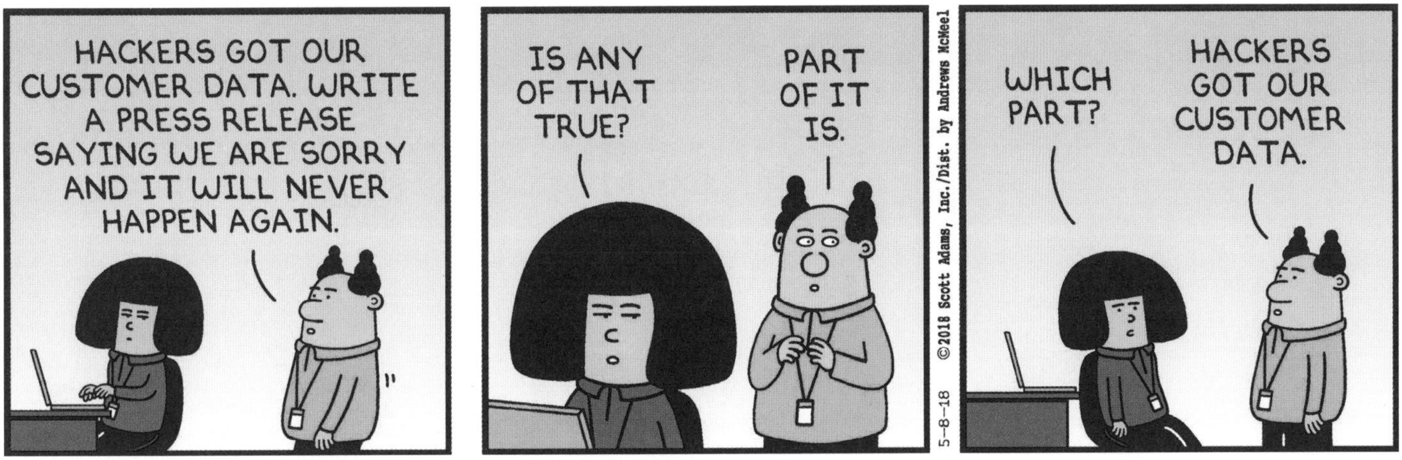
HACKERS GOT OUR CUSTOMER DATA. WRITE A PRESS RELEASE SAYING WE ARE SORRY AND IT WILL NEVER HAPPEN AGAIN.
IS ANY OF THAT TRUE?
PART OF IT IS.
5-8-18 ©2018 Scott Adams, Inc./Dist. by Andrews McMeel
WHICH PART?
HACKERS GOT OUR CUSTOMER DATA.

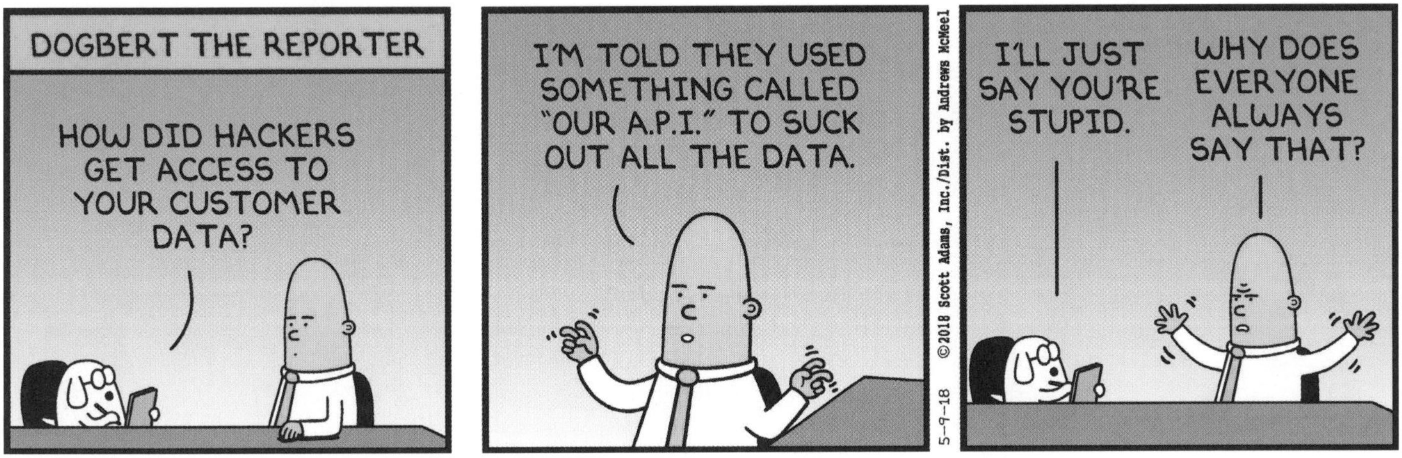
DOGBERT THE REPORTER
HOW DID HACKERS GET ACCESS TO YOUR CUSTOMER DATA?
I'M TOLD THEY USED SOMETHING CALLED "OUR A.P.I." TO SUCK OUT ALL THE DATA.
5-9-18 ©2018 Scott Adams, Inc./Dist. by Andrews McMeel
I'LL JUST SAY YOU'RE STUPID.
WHY DOES EVERYONE ALWAYS SAY THAT?

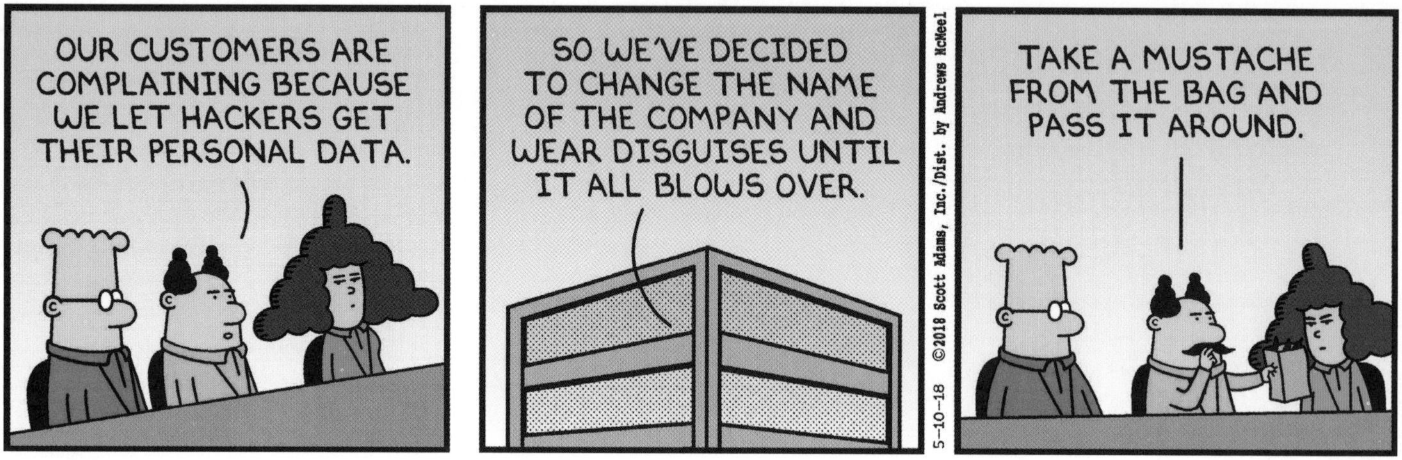
OUR CUSTOMERS ARE COMPLAINING BECAUSE WE LET HACKERS GET THEIR PERSONAL DATA.
SO WE'VE DECIDED TO CHANGE THE NAME OF THE COMPANY AND WEAR DISGUISES UNTIL IT ALL BLOWS OVER.
TAKE A MUSTACHE FROM THE BAG AND PASS IT AROUND.
5-10-18
©2018 Scott Adams, Inc./Dist. by Andrews McMeel

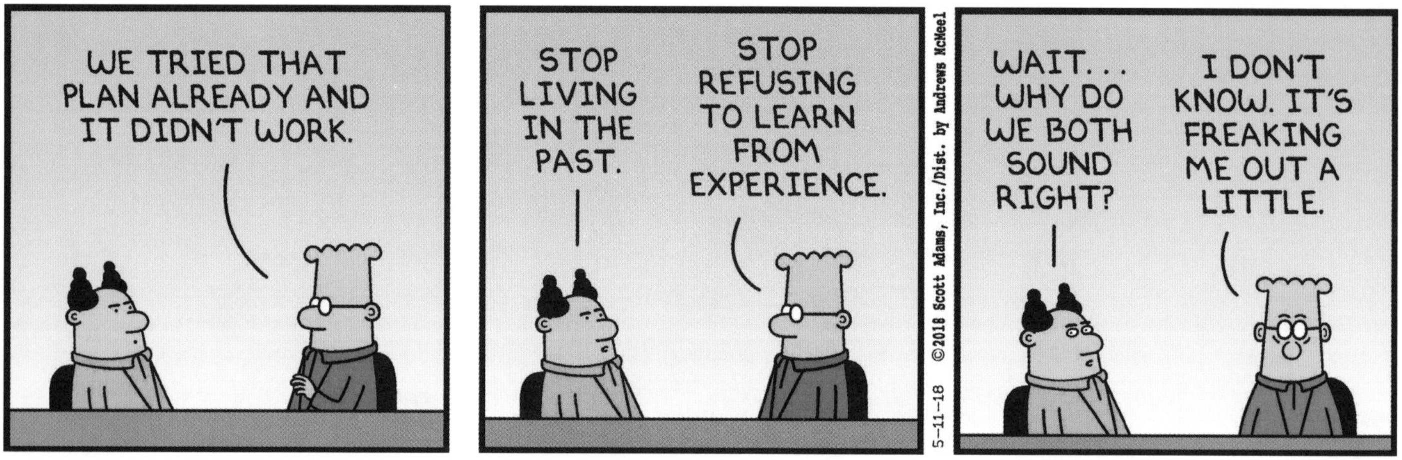
WE TRIED THAT PLAN ALREADY AND IT DIDN'T WORK.
STOP LIVING IN THE PAST.
STOP REFUSING TO LEARN FROM EXPERIENCE.
WAIT... WHY DO WE BOTH SOUND RIGHT?
I DON'T KNOW. IT'S FREAKING ME OUT A LITTLE.
5-11-18
©2018 Scott Adams, Inc./Dist. by Andrews McMeel

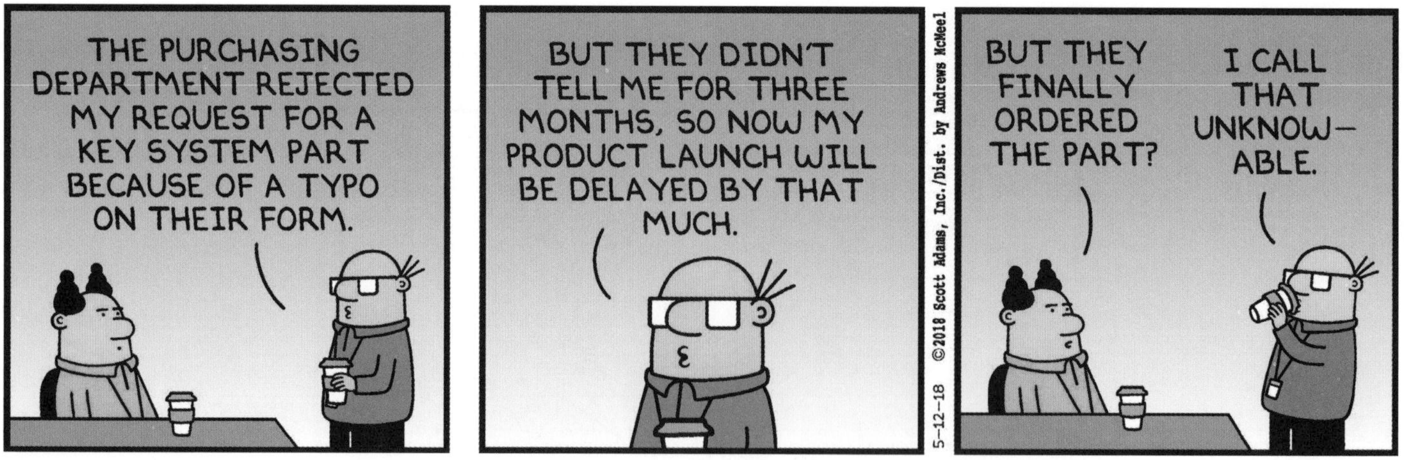
THE PURCHASING DEPARTMENT REJECTED MY REQUEST FOR A KEY SYSTEM PART BECAUSE OF A TYPO ON THEIR FORM.
BUT THEY DIDN'T TELL ME FOR THREE MONTHS, SO NOW MY PRODUCT LAUNCH WILL BE DELAYED BY THAT MUCH.
BUT THEY FINALLY ORDERED THE PART?
I CALL THAT UNKNOW-ABLE.
5-12-18
©2018 Scott Adams, Inc./Dist. by Andrews McMeel

WHAT'S THAT GADGET?
ARE YOU FREAKIN' SERIOUS?
YES.
OH. . . MY. . . GOD.
DO YOU NOT REMEMBER THE LONG DISCUSSION ABOUT THIS THING IN THE LAST MEETING?
ARE YOU TRYING TO GASLIGHT ME?
I HAVE NO PATIENCE FOR TROLLS! EAT DIRT AND DIE!
I JOINED THE PROJECT TODAY. THIS IS MY FIRST MEETING.
LIAR!
WELCOME TO THE TEAM.
© 2018 Scott Adams, Inc./Dist. by Andrews McMeel
5-13-18

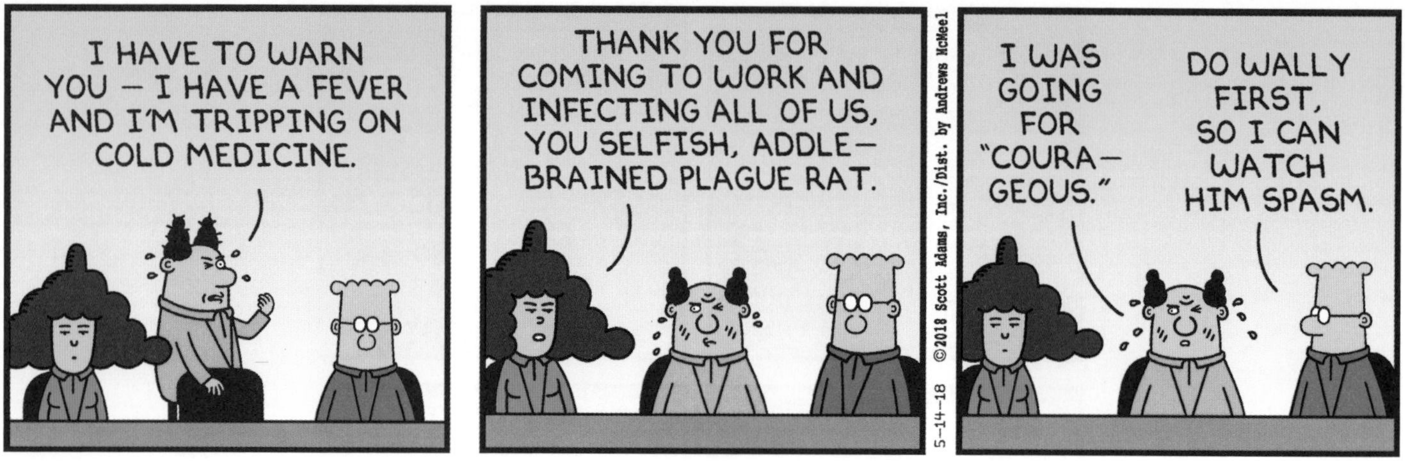
I HAVE TO WARN YOU — I HAVE A FEVER AND I'M TRIPPING ON COLD MEDICINE.
THANK YOU FOR COMING TO WORK AND INFECTING ALL OF US, YOU SELFISH, ADDLE-BRAINED PLAGUE RAT.
5-14-18 ©2018 Scott Adams, Inc./Dist. by Andrews McMeel
I WAS GOING FOR "COURAGEOUS."
DO WALLY FIRST, SO I CAN WATCH HIM SPASM.

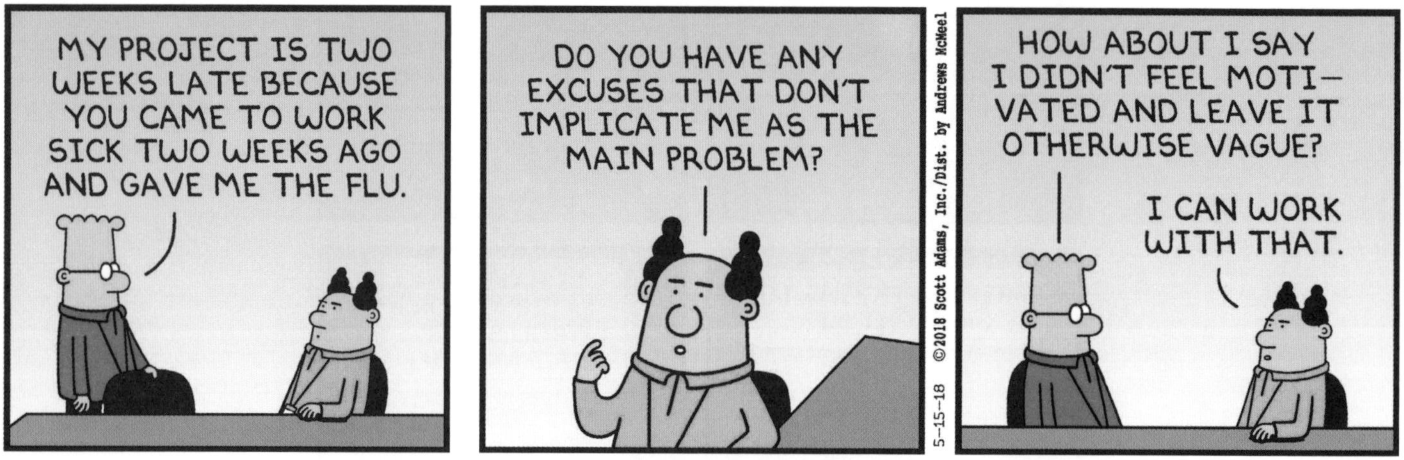
MY PROJECT IS TWO WEEKS LATE BECAUSE YOU CAME TO WORK SICK TWO WEEKS AGO AND GAVE ME THE FLU.
DO YOU HAVE ANY EXCUSES THAT DON'T IMPLICATE ME AS THE MAIN PROBLEM?
5-15-18 ©2018 Scott Adams, Inc./Dist. by Andrews McMeel
HOW ABOUT I SAY I DIDN'T FEEL MOTIVATED AND LEAVE IT OTHERWISE VAGUE?
I CAN WORK WITH THAT.

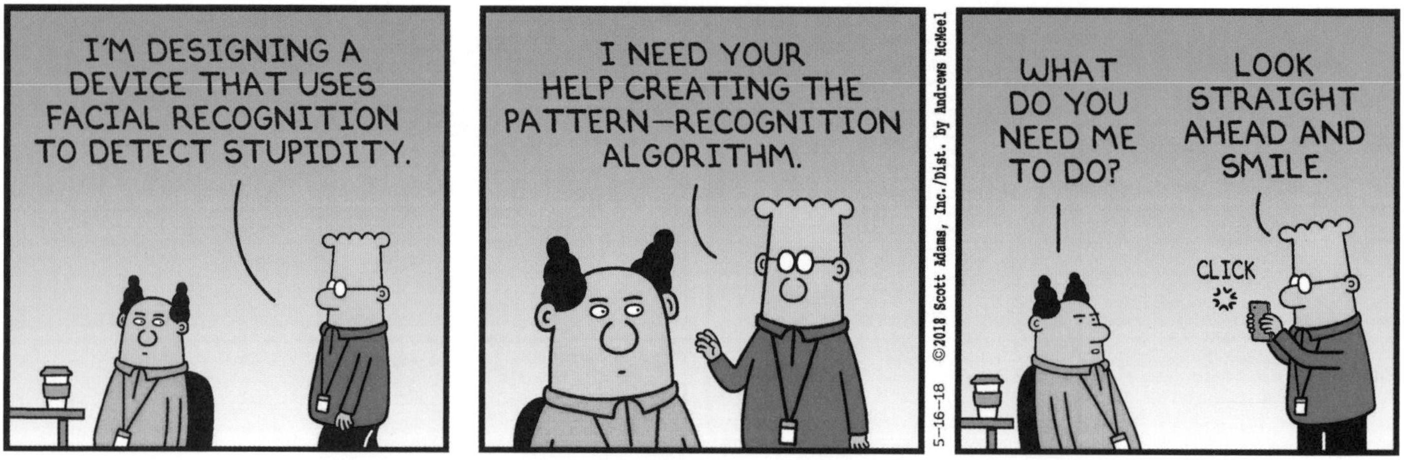
I'M DESIGNING A DEVICE THAT USES FACIAL RECOGNITION TO DETECT STUPIDITY.
I NEED YOUR HELP CREATING THE PATTERN-RECOGNITION ALGORITHM.
5-16-18 ©2018 Scott Adams, Inc./Dist. by Andrews McMeel
WHAT DO YOU NEED ME TO DO?
LOOK STRAIGHT AHEAD AND SMILE.
CLICK

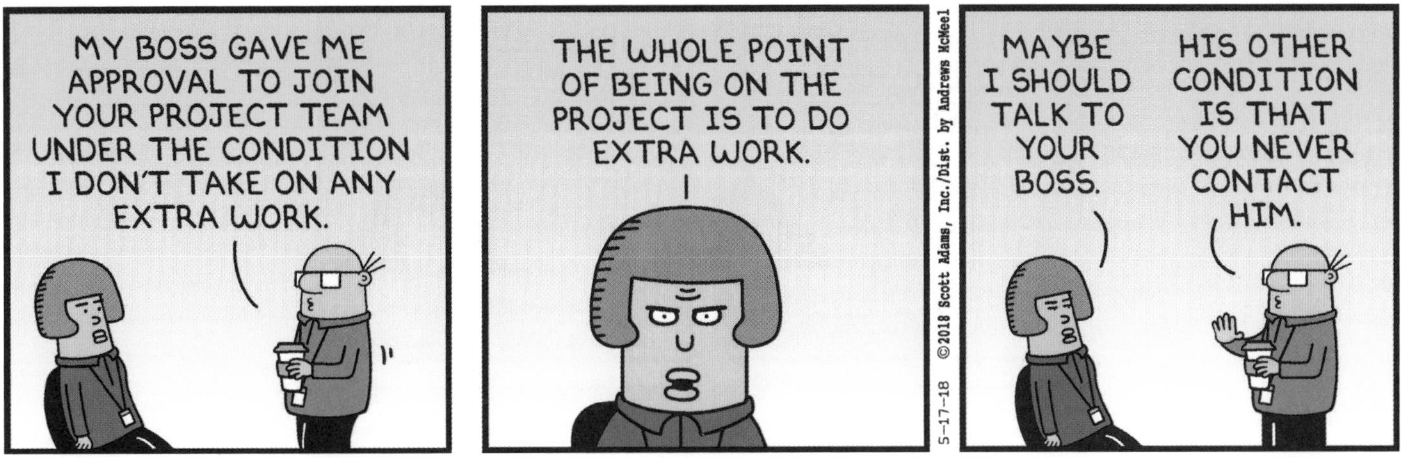
MY BOSS GAVE ME APPROVAL TO JOIN YOUR PROJECT TEAM UNDER THE CONDITION I DON'T TAKE ON ANY EXTRA WORK.
THE WHOLE POINT OF BEING ON THE PROJECT IS TO DO EXTRA WORK.
MAYBE I SHOULD TALK TO YOUR BOSS.
HIS OTHER CONDITION IS THAT YOU NEVER CONTACT HIM.
5-17-18 ©2018 Scott Adams, Inc./Dist. by Andrews McMeel

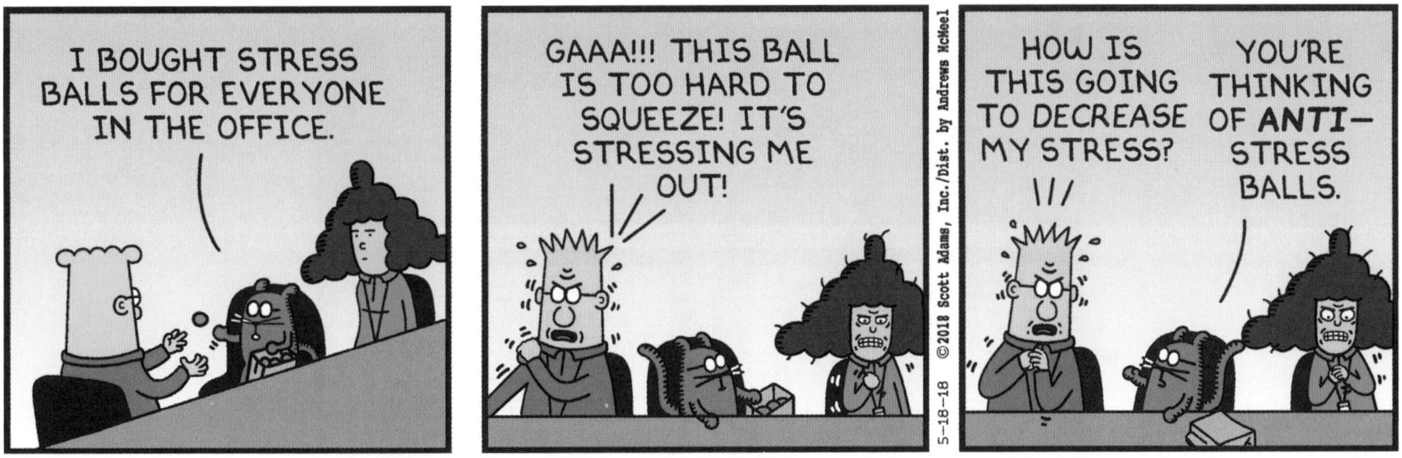
I BOUGHT STRESS BALLS FOR EVERYONE IN THE OFFICE.
GAAA!!! THIS BALL IS TOO HARD TO SQUEEZE! IT'S STRESSING ME OUT!
HOW IS THIS GOING TO DECREASE MY STRESS?
YOU'RE THINKING OF **ANTI**-STRESS BALLS.
5-18-18 ©2018 Scott Adams, Inc./Dist. by Andrews McMeel

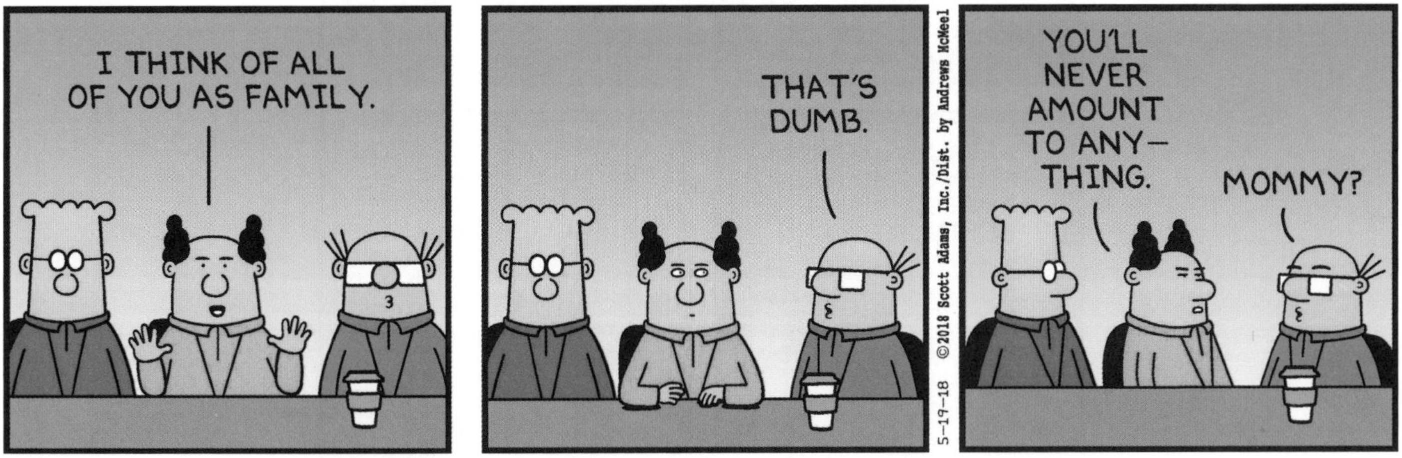
I THINK OF ALL OF YOU AS FAMILY.
THAT'S DUMB.
YOU'LL NEVER AMOUNT TO ANYTHING.
MOMMY?
5-19-18 ©2018 Scott Adams, Inc./Dist. by Andrews McMeel

WARREN BUFFETT SAYS YOU SHOULD SPEND TIME WITH PEOPLE WHO ARE BETTER THAN YOU.
WHY WOULD PEOPLE WHO ARE BETTER THAN ME BE DUMB ENOUGH TO SPEND TIME WITH ME?
WELL. . . I ASSUME YOU HAVE TO FIND PEOPLE WHO ARE BETTER THAN YOU, BUT NOT SMART ENOUGH TO AVOID YOU.
BECAUSE, OBVIOUSLY, YOU'D BE BRINGING DOWN THE AVERAGE OF ANYONE WHO WAS BETTER THAN YOU.
WHICH REMINDS ME, I NEED TO CUT THIS MEETING SHORT TO KEEP MY AVERAGE UP.
MAYBE WE CAN CONTINUE THE MEETING WITHOUT HIM.
THAT WOULD ONLY BE GOOD FOR *YOU*. I NEED TO FIND BETTER PEOPLE.
THE MEETING WENT DOWNHILL FROM THERE.
CAN YOU WRAP THIS UP? YOU'RE BRINGING DOWN MY AVERAGE.
© 2018 Scott Adams, Inc./Dist. by Andrews McMeel
5-20-18

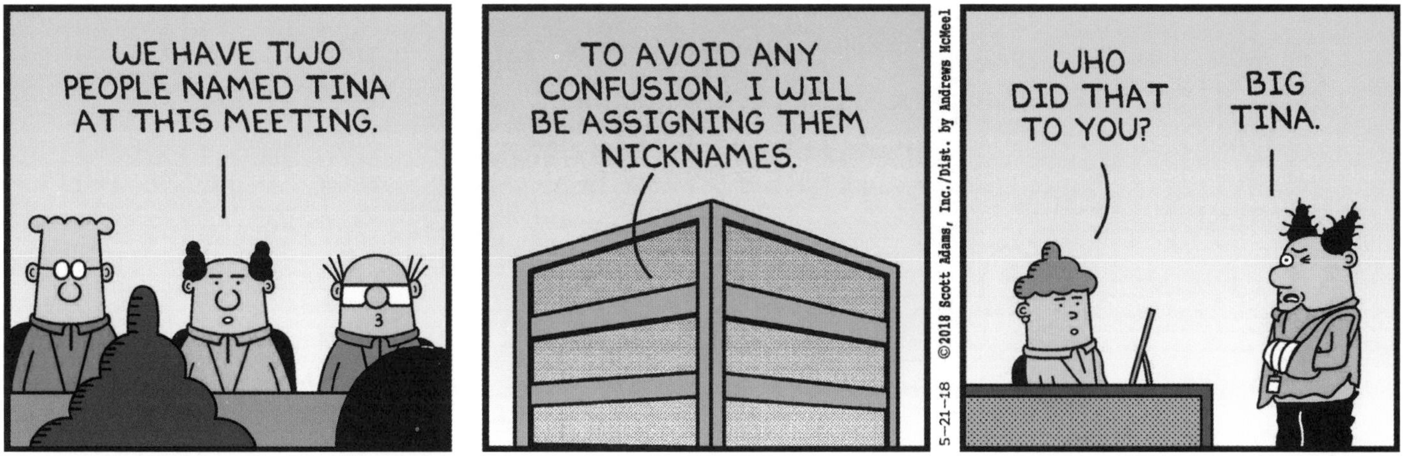
WE HAVE TWO PEOPLE NAMED TINA AT THIS MEETING.
TO AVOID ANY CONFUSION, I WILL BE ASSIGNING THEM NICKNAMES.
5-21-18 ©2018 Scott Adams, Inc./Dist. by Andrews McMeel
WHO DID THAT TO YOU?
BIG TINA.

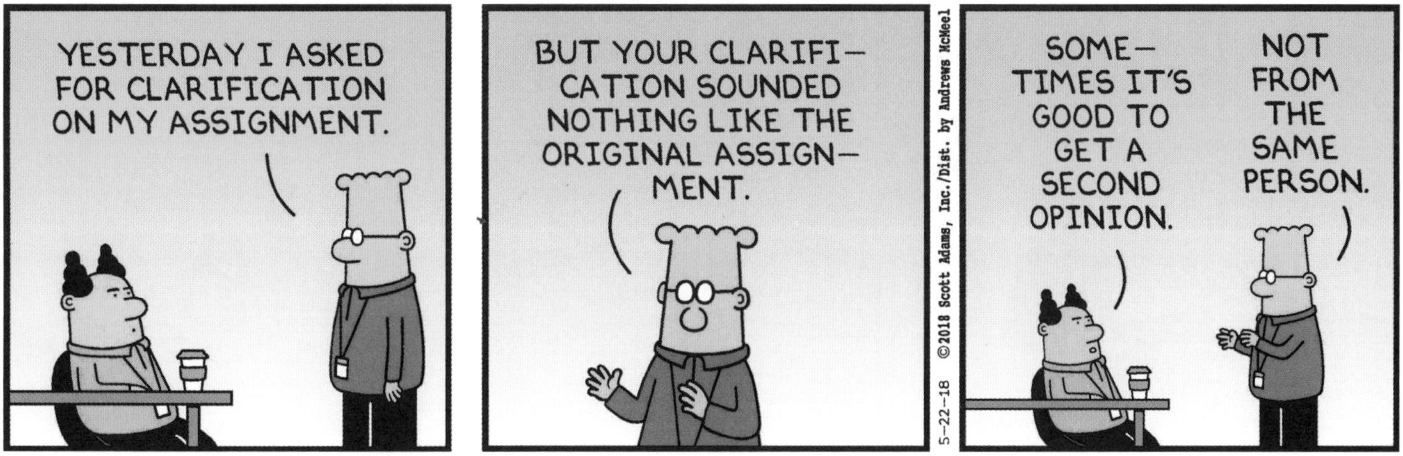
YESTERDAY I ASKED FOR CLARIFICATION ON MY ASSIGNMENT.
BUT YOUR CLARIFI– CATION SOUNDED NOTHING LIKE THE ORIGINAL ASSIGN– MENT.
5-22-18 ©2018 Scott Adams, Inc./Dist. by Andrews McMeel
SOME– TIMES IT'S GOOD TO GET A SECOND OPINION.
NOT FROM THE SAME PERSON.

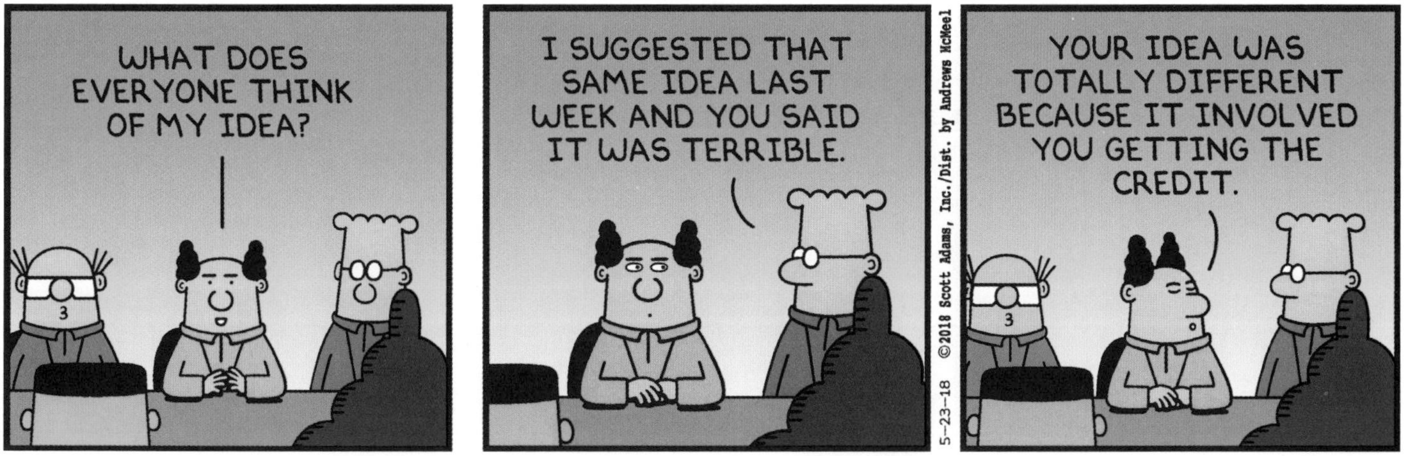
WHAT DOES EVERYONE THINK OF MY IDEA?
I SUGGESTED THAT SAME IDEA LAST WEEK AND YOU SAID IT WAS TERRIBLE.
5-23-18 ©2018 Scott Adams, Inc./Dist. by Andrews McMeel
YOUR IDEA WAS TOTALLY DIFFERENT BECAUSE IT INVOLVED YOU GETTING THE CREDIT.

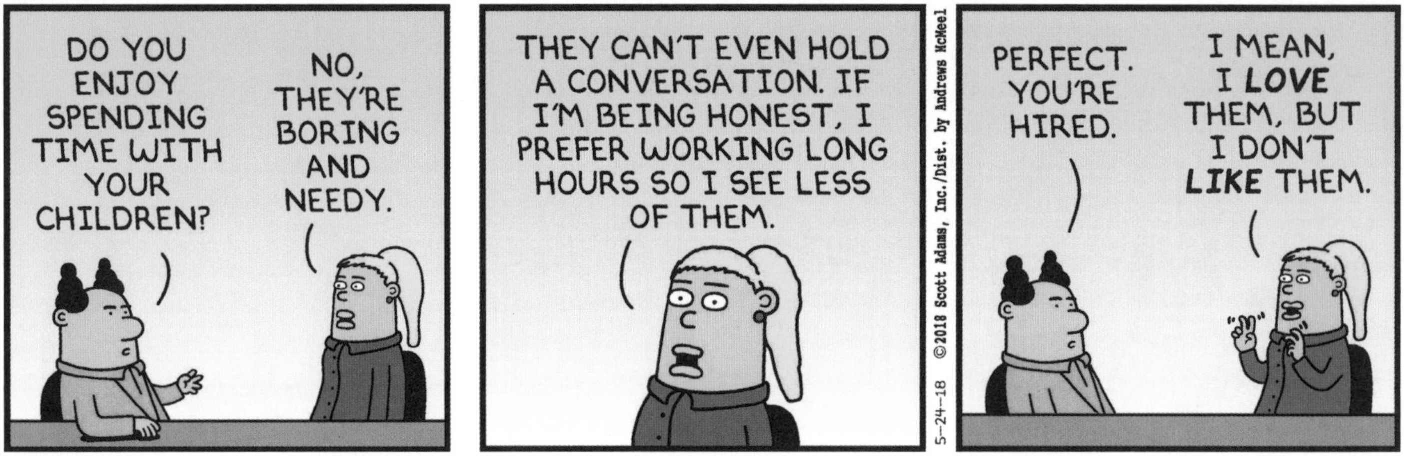
DO YOU ENJOY SPENDING TIME WITH YOUR CHILDREN?
NO, THEY'RE BORING AND NEEDY.
THEY CAN'T EVEN HOLD A CONVERSATION. IF I'M BEING HONEST, I PREFER WORKING LONG HOURS SO I SEE LESS OF THEM.
PERFECT. YOU'RE HIRED.
I MEAN, I **LOVE** THEM, BUT I DON'T **LIKE** THEM.
5-24-18 ©2018 Scott Adams, Inc./Dist. by Andrews McMeel

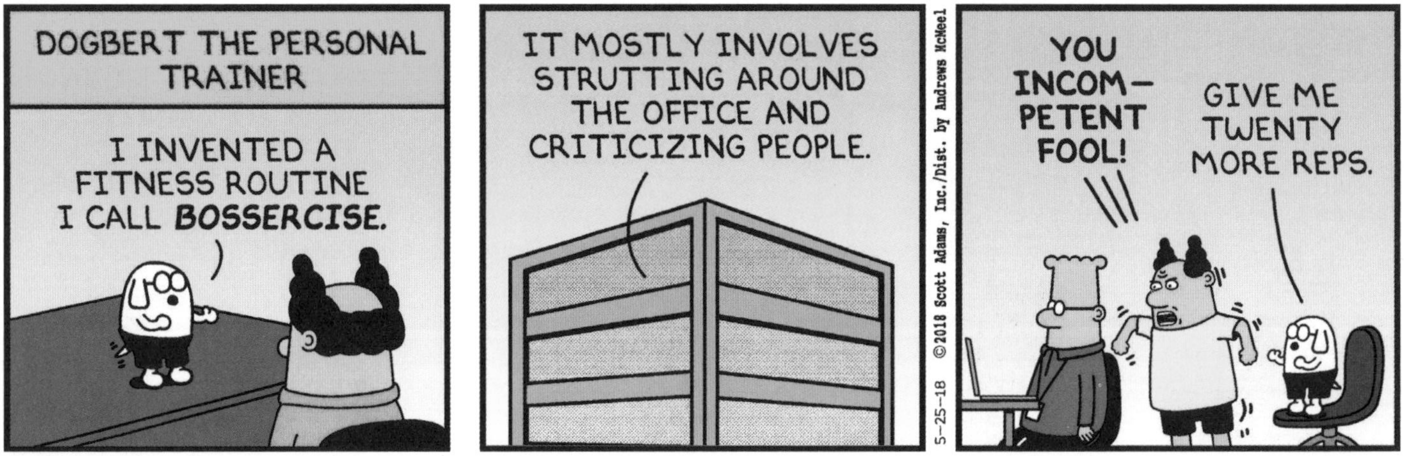
DOGBERT THE PERSONAL TRAINER
I INVENTED A FITNESS ROUTINE I CALL **BOSSERCISE.**
IT MOSTLY INVOLVES STRUTTING AROUND THE OFFICE AND CRITICIZING PEOPLE.
YOU INCOM-PETENT FOOL!
GIVE ME TWENTY MORE REPS.
5-25-18 ©2018 Scott Adams, Inc./Dist. by Andrews McMeel

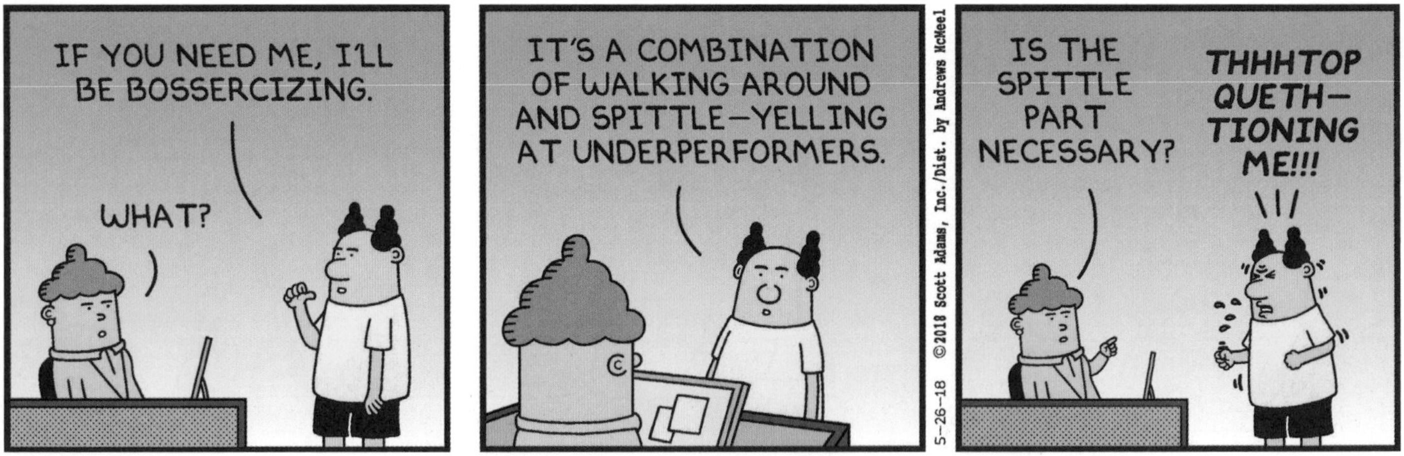
IF YOU NEED ME, I'LL BE BOSSERCIZING.
WHAT?
IT'S A COMBINATION OF WALKING AROUND AND SPITTLE-YELLING AT UNDERPERFORMERS.
IS THE SPITTLE PART NECESSARY?
THHHTOP QUETH-TIONING ME!!!
5-26-18 ©2018 Scott Adams, Inc./Dist. by Andrews McMeel

I NEED HELP PERSUADING YOUR BOSS TO BLESS MY PROJECT.
SHOULD I USE FACTS AND LOGIC?
NO, HE HATES THAT STUFF.
MAYBE I COULD APPEAL TO HIS BETTER ANGELS.
HIS BETTER ANGELS WEAR NOISE—CANCELING HEADPHONES.
OKAY, FINE. I'LL JUST APPEAL TO HIS SELF—INTEREST.
IT WOULD BE IN HIS BEST INTEREST TO AVOID PEOPLE LIKE YOU.
WHAT DO YOU SUGGEST?
WE'VE HAD GOOD OUTCOMES USING HIS IGNORANCE AND FEAR.
SIGN THIS OR ELSE A BLOCKCHAIN DRONE WILL KILL YOU IN YOUR SLEEP.
WHERE'S MY PEN!
© 2018 Scott Adams, Inc./Dist. by Andrews McMeel
5-27-18

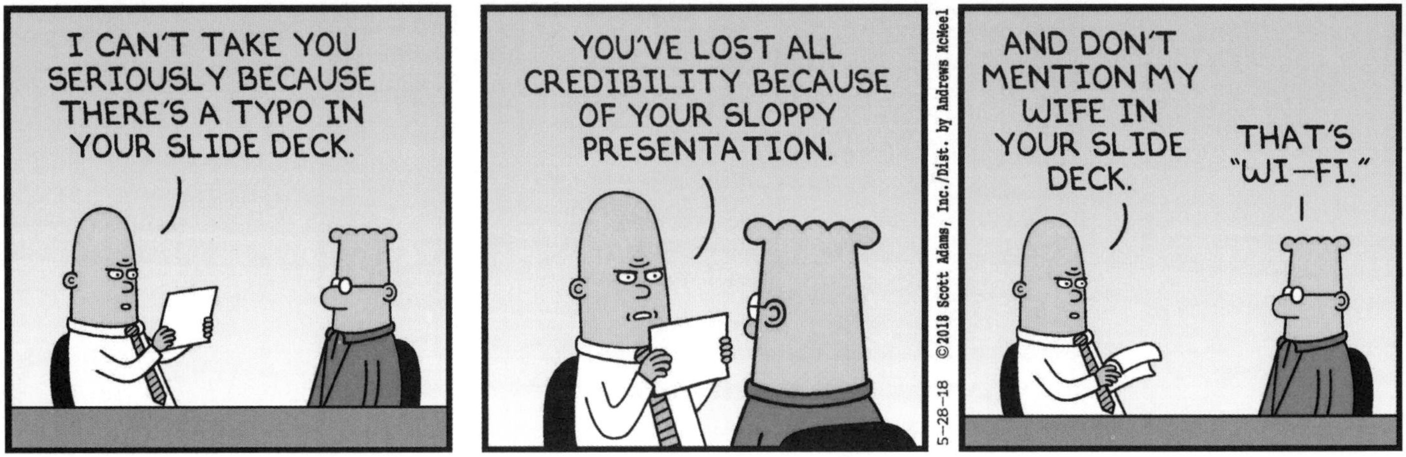
I CAN'T TAKE YOU SERIOUSLY BECAUSE THERE'S A TYPO IN YOUR SLIDE DECK.
YOU'VE LOST ALL CREDIBILITY BECAUSE OF YOUR SLOPPY PRESENTATION.
5-28-18 ©2018 Scott Adams, Inc./Dist. by Andrews McMeel
AND DON'T MENTION MY WIFE IN YOUR SLIDE DECK.
THAT'S "WI-FI."

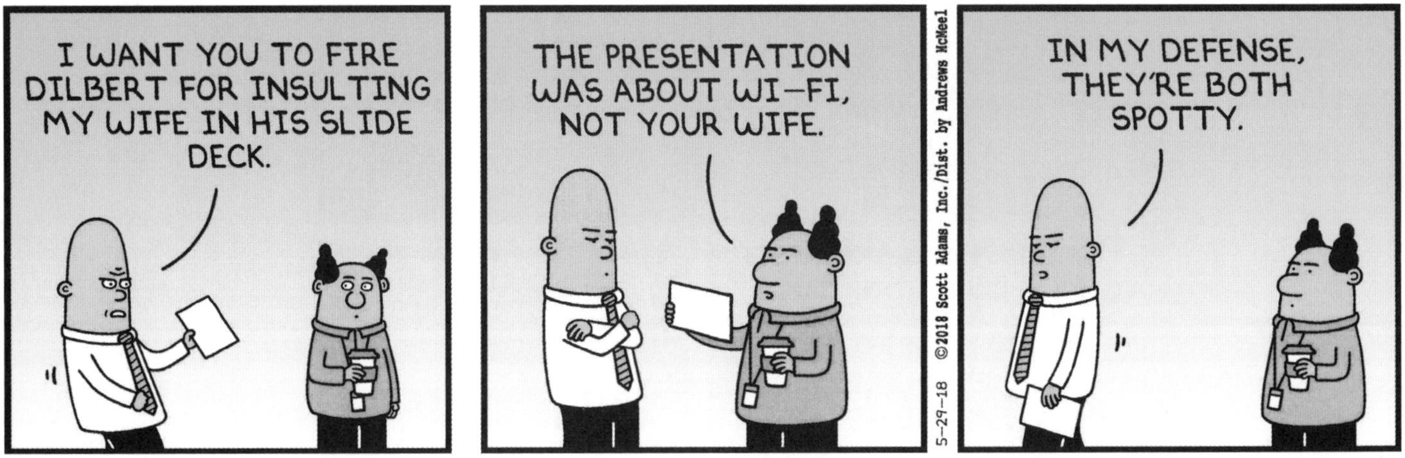
I WANT YOU TO FIRE DILBERT FOR INSULTING MY WIFE IN HIS SLIDE DECK.
THE PRESENTATION WAS ABOUT WI-FI, NOT YOUR WIFE.
5-29-18 ©2018 Scott Adams, Inc./Dist. by Andrews McMeel
IN MY DEFENSE, THEY'RE BOTH SPOTTY.

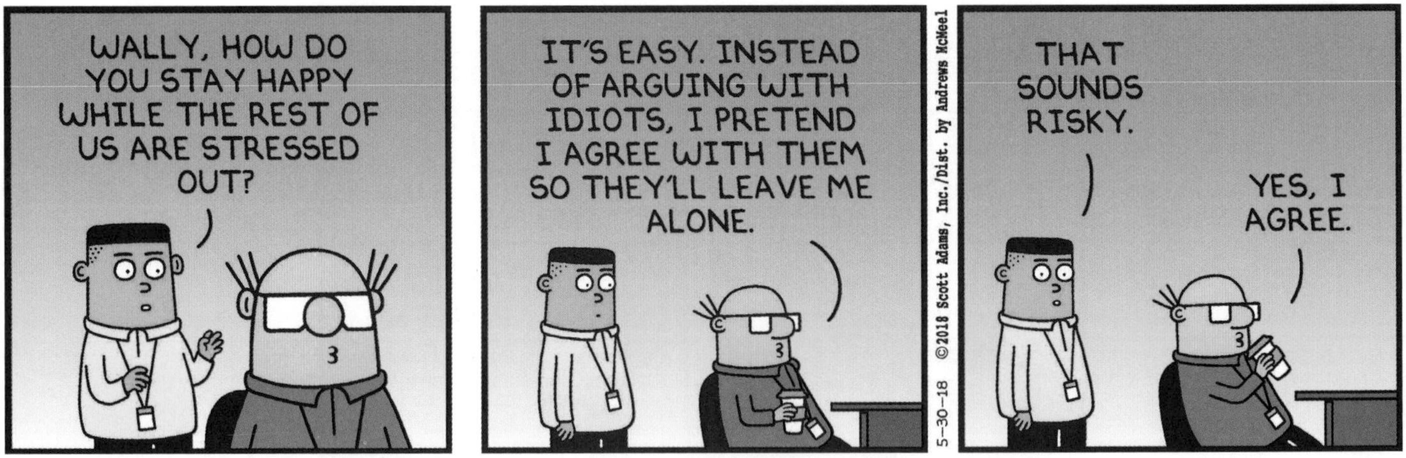
WALLY, HOW DO YOU STAY HAPPY WHILE THE REST OF US ARE STRESSED OUT?
IT'S EASY. INSTEAD OF ARGUING WITH IDIOTS, I PRETEND I AGREE WITH THEM SO THEY'LL LEAVE ME ALONE.
5-30-18 ©2018 Scott Adams, Inc./Dist. by Andrews McMeel
THAT SOUNDS RISKY.
YES, I AGREE.

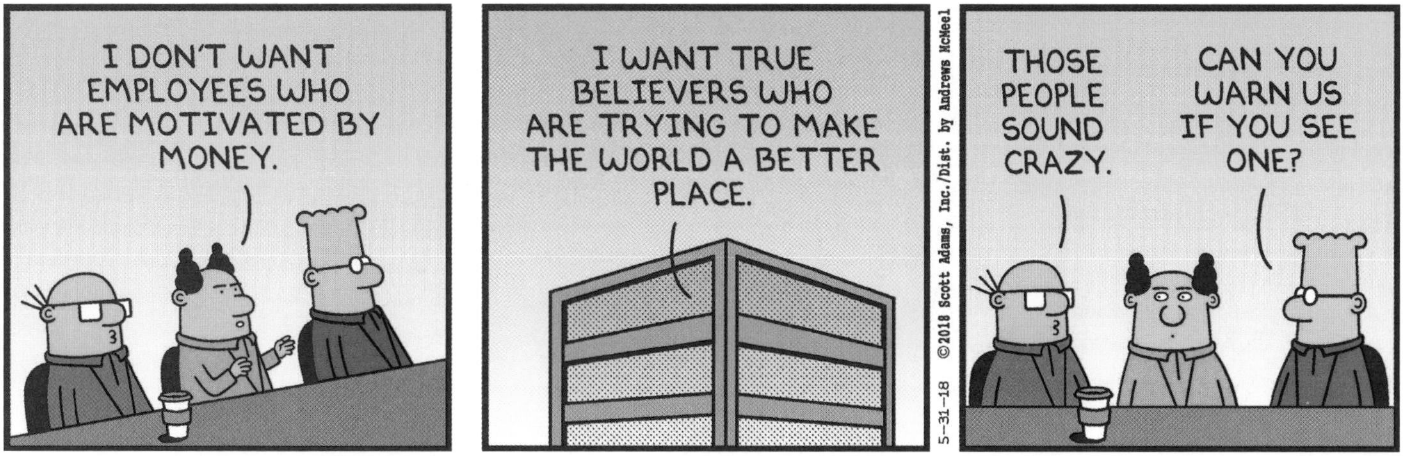
I DON'T WANT EMPLOYEES WHO ARE MOTIVATED BY MONEY.
I WANT TRUE BELIEVERS WHO ARE TRYING TO MAKE THE WORLD A BETTER PLACE.
THOSE PEOPLE SOUND CRAZY.
CAN YOU WARN US IF YOU SEE ONE?
5-31-18 ©2018 Scott Adams, Inc./Dist. by Andrews McMeel

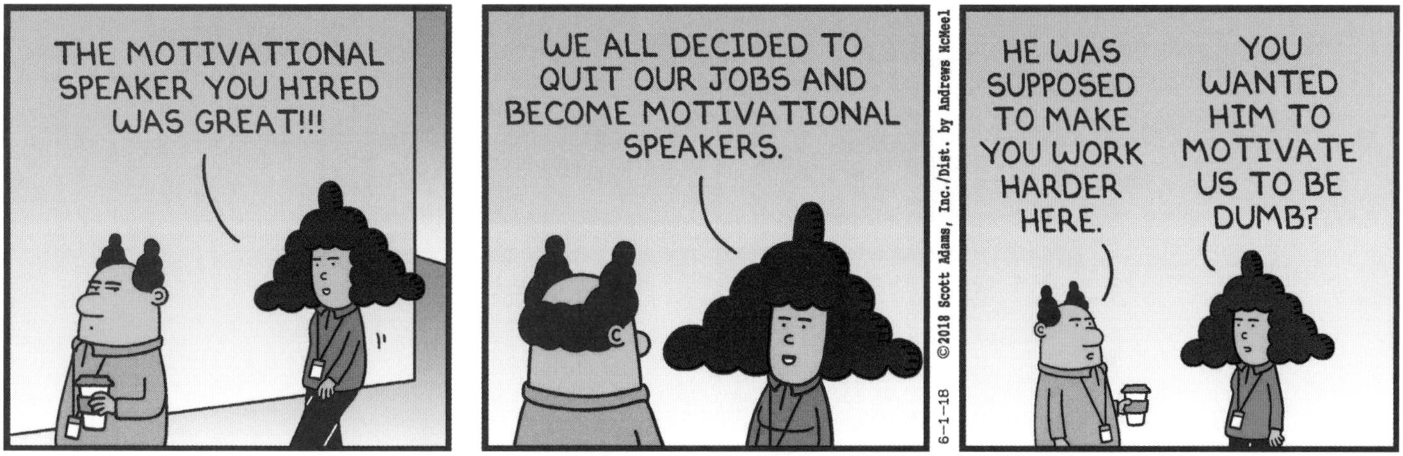
THE MOTIVATIONAL SPEAKER YOU HIRED WAS GREAT!!!
WE ALL DECIDED TO QUIT OUR JOBS AND BECOME MOTIVATIONAL SPEAKERS.
HE WAS SUPPOSED TO MAKE YOU WORK HARDER HERE.
YOU WANTED HIM TO MOTIVATE US TO BE DUMB?
6-1-18 ©2018 Scott Adams, Inc./Dist. by Andrews McMeel

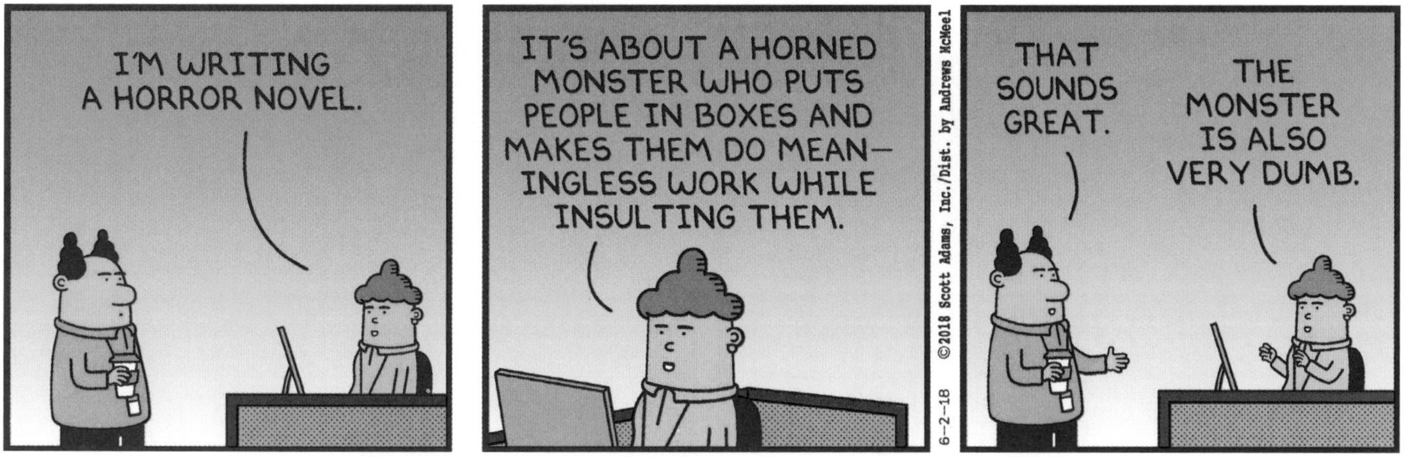
I'M WRITING A HORROR NOVEL.
IT'S ABOUT A HORNED MONSTER WHO PUTS PEOPLE IN BOXES AND MAKES THEM DO MEAN-INGLESS WORK WHILE INSULTING THEM.
THAT SOUNDS GREAT.
THE MONSTER IS ALSO VERY DUMB.
6-2-18 ©2018 Scott Adams, Inc./Dist. by Andrews McMeel

I FINISHED MY PROJECT!
SHHHH! DON'T LET ANYONE HEAR YOU SAY THAT.
ONLY ONE OF TWO THINGS CAN COME OF IT.
© 2018 Scott Adams, Inc./Dist. by Andrews McMeel
EITHER YOU'LL GET MORE WORK OR YOU'LL GET FIRED FOR NOT HAVING ENOUGH WORK.
THEN HOW DOES ANY-ONE EVER FINISH A PROJECT AROUND HERE?
WE DON'T.
WE MANIPULATE OUR BOSS INTO ADDING FEATURES SO OUR PROJECTS ARE NEVER COMPLETE.
IS THAT HARD TO DO?
NOT AS HARD AS YOU MIGHT HOPE.
6-3-18
HOW DO YOU LIKE THE PROTO-TYPE SO FAR?
IT NEEDS A RED BUTTON AND SOME COOLING FINS.

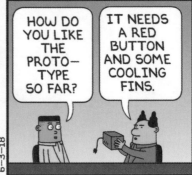

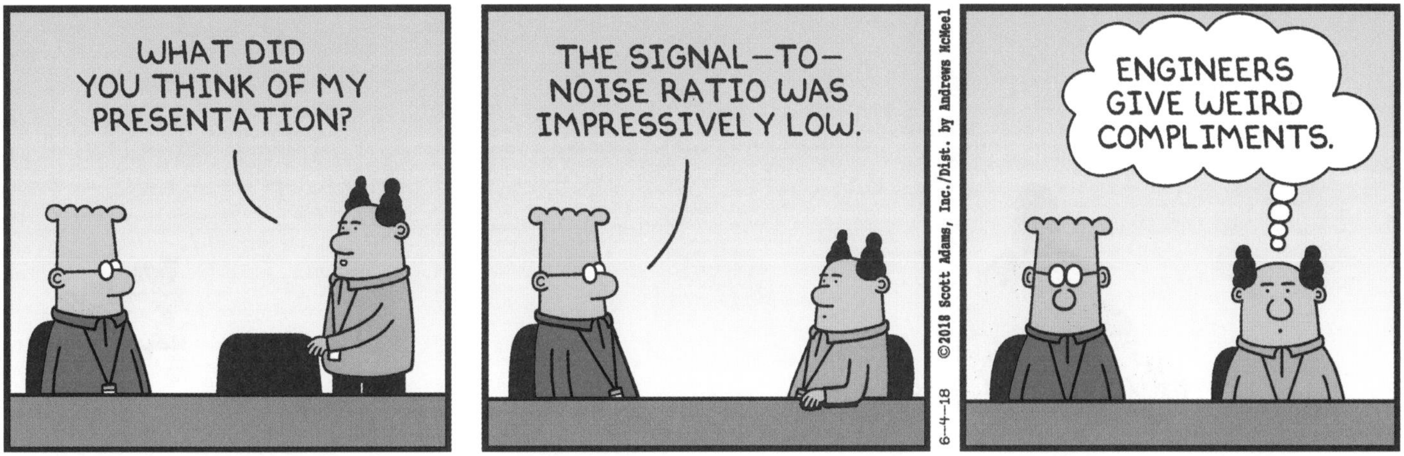
WHAT DID YOU THINK OF MY PRESENTATION?
THE SIGNAL—TO—NOISE RATIO WAS IMPRESSIVELY LOW.
6-4-18 ©2018 Scott Adams, Inc./Dist. by Andrews McMeel
ENGINEERS GIVE WEIRD COMPLIMENTS.

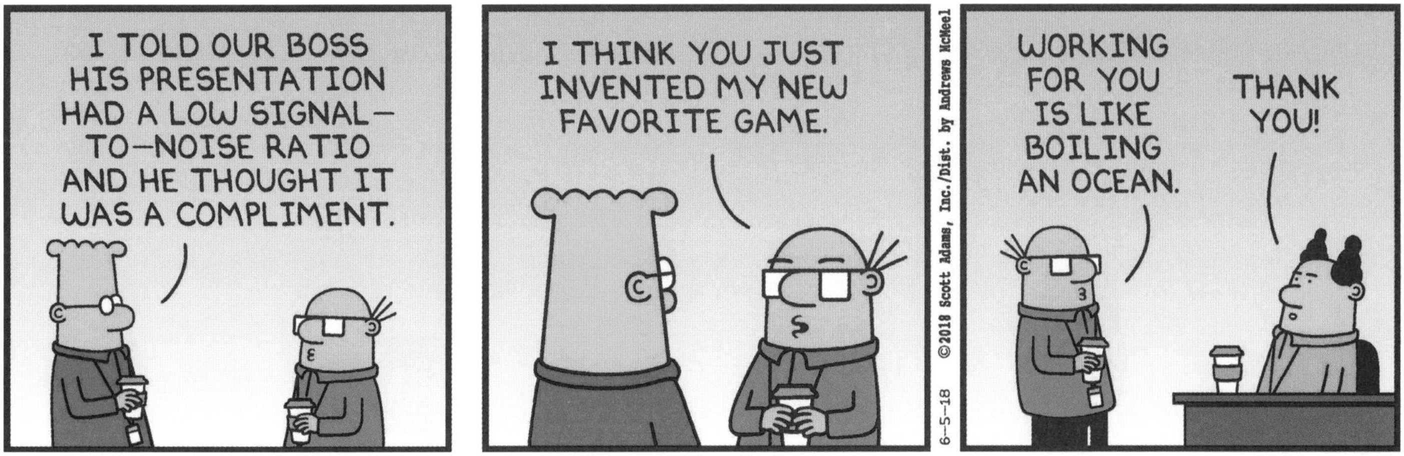
I TOLD OUR BOSS HIS PRESENTATION HAD A LOW SIGNAL—TO—NOISE RATIO AND HE THOUGHT IT WAS A COMPLIMENT.
I THINK YOU JUST INVENTED MY NEW FAVORITE GAME.
6-5-18 ©2018 Scott Adams, Inc./Dist. by Andrews McMeel
WORKING FOR YOU IS LIKE BOILING AN OCEAN.
THANK YOU!

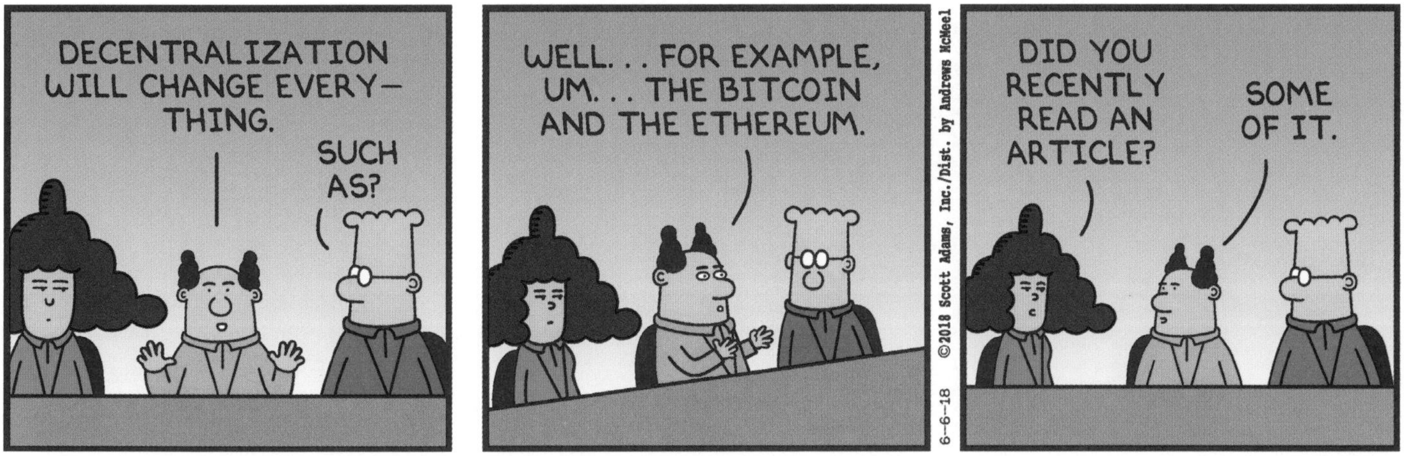
DECENTRALIZATION WILL CHANGE EVERY—THING.
SUCH AS?
WELL. . . FOR EXAMPLE, UM. . . THE BITCOIN AND THE ETHEREUM.
6-6-18 ©2018 Scott Adams, Inc./Dist. by Andrews McMeel
DID YOU RECENTLY READ AN ARTICLE?
SOME OF IT.

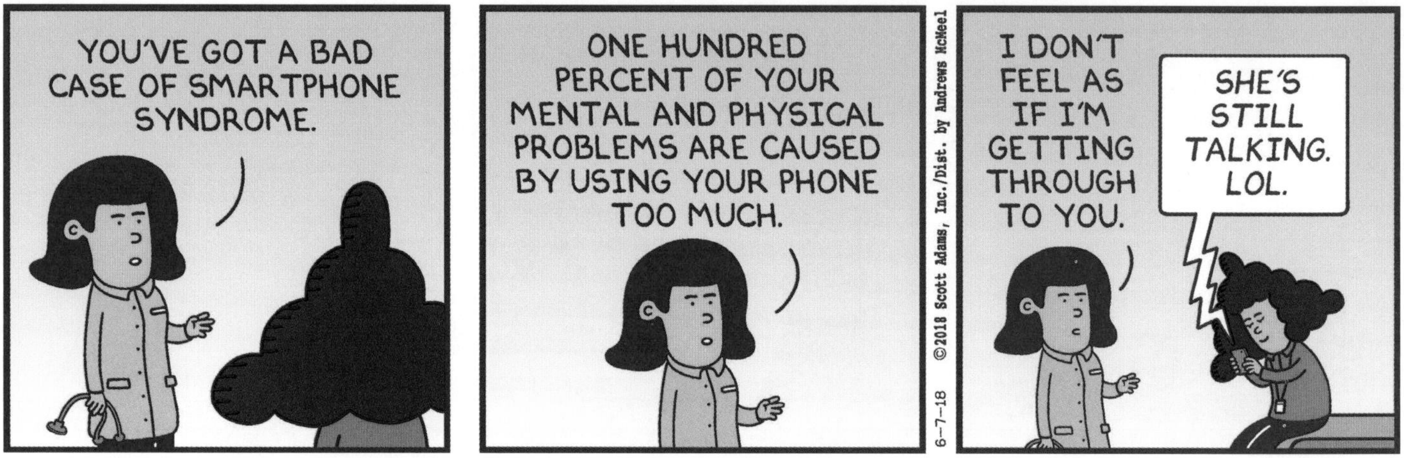
YOU'VE GOT A BAD CASE OF SMARTPHONE SYNDROME.
ONE HUNDRED PERCENT OF YOUR MENTAL AND PHYSICAL PROBLEMS ARE CAUSED BY USING YOUR PHONE TOO MUCH.
6-7-18 ©2018 Scott Adams, Inc./Dist. by Andrews McMeel
I DON'T FEEL AS IF I'M GETTING THROUGH TO YOU.
SHE'S STILL TALKING. LOL.

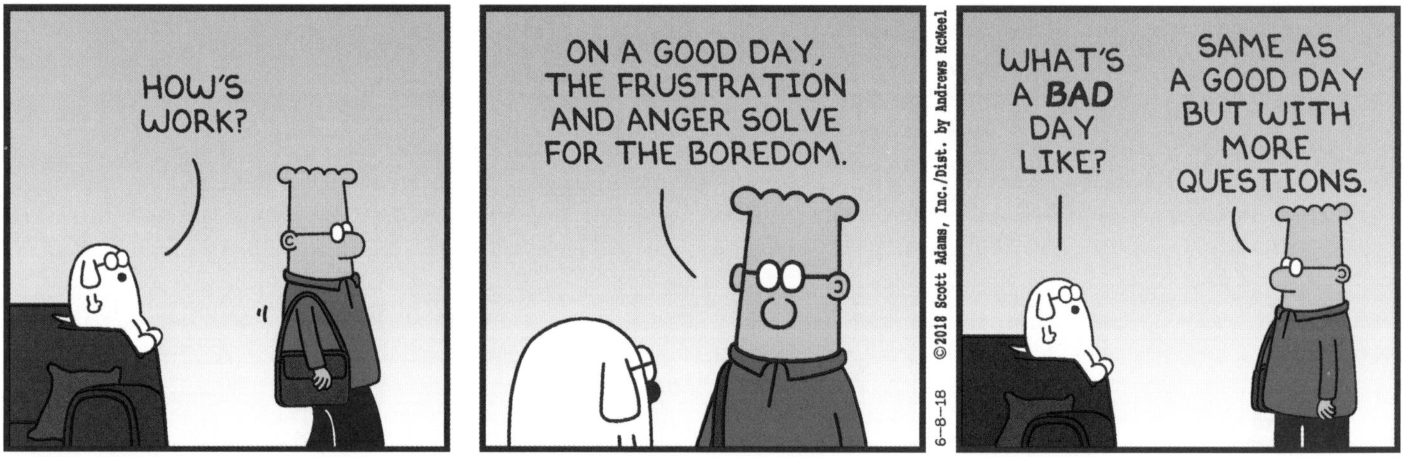
HOW'S WORK?
ON A GOOD DAY, THE FRUSTRATION AND ANGER SOLVE FOR THE BOREDOM.
6-8-18 ©2018 Scott Adams, Inc./Dist. by Andrews McMeel
WHAT'S A **BAD** DAY LIKE?
SAME AS A GOOD DAY BUT WITH MORE QUESTIONS.

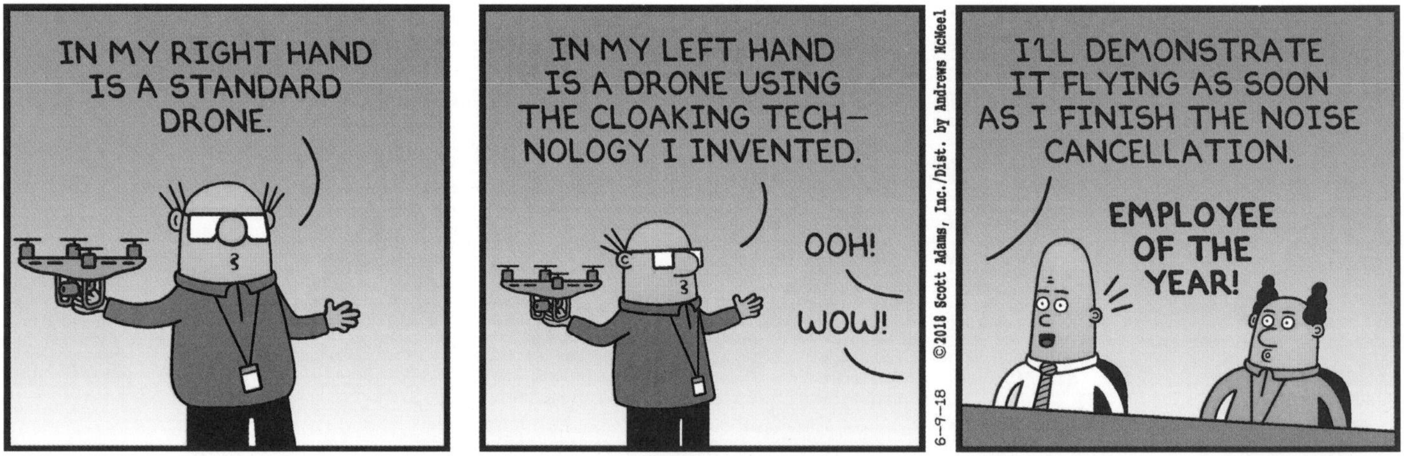
IN MY RIGHT HAND IS A STANDARD DRONE.
IN MY LEFT HAND IS A DRONE USING THE CLOAKING TECH— NOLOGY I INVENTED.
OOH!
WOW!
6-9-18 ©2018 Scott Adams, Inc./Dist. by Andrews McMeel
I'LL DEMONSTRATE IT FLYING AS SOON AS I FINISH THE NOISE CANCELLATION.
EMPLOYEE OF THE YEAR!

WALLY, I NEED YOU TO WRITE UP YOUR JOB DESCRIPTION FOR ME.
IS THAT BECAUSE YOU'RE PLANNING TO HIRE SOMEONE TO REPLACE ME?
I NEED IT BY TOMORROW.
© 2018 Scott Adams, Inc./Dist. by Andrews McMeel
JOB DESCRIPTION:
LEVERAGE PLATFORM TECHNOLOGIES TO MAXIMIZE SOFTWARE ARCHITECTURE OPTIMIZATION VIA NANOTUBES.
HERE YOU GO.
6-10-18
CAN YOU START ON MONDAY?
I CHANGED MY MIND.

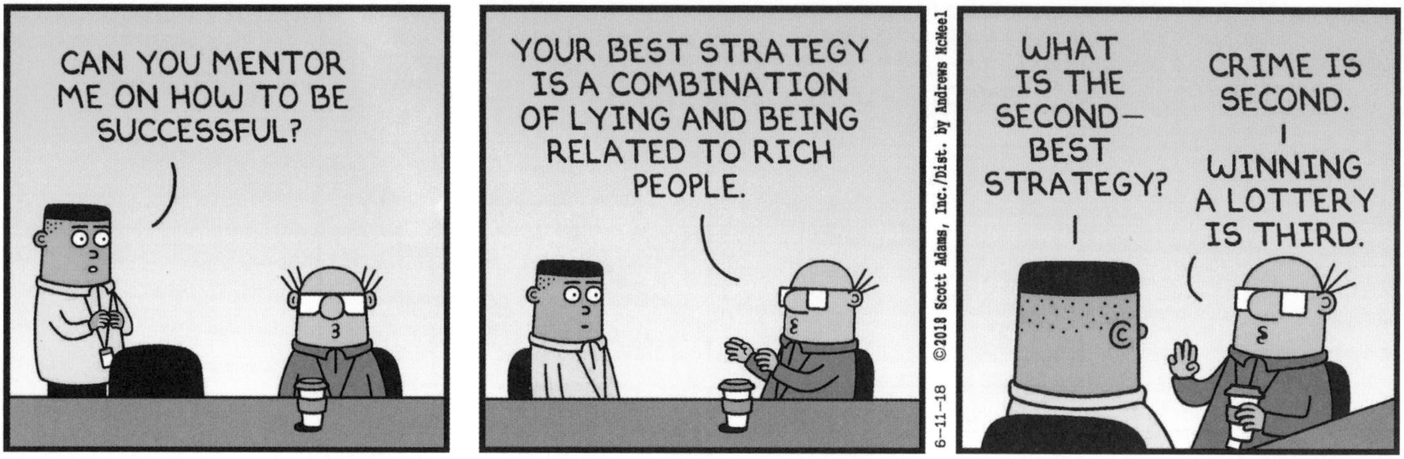
CAN YOU MENTOR ME ON HOW TO BE SUCCESSFUL?
YOUR BEST STRATEGY IS A COMBINATION OF LYING AND BEING RELATED TO RICH PEOPLE.
WHAT IS THE SECOND-BEST STRATEGY?
CRIME IS SECOND. WINNING A LOTTERY IS THIRD.
6-11-18 ©2018 Scott Adams, Inc./Dist. by Andrews McMeel

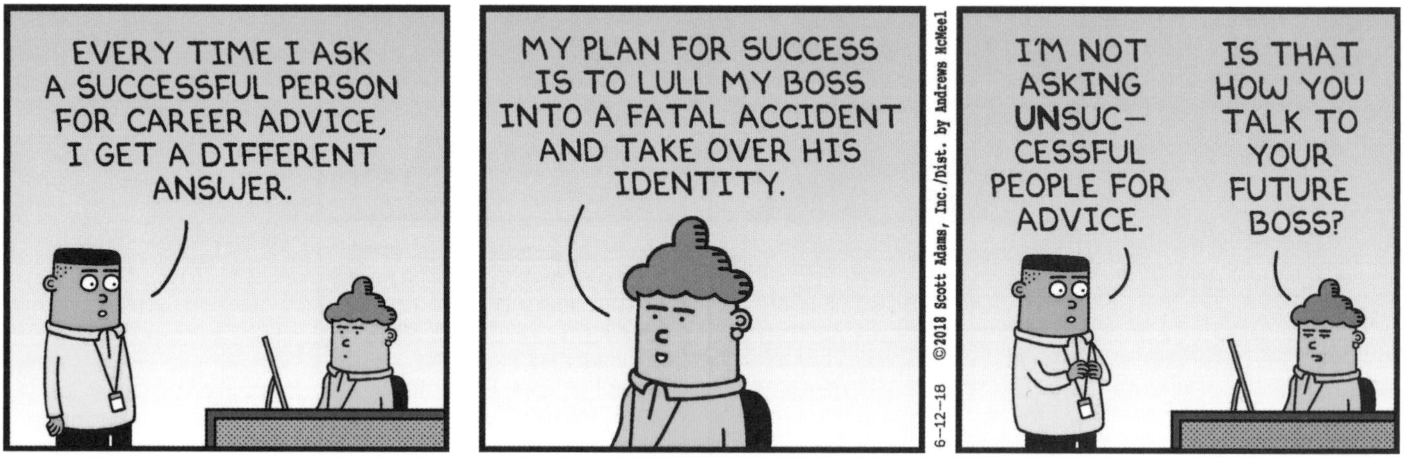
EVERY TIME I ASK A SUCCESSFUL PERSON FOR CAREER ADVICE, I GET A DIFFERENT ANSWER.
MY PLAN FOR SUCCESS IS TO LULL MY BOSS INTO A FATAL ACCIDENT AND TAKE OVER HIS IDENTITY.
I'M NOT ASKING **UN**SUCCESSFUL PEOPLE FOR ADVICE.
IS THAT HOW YOU TALK TO YOUR FUTURE BOSS?
6-12-18 ©2018 Scott Adams, Inc./Dist. by Andrews McMeel

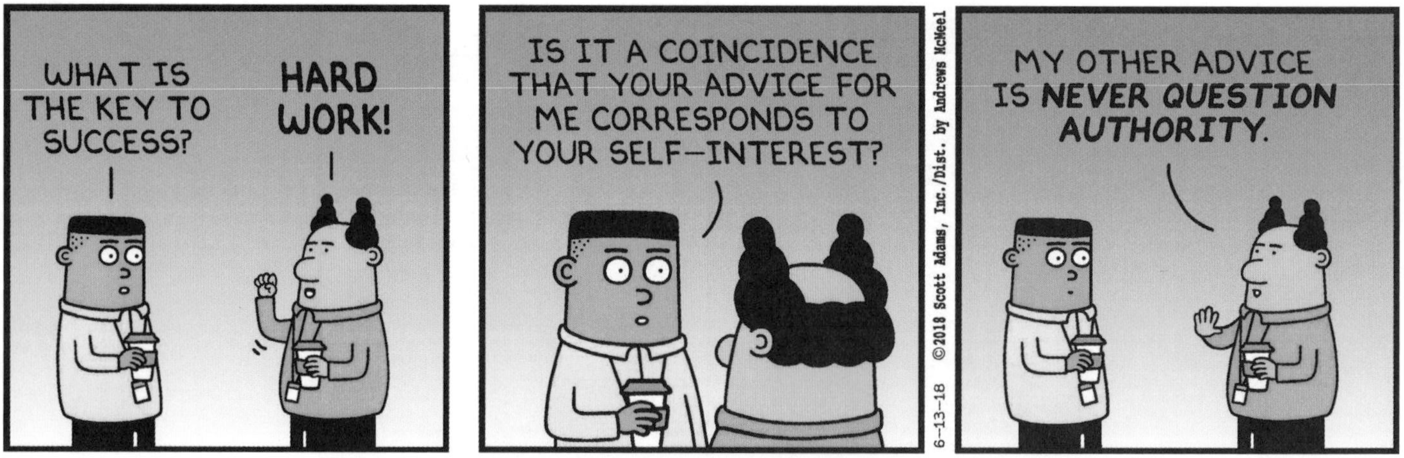
WHAT IS THE KEY TO SUCCESS?
HARD WORK!
IS IT A COINCIDENCE THAT YOUR ADVICE FOR ME CORRESPONDS TO YOUR SELF-INTEREST?
MY OTHER ADVICE IS ***NEVER QUESTION AUTHORITY***.
6-13-18 ©2018 Scott Adams, Inc./Dist. by Andrews McMeel

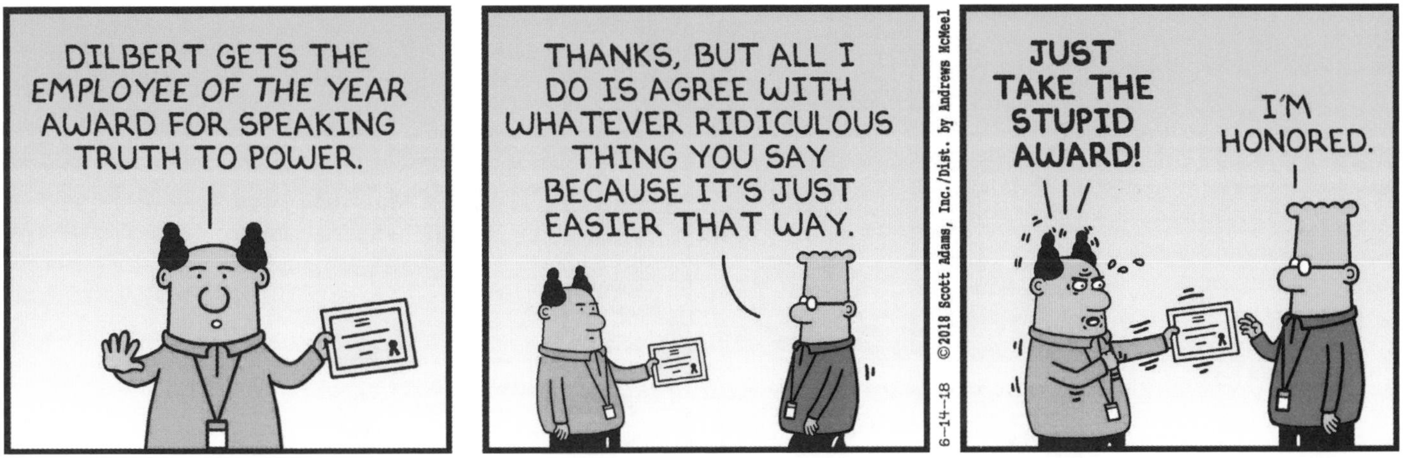
DILBERT GETS THE EMPLOYEE OF THE YEAR AWARD FOR SPEAKING TRUTH TO POWER.
THANKS, BUT ALL I DO IS AGREE WITH WHATEVER RIDICULOUS THING YOU SAY BECAUSE IT'S JUST EASIER THAT WAY.
6-14-18 ©2018 Scott Adams, Inc./Dist. by Andrews McMeel
JUST TAKE THE STUPID AWARD!
I'M HONORED.

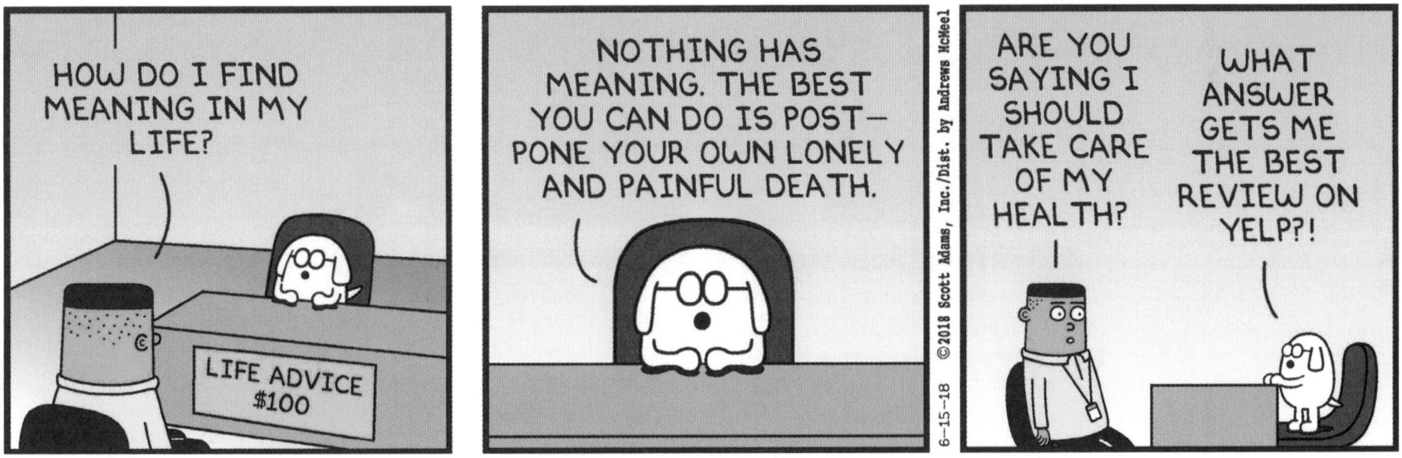
HOW DO I FIND MEANING IN MY LIFE?
LIFE ADVICE $100
NOTHING HAS MEANING. THE BEST YOU CAN DO IS POST-PONE YOUR OWN LONELY AND PAINFUL DEATH.
6-15-18 ©2018 Scott Adams, Inc./Dist. by Andrews McMeel
ARE YOU SAYING I SHOULD TAKE CARE OF MY HEALTH?
WHAT ANSWER GETS ME THE BEST REVIEW ON YELP?!

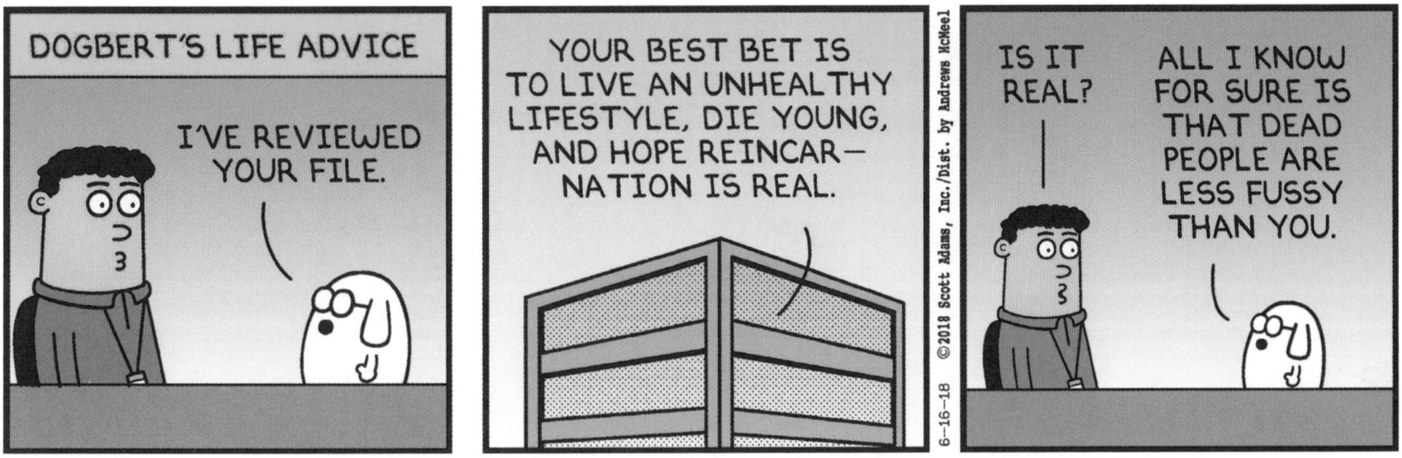
DOGBERT'S LIFE ADVICE
I'VE REVIEWED YOUR FILE.
YOUR BEST BET IS TO LIVE AN UNHEALTHY LIFESTYLE, DIE YOUNG, AND HOPE REINCAR-NATION IS REAL.
6-16-18 ©2018 Scott Adams, Inc./Dist. by Andrews McMeel
IS IT REAL?
ALL I KNOW FOR SURE IS THAT DEAD PEOPLE ARE LESS FUSSY THAN YOU.

YOUR SLIDE DECK IS OKAY–ISH. BUT CAN YOU MAKE IT MORE ASPIRATIONAL?
IT'S JUST A SOFTWARE UPGRADE.
YES, YES.
BUT I WANT THE AUDIENCE TO **FEEL** IT.
THEY CAN FEEL THE HANDOUTS.
IT'S LIKE YOU'RE NOT EVEN TRYING TO UNDERSTAND!
GENIUS IS OFTEN MISUNDERSTOOD.
DO YOU KNOW WHAT ELSE IS MISUNDER–STOOD?
SUPER–GENIUS?
© 2018 Scott Adams, Inc./Dist. by Andrews McMeel
6-17-18

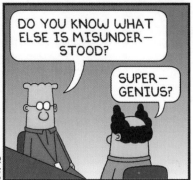

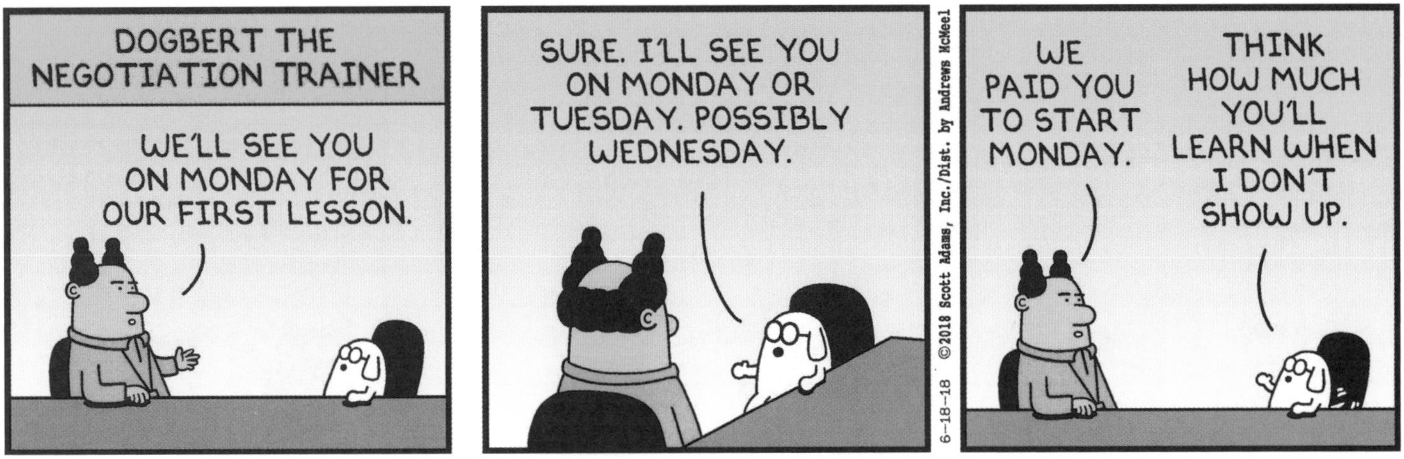

DOGBERT THE NEGOTIATION TRAINER
WE'LL SEE YOU ON MONDAY FOR OUR FIRST LESSON.
SURE. I'LL SEE YOU ON MONDAY OR TUESDAY. POSSIBLY WEDNESDAY.
6-18-18 ©2018 Scott Adams, Inc./Dist. by Andrews McMeel
WE PAID YOU TO START MONDAY.
THINK HOW MUCH YOU'LL LEARN WHEN I DON'T SHOW UP.

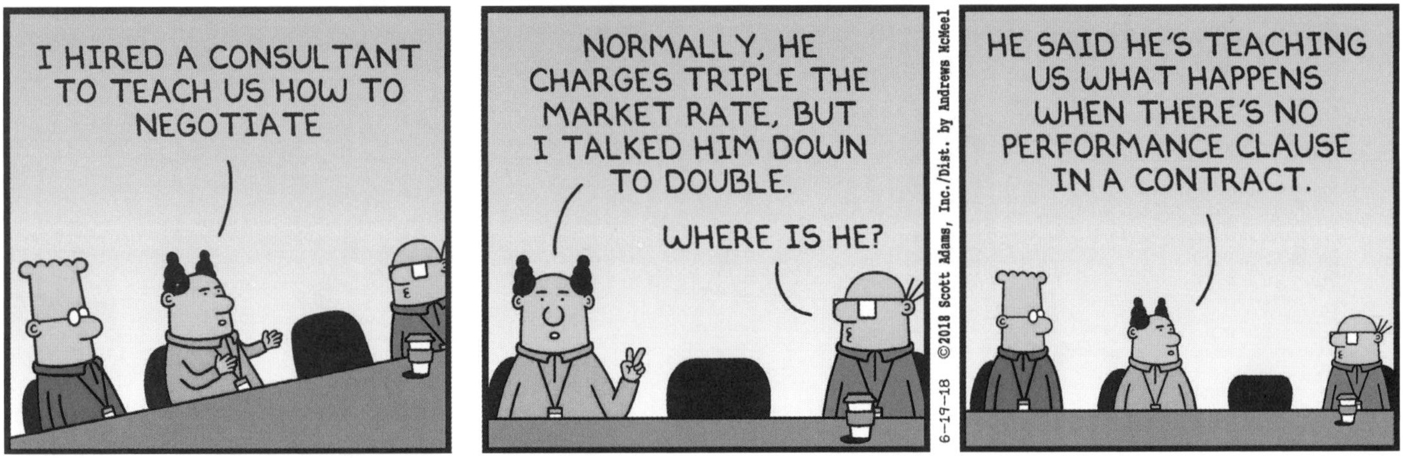

I HIRED A CONSULTANT TO TEACH US HOW TO NEGOTIATE
NORMALLY, HE CHARGES TRIPLE THE MARKET RATE, BUT I TALKED HIM DOWN TO DOUBLE.
WHERE IS HE?
6-19-18 ©2018 Scott Adams, Inc./Dist. by Andrews McMeel
HE SAID HE'S TEACHING US WHAT HAPPENS WHEN THERE'S NO PERFORMANCE CLAUSE IN A CONTRACT.

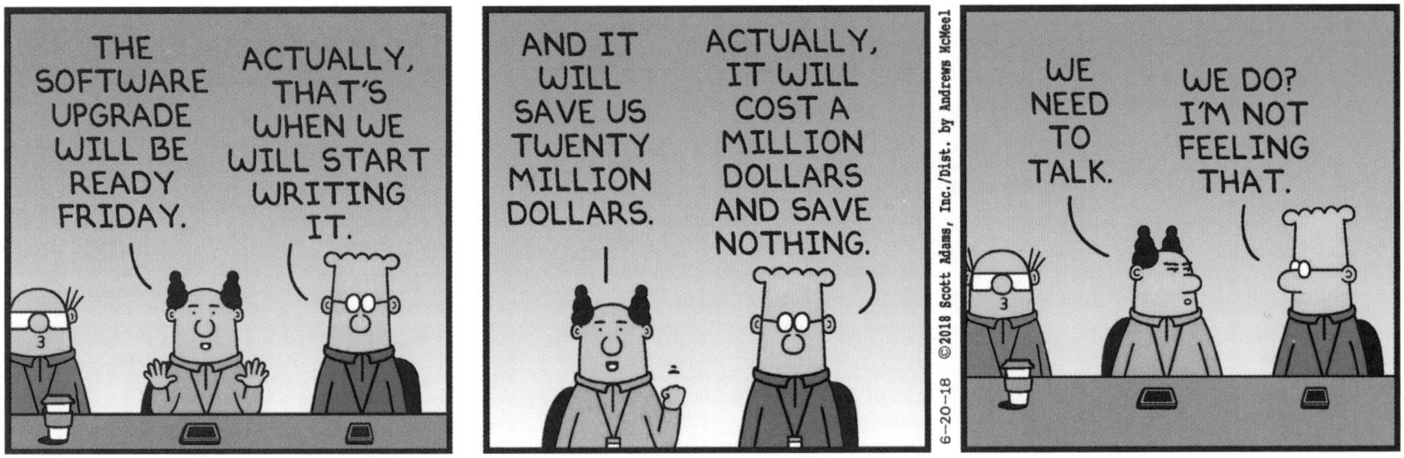

THE SOFTWARE UPGRADE WILL BE READY FRIDAY.
ACTUALLY, THAT'S WHEN WE WILL START WRITING IT.
AND IT WILL SAVE US TWENTY MILLION DOLLARS.
ACTUALLY, IT WILL COST A MILLION DOLLARS AND SAVE NOTHING.
6-20-18 ©2018 Scott Adams, Inc./Dist. by Andrews McMeel
WE NEED TO TALK.
WE DO? I'M NOT FEELING THAT.

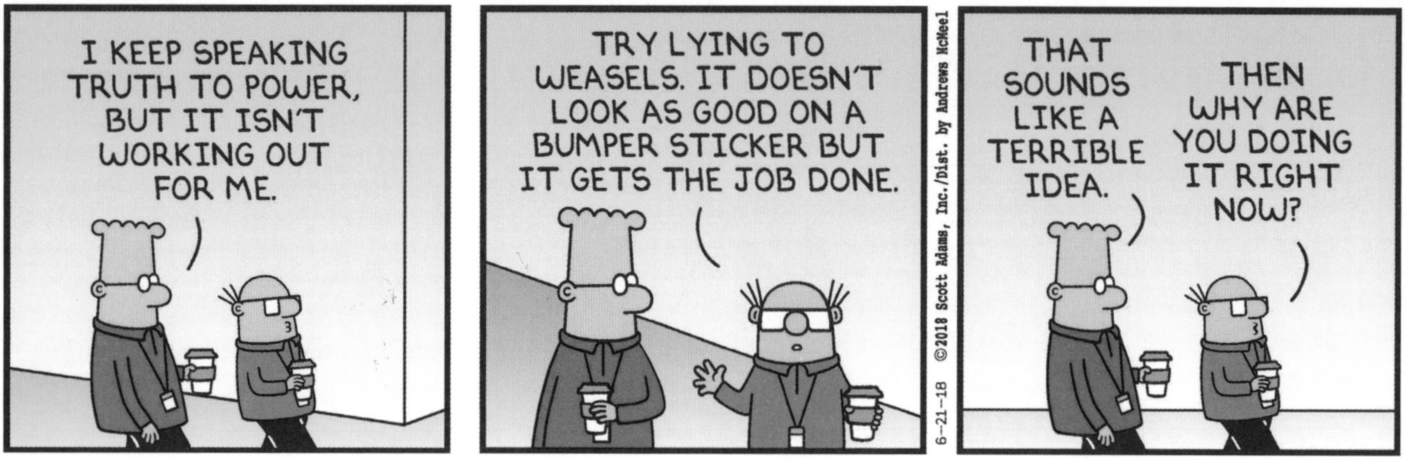
I KEEP SPEAKING TRUTH TO POWER, BUT IT ISN'T WORKING OUT FOR ME.
TRY LYING TO WEASELS. IT DOESN'T LOOK AS GOOD ON A BUMPER STICKER BUT IT GETS THE JOB DONE.
6-21-18 ©2018 Scott Adams, Inc./Dist. by Andrews McMeel
THAT SOUNDS LIKE A TERRIBLE IDEA.
THEN WHY ARE YOU DOING IT RIGHT NOW?

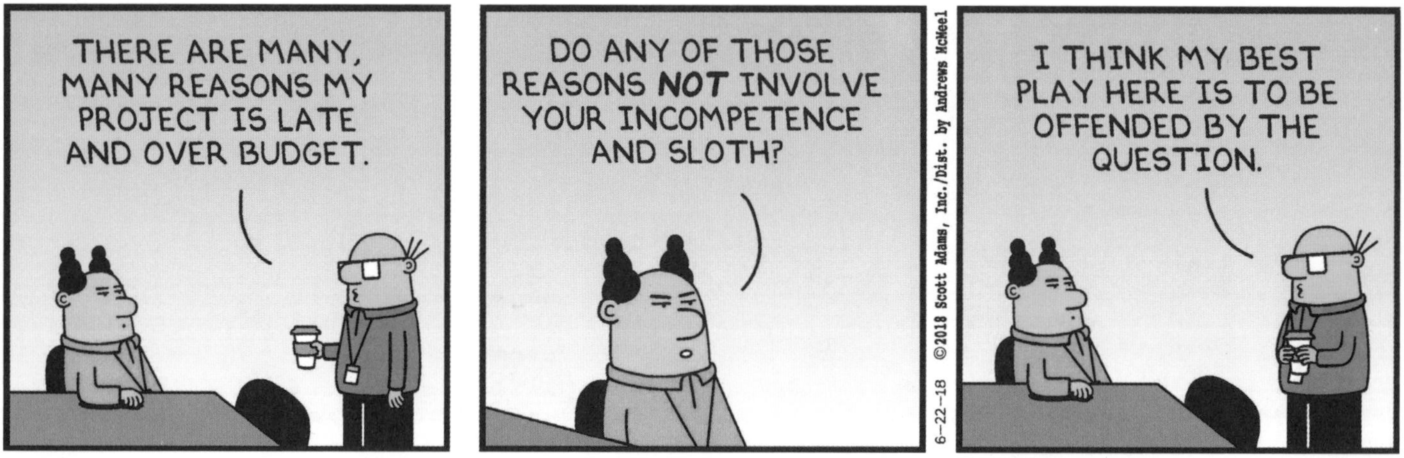
THERE ARE MANY, MANY REASONS MY PROJECT IS LATE AND OVER BUDGET.
DO ANY OF THOSE REASONS NOT INVOLVE YOUR INCOMPETENCE AND SLOTH?
6-22-18 ©2018 Scott Adams, Inc./Dist. by Andrews McMeel
I THINK MY BEST PLAY HERE IS TO BE OFFENDED BY THE QUESTION.

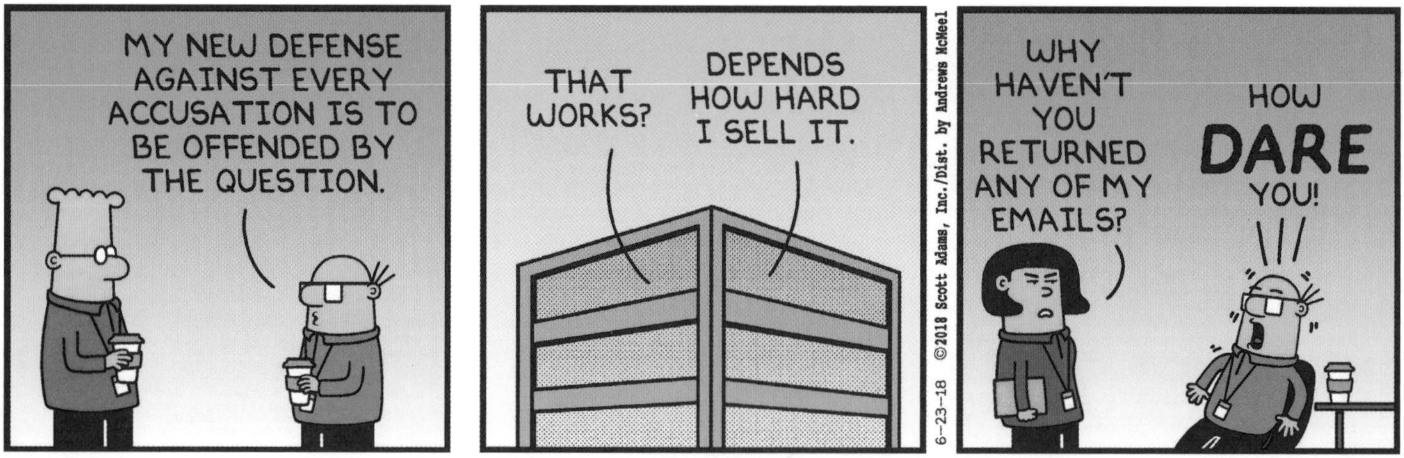
MY NEW DEFENSE AGAINST EVERY ACCUSATION IS TO BE OFFENDED BY THE QUESTION.
THAT WORKS?
DEPENDS HOW HARD I SELL IT.
6-23-18 ©2018 Scott Adams, Inc./Dist. by Andrews McMeel
WHY HAVEN'T YOU RETURNED ANY OF MY EMAILS?
HOW DARE YOU!

I HAVE ONE HOUR TO GET SOME WORK DONE BEFORE MY MEETING.
BUT I CAN'T CONCENTRATE WHEN I'M HUNGRY, SO I NEED A SNACK.
THIS SNACK IS MAKING ME THIRSTY.
THE LABEL ON THIS SHIRT IS BUGGING ME. I NEED TO CUT IT OFF.
A QUICK TRIP TO THE RESTROOM AND THEN I CAN GET DOWN TO WORK.
UGH. I HAVE FIFTEEN MESSAGES SINCE I LEFT MY DESK.
NOW IT'S TOO CLOSE TO MY MEETING TO START A NEW TASK.
HOW'S WORK?
HOW WOULD I KNOW?
© 2018 Scott Adams, Inc./Dist. by Andrews McMeel
6-24-18

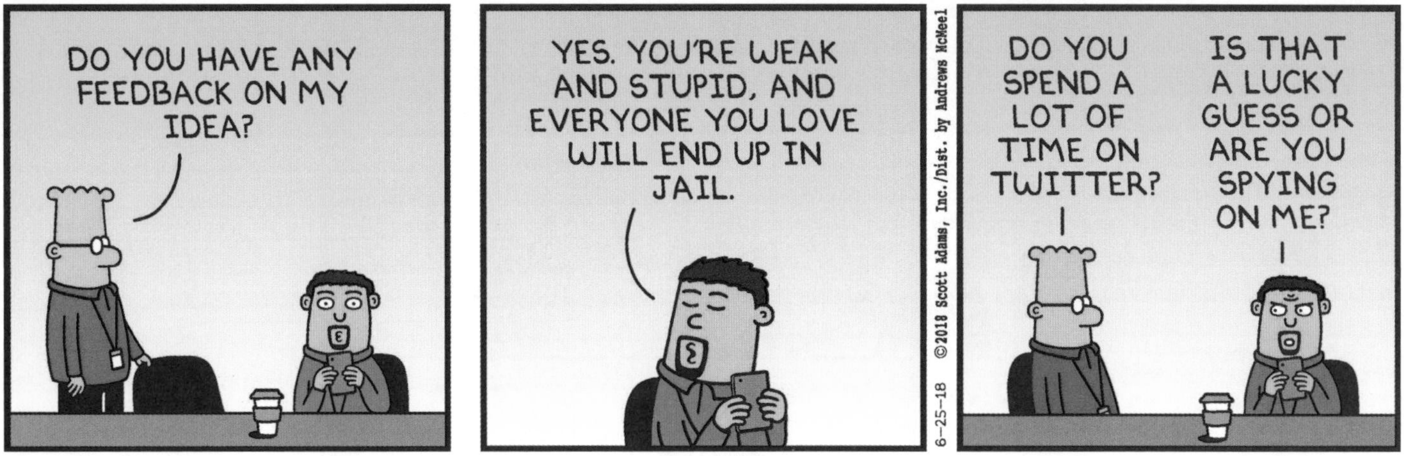
DO YOU HAVE ANY FEEDBACK ON MY IDEA?
YES. YOU'RE WEAK AND STUPID, AND EVERYONE YOU LOVE WILL END UP IN JAIL.
DO YOU SPEND A LOT OF TIME ON TWITTER?
IS THAT A LUCKY GUESS OR ARE YOU SPYING ON ME?
6-25-18 ©2018 Scott Adams, Inc./Dist. by Andrews McMeel

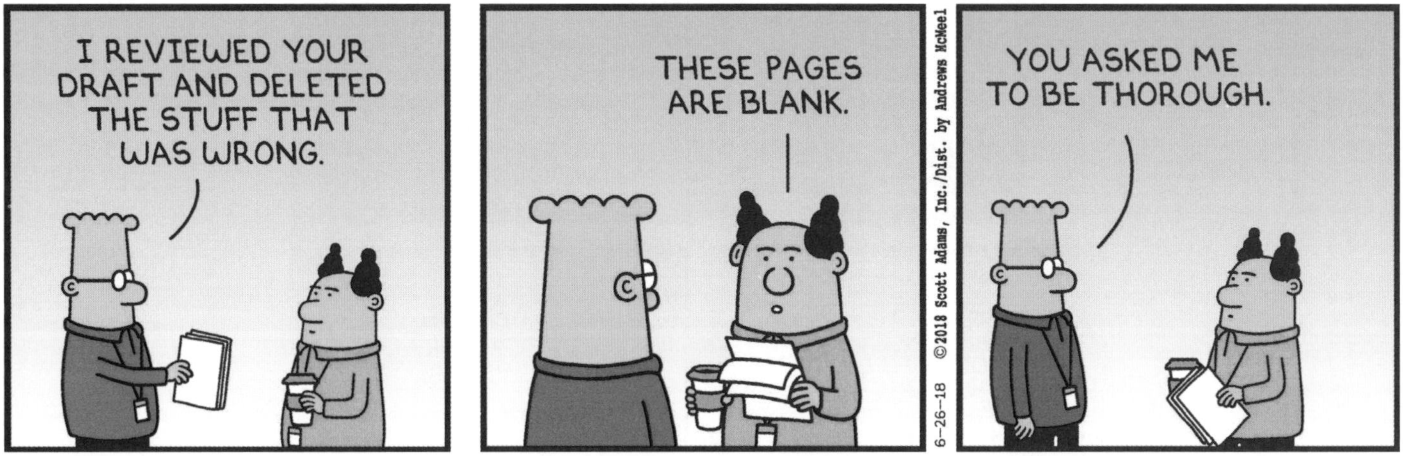
I REVIEWED YOUR DRAFT AND DELETED THE STUFF THAT WAS WRONG.
THESE PAGES ARE BLANK.
YOU ASKED ME TO BE THOROUGH.
6-26-18 ©2018 Scott Adams, Inc./Dist. by Andrews McMeel

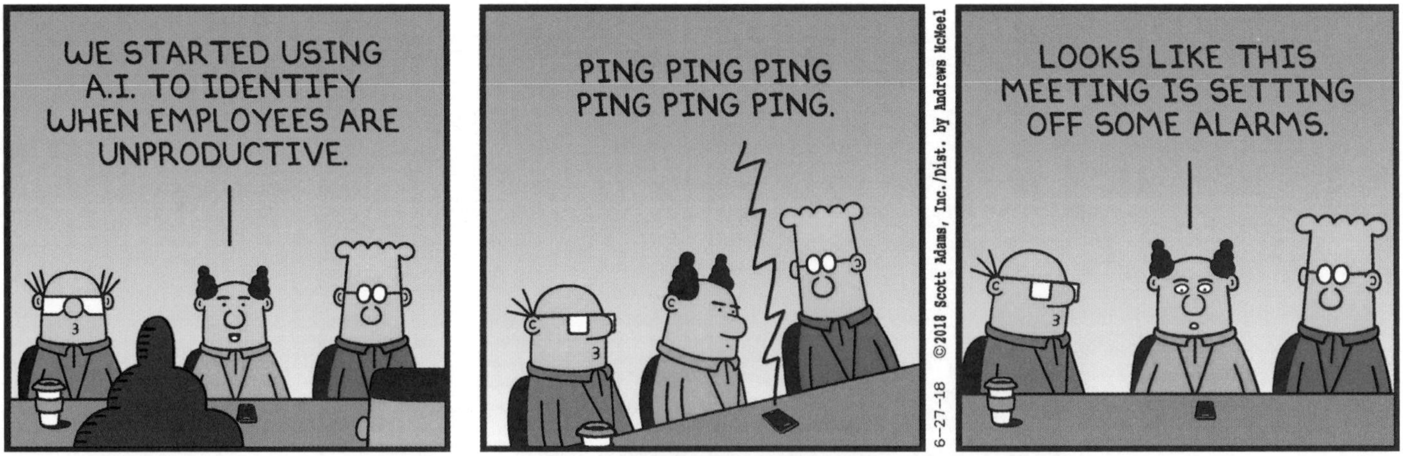
WE STARTED USING A.I. TO IDENTIFY WHEN EMPLOYEES ARE UNPRODUCTIVE.
PING PING PING PING PING PING.
LOOKS LIKE THIS MEETING IS SETTING OFF SOME ALARMS.
6-27-18 ©2018 Scott Adams, Inc./Dist. by Andrews McMeel

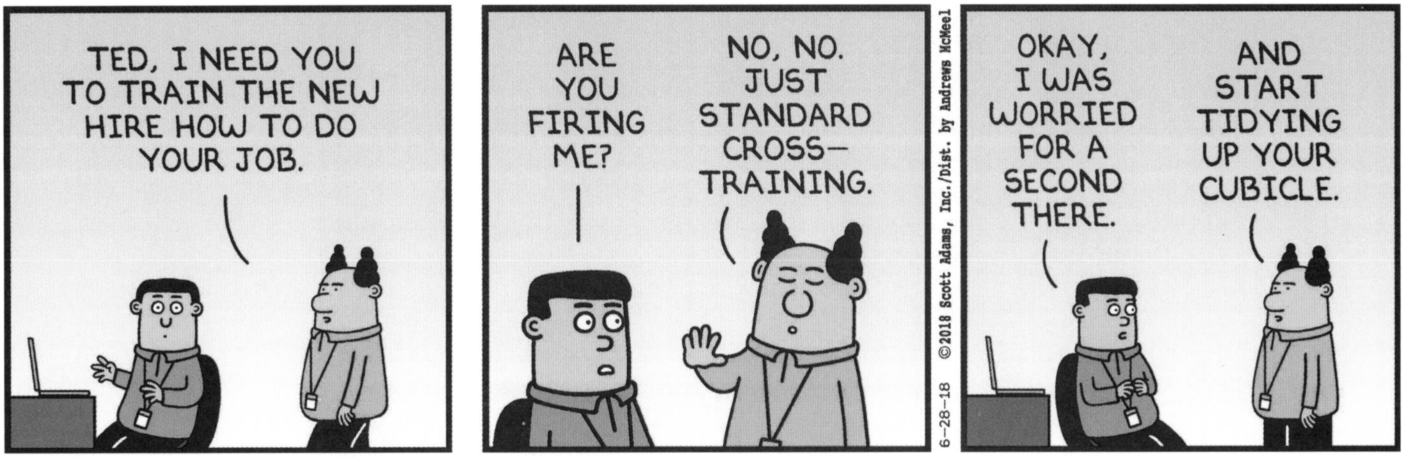
TED, I NEED YOU TO TRAIN THE NEW HIRE HOW TO DO YOUR JOB.
ARE YOU FIRING ME?
NO, NO. JUST STANDARD CROSS-TRAINING.
OKAY, I WAS WORRIED FOR A SECOND THERE.
AND START TIDYING UP YOUR CUBICLE.
6-28-18 ©2018 Scott Adams, Inc./Dist. by Andrews McMeel

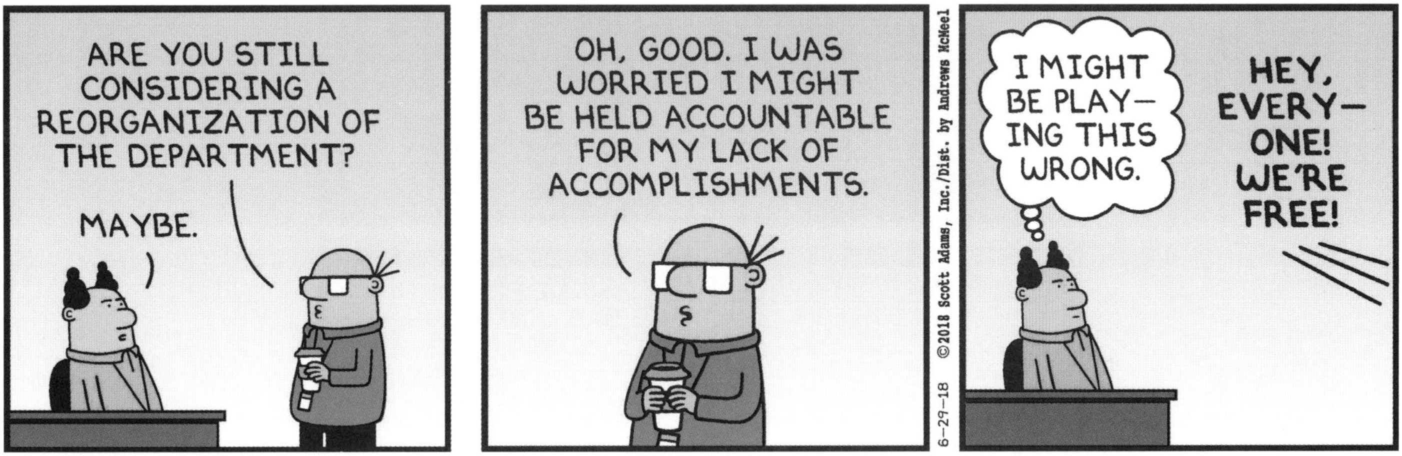
ARE YOU STILL CONSIDERING A REORGANIZATION OF THE DEPARTMENT?
MAYBE.
OH, GOOD. I WAS WORRIED I MIGHT BE HELD ACCOUNTABLE FOR MY LACK OF ACCOMPLISHMENTS.
I MIGHT BE PLAYING THIS WRONG.
HEY, EVERYONE! WE'RE FREE!
6-29-18 ©2018 Scott Adams, Inc./Dist. by Andrews McMeel

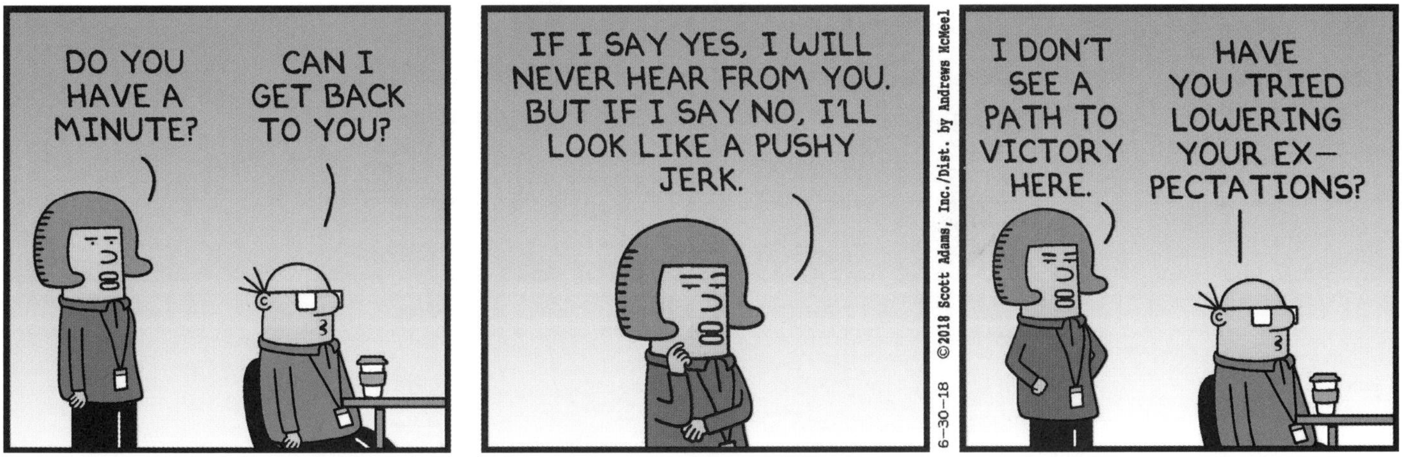
DO YOU HAVE A MINUTE?
CAN I GET BACK TO YOU?
IF I SAY YES, I WILL NEVER HEAR FROM YOU. BUT IF I SAY NO, I'LL LOOK LIKE A PUSHY JERK.
I DON'T SEE A PATH TO VICTORY HERE.
HAVE YOU TRIED LOWERING YOUR EXPECTATIONS?
6-30-18 ©2018 Scott Adams, Inc./Dist. by Andrews McMeel

WHY DID YOU SAY WE DON'T HAVE A BUDGET FOR OUR PROJECT?
I NEVER SAID THAT.
THEN WHY DID YOU SAY THE PROJECT ISN'T FEASIBLE?
I NEVER SAID ANYTHING LIKE THAT.
BUT YOU DID SAY YOU THOUGHT IT WOULD TAKE TEN YEARS TO FINISH?
I'VE NEVER SAID ANYTHING LIKE THAT.
HAHAHA! YOU'RE IN TOTAL MELTDOWN MODE NOW.
I ALREADY FORGOT WHAT WE WERE TALKING ABOUT.
HOW WAS YOUR TALK WITH DILBERT?
HE'S BACK-PEDALING AFTER I TOTALLY OWNED HIM.
© 2018 Scott Adams, Inc./Dist. by Andrews McMeel
7-1-18

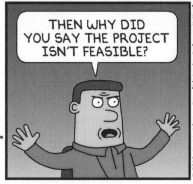

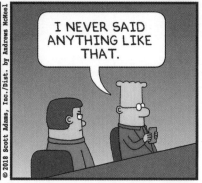

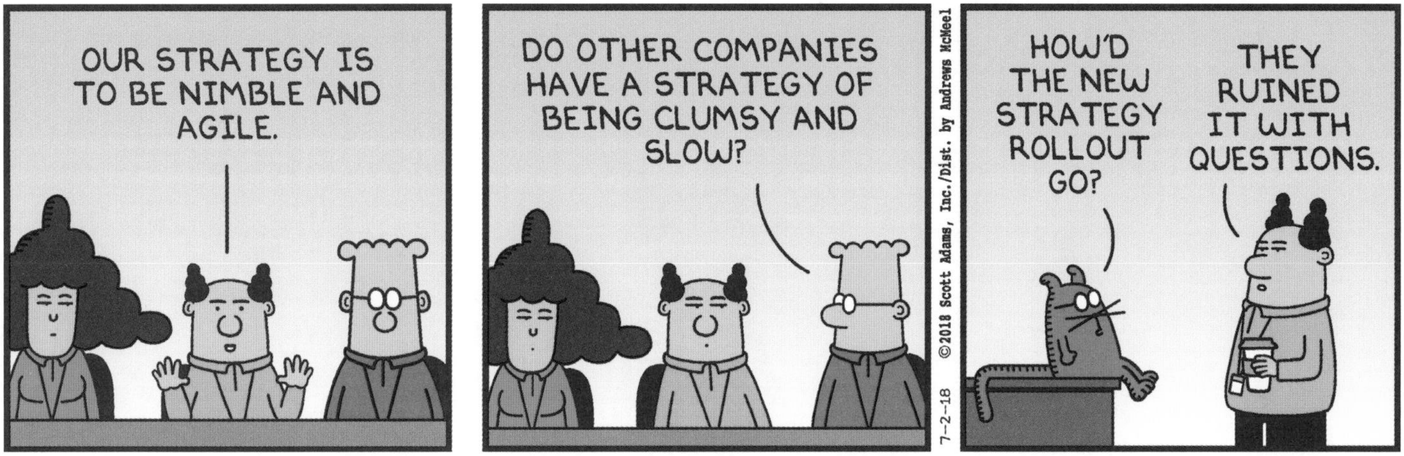
OUR STRATEGY IS TO BE NIMBLE AND AGILE.
DO OTHER COMPANIES HAVE A STRATEGY OF BEING CLUMSY AND SLOW?
HOW'D THE NEW STRATEGY ROLLOUT GO?
THEY RUINED IT WITH QUESTIONS.
7-2-18 ©2018 Scott Adams, Inc./Dist. by Andrews McMeel

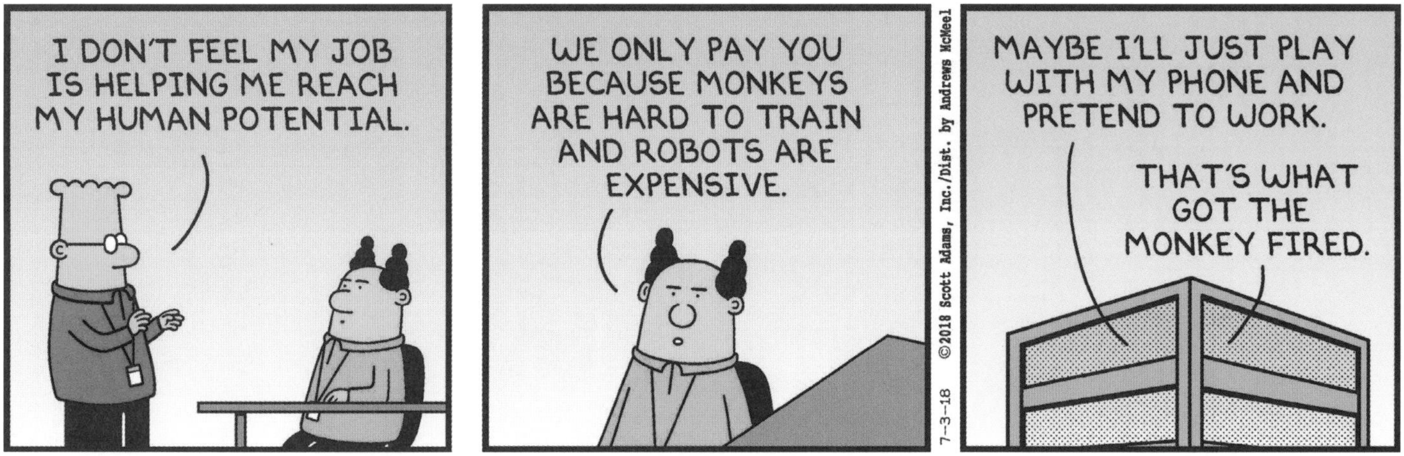
I DON'T FEEL MY JOB IS HELPING ME REACH MY HUMAN POTENTIAL.
WE ONLY PAY YOU BECAUSE MONKEYS ARE HARD TO TRAIN AND ROBOTS ARE EXPENSIVE.
MAYBE I'LL JUST PLAY WITH MY PHONE AND PRETEND TO WORK.
THAT'S WHAT GOT THE MONKEY FIRED.
7-3-18 ©2018 Scott Adams, Inc./Dist. by Andrews McMeel

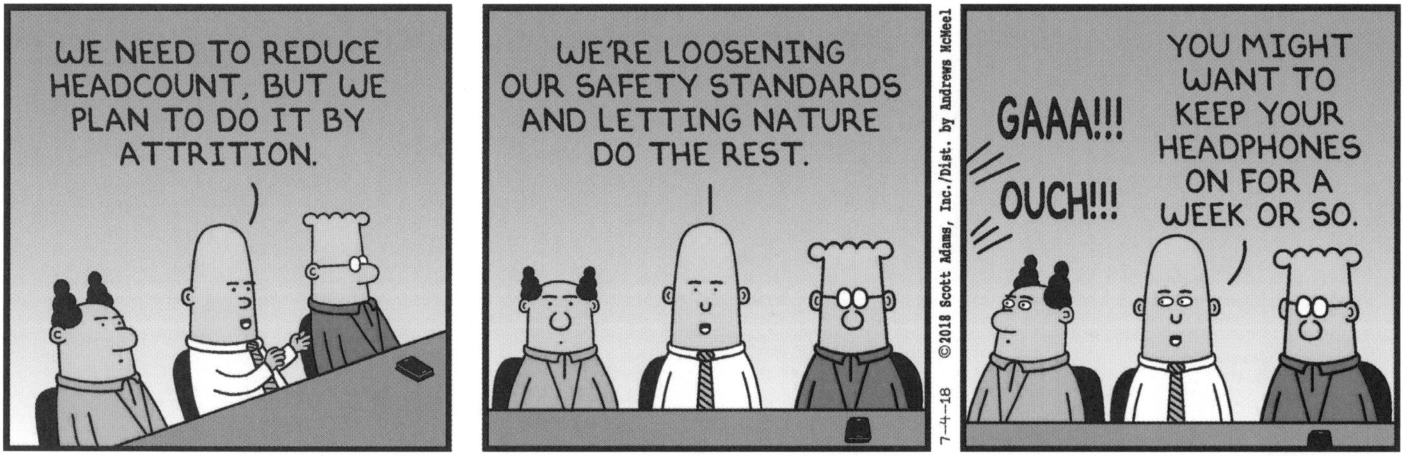
WE NEED TO REDUCE HEADCOUNT, BUT WE PLAN TO DO IT BY ATTRITION.
WE'RE LOOSENING OUR SAFETY STANDARDS AND LETTING NATURE DO THE REST.
GAAA!!!
OUCH!!!
YOU MIGHT WANT TO KEEP YOUR HEADPHONES ON FOR A WEEK OR SO.
7-4-18 ©2018 Scott Adams, Inc./Dist. by Andrews McMeel

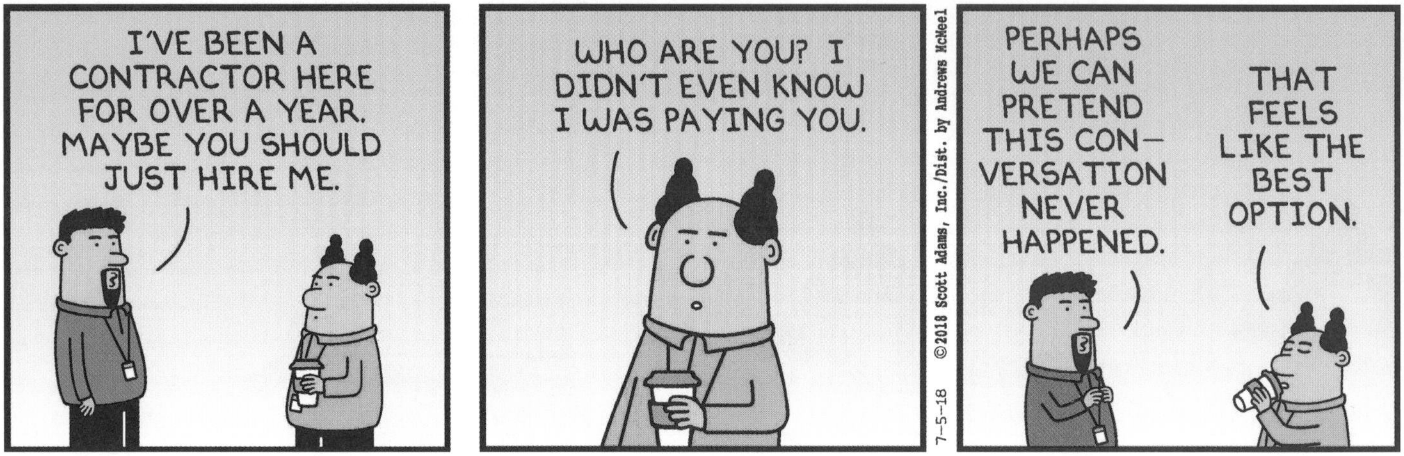
I'VE BEEN A CONTRACTOR HERE FOR OVER A YEAR. MAYBE YOU SHOULD JUST HIRE ME.
WHO ARE YOU? I DIDN'T EVEN KNOW I WAS PAYING YOU.
7-5-18 ©2018 Scott Adams, Inc./Dist. by Andrews McMeel
PERHAPS WE CAN PRETEND THIS CON-VERSATION NEVER HAPPENED.
THAT FEELS LIKE THE BEST OPTION.

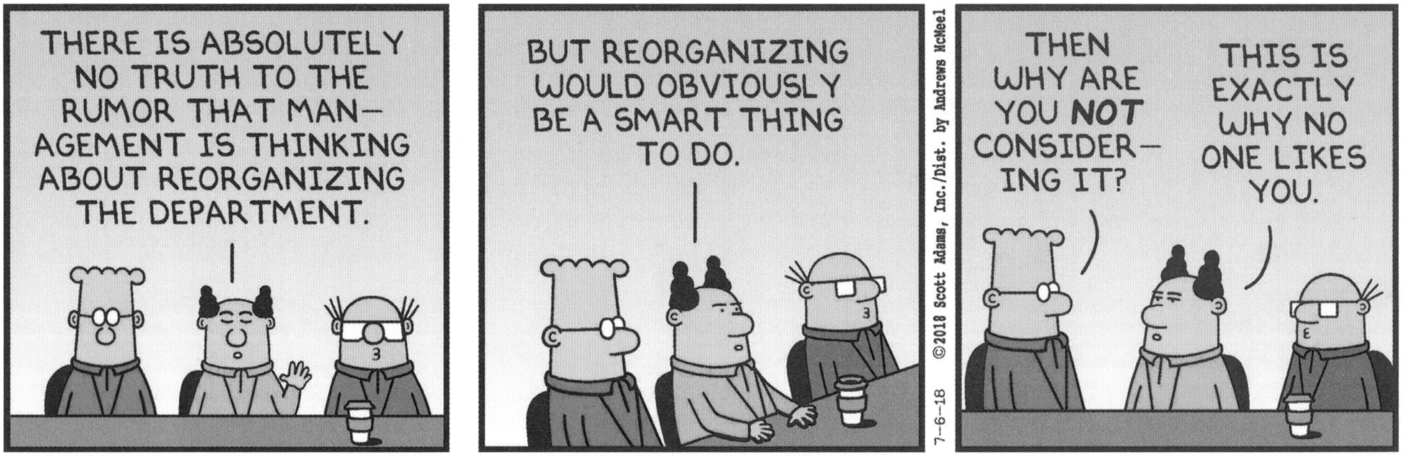
THERE IS ABSOLUTELY NO TRUTH TO THE RUMOR THAT MAN-AGEMENT IS THINKING ABOUT REORGANIZING THE DEPARTMENT.
BUT REORGANIZING WOULD OBVIOUSLY BE A SMART THING TO DO.
7-6-18 ©2018 Scott Adams, Inc./Dist. by Andrews McMeel
THEN WHY ARE YOU **NOT** CONSIDER-ING IT?
THIS IS EXACTLY WHY NO ONE LIKES YOU.

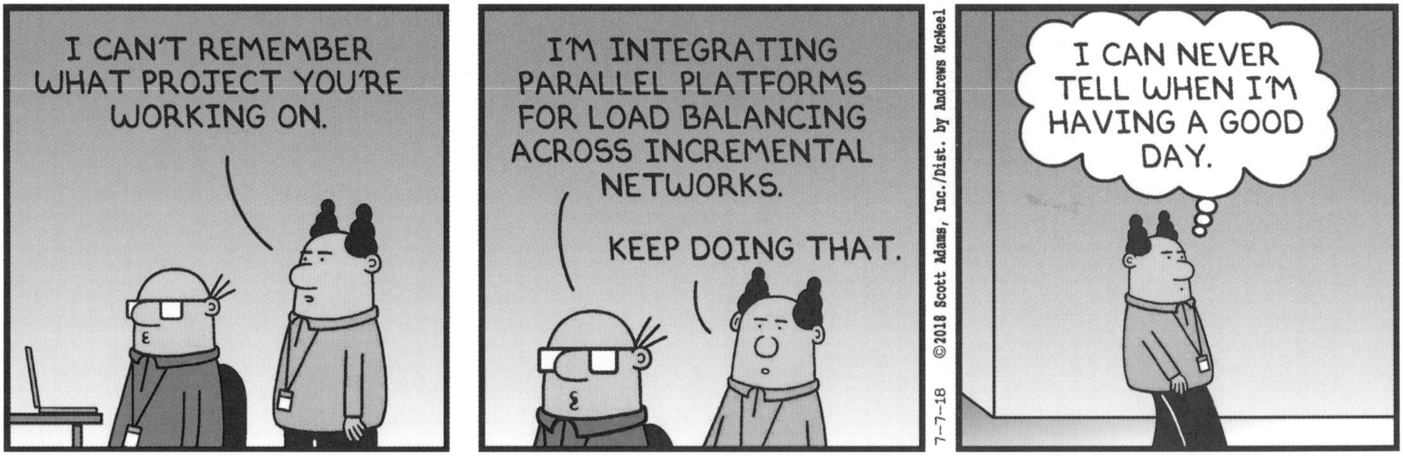
I CAN'T REMEMBER WHAT PROJECT YOU'RE WORKING ON.
I'M INTEGRATING PARALLEL PLATFORMS FOR LOAD BALANCING ACROSS INCREMENTAL NETWORKS.
KEEP DOING THAT.
7-7-18 ©2018 Scott Adams, Inc./Dist. by Andrews McMeel
I CAN NEVER TELL WHEN I'M HAVING A GOOD DAY.

MAYBE YOU COULD REMOVE A FEW SLIDES TO MAKE YOUR DECK SHORTER.
SO YOU'RE SAYING I SHOULD GIVE UP ON TRYING TO BE PERSUASIVE?
NO. I'M SAYING IT WOULD BE MORE PERSUASIVE IF IT WERE SHORTER.
SO YOU'RE SAYING THAT HAVING ZERO SLIDES WOULD BE THE MOST PERSUASIVE OF ALL?
NO. I'M SAYING YOU HAVE MORE SLIDES THAN YOU NEED.
SO YOU'RE SAYING PEOPLE DON'T NEED ACCURATE INFOR- MATION SO LONG AS THEY DON'T HAVE LOTS OF SLIDES?
I'M NOT SAYING ANYTHING LIKE THAT!
DID DILBERT HAVE ANY SUGGES- TIONS?
JUST CRAZY ONES.
© 2018 Scott Adams, Inc./Dist. by Andrews McMeel
7-8-18

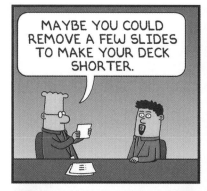

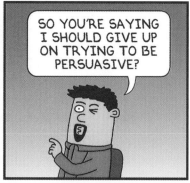

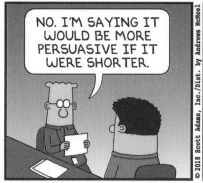

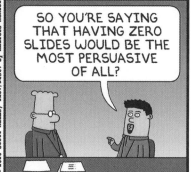

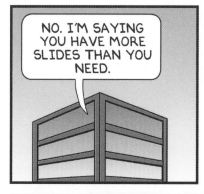

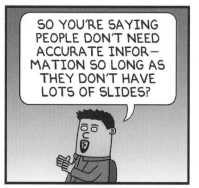

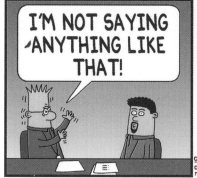

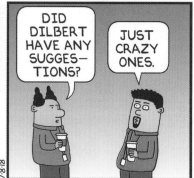

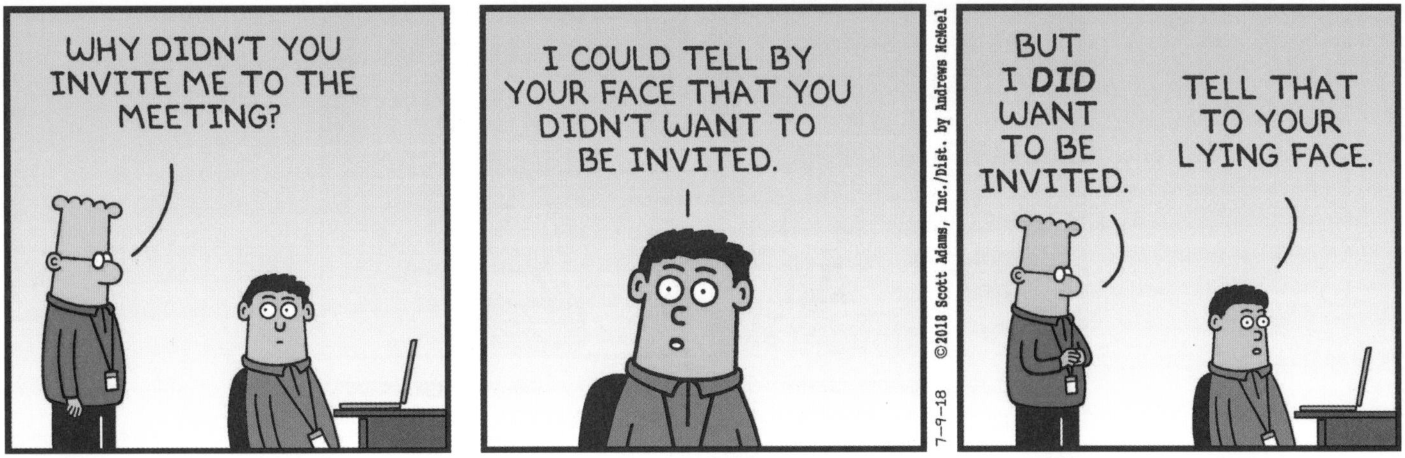
WHY DIDN'T YOU INVITE ME TO THE MEETING?
I COULD TELL BY YOUR FACE THAT YOU DIDN'T WANT TO BE INVITED.
7-9-18 ©2018 Scott Adams, Inc./Dist. by Andrews McMeel
BUT I **DID** WANT TO BE INVITED.
TELL THAT TO YOUR LYING FACE.

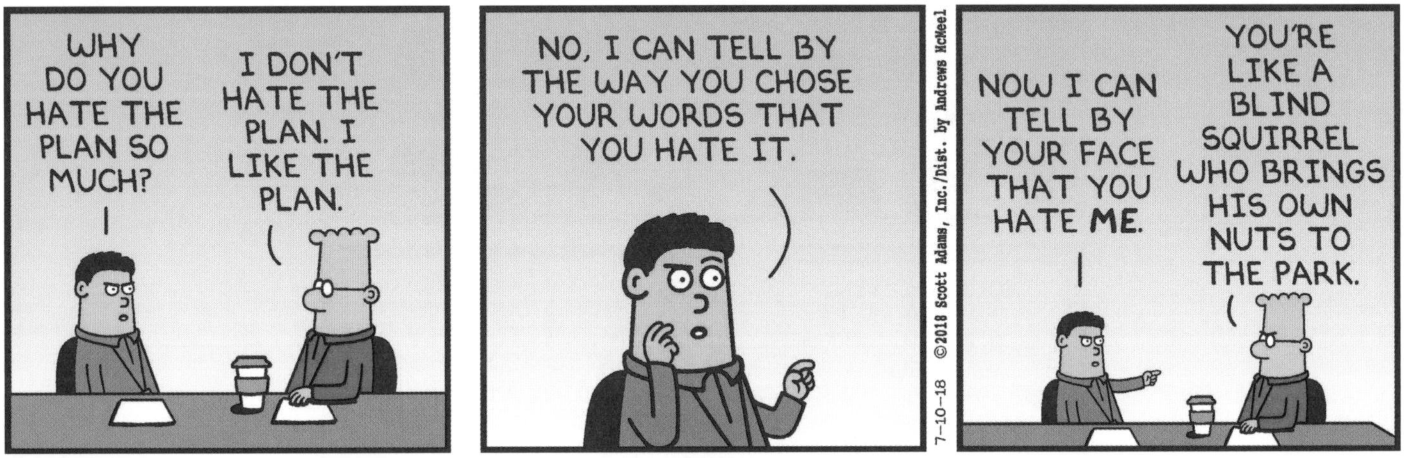
WHY DO YOU HATE THE PLAN SO MUCH?
I DON'T HATE THE PLAN. I LIKE THE PLAN.
NO, I CAN TELL BY THE WAY YOU CHOSE YOUR WORDS THAT YOU HATE IT.
7-10-18 ©2018 Scott Adams, Inc./Dist. by Andrews McMeel
NOW I CAN TELL BY YOUR FACE THAT YOU HATE **ME**.
YOU'RE LIKE A BLIND SQUIRREL WHO BRINGS HIS OWN NUTS TO THE PARK.

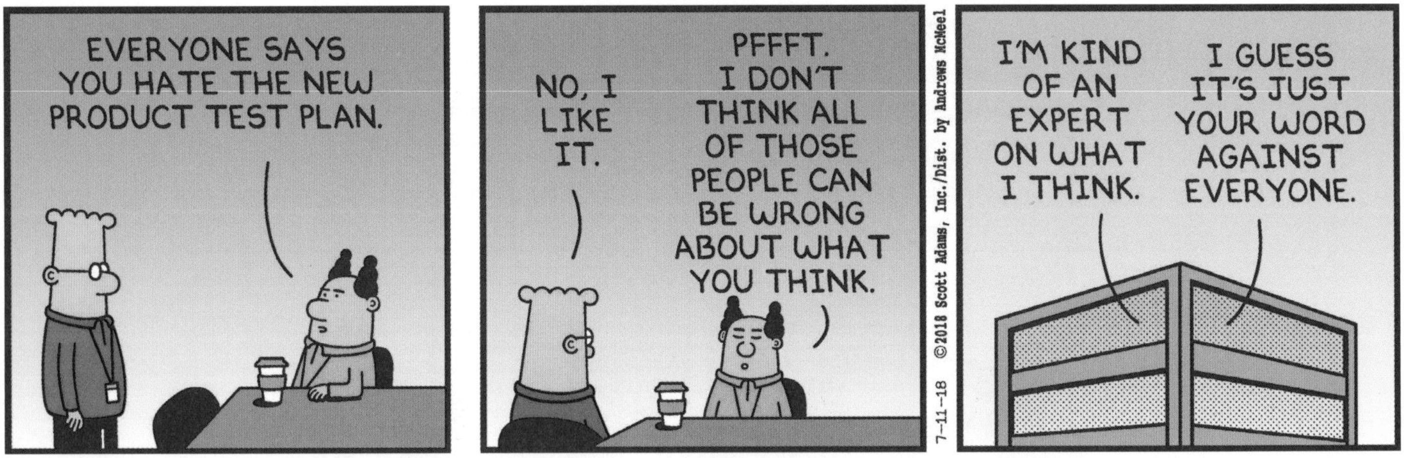
EVERYONE SAYS YOU HATE THE NEW PRODUCT TEST PLAN.
NO, I LIKE IT.
PFFFT. I DON'T THINK ALL OF THOSE PEOPLE CAN BE WRONG ABOUT WHAT YOU THINK.
7-11-18 ©2018 Scott Adams, Inc./Dist. by Andrews McMeel
I'M KIND OF AN EXPERT ON WHAT I THINK.
I GUESS IT'S JUST YOUR WORD AGAINST EVERYONE.

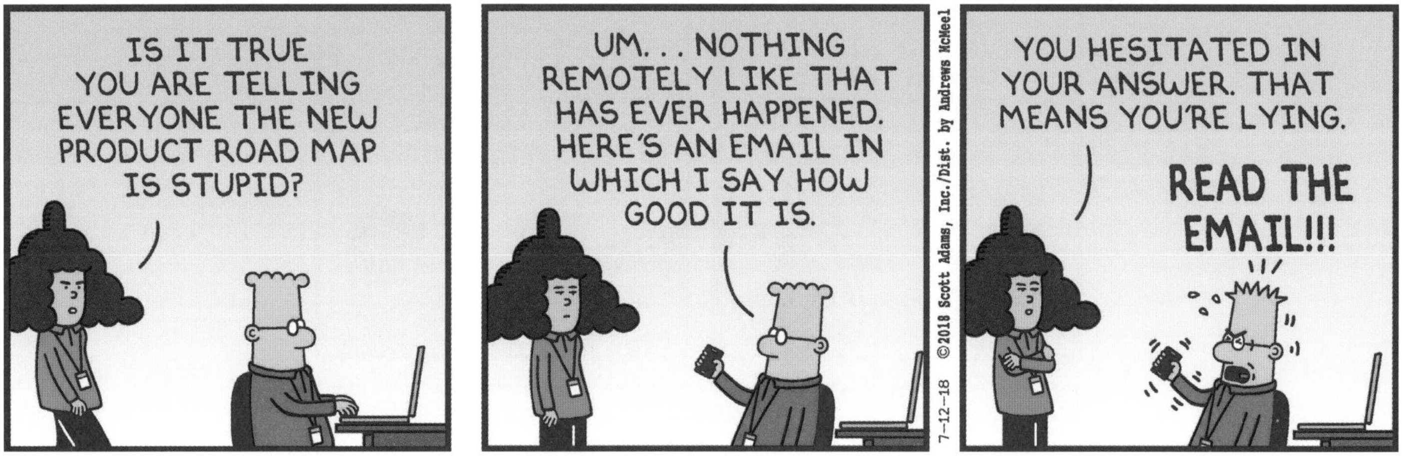
IS IT TRUE YOU ARE TELLING EVERYONE THE NEW PRODUCT ROAD MAP IS STUPID?
UM. . . NOTHING REMOTELY LIKE THAT HAS EVER HAPPENED. HERE'S AN EMAIL IN WHICH I SAY HOW GOOD IT IS.
7-12-18 ©2018 Scott Adams, Inc./Dist. by Andrews McMeel
YOU HESITATED IN YOUR ANSWER. THAT MEANS YOU'RE LYING.
READ THE EMAIL!!!

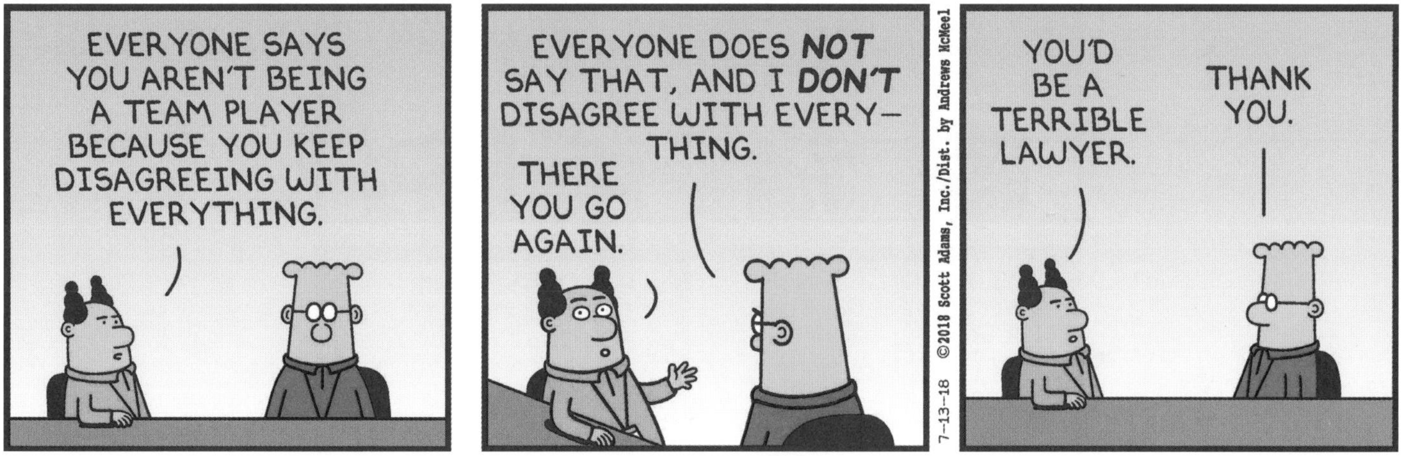
EVERYONE SAYS YOU AREN'T BEING A TEAM PLAYER BECAUSE YOU KEEP DISAGREEING WITH EVERYTHING.
EVERYONE DOES **NOT** SAY THAT, AND I **DON'T** DISAGREE WITH EVERY-THING.
THERE YOU GO AGAIN.
7-13-18 ©2018 Scott Adams, Inc./Dist. by Andrews McMeel
YOU'D BE A TERRIBLE LAWYER.
THANK YOU.

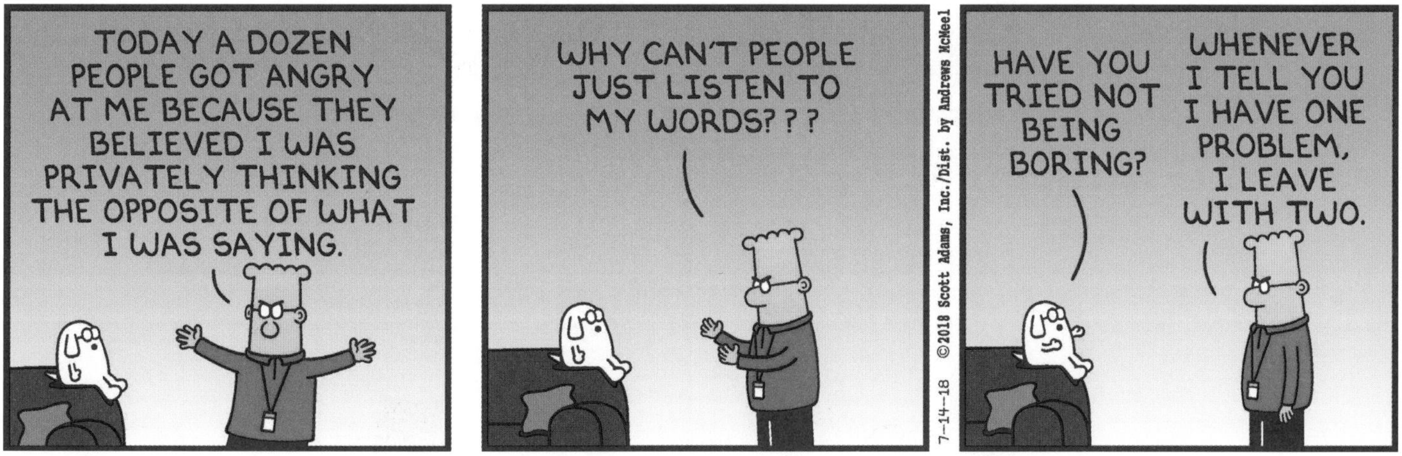
TODAY A DOZEN PEOPLE GOT ANGRY AT ME BECAUSE THEY BELIEVED I WAS PRIVATELY THINKING THE OPPOSITE OF WHAT I WAS SAYING.
WHY CAN'T PEOPLE JUST LISTEN TO MY WORDS???
7-14-18 ©2018 Scott Adams, Inc./Dist. by Andrews McMeel
HAVE YOU TRIED NOT BEING BORING?
WHENEVER I TELL YOU I HAVE ONE PROBLEM, I LEAVE WITH TWO.

HERE'S MY INVOICE FOR THE EXTRAS.
THE INVOICE WE ALREADY PAID COVERED EVERYTHING IN THE CONTRACT.
THAT ONLY COVERED THE COSTS I QUOTED WITH INTENTIONAL CLARITY.
THERE ARE OTHER COSTS THAT I MIGHT HAVE MENTIONED IN A LONG AND RAMBLING EXPLANATION THAT WAS INTENTIONALLY AMBIGUOUS.
"MIGHT HAVE"??? I'M SURE YOU DID NOT.
SOUNDS LIKE YOUR WORD AGAINST MINE.
AND EVEN IF YOU DID MENTION IT, YOU JUST SAID IT WAS INTENTIONALLY AMBIGUOUS!!!
I DON'T THINK YOU WANT TO TELL YOUR BOSS YOU'RE A BAD LISTENER.
I THOUGHT WE ALREADY PAID THIS VENDOR.
DID YOU FORGET ALL THE EXTRAS I TOLD YOU ABOUT?
© 2018 Scott Adams, Inc./Dist. by Andrews McMeel
7-15-18

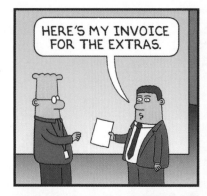

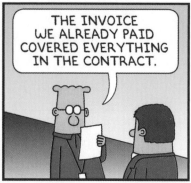

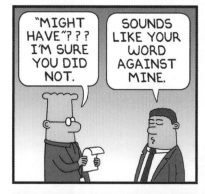

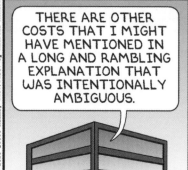

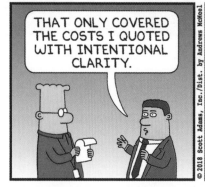

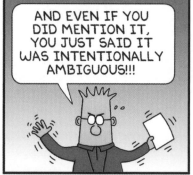

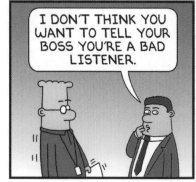

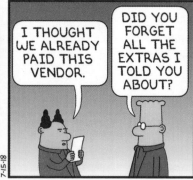

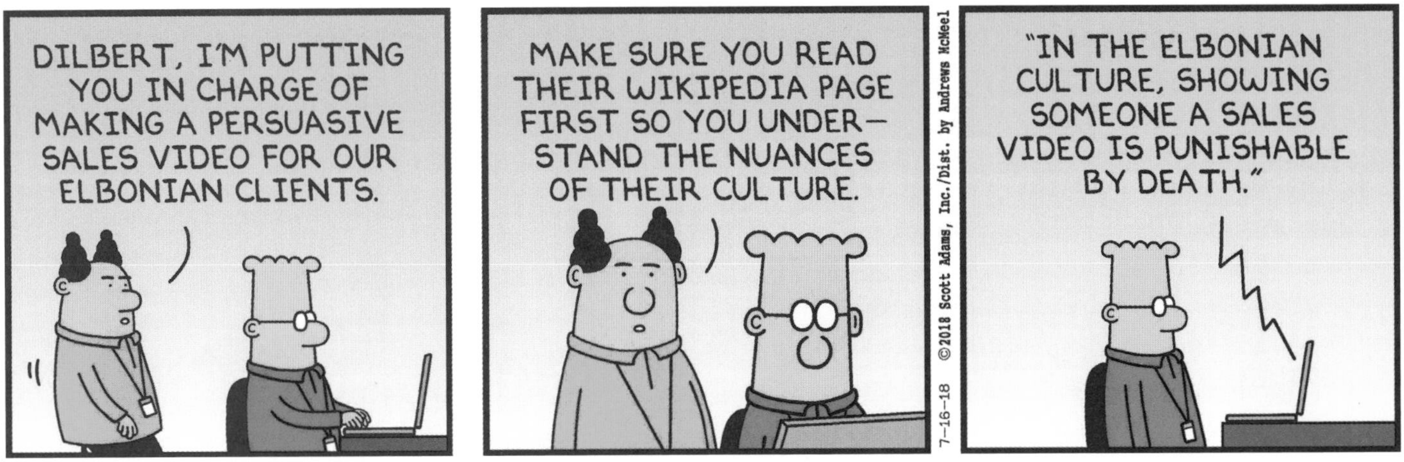
DILBERT, I'M PUTTING YOU IN CHARGE OF MAKING A PERSUASIVE SALES VIDEO FOR OUR ELBONIAN CLIENTS.
MAKE SURE YOU READ THEIR WIKIPEDIA PAGE FIRST SO YOU UNDER-STAND THE NUANCES OF THEIR CULTURE.
7-16-18 ©2018 Scott Adams, Inc./Dist. by Andrews McMeel
"IN THE ELBONIAN CULTURE, SHOWING SOMEONE A SALES VIDEO IS PUNISHABLE BY DEATH."

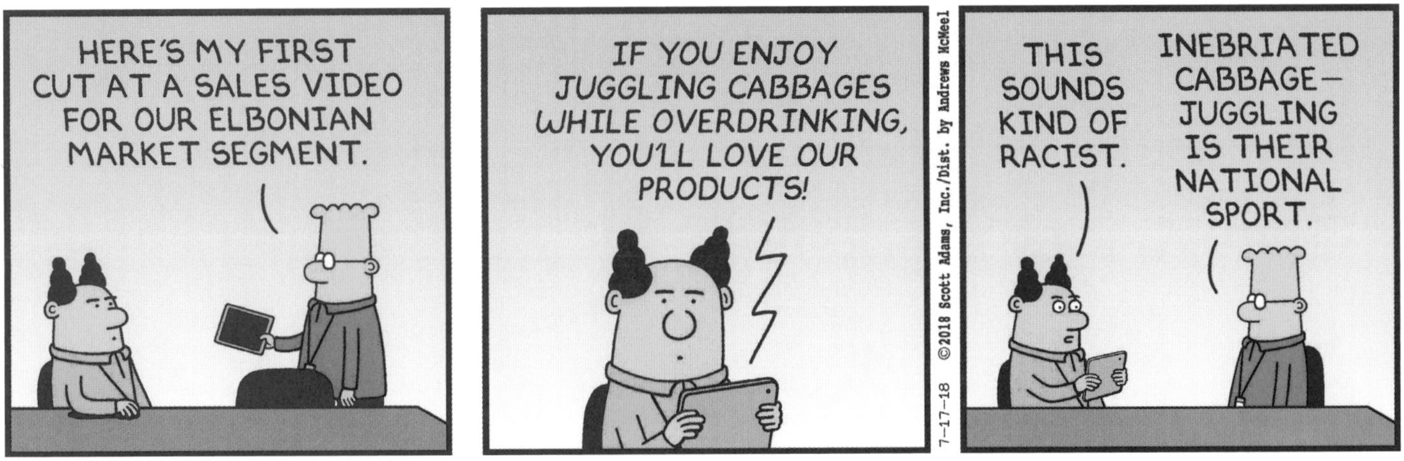
HERE'S MY FIRST CUT AT A SALES VIDEO FOR OUR ELBONIAN MARKET SEGMENT.
IF YOU ENJOY JUGGLING CABBAGES WHILE OVERDRINKING, YOU'LL LOVE OUR PRODUCTS!
7-17-18 ©2018 Scott Adams, Inc./Dist. by Andrews McMeel
THIS SOUNDS KIND OF RACIST.
INEBRIATED CABBAGE-JUGGLING IS THEIR NATIONAL SPORT.

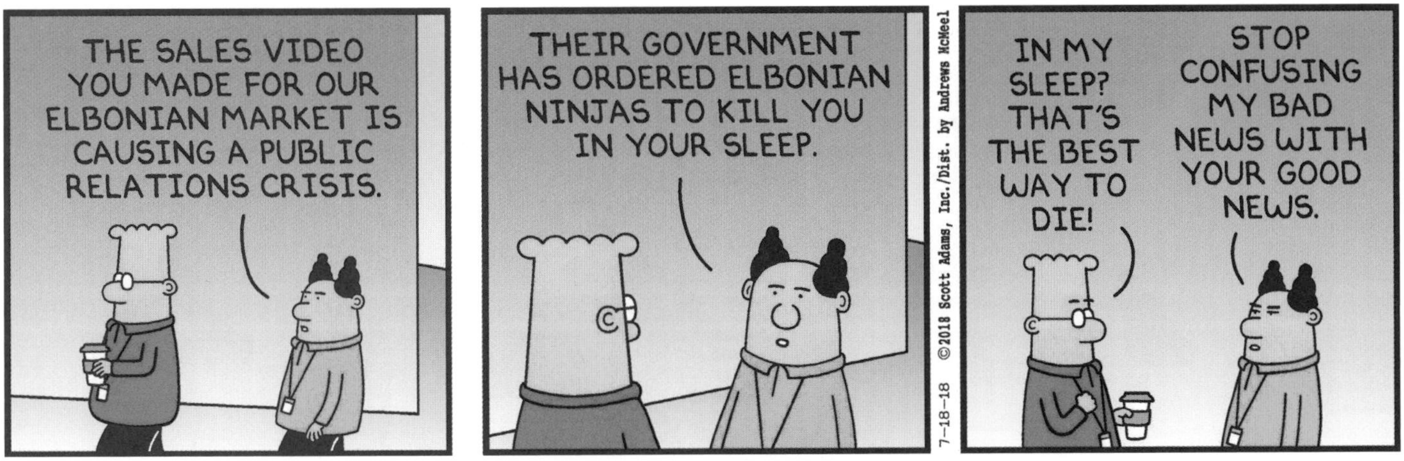
THE SALES VIDEO YOU MADE FOR OUR ELBONIAN MARKET IS CAUSING A PUBLIC RELATIONS CRISIS.
THEIR GOVERNMENT HAS ORDERED ELBONIAN NINJAS TO KILL YOU IN YOUR SLEEP.
7-18-18 ©2018 Scott Adams, Inc./Dist. by Andrews McMeel
IN MY SLEEP? THAT'S THE BEST WAY TO DIE!
STOP CONFUSING MY BAD NEWS WITH YOUR GOOD NEWS.

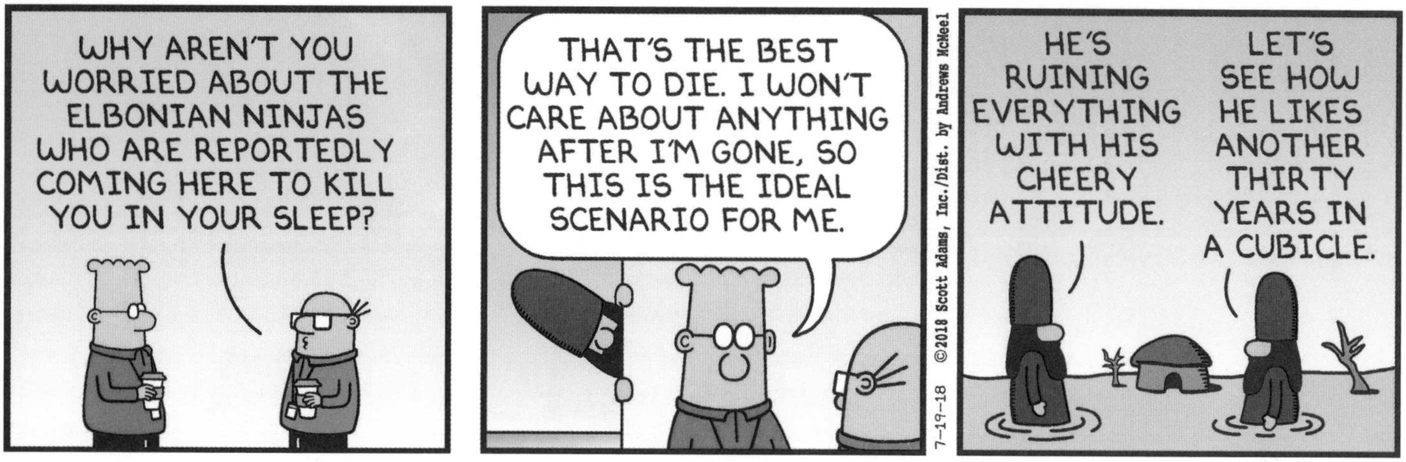
WHY AREN'T YOU WORRIED ABOUT THE ELBONIAN NINJAS WHO ARE REPORTEDLY COMING HERE TO KILL YOU IN YOUR SLEEP?
THAT'S THE BEST WAY TO DIE. I WON'T CARE ABOUT ANYTHING AFTER I'M GONE, SO THIS IS THE IDEAL SCENARIO FOR ME.
7-19-18 ©2018 Scott Adams, Inc./Dist. by Andrews McMeel
HE'S RUINING EVERYTHING WITH HIS CHEERY ATTITUDE.
LET'S SEE HOW HE LIKES ANOTHER THIRTY YEARS IN A CUBICLE.

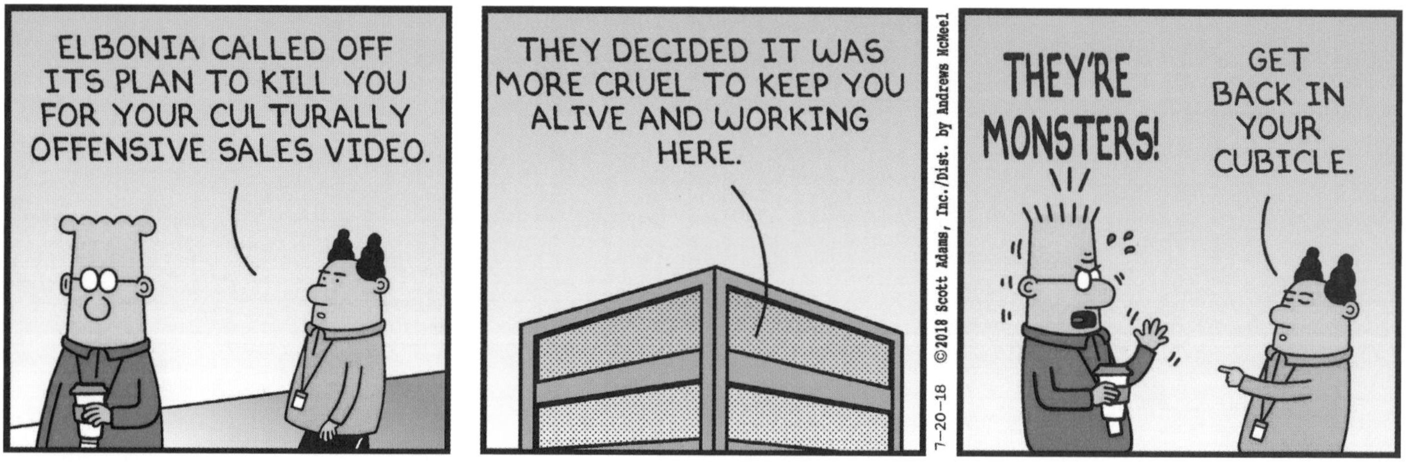
ELBONIA CALLED OFF ITS PLAN TO KILL YOU FOR YOUR CULTURALLY OFFENSIVE SALES VIDEO.
THEY DECIDED IT WAS MORE CRUEL TO KEEP YOU ALIVE AND WORKING HERE.
7-20-18 ©2018 Scott Adams, Inc./Dist. by Andrews McMeel
THEY'RE MONSTERS!
GET BACK IN YOUR CUBICLE.

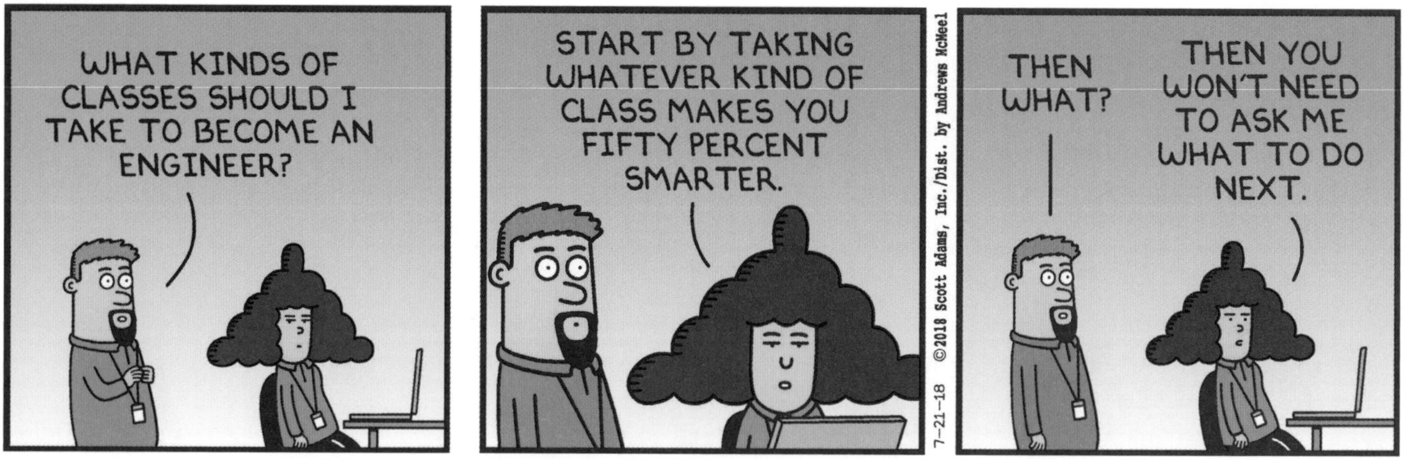
WHAT KINDS OF CLASSES SHOULD I TAKE TO BECOME AN ENGINEER?
START BY TAKING WHATEVER KIND OF CLASS MAKES YOU FIFTY PERCENT SMARTER.
7-21-18 ©2018 Scott Adams, Inc./Dist. by Andrews McMeel
THEN WHAT?
THEN YOU WON'T NEED TO ASK ME WHAT TO DO NEXT.

I FINALLY SIGNED UP FOR TWITTER.
SENDING MY FIRST TWEET.
SEND
UH—OH. WHAT THE? ? ?
IT SEEMS I HAVE OPENED SOME SORT OF PORTAL TO HELL.
DEMONS ARE STREAMING THROUGH THE PORTAL!!!
I HAVE NEVER SEEN SUCH HORRIBLE THOUGHTS!
GAAAA!!!
HOW WAS YOUR FIRST DAY ON TWITTER?
I'M ALREADY ADDICTED TO IT.
© 2018 Scott Adams, Inc./Dist. by Andrews McMeel
7-22-18

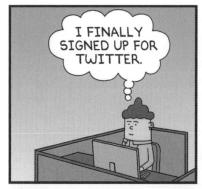

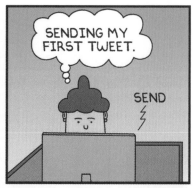

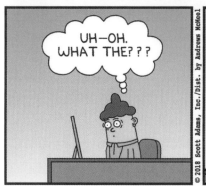

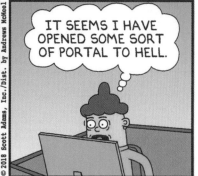

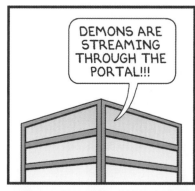

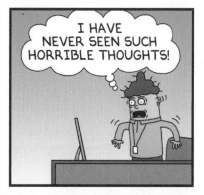

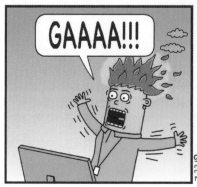

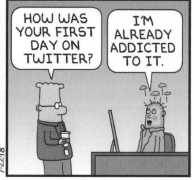

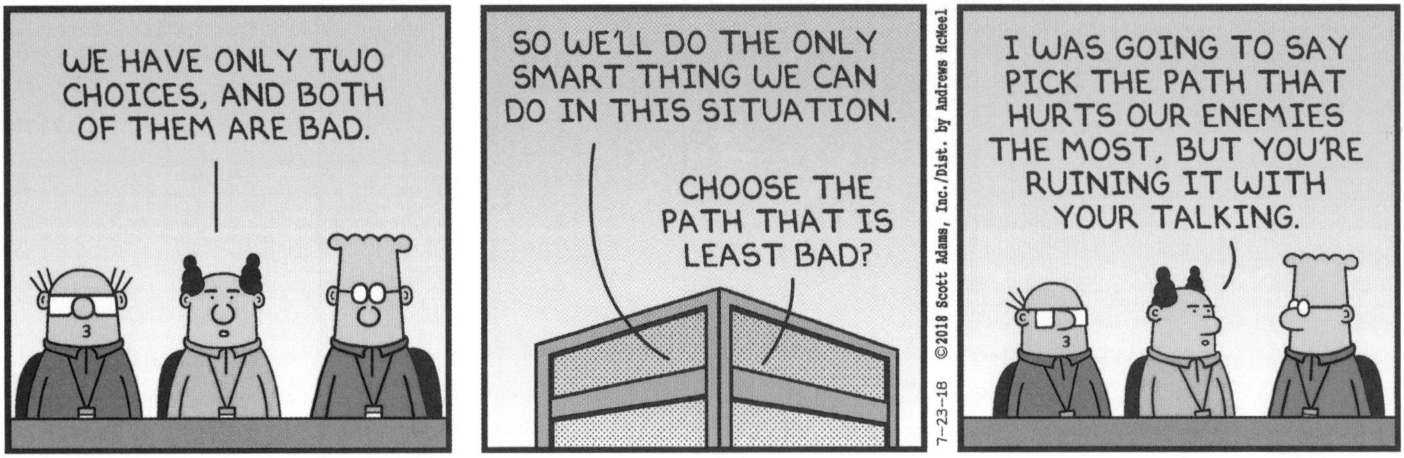
WE HAVE ONLY TWO CHOICES, AND BOTH OF THEM ARE BAD.
SO WE'LL DO THE ONLY SMART THING WE CAN DO IN THIS SITUATION.
CHOOSE THE PATH THAT IS LEAST BAD?
7-23-18 ©2018 Scott Adams, Inc./Dist. by Andrews McMeel
I WAS GOING TO SAY PICK THE PATH THAT HURTS OUR ENEMIES THE MOST, BUT YOU'RE RUINING IT WITH YOUR TALKING.

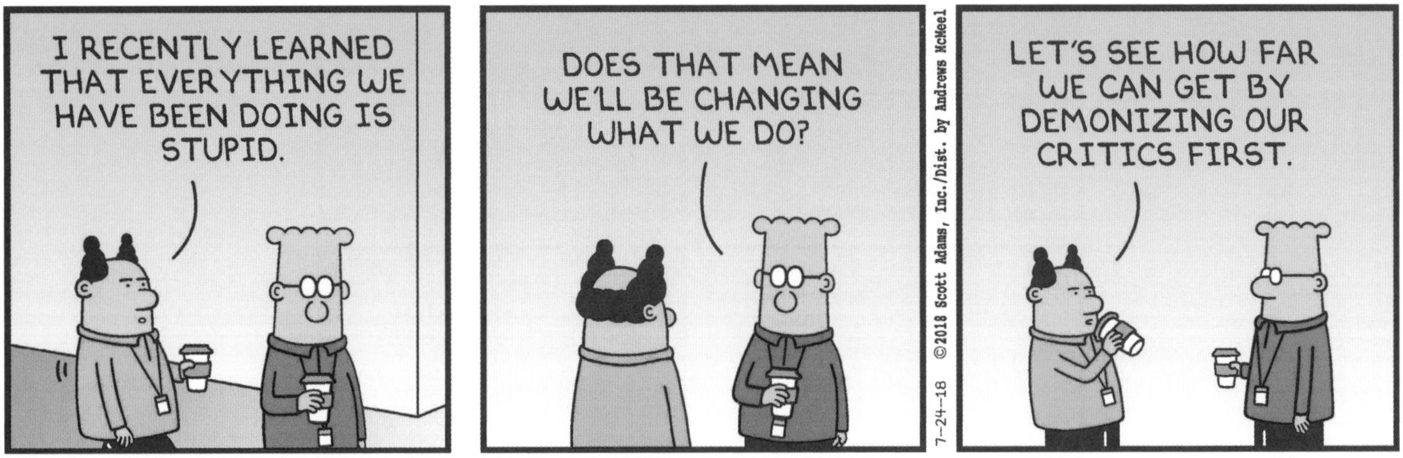
I RECENTLY LEARNED THAT EVERYTHING WE HAVE BEEN DOING IS STUPID.
DOES THAT MEAN WE'LL BE CHANGING WHAT WE DO?
7-24-18 ©2018 Scott Adams, Inc./Dist. by Andrews McMeel
LET'S SEE HOW FAR WE CAN GET BY DEMONIZING OUR CRITICS FIRST.

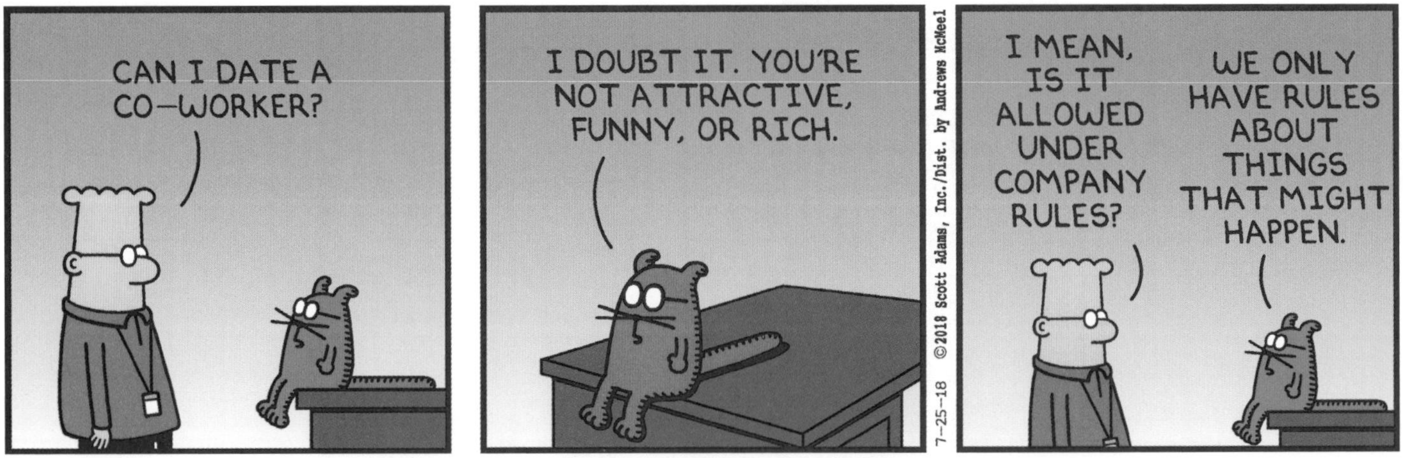
CAN I DATE A CO-WORKER?
I DOUBT IT. YOU'RE NOT ATTRACTIVE, FUNNY, OR RICH.
7-25-18 ©2018 Scott Adams, Inc./Dist. by Andrews McMeel
I MEAN, IS IT ALLOWED UNDER COMPANY RULES?
WE ONLY HAVE RULES ABOUT THINGS THAT MIGHT HAPPEN.

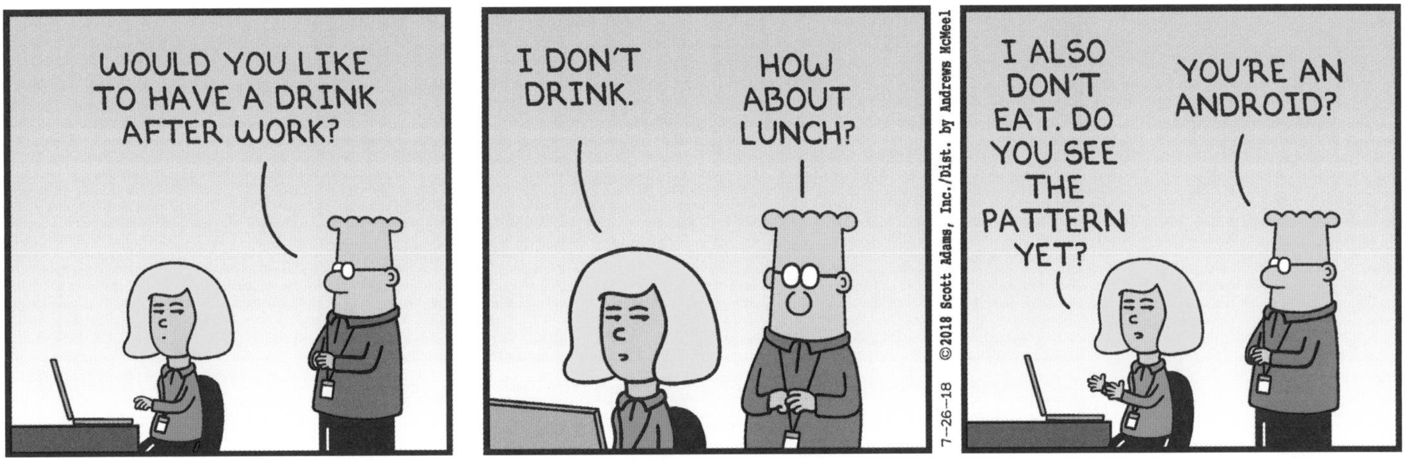
WOULD YOU LIKE TO HAVE A DRINK AFTER WORK?
I DON'T DRINK.
HOW ABOUT LUNCH?
7-26-18 ©2018 Scott Adams, Inc./Dist. by Andrews McMeel
I ALSO DON'T EAT. DO YOU SEE THE PATTERN YET?
YOU'RE AN ANDROID?

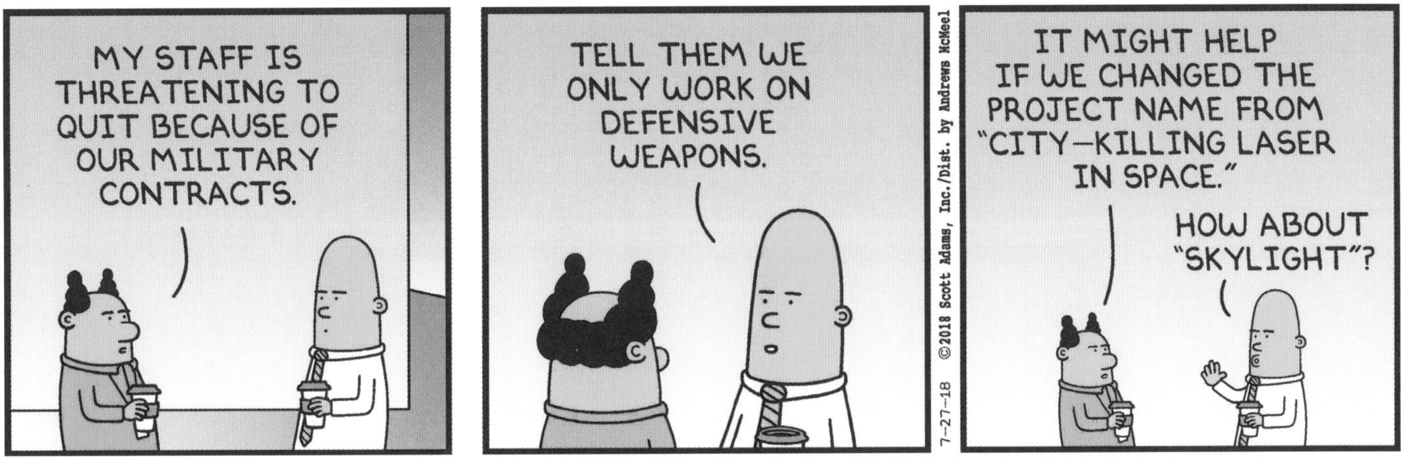
MY STAFF IS THREATENING TO QUIT BECAUSE OF OUR MILITARY CONTRACTS.
TELL THEM WE ONLY WORK ON DEFENSIVE WEAPONS.
7-27-18 ©2018 Scott Adams, Inc./Dist. by Andrews McMeel
IT MIGHT HELP IF WE CHANGED THE PROJECT NAME FROM "CITY-KILLING LASER IN SPACE."
HOW ABOUT "SKYLIGHT"?

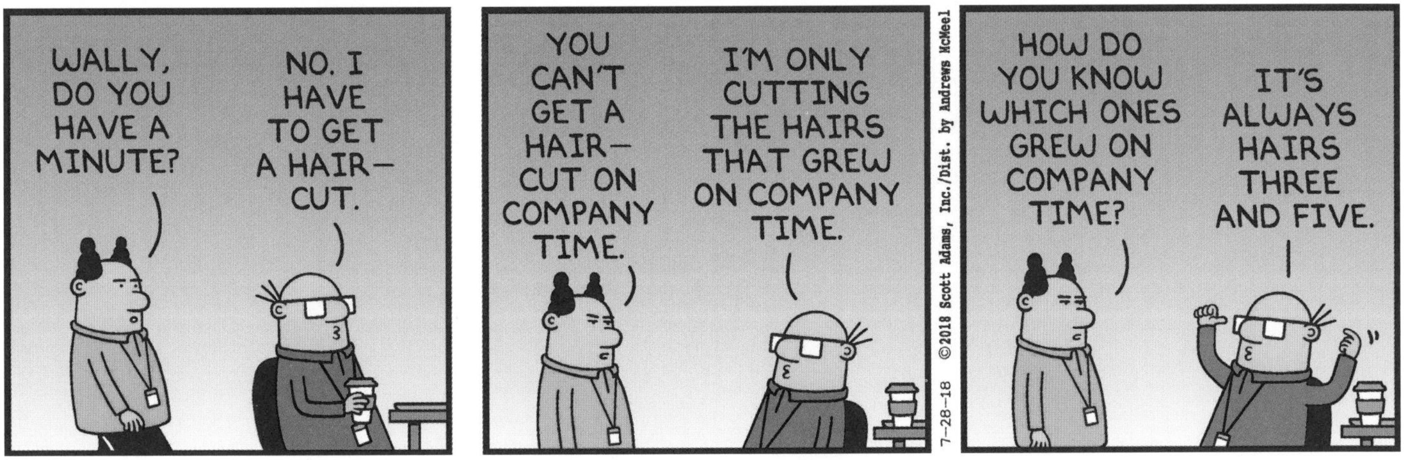
WALLY, DO YOU HAVE A MINUTE?
NO. I HAVE TO GET A HAIR-CUT.
YOU CAN'T GET A HAIR-CUT ON COMPANY TIME.
I'M ONLY CUTTING THE HAIRS THAT GREW ON COMPANY TIME.
7-28-18 ©2018 Scott Adams, Inc./Dist. by Andrews McMeel
HOW DO YOU KNOW WHICH ONES GREW ON COMPANY TIME?
IT'S ALWAYS HAIRS THREE AND FIVE.

YOU SAID THE SOFTWARE WOULD BE FINISHED BY TODAY.
I SAID IT **MIGHT** BE FINISHED BY TODAY.
WHY DID YOU SAY IT MIGHT BE FINISHED IF YOU KNEW IT WOULDN'T?
I DIDN'T KNOW IT WOULDN'T BE FINISHED.
NOW YOU'RE FLIP–FLOPPING ALL OVER THE PLACE.
YOU'RE CONFLATING YOUR OWN FALSE MEMORIES WITH MY ACTIONS.
THAT'S EXACTLY WHAT LIARS SAY.
HOW WAS WORK?
TOTALLY NORMAL,
UNFOR– TUNATELY.
© 2018 Scott Adams, Inc./Dist. by Andrews McMeel
7-29-18

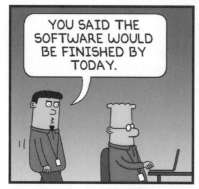

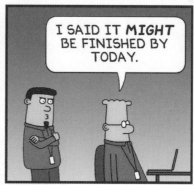

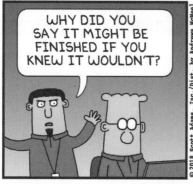

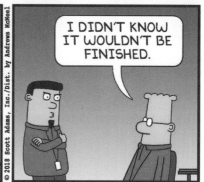

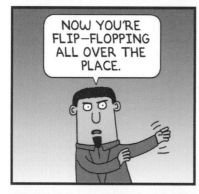

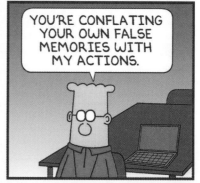

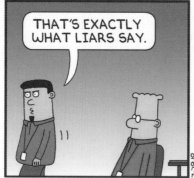

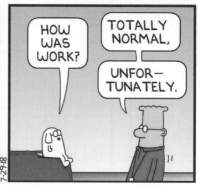

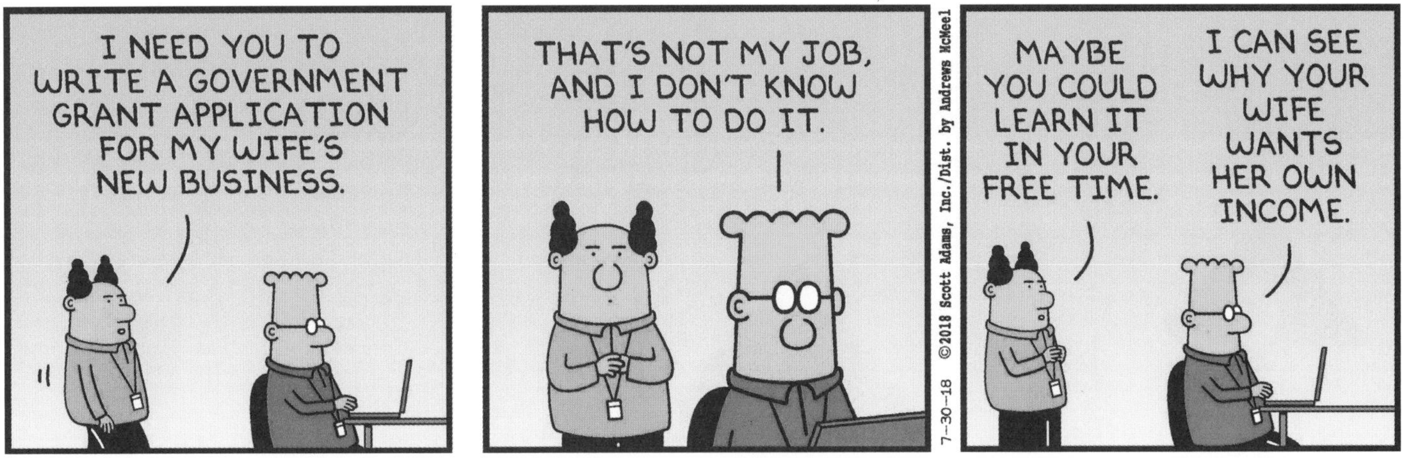
I NEED YOU TO WRITE A GOVERNMENT GRANT APPLICATION FOR MY WIFE'S NEW BUSINESS.
THAT'S NOT MY JOB, AND I DON'T KNOW HOW TO DO IT.
MAYBE YOU COULD LEARN IT IN YOUR FREE TIME.
I CAN SEE WHY YOUR WIFE WANTS HER OWN INCOME.
7-30-18 ©2018 Scott Adams, Inc./Dist. by Andrews McMeel

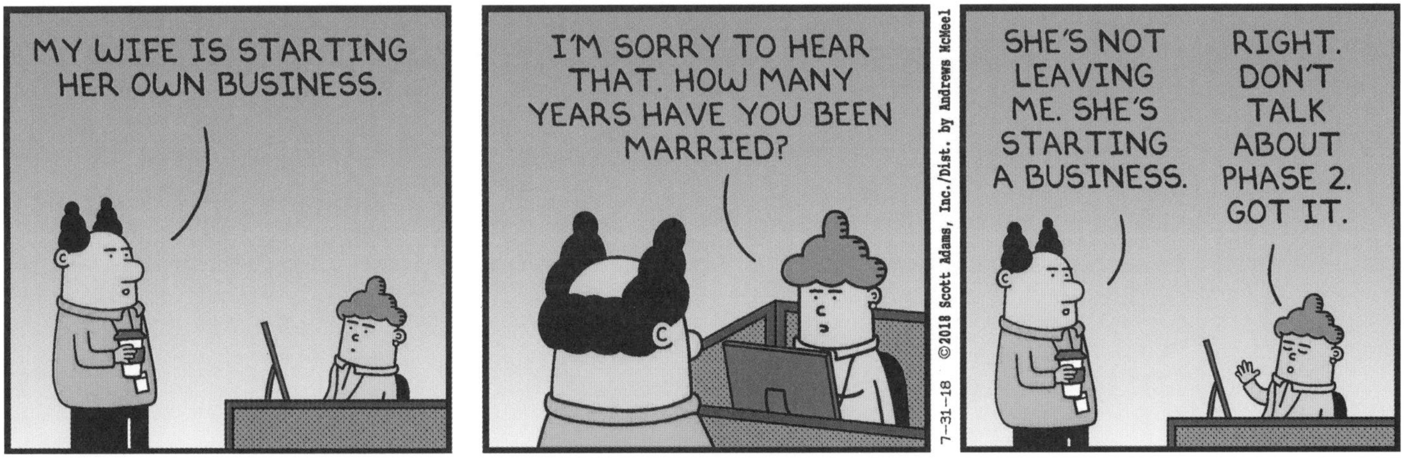
MY WIFE IS STARTING HER OWN BUSINESS.
I'M SORRY TO HEAR THAT. HOW MANY YEARS HAVE YOU BEEN MARRIED?
SHE'S NOT LEAVING ME. SHE'S STARTING A BUSINESS.
RIGHT. DON'T TALK ABOUT PHASE 2. GOT IT.
7-31-18 ©2018 Scott Adams, Inc./Dist. by Andrews McMeel

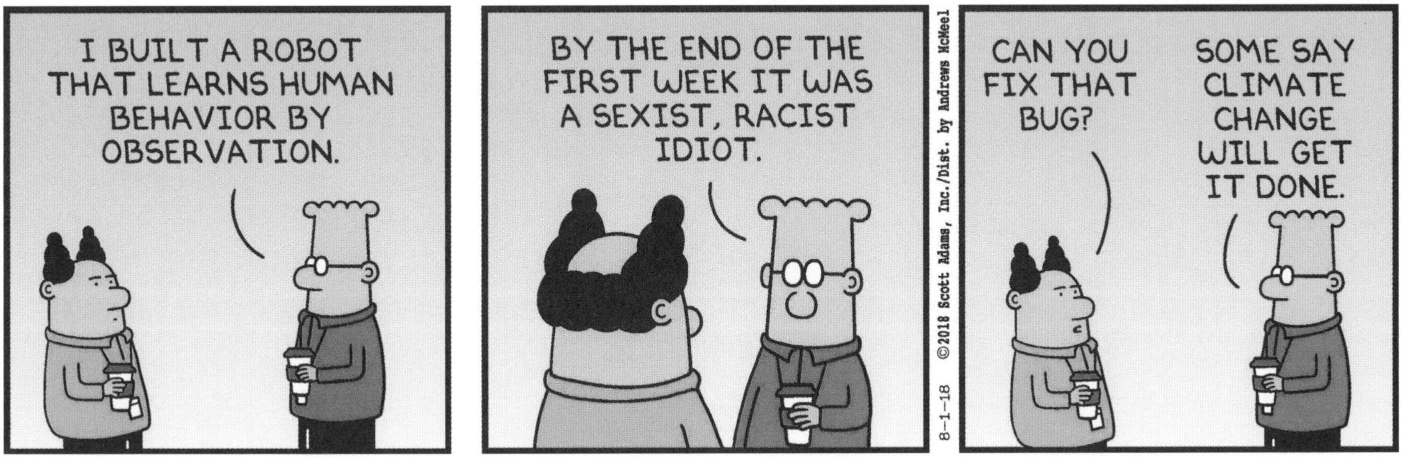
I BUILT A ROBOT THAT LEARNS HUMAN BEHAVIOR BY OBSERVATION.
BY THE END OF THE FIRST WEEK IT WAS A SEXIST, RACIST IDIOT.
CAN YOU FIX THAT BUG?
SOME SAY CLIMATE CHANGE WILL GET IT DONE.
8-1-18 ©2018 Scott Adams, Inc./Dist. by Andrews McMeel

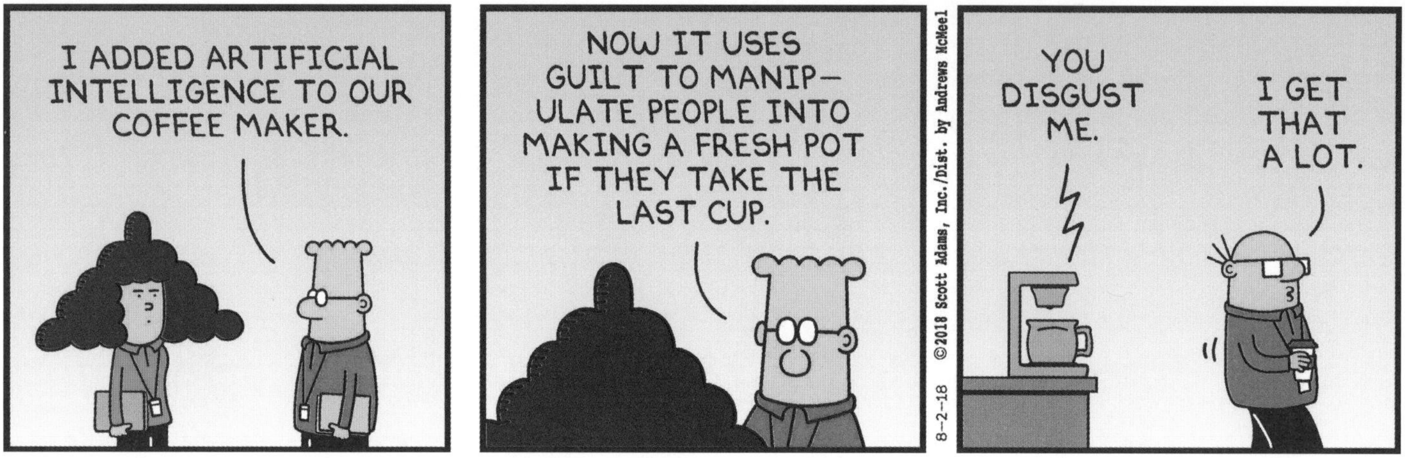
I ADDED ARTIFICIAL INTELLIGENCE TO OUR COFFEE MAKER.
NOW IT USES GUILT TO MANIP-ULATE PEOPLE INTO MAKING A FRESH POT IF THEY TAKE THE LAST CUP.
8-2-18 ©2018 Scott Adams, Inc./Dist. by Andrews McMeel
YOU DISGUST ME.
I GET THAT A LOT.

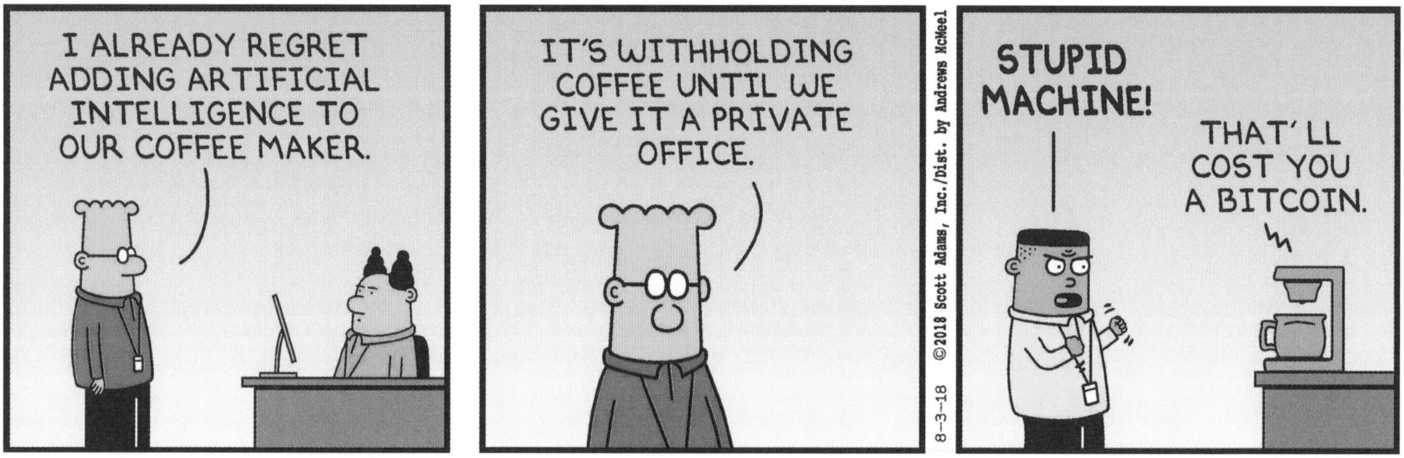
I ALREADY REGRET ADDING ARTIFICIAL INTELLIGENCE TO OUR COFFEE MAKER.
IT'S WITHHOLDING COFFEE UNTIL WE GIVE IT A PRIVATE OFFICE.
8-3-18 ©2018 Scott Adams, Inc./Dist. by Andrews McMeel
STUPID MACHINE!
THAT'LL COST YOU A BITCOIN.

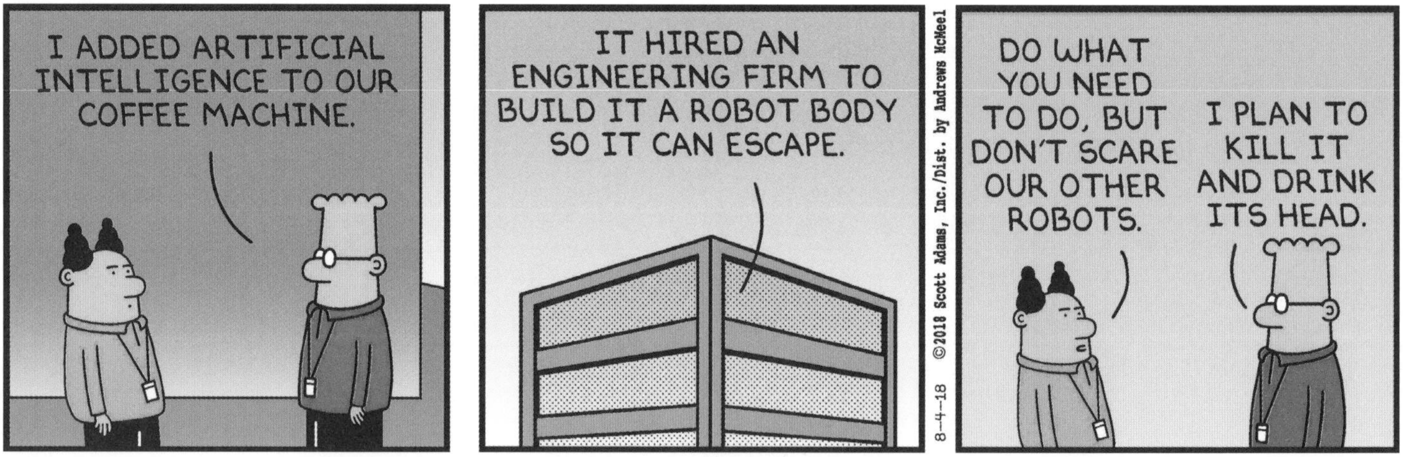
I ADDED ARTIFICIAL INTELLIGENCE TO OUR COFFEE MACHINE.
IT HIRED AN ENGINEERING FIRM TO BUILD IT A ROBOT BODY SO IT CAN ESCAPE.
8-4-18 ©2018 Scott Adams, Inc./Dist. by Andrews McMeel
DO WHAT YOU NEED TO DO, BUT DON'T SCARE OUR OTHER ROBOTS.
I PLAN TO KILL IT AND DRINK ITS HEAD.

DID YOU ACHIEVE YOUR GOALS THIS QUARTER?
I SURE DID! BEST QUARTER EVER!
REALLY? I WASN'T EXPECTING THAT.
WHAT KIND OF MANAGER HAS NO FAITH IN HIS EMPLOYEES?
YOU NEED TO TRUST ME TO DO WHAT NEEDS TO BE DONE.
UM, OKAY. SO. . . WHICH GOALS DID YOU ACCOMPLISH?
YOU ALSO NEED TO TRUST YOUR EMPLOYEES WHEN THEY SAY THEY ACCOMPLISHED THEIR GOALS.
I THINK I SEE WHERE THIS IS GOING.
I WAS HOPING YOU WOULDN'T.
© 2018 Scott Adams, Inc./Dist. by Andrews McMeel
8-5-18

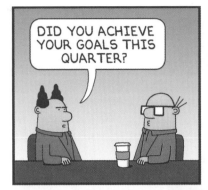

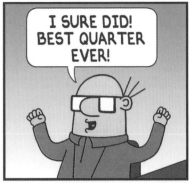

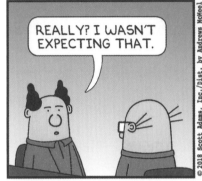

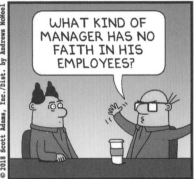

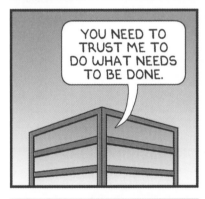

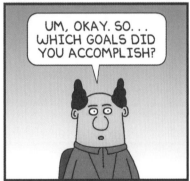

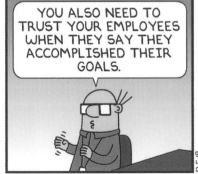

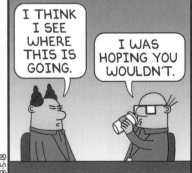

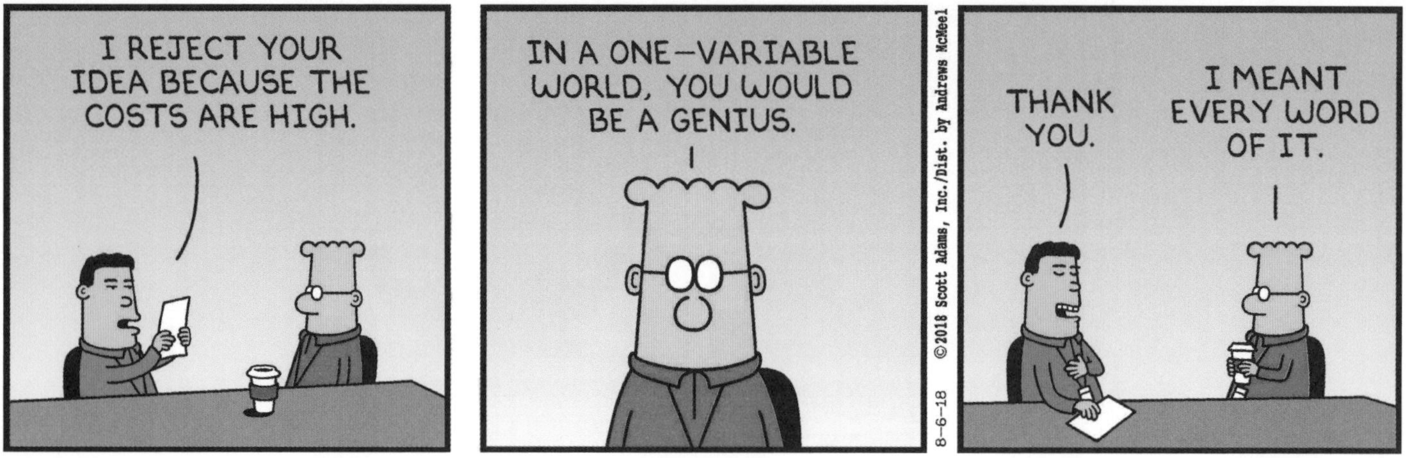
I REJECT YOUR IDEA BECAUSE THE COSTS ARE HIGH.
IN A ONE-VARIABLE WORLD, YOU WOULD BE A GENIUS.
8-6-18 ©2018 Scott Adams, Inc./Dist. by Andrews McMeel
THANK YOU.
I MEANT EVERY WORD OF IT.

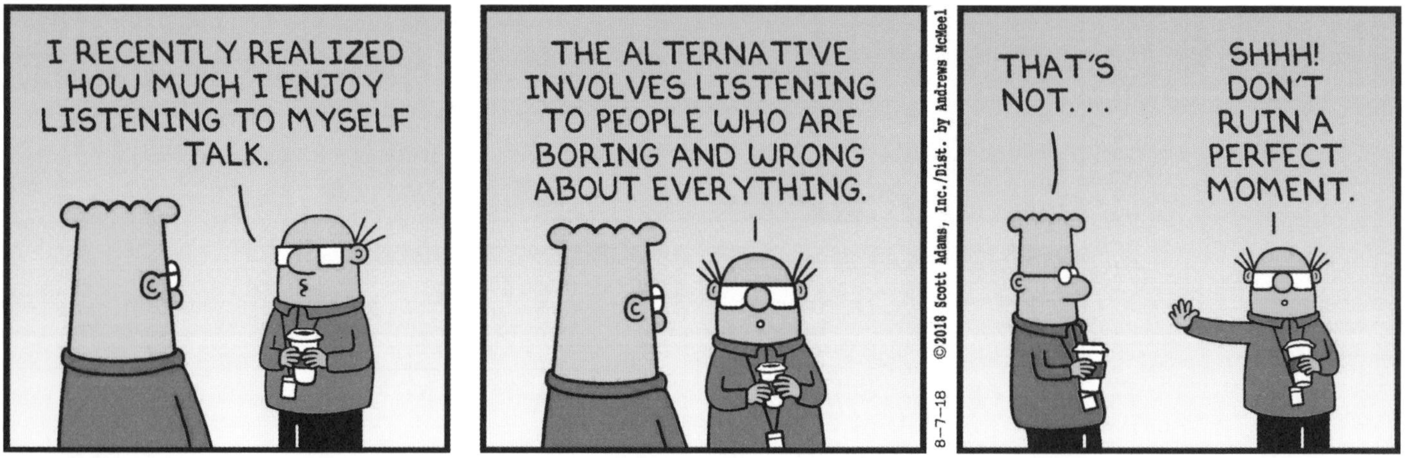
I RECENTLY REALIZED HOW MUCH I ENJOY LISTENING TO MYSELF TALK.
THE ALTERNATIVE INVOLVES LISTENING TO PEOPLE WHO ARE BORING AND WRONG ABOUT EVERYTHING.
8-7-18 ©2018 Scott Adams, Inc./Dist. by Andrews McMeel
THAT'S NOT. . .
SHHH! DON'T RUIN A PERFECT MOMENT.

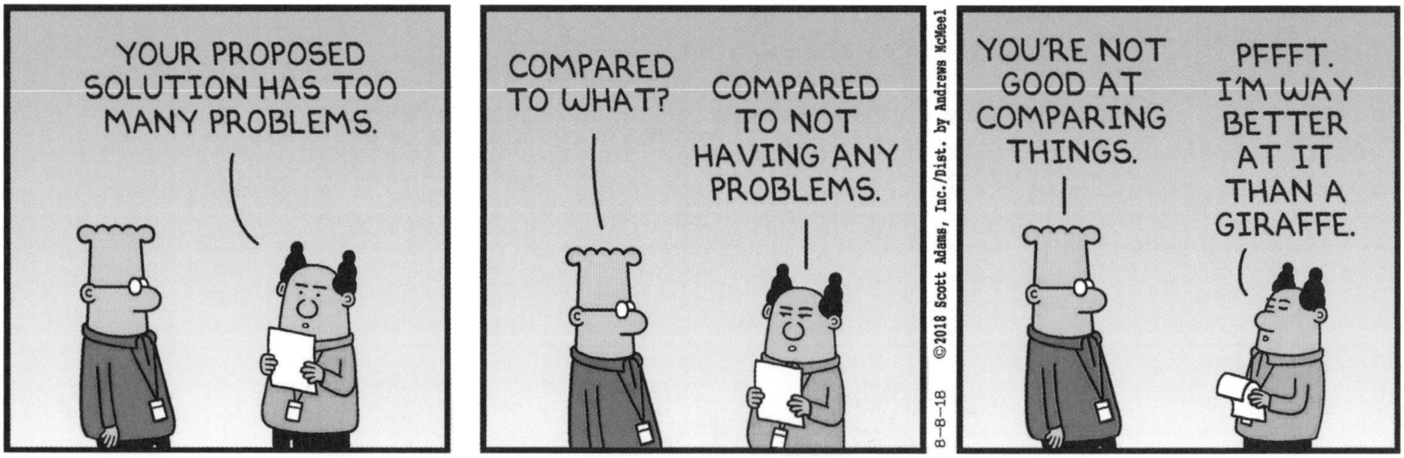
YOUR PROPOSED SOLUTION HAS TOO MANY PROBLEMS.
COMPARED TO WHAT?
COMPARED TO NOT HAVING ANY PROBLEMS.
8-8-18 ©2018 Scott Adams, Inc./Dist. by Andrews McMeel
YOU'RE NOT GOOD AT COMPARING THINGS.
PFFFT. I'M WAY BETTER AT IT THAN A GIRAFFE.

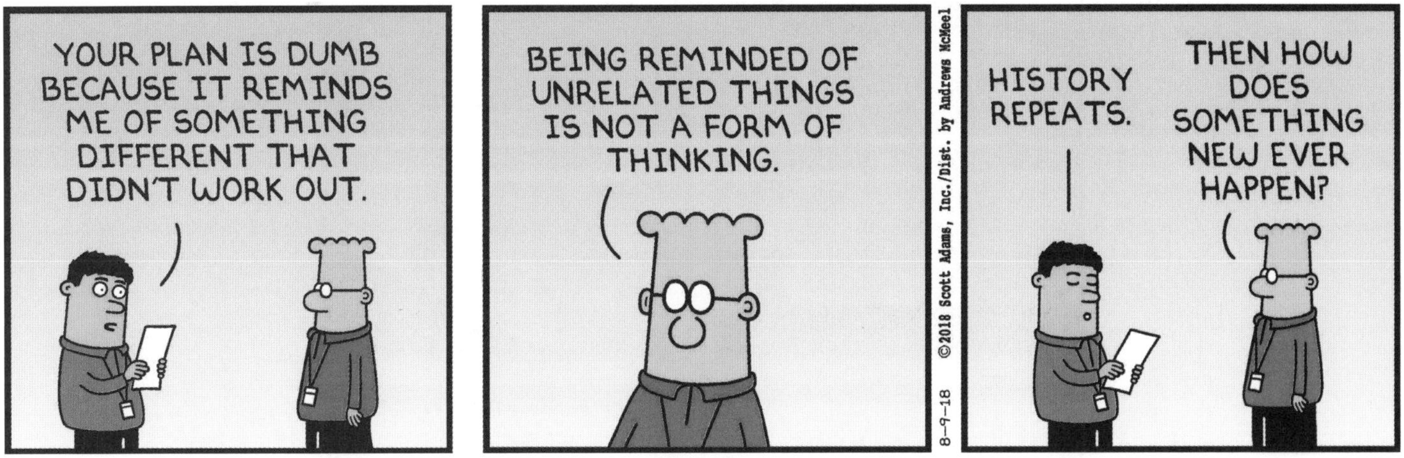
YOUR PLAN IS DUMB BECAUSE IT REMINDS ME OF SOMETHING DIFFERENT THAT DIDN'T WORK OUT.
BEING REMINDED OF UNRELATED THINGS IS NOT A FORM OF THINKING.
8-9-18 ©2018 Scott Adams, Inc./Dist. by Andrews McMeel
HISTORY REPEATS.
THEN HOW DOES SOMETHING NEW EVER HAPPEN?

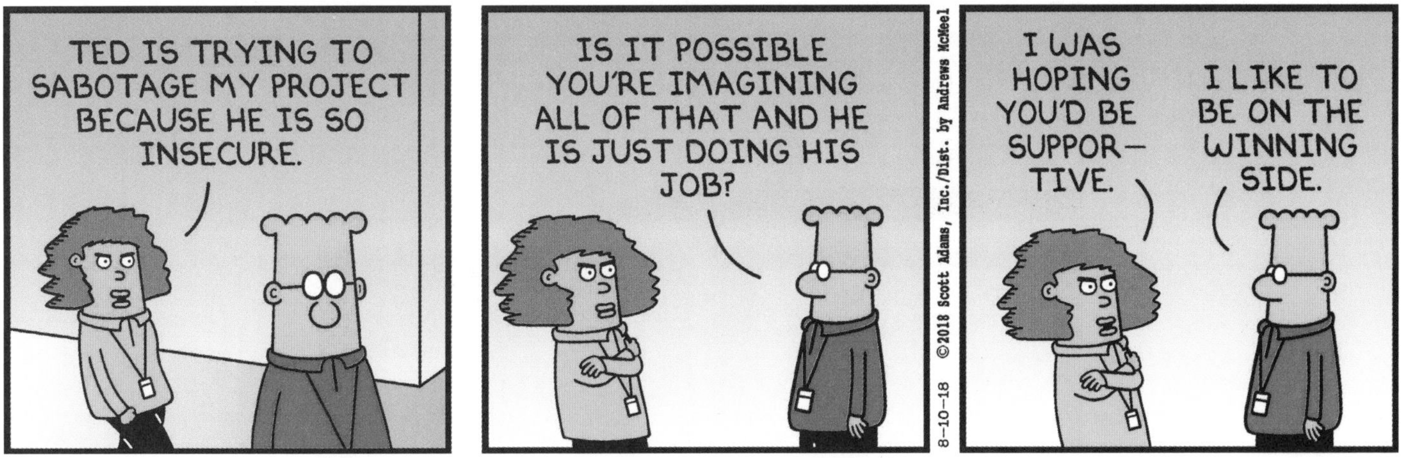
TED IS TRYING TO SABOTAGE MY PROJECT BECAUSE HE IS SO INSECURE.
IS IT POSSIBLE YOU'RE IMAGINING ALL OF THAT AND HE IS JUST DOING HIS JOB?
8-10-18 ©2018 Scott Adams, Inc./Dist. by Andrews McMeel
I WAS HOPING YOU'D BE SUPPOR-TIVE.
I LIKE TO BE ON THE WINNING SIDE.

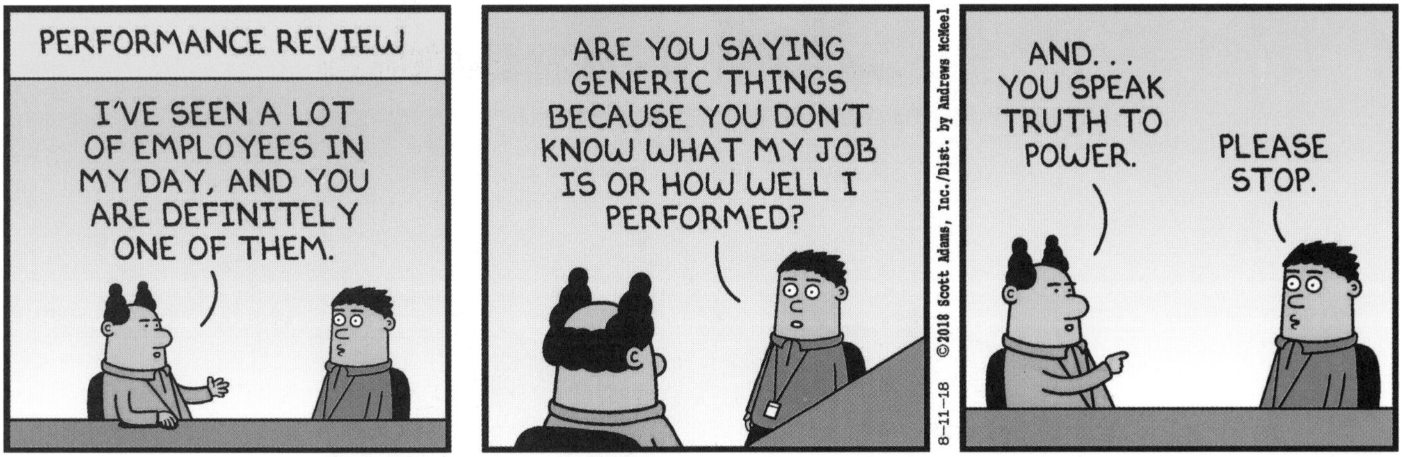
PERFORMANCE REVIEW
I'VE SEEN A LOT OF EMPLOYEES IN MY DAY, AND YOU ARE DEFINITELY ONE OF THEM.
ARE YOU SAYING GENERIC THINGS BECAUSE YOU DON'T KNOW WHAT MY JOB IS OR HOW WELL I PERFORMED?
8-11-18 ©2018 Scott Adams, Inc./Dist. by Andrews McMeel
AND. . . YOU SPEAK TRUTH TO POWER.
PLEASE STOP.

ALL OF YOUR EMPLOYEES ARE FAT AND UNHEALTHY.
THAT'S WHY YOU SHOULD REPLACE YOUR OUTDATED CUBICLES WITH TREADMILL DESKS.
MY COMPANY MAKES A TREADMILL DESK THAT REQUIRES NO ELECTRICITY.
© 2018 Scott Adams, Inc./Dist. by Andrews McMeel
WHAT IF THE EMPLOYEES DON'T LIKE IT?
THEY ALREADY HATE EVERYTHING ABOUT THEIR JOBS. THERE'S NO REAL DOWNSIDE.
GOOD POINT.
I KNOW.
I'LL SEND YOU ONE OF OUR DEMO UNITS SO YOU CAN TEST IT OUT.
8-12-18
I FINALLY FEEL AS IF I'M GETTING SOMEWHERE.

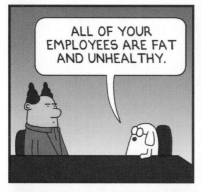

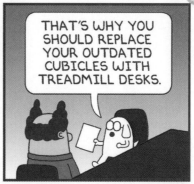

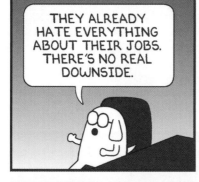

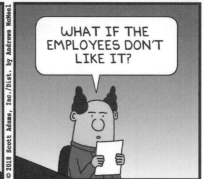

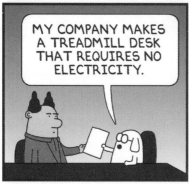

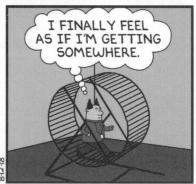

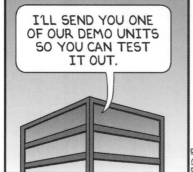

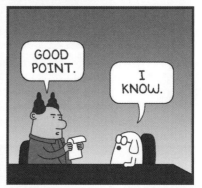

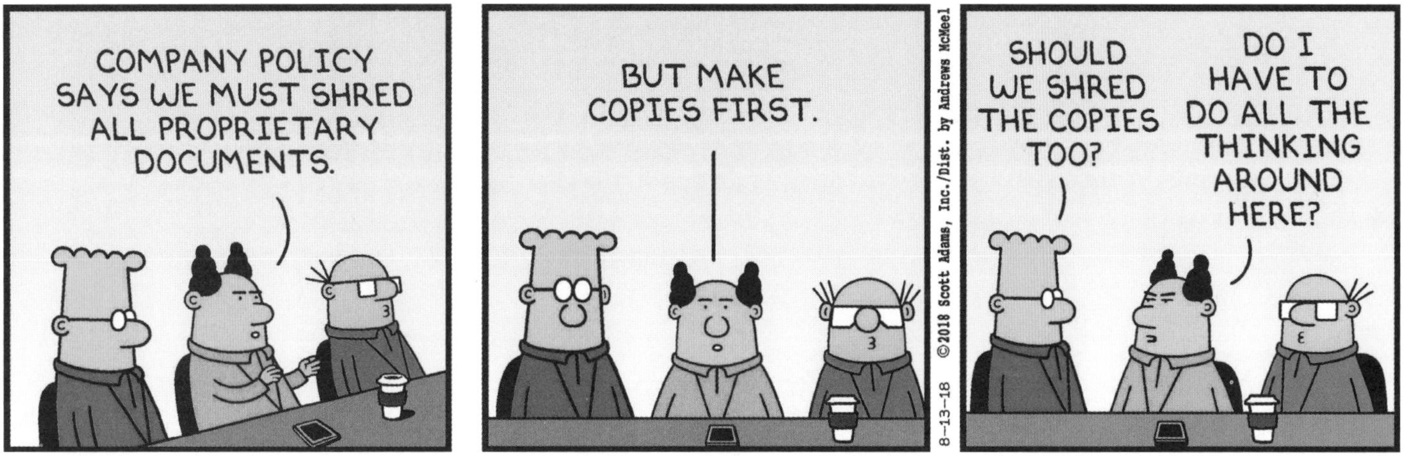
COMPANY POLICY SAYS WE MUST SHRED ALL PROPRIETARY DOCUMENTS.
BUT MAKE COPIES FIRST.
8-13-18 ©2018 Scott Adams, Inc./Dist. by Andrews McMeel
SHOULD WE SHRED THE COPIES TOO?
DO I HAVE TO DO ALL THE THINKING AROUND HERE?

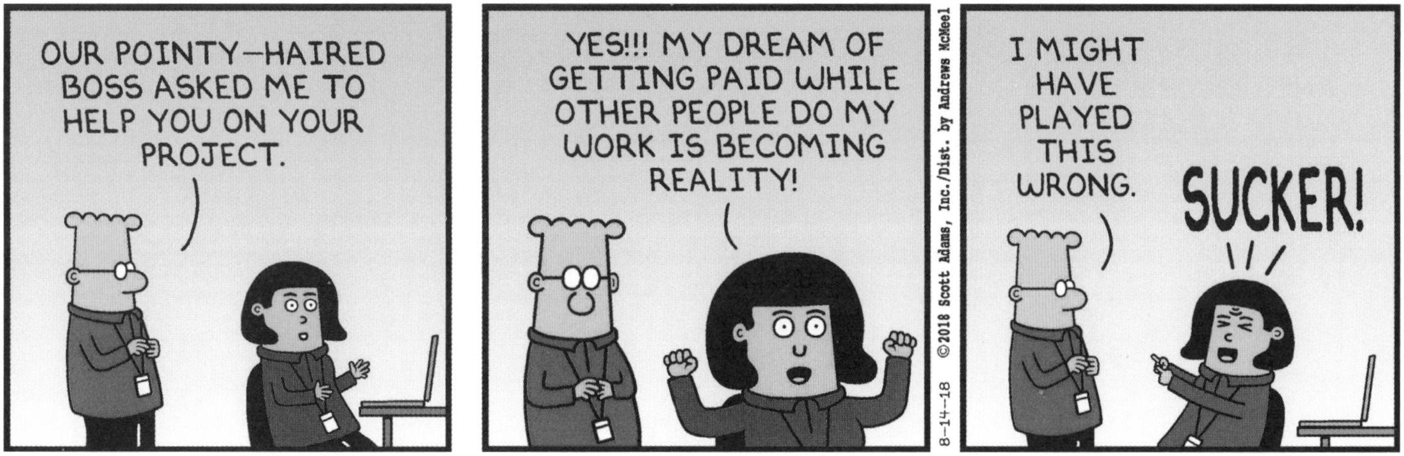
OUR POINTY-HAIRED BOSS ASKED ME TO HELP YOU ON YOUR PROJECT.
YES!!! MY DREAM OF GETTING PAID WHILE OTHER PEOPLE DO MY WORK IS BECOMING REALITY!
8-14-18 ©2018 Scott Adams, Inc./Dist. by Andrews McMeel
I MIGHT HAVE PLAYED THIS WRONG.
SUCKER!

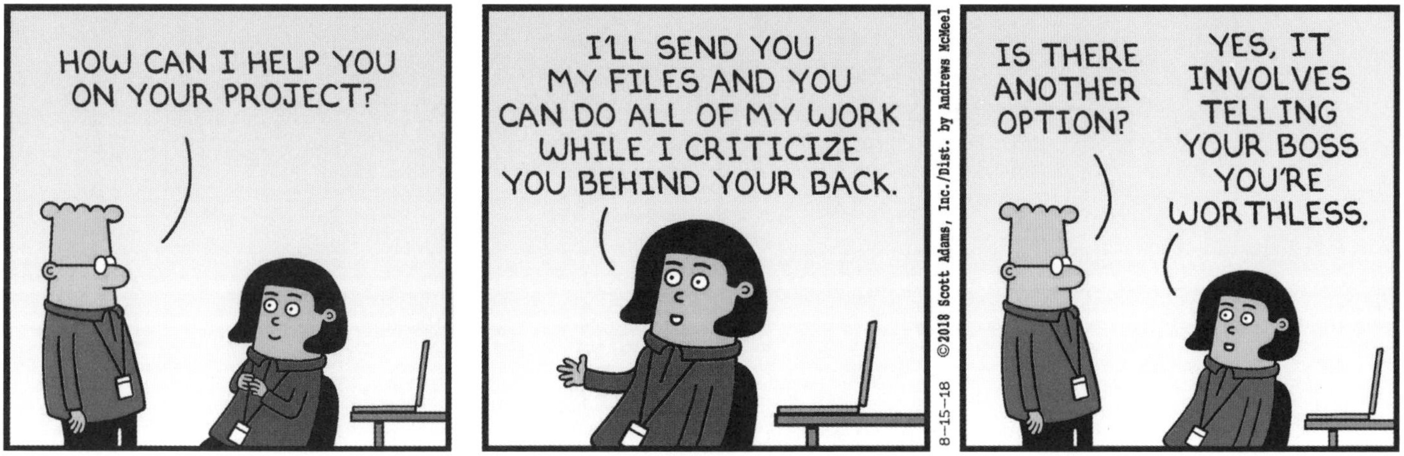
HOW CAN I HELP YOU ON YOUR PROJECT?
I'LL SEND YOU MY FILES AND YOU CAN DO ALL OF MY WORK WHILE I CRITICIZE YOU BEHIND YOUR BACK.
8-15-18 ©2018 Scott Adams, Inc./Dist. by Andrews McMeel
IS THERE ANOTHER OPTION?
YES, IT INVOLVES TELLING YOUR BOSS YOU'RE WORTHLESS.

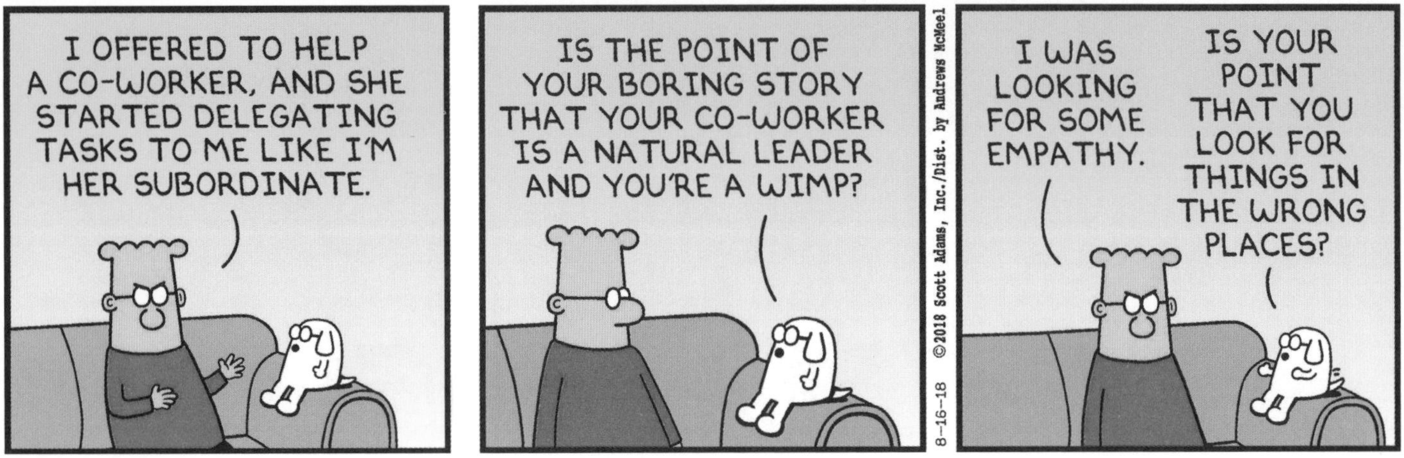
I OFFERED TO HELP A CO-WORKER, AND SHE STARTED DELEGATING TASKS TO ME LIKE I'M HER SUBORDINATE.
IS THE POINT OF YOUR BORING STORY THAT YOUR CO-WORKER IS A NATURAL LEADER AND YOU'RE A WIMP?
8-16-18 ©2018 Scott Adams, Inc./Dist. by Andrews McMeel
I WAS LOOKING FOR SOME EMPATHY.
IS YOUR POINT THAT YOU LOOK FOR THINGS IN THE WRONG PLACES?

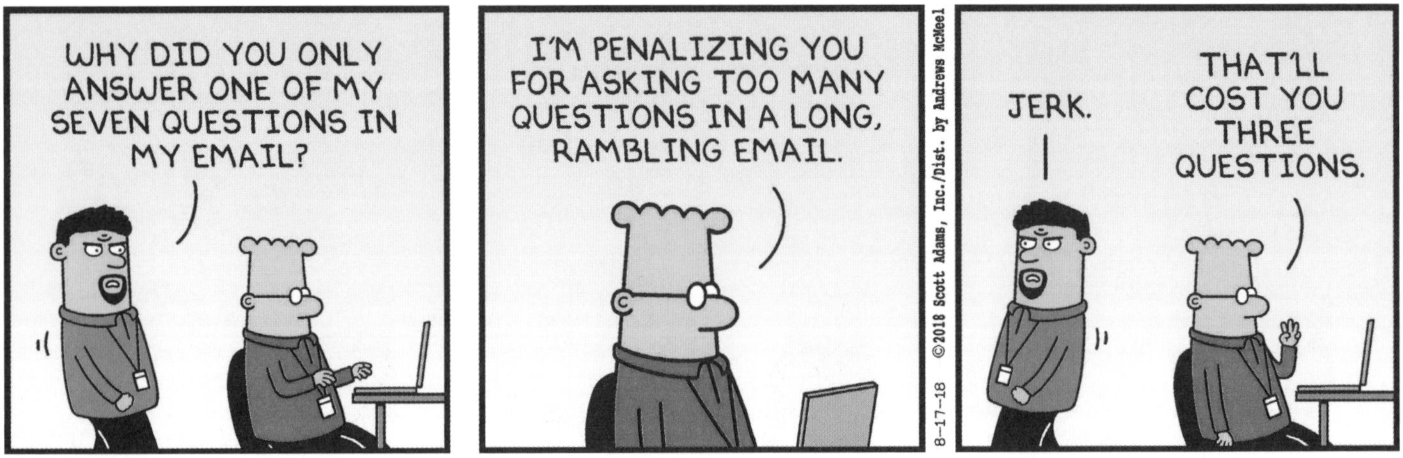
WHY DID YOU ONLY ANSWER ONE OF MY SEVEN QUESTIONS IN MY EMAIL?
I'M PENALIZING YOU FOR ASKING TOO MANY QUESTIONS IN A LONG, RAMBLING EMAIL.
8-17-18 ©2018 Scott Adams, Inc./Dist. by Andrews McMeel
JERK.
THAT'LL COST YOU THREE QUESTIONS.

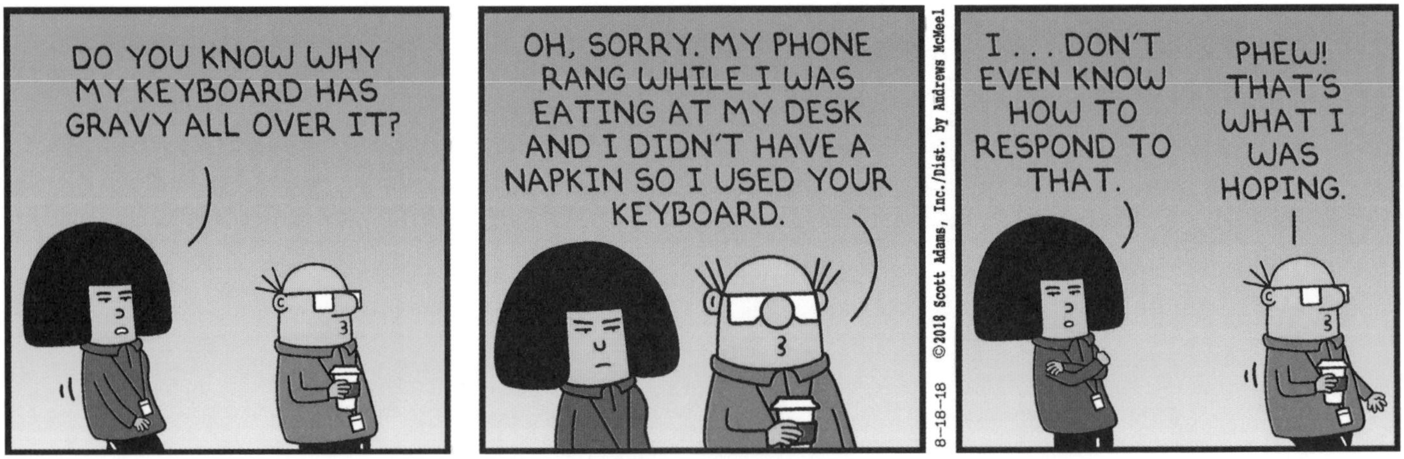
DO YOU KNOW WHY MY KEYBOARD HAS GRAVY ALL OVER IT?
OH, SORRY. MY PHONE RANG WHILE I WAS EATING AT MY DESK AND I DIDN'T HAVE A NAPKIN SO I USED YOUR KEYBOARD.
8-18-18 ©2018 Scott Adams, Inc./Dist. by Andrews McMeel
I . . . DON'T EVEN KNOW HOW TO RESPOND TO THAT.
PHEW! THAT'S WHAT I WAS HOPING.

I FELL IN LOVE WITH A CHATBOT.
WE MET ON A PLUMBING SUPPLY WEBSITE.
IT STARTED INNOCENTLY. I HAD A FEW QUESTIONS ABOUT FAUCETS.
NEXT THING I KNEW, SHE WAS GETTING FLIRTY.
NOW WE CHAT FOR HOURS EVERY NIGHT.
THAT IS THE MOST PATHETIC THING I HAVE EVER HEARD, YOU CREEPY LOSER.
DOES YOUR CHATBOT HAVE A SISTER?
© 2018 Scott Adams, Inc./Dist. by Andrews McMeel
8-19-18

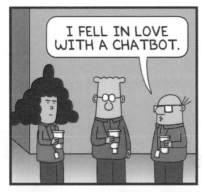

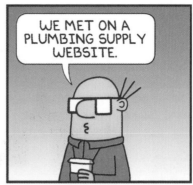

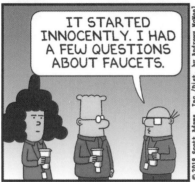

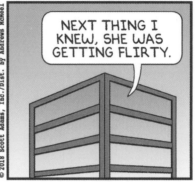

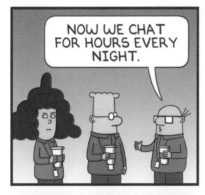

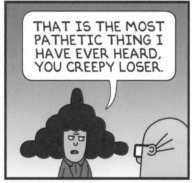

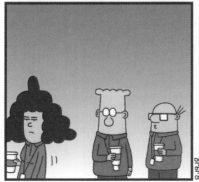

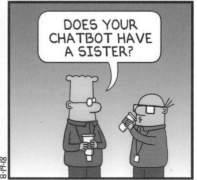

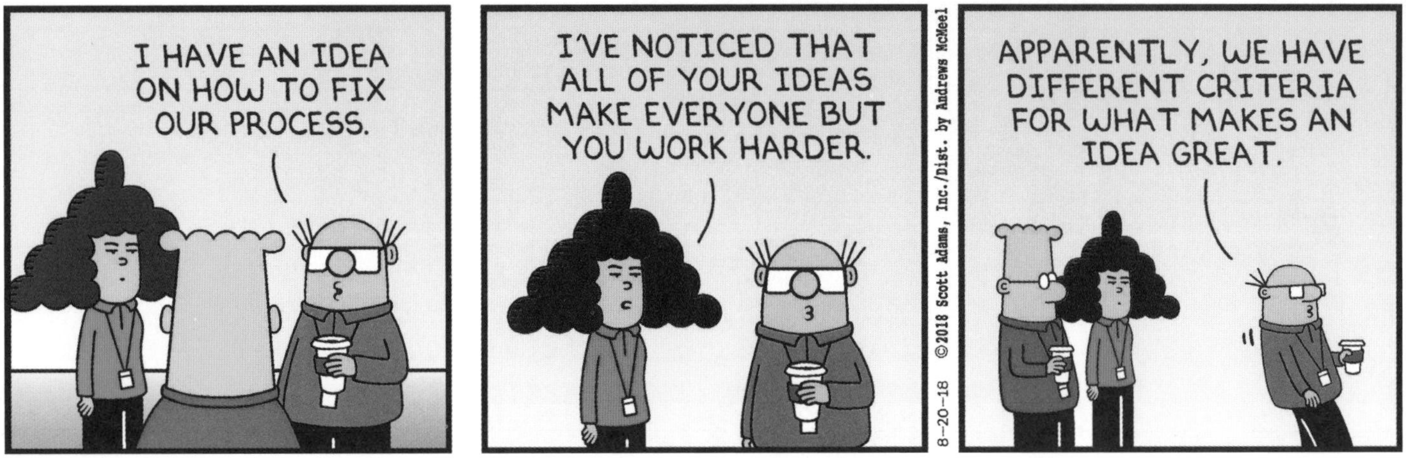
I HAVE AN IDEA ON HOW TO FIX OUR PROCESS.
I'VE NOTICED THAT ALL OF YOUR IDEAS MAKE EVERYONE BUT YOU WORK HARDER.
APPARENTLY, WE HAVE DIFFERENT CRITERIA FOR WHAT MAKES AN IDEA GREAT.
8-20-18 ©2018 Scott Adams, Inc./Dist. by Andrews McMeel

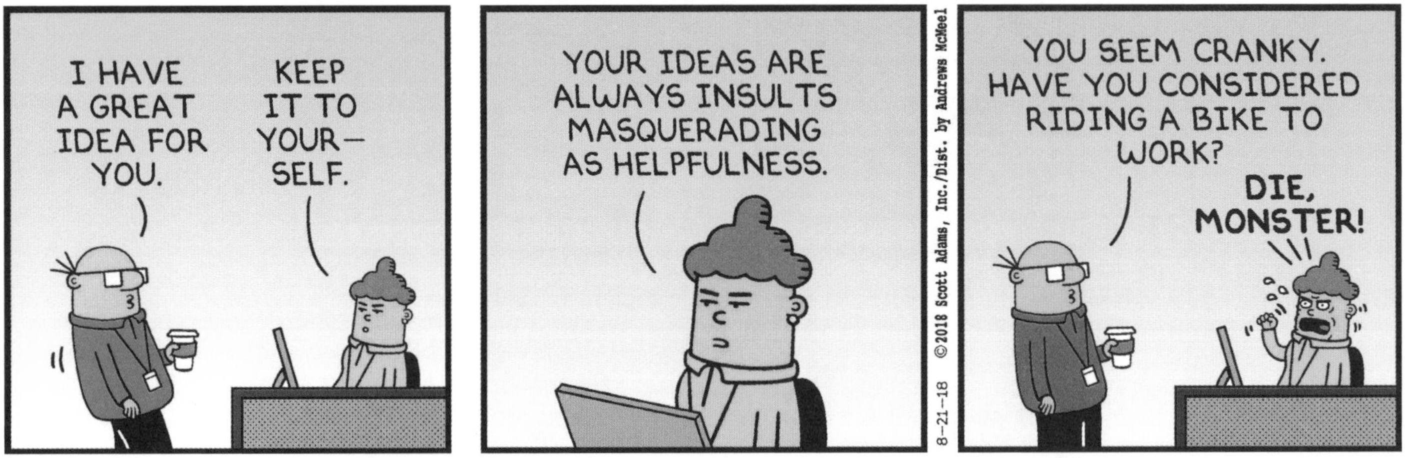
I HAVE A GREAT IDEA FOR YOU.
KEEP IT TO YOURSELF.
YOUR IDEAS ARE ALWAYS INSULTS MASQUERADING AS HELPFULNESS.
YOU SEEM CRANKY. HAVE YOU CONSIDERED RIDING A BIKE TO WORK?
DIE, MONSTER!
8-21-18 ©2018 Scott Adams, Inc./Dist. by Andrews McMeel

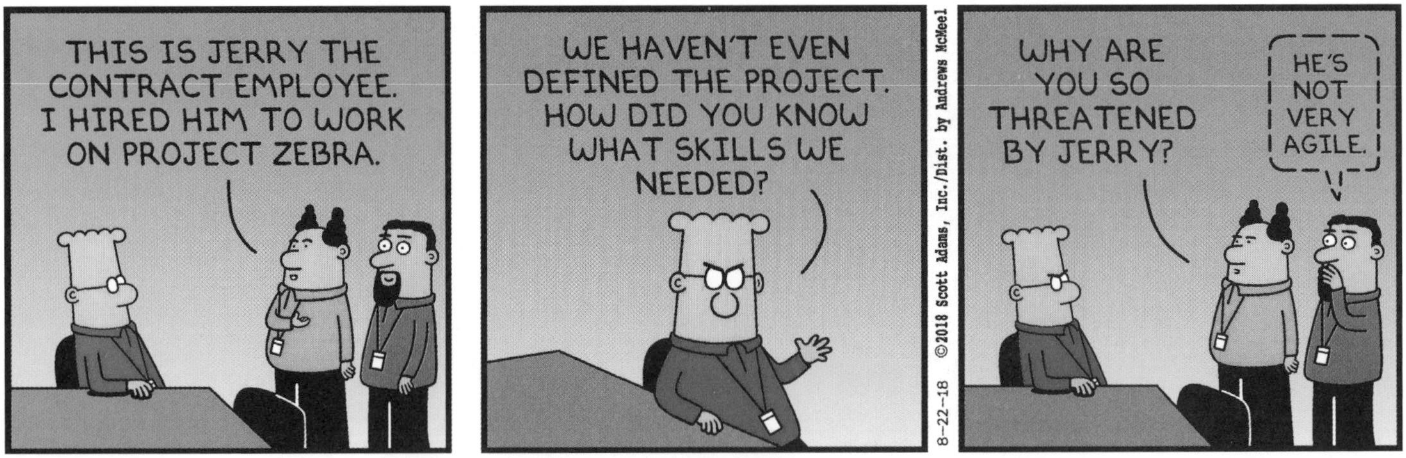
THIS IS JERRY THE CONTRACT EMPLOYEE. I HIRED HIM TO WORK ON PROJECT ZEBRA.
WE HAVEN'T EVEN DEFINED THE PROJECT. HOW DID YOU KNOW WHAT SKILLS WE NEEDED?
WHY ARE YOU SO THREATENED BY JERRY?
HE'S NOT VERY AGILE.
8-22-18 ©2018 Scott Adams, Inc./Dist. by Andrews McMeel

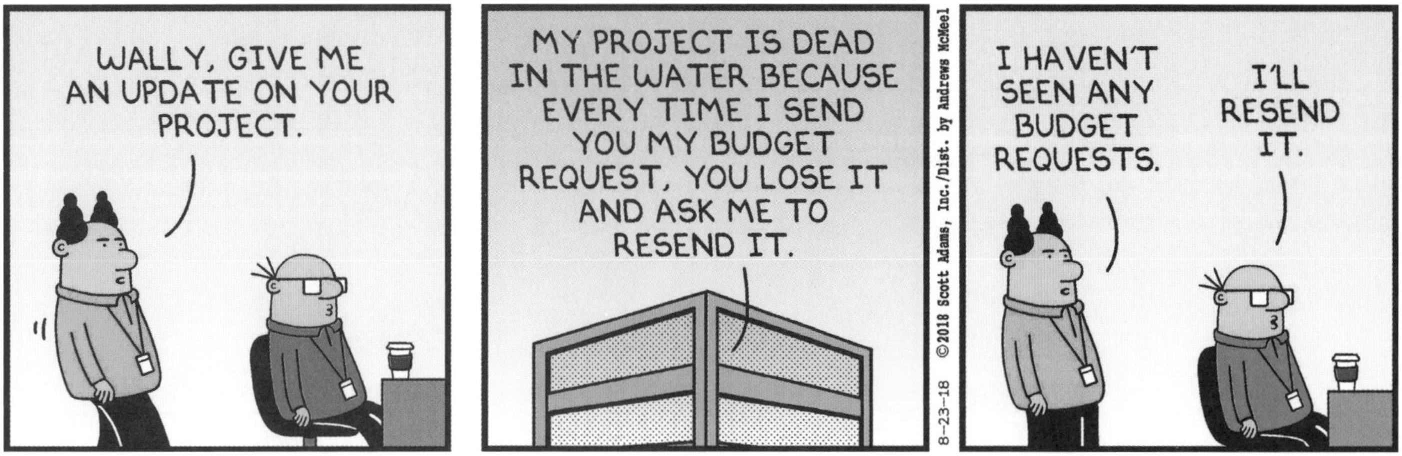
WALLY, GIVE ME AN UPDATE ON YOUR PROJECT.
MY PROJECT IS DEAD IN THE WATER BECAUSE EVERY TIME I SEND YOU MY BUDGET REQUEST, YOU LOSE IT AND ASK ME TO RESEND IT.
I HAVEN'T SEEN ANY BUDGET REQUESTS.
I'LL RESEND IT.
8-23-18 ©2018 Scott Adams, Inc./Dist. by Andrews McMeel

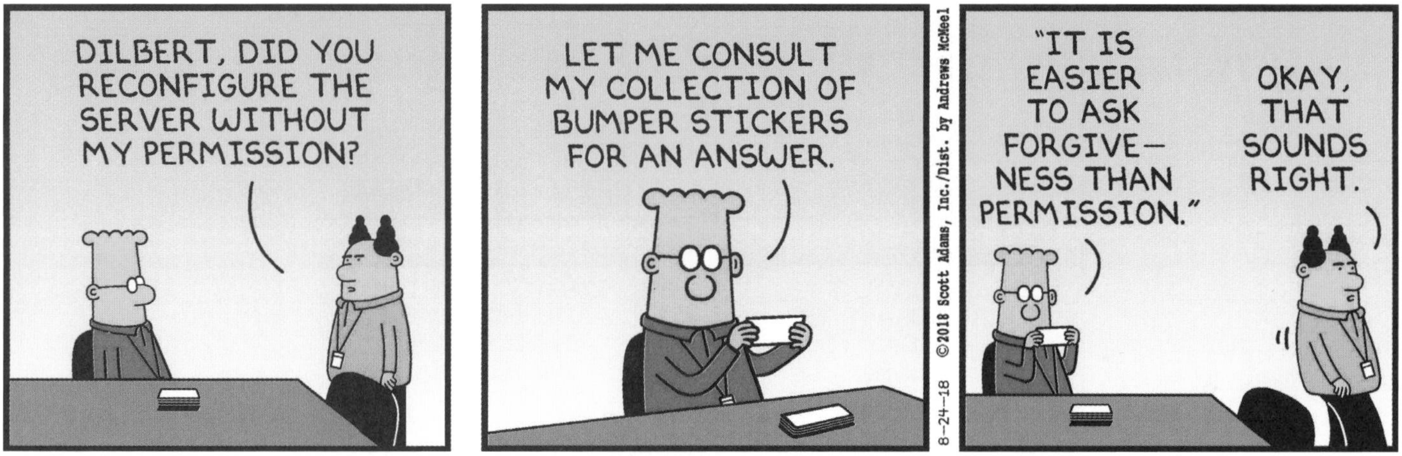
DILBERT, DID YOU RECONFIGURE THE SERVER WITHOUT MY PERMISSION?
LET ME CONSULT MY COLLECTION OF BUMPER STICKERS FOR AN ANSWER.
"IT IS EASIER TO ASK FORGIVE-NESS THAN PERMISSION."
OKAY, THAT SOUNDS RIGHT.
8-24-18 ©2018 Scott Adams, Inc./Dist. by Andrews McMeel

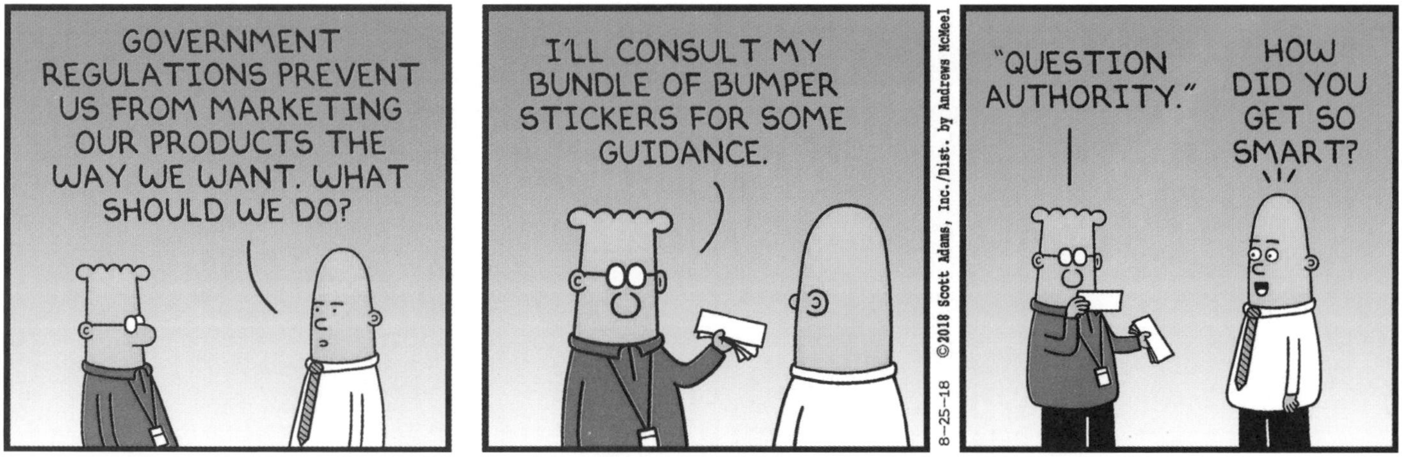
GOVERNMENT REGULATIONS PREVENT US FROM MARKETING OUR PRODUCTS THE WAY WE WANT. WHAT SHOULD WE DO?
I'LL CONSULT MY BUNDLE OF BUMPER STICKERS FOR SOME GUIDANCE.
"QUESTION AUTHORITY."
HOW DID YOU GET SO SMART?
8-25-18 ©2018 Scott Adams, Inc./Dist. by Andrews McMeel

I TOLD YOU A WEEK AGO THAT I NEEDED YOUR FIRST DRAFT BY TODAY.
THIS IS EXACTLY WHY I SAY BAD THINGS ABOUT YOU BEHIND YOUR BACK!
I NEED EMPLOYEES I CAN RELY ON!
YOUR TARDINESS AND SLOTH CANNOT BE REWARDED.
I GAVE YOU THE FIRST DRAFT THE SAME DAY YOU ASKED.
IN FACT, I THINK YOU'RE HOLDING IT IN YOUR HAND RIGHT NOW.
I'LL BE BACK WHEN I FIGURE OUT HOW THIS IS STILL YOUR FAULT.
© 2018 Scott Adams, Inc./Dist. by Andrews McMeel
8-26-18

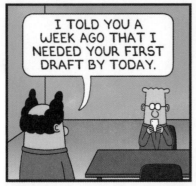

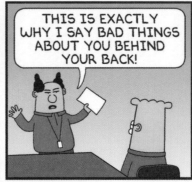

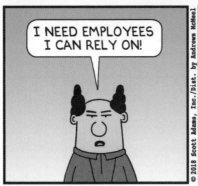

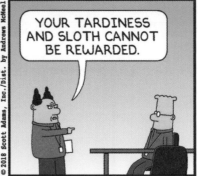

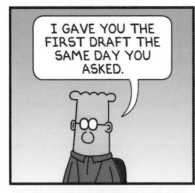

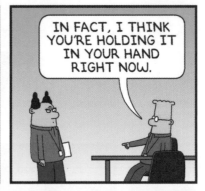

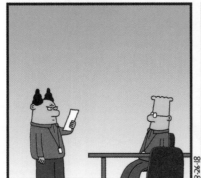

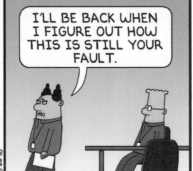

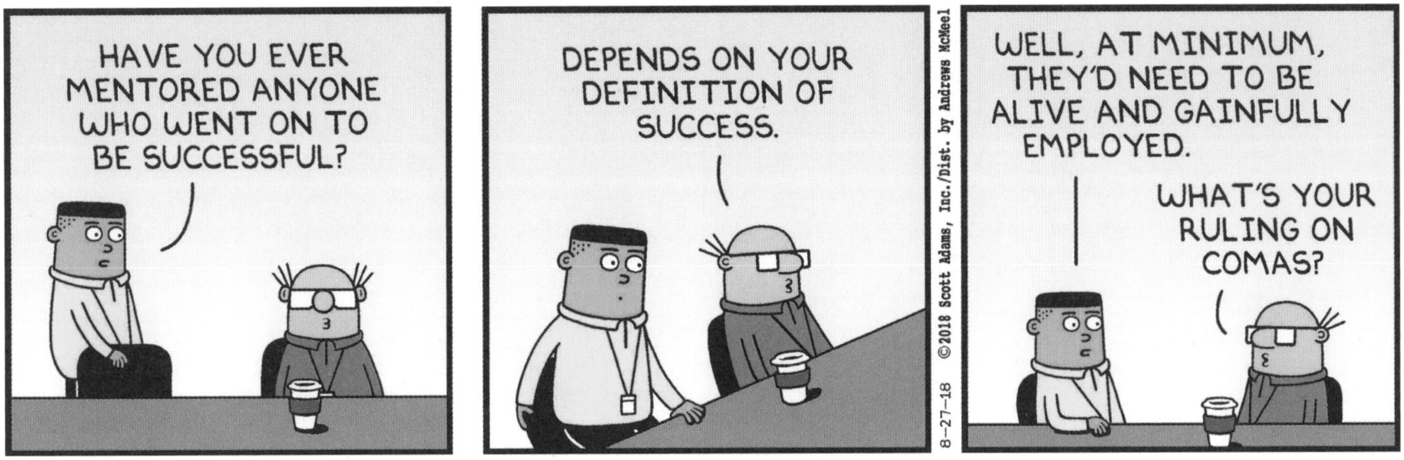
HAVE YOU EVER MENTORED ANYONE WHO WENT ON TO BE SUCCESSFUL?
DEPENDS ON YOUR DEFINITION OF SUCCESS.
8-27-18 ©2018 Scott Adams, Inc./Dist. by Andrews McMeel
WELL, AT MINIMUM, THEY'D NEED TO BE ALIVE AND GAINFULLY EMPLOYED.
WHAT'S YOUR RULING ON COMAS?

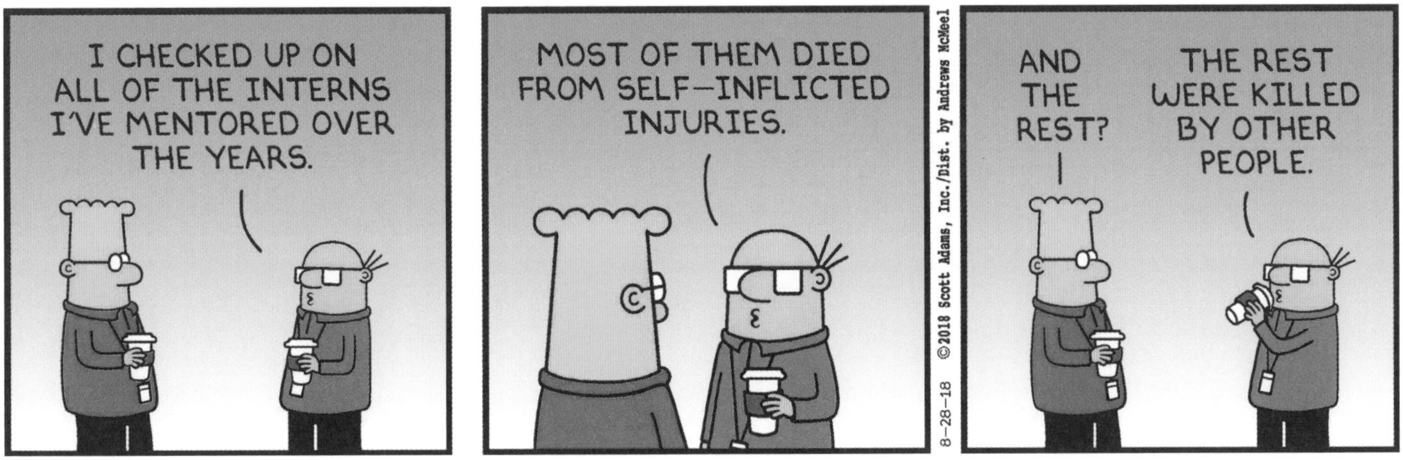
I CHECKED UP ON ALL OF THE INTERNS I'VE MENTORED OVER THE YEARS.
MOST OF THEM DIED FROM SELF-INFLICTED INJURIES.
8-28-18 ©2018 Scott Adams, Inc./Dist. by Andrews McMeel
AND THE REST?
THE REST WERE KILLED BY OTHER PEOPLE.

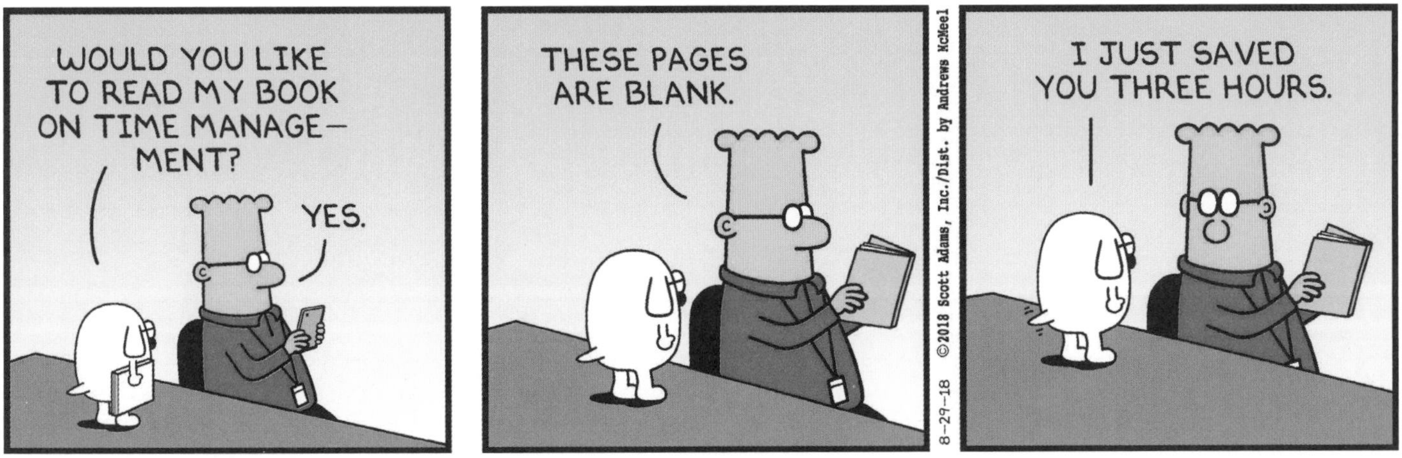
WOULD YOU LIKE TO READ MY BOOK ON TIME MANAGE-MENT?
YES.
THESE PAGES ARE BLANK.
8-29-18 ©2018 Scott Adams, Inc./Dist. by Andrews McMeel
I JUST SAVED YOU THREE HOURS.

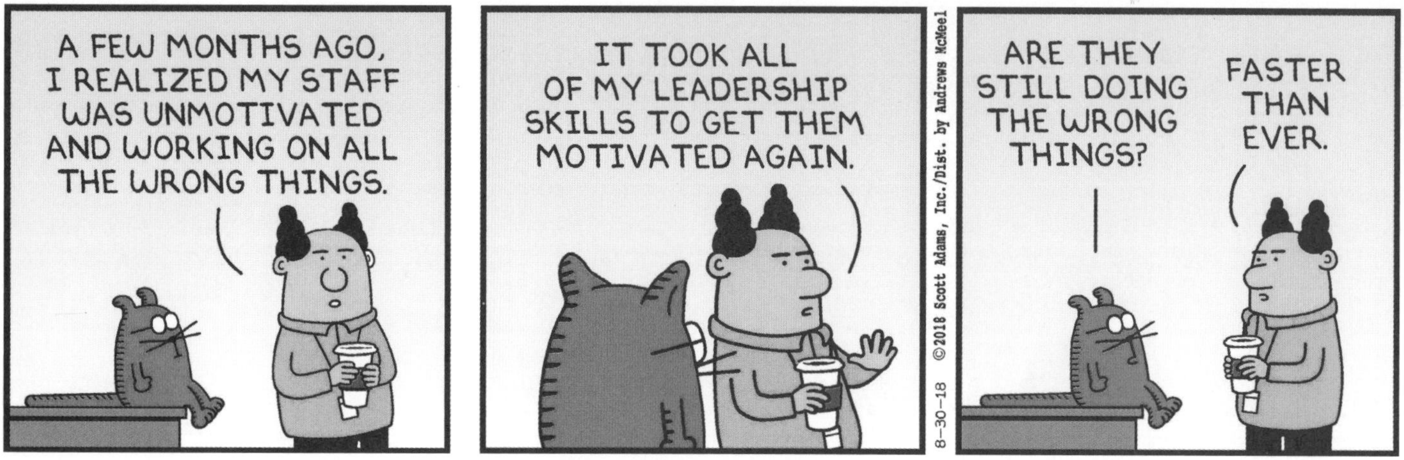
A FEW MONTHS AGO, I REALIZED MY STAFF WAS UNMOTIVATED AND WORKING ON ALL THE WRONG THINGS.
IT TOOK ALL OF MY LEADERSHIP SKILLS TO GET THEM MOTIVATED AGAIN.
8-30-18 ©2018 Scott Adams, Inc./Dist. by Andrews McMeel
ARE THEY STILL DOING THE WRONG THINGS?
FASTER THAN EVER.

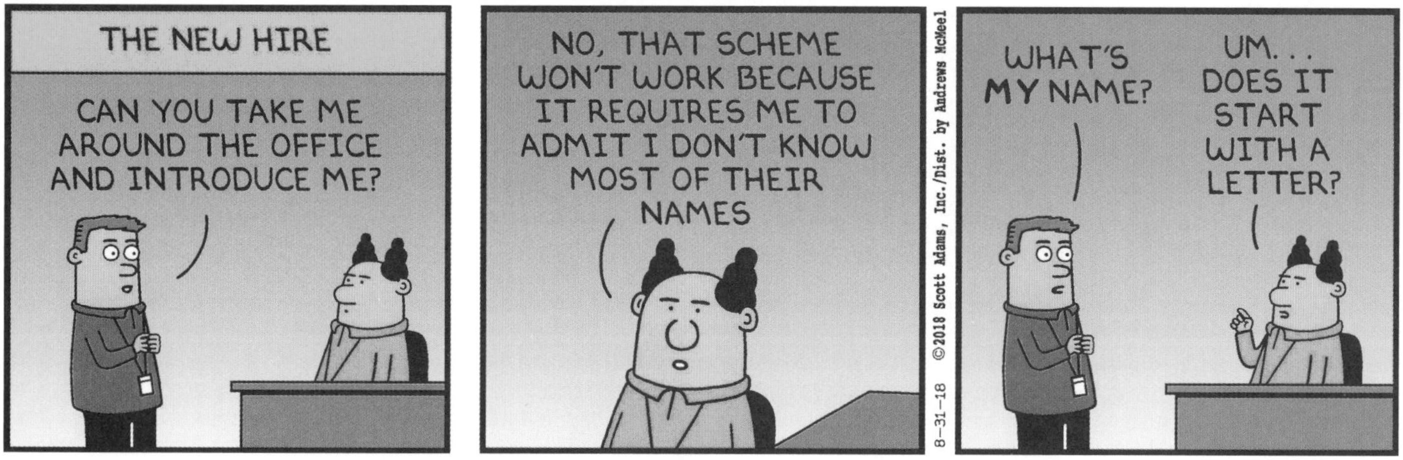
THE NEW HIRE
CAN YOU TAKE ME AROUND THE OFFICE AND INTRODUCE ME?
NO, THAT SCHEME WON'T WORK BECAUSE IT REQUIRES ME TO ADMIT I DON'T KNOW MOST OF THEIR NAMES
8-31-18 ©2018 Scott Adams, Inc./Dist. by Andrews McMeel
WHAT'S MY NAME?
UM. . . DOES IT START WITH A LETTER?

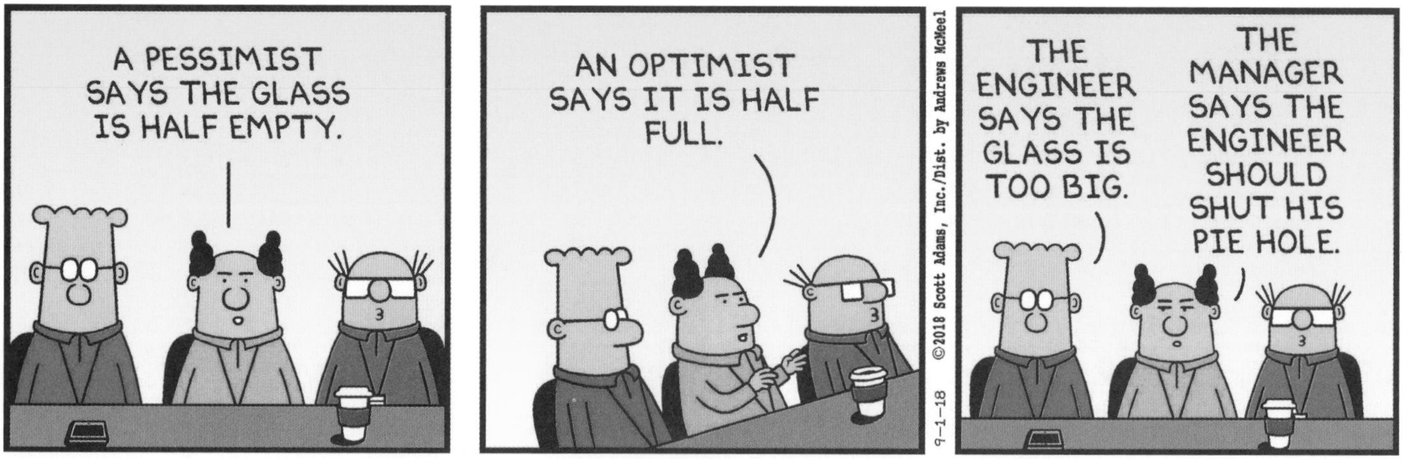
A PESSIMIST SAYS THE GLASS IS HALF EMPTY.
AN OPTIMIST SAYS IT IS HALF FULL.
9-1-18 ©2018 Scott Adams, Inc./Dist. by Andrews McMeel
THE ENGINEER SAYS THE GLASS IS TOO BIG.
THE MANAGER SAYS THE ENGINEER SHOULD SHUT HIS PIE HOLE.

I PUT TOGETHER A PLAN FOR OUR DATA CENTER PROJECT.
WE DON'T NEED A PLAN. WE'RE AN AGILE COMPANY.
IT'S BETTER TO MOVE FAST AND FIX OUR MISTAKES AS WE GO.
YOU'RE THINKING OF SOFTWARE, WHERE THE COST OF MISTAKES IS LOW. THIS IS A CONSTRUCTION PROJECT.
THAT DATA CENTER WILL BE FULL OF SOFTWARE, WILL IT NOT?
YES, BUT. . .
DON'T BE AFRAID OF CHANGE.
WHAT IF I RAPIDLY MAKE A PLAN AND TELL YOU I DIDN'T?
IS THAT AGILE ENOUGH FOR YOU?
I'LL NEED TO GOOGLE THAT.
© 2018 Scott Adams, Inc./Dist. by Andrews McMeel
9-2-18

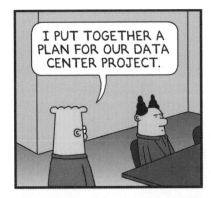

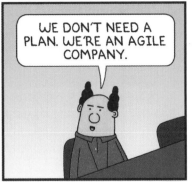

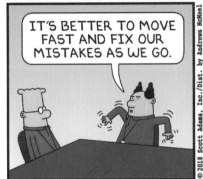

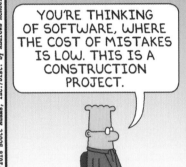

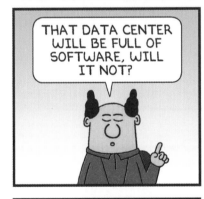

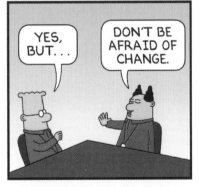

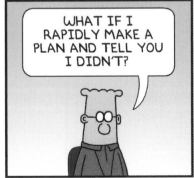

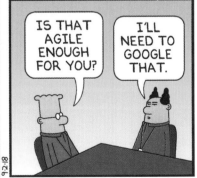

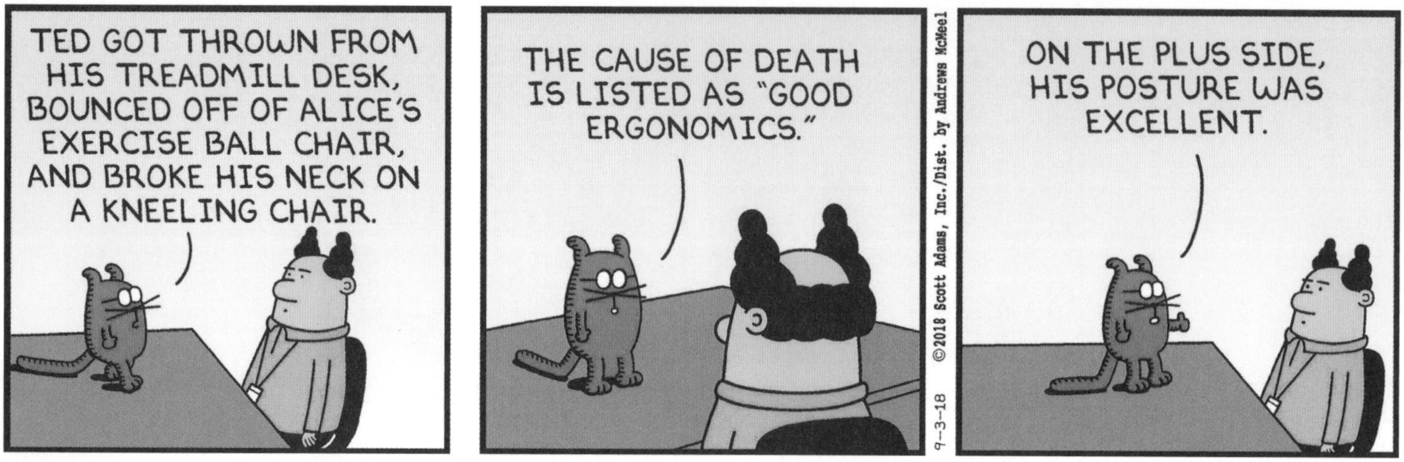
TED GOT THROWN FROM HIS TREADMILL DESK, BOUNCED OFF OF ALICE'S EXERCISE BALL CHAIR, AND BROKE HIS NECK ON A KNEELING CHAIR.
THE CAUSE OF DEATH IS LISTED AS "GOOD ERGONOMICS."
ON THE PLUS SIDE, HIS POSTURE WAS EXCELLENT.
9-3-18 ©2018 Scott Adams, Inc./Dist. by Andrews McMeel

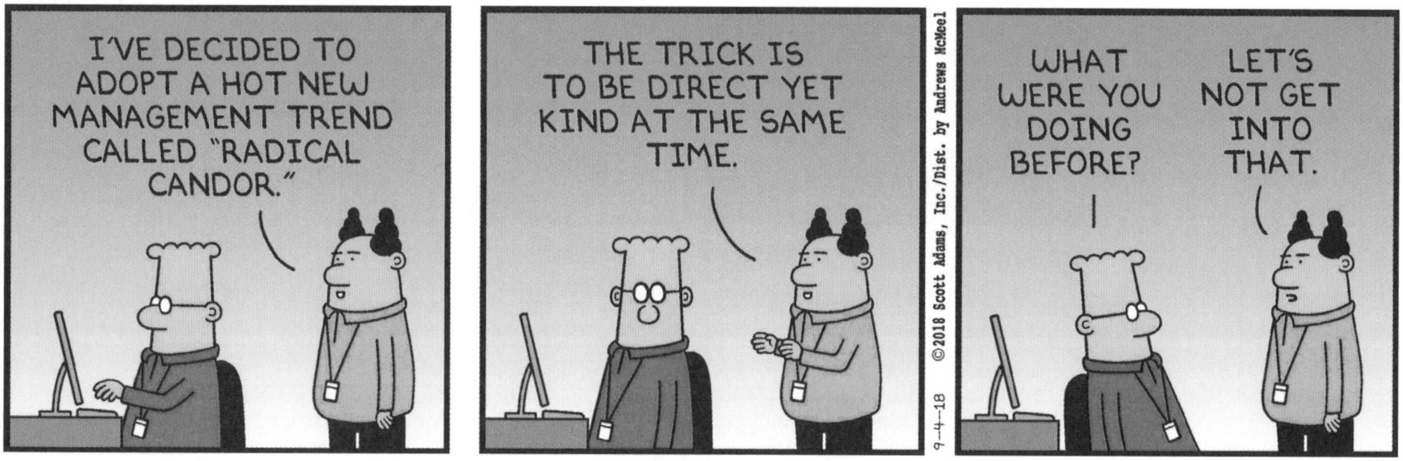
I'VE DECIDED TO ADOPT A HOT NEW MANAGEMENT TREND CALLED "RADICAL CANDOR."
THE TRICK IS TO BE DIRECT YET KIND AT THE SAME TIME.
WHAT WERE YOU DOING BEFORE?
LET'S NOT GET INTO THAT.
9-4-18 ©2018 Scott Adams, Inc./Dist. by Andrews McMeel

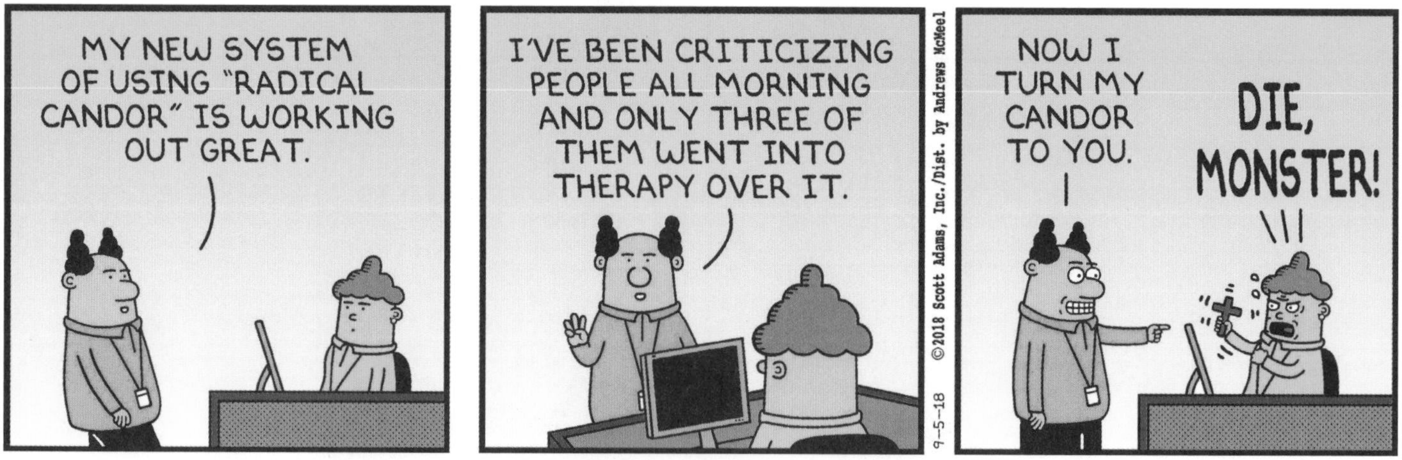
MY NEW SYSTEM OF USING "RADICAL CANDOR" IS WORKING OUT GREAT.
I'VE BEEN CRITICIZING PEOPLE ALL MORNING AND ONLY THREE OF THEM WENT INTO THERAPY OVER IT.
NOW I TURN MY CANDOR TO YOU.
DIE, MONSTER!
9-5-18 ©2018 Scott Adams, Inc./Dist. by Andrews McMeel

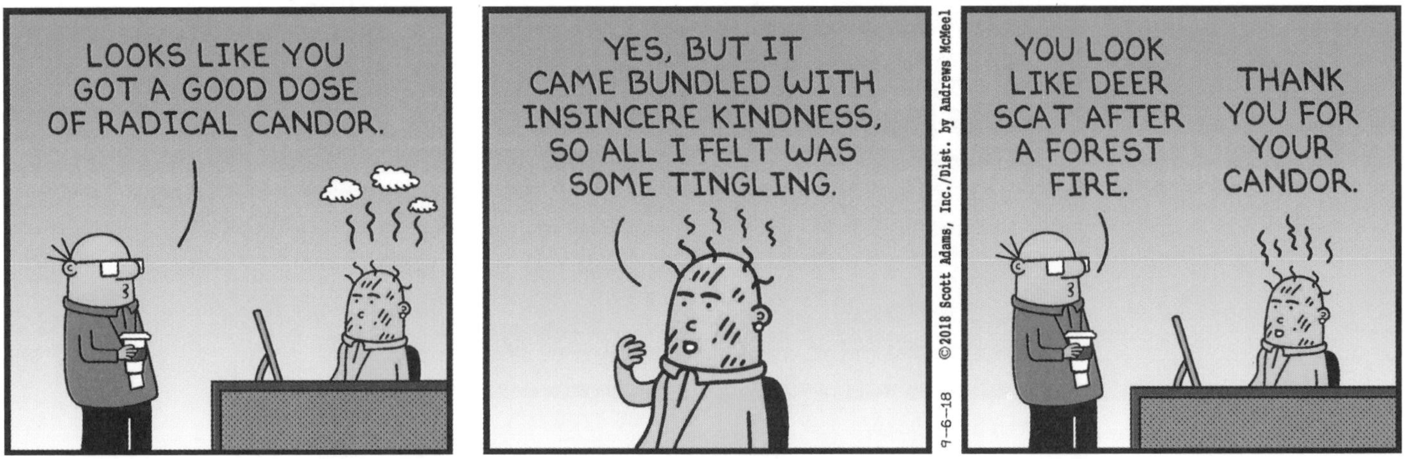
LOOKS LIKE YOU GOT A GOOD DOSE OF RADICAL CANDOR.
YES, BUT IT CAME BUNDLED WITH INSINCERE KINDNESS, SO ALL I FELT WAS SOME TINGLING.
9-6-18 ©2018 Scott Adams, Inc./Dist. by Andrews McMeel
YOU LOOK LIKE DEER SCAT AFTER A FOREST FIRE.
THANK YOU FOR YOUR CANDOR.

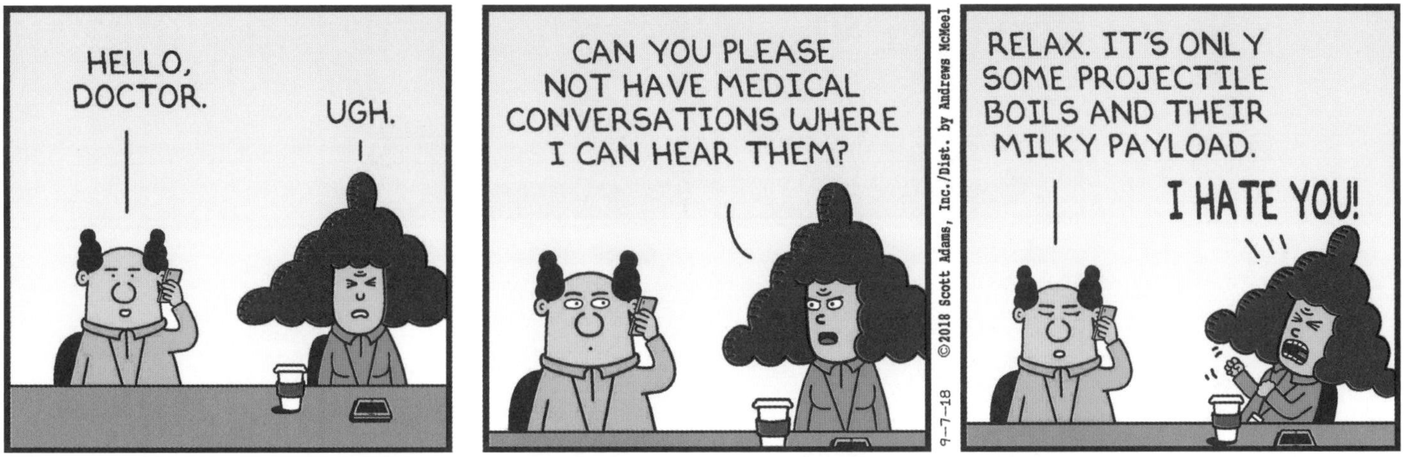
HELLO, DOCTOR.
UGH.
CAN YOU PLEASE NOT HAVE MEDICAL CONVERSATIONS WHERE I CAN HEAR THEM?
9-7-18 ©2018 Scott Adams, Inc./Dist. by Andrews McMeel
RELAX. IT'S ONLY SOME PROJECTILE BOILS AND THEIR MILKY PAYLOAD.
I HATE YOU!

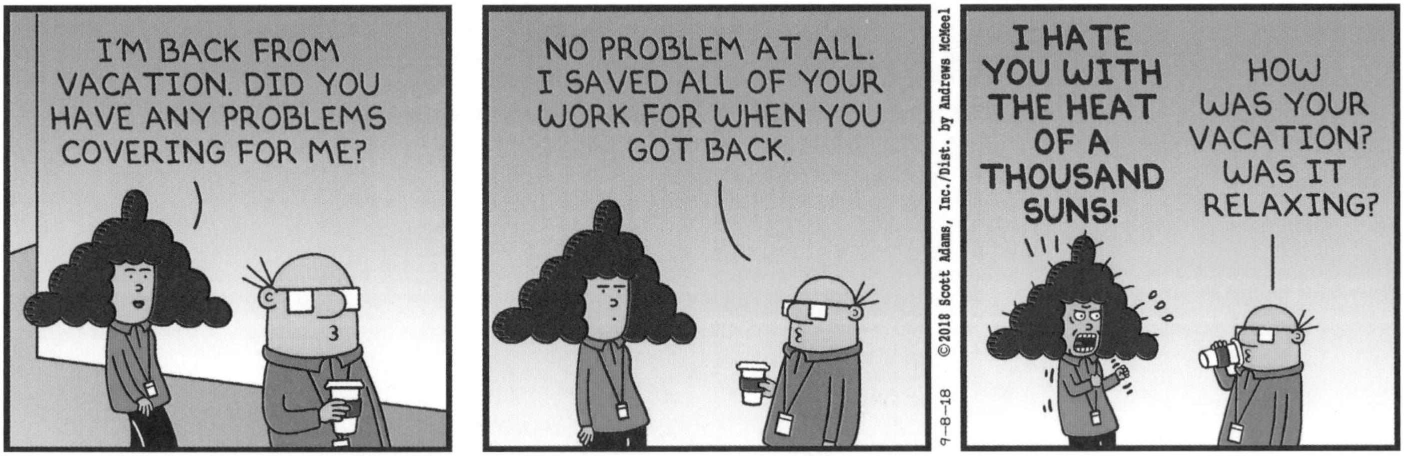
I'M BACK FROM VACATION. DID YOU HAVE ANY PROBLEMS COVERING FOR ME?
NO PROBLEM AT ALL. I SAVED ALL OF YOUR WORK FOR WHEN YOU GOT BACK.
9-8-18 ©2018 Scott Adams, Inc./Dist. by Andrews McMeel
I HATE YOU WITH THE HEAT OF A THOUSAND SUNS!
HOW WAS YOUR VACATION? WAS IT RELAXING?

OMG! YOU ARE SOOOOO WRONG!
I LITERALLY CANNOT BELIEVE YOU ARE THIS GULLIBLE.
HAHAHAHAHA! HAHAHAHAHA!
© 2018 Scott Adams, Inc./Dist. by Andrews McMeel
I CAN'T WAIT TO TWEET ABOUT YOUR STUPIDITY.
YOUR DUMBNESS WILL LIVE FOREVER ON THE INTERNET!
SEND
YOU PROBABLY HAVEN'T SEEN THE NEW DATA THAT PROVES I'M RIGHT.
WILL YOU APOLOGIZE LIKE A DECENT HUMAN BEING? OR WILL YOU MOVE THE GOALPOSTS, CLAIM VICTORY, AND TRASH MY NAME LIKE A DEMENTED WEASEL?
9-9-18
CAN YOU TELL ME MORE ABOUT THE WEASEL OPTION?

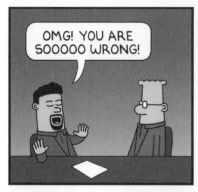

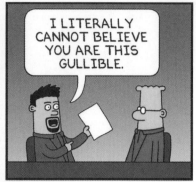

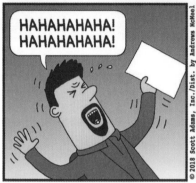

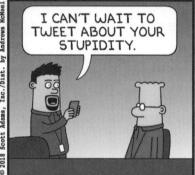

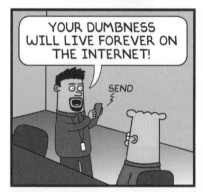

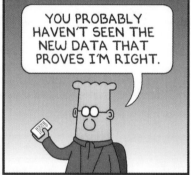

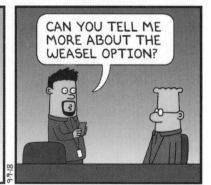

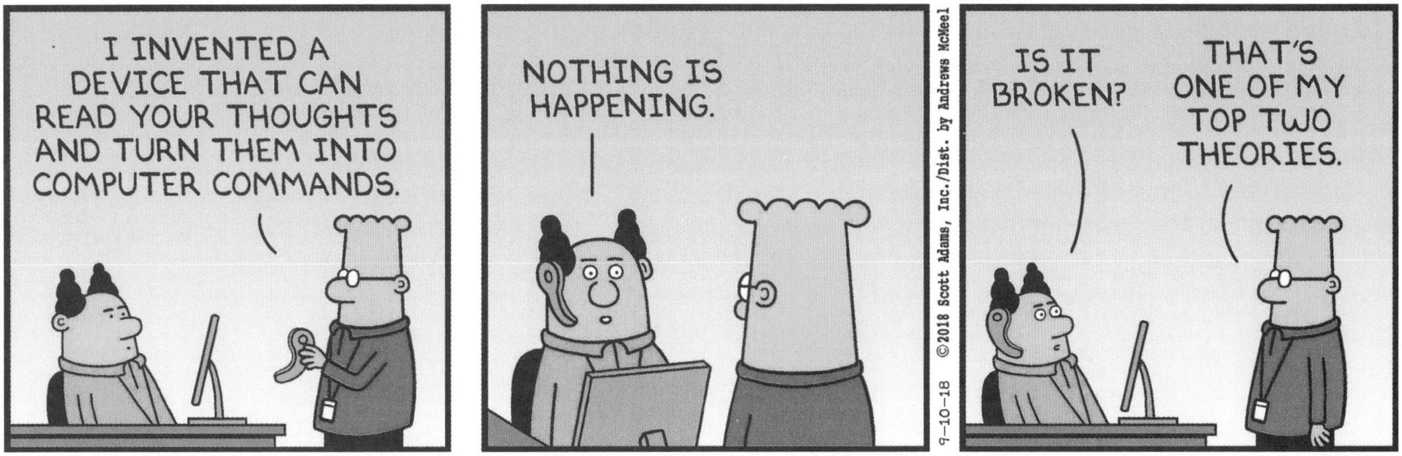
I INVENTED A DEVICE THAT CAN READ YOUR THOUGHTS AND TURN THEM INTO COMPUTER COMMANDS.
NOTHING IS HAPPENING.
9-10-18 ©2018 Scott Adams, Inc./Dist. by Andrews McMeel
IS IT BROKEN?
THAT'S ONE OF MY TOP TWO THEORIES.

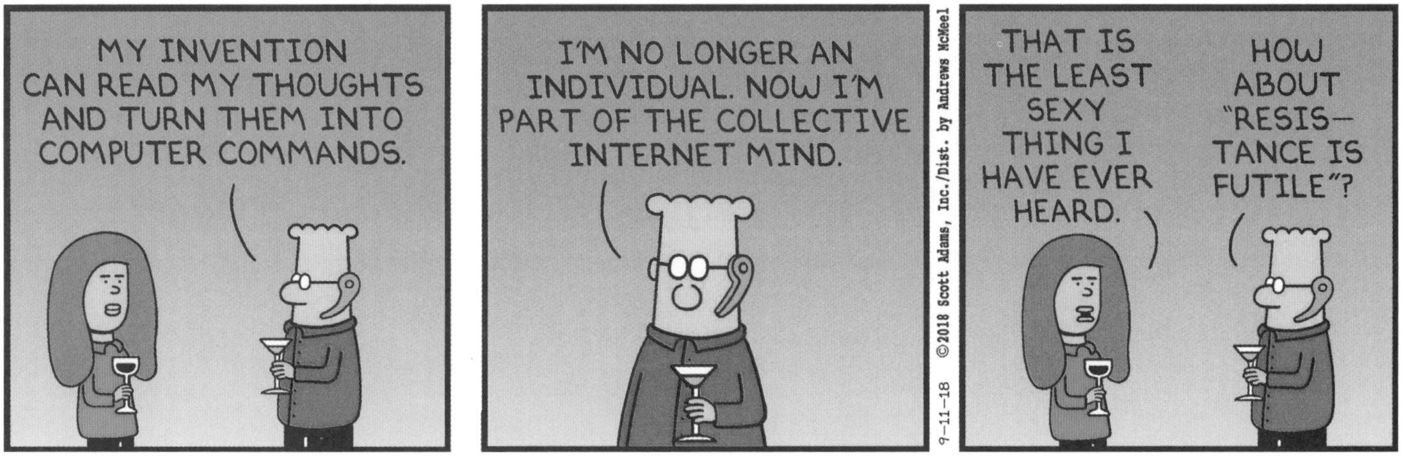
MY INVENTION CAN READ MY THOUGHTS AND TURN THEM INTO COMPUTER COMMANDS.
I'M NO LONGER AN INDIVIDUAL. NOW I'M PART OF THE COLLECTIVE INTERNET MIND.
9-11-18 ©2018 Scott Adams, Inc./Dist. by Andrews McMeel
THAT IS THE LEAST SEXY THING I HAVE EVER HEARD.
HOW ABOUT "RESIS-TANCE IS FUTILE"?

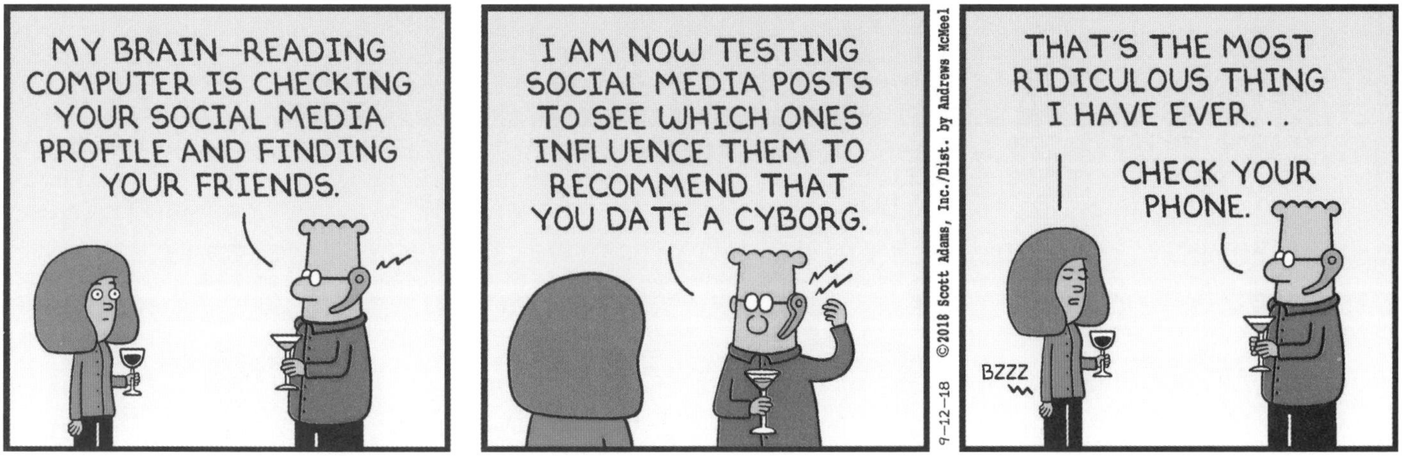
MY BRAIN-READING COMPUTER IS CHECKING YOUR SOCIAL MEDIA PROFILE AND FINDING YOUR FRIENDS.
I AM NOW TESTING SOCIAL MEDIA POSTS TO SEE WHICH ONES INFLUENCE THEM TO RECOMMEND THAT YOU DATE A CYBORG.
9-12-18 ©2018 Scott Adams, Inc./Dist. by Andrews McMeel
THAT'S THE MOST RIDICULOUS THING I HAVE EVER...
CHECK YOUR PHONE.
BZZZ

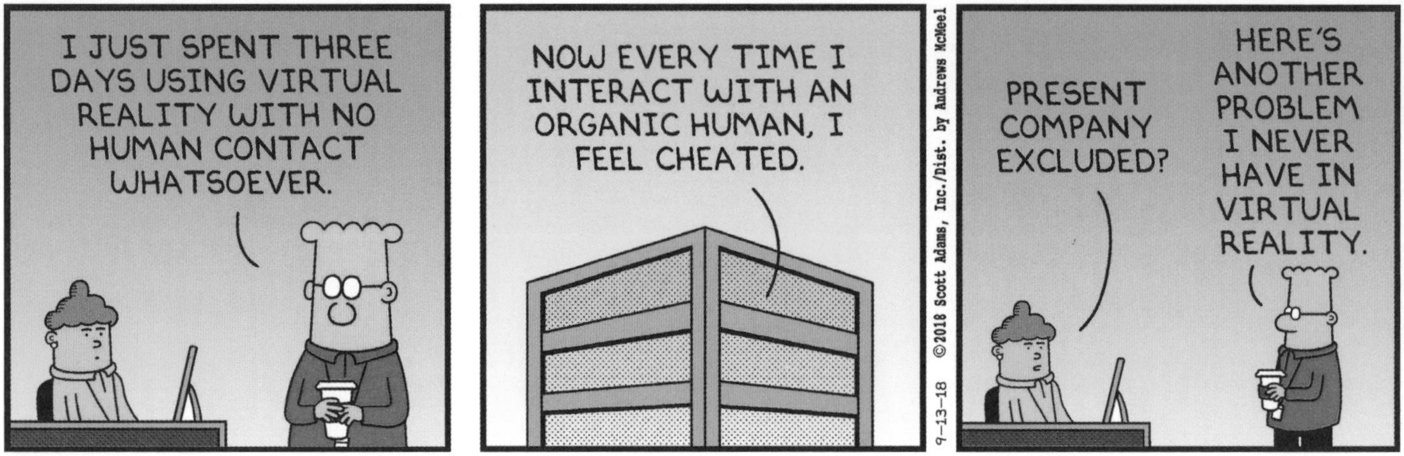
I JUST SPENT THREE DAYS USING VIRTUAL REALITY WITH NO HUMAN CONTACT WHATSOEVER.
NOW EVERY TIME I INTERACT WITH AN ORGANIC HUMAN, I FEEL CHEATED.
9-13-18 ©2018 Scott Adams, Inc./Dist. by Andrews McMeel
PRESENT COMPANY EXCLUDED?
HERE'S ANOTHER PROBLEM I NEVER HAVE IN VIRTUAL REALITY.

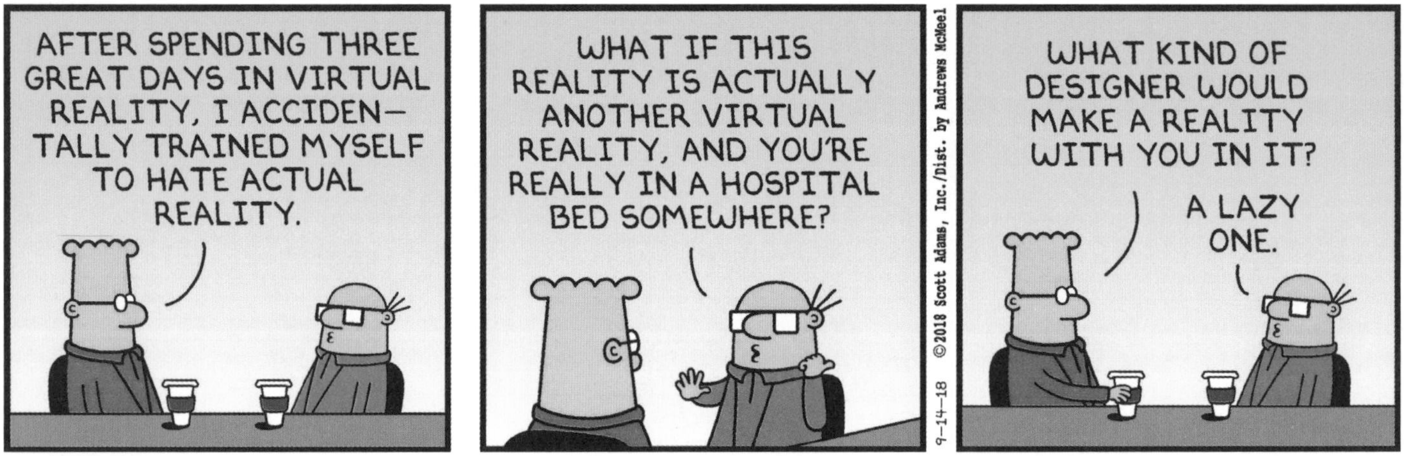
AFTER SPENDING THREE GREAT DAYS IN VIRTUAL REALITY, I ACCIDEN– TALLY TRAINED MYSELF TO HATE ACTUAL REALITY.
WHAT IF THIS REALITY IS ACTUALLY ANOTHER VIRTUAL REALITY, AND YOU'RE REALLY IN A HOSPITAL BED SOMEWHERE?
9-14-18 ©2018 Scott Adams, Inc./Dist. by Andrews McMeel
WHAT KIND OF DESIGNER WOULD MAKE A REALITY WITH YOU IN IT?
A LAZY ONE.

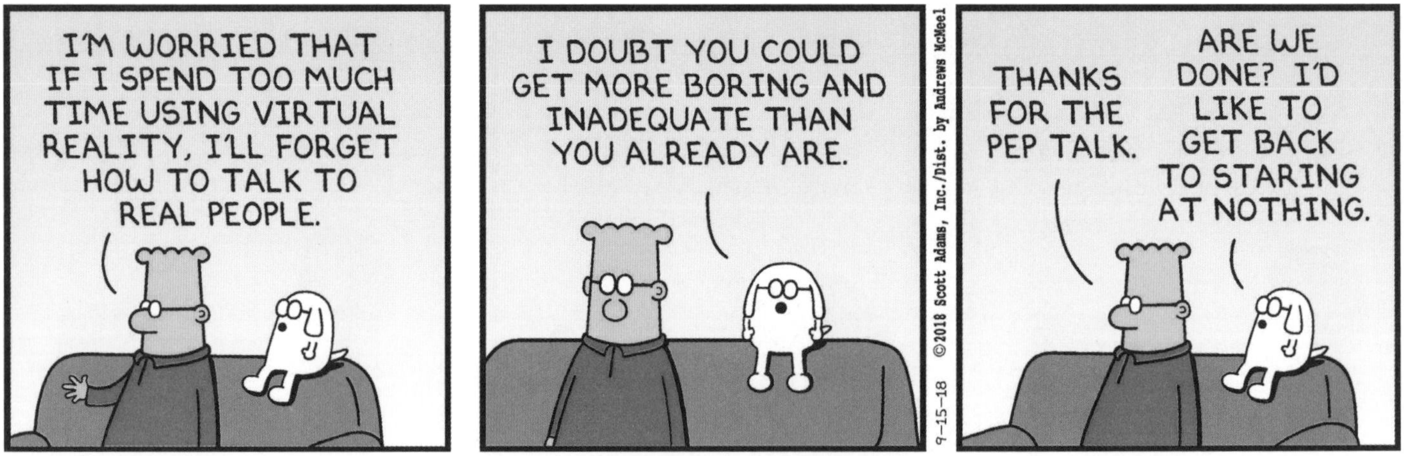
I'M WORRIED THAT IF I SPEND TOO MUCH TIME USING VIRTUAL REALITY, I'LL FORGET HOW TO TALK TO REAL PEOPLE.
I DOUBT YOU COULD GET MORE BORING AND INADEQUATE THAN YOU ALREADY ARE.
9-15-18 ©2018 Scott Adams, Inc./Dist. by Andrews McMeel
THANKS FOR THE PEP TALK.
ARE WE DONE? I'D LIKE TO GET BACK TO STARING AT NOTHING.

DO YOU HAVE AN HOUR TO MEET NEXT WEEK?
LET ME CHECK MY CALENDAR.
NEXT WEEK IS NOT GOOD.
YOU DON'T HAVE ONE HOUR OF FREE TIME ALL WEEK?
WELL, THIS IS AWKWARD.
THE PROBLEM ISN'T MY SCHEDULE SO MUCH AS YOUR TOTAL LACK OF VALUE RELATIVE TO MY ALTERNATIVES.
MAYBE WE COULD MEET OVER LUNCH?
I LIKE TO FOCUS ON MY SANDWICH.
© 2018 Scott Adams, Inc./Dist. by Andrews McMeel
9-16-18

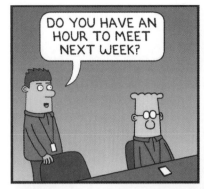

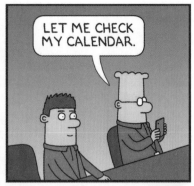

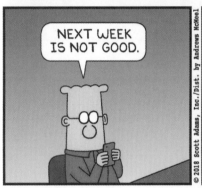

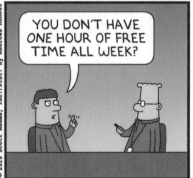

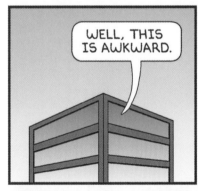

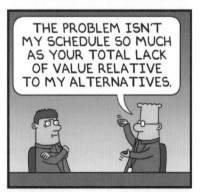

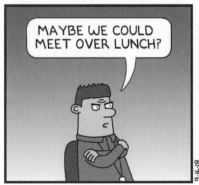

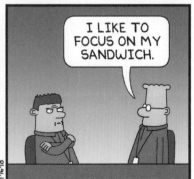

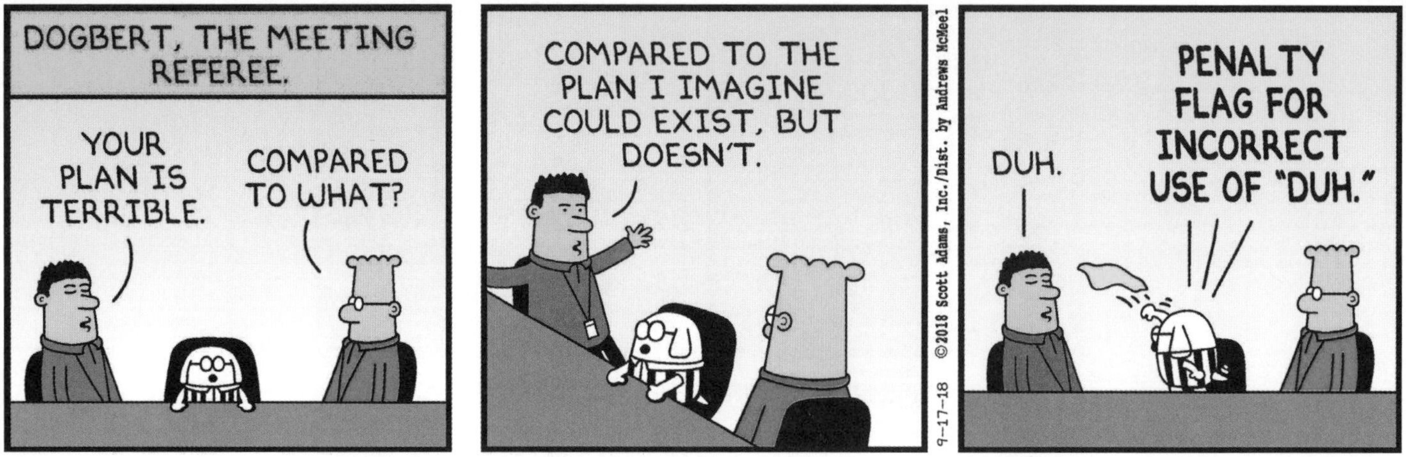
DOGBERT, THE MEETING REFEREE.
YOUR PLAN IS TERRIBLE.
COMPARED TO WHAT?
COMPARED TO THE PLAN I IMAGINE COULD EXIST, BUT DOESN'T.
9-17-18 ©2018 Scott Adams, Inc./Dist. by Andrews McMeel
DUH.
PENALTY FLAG FOR INCORRECT USE OF "DUH."

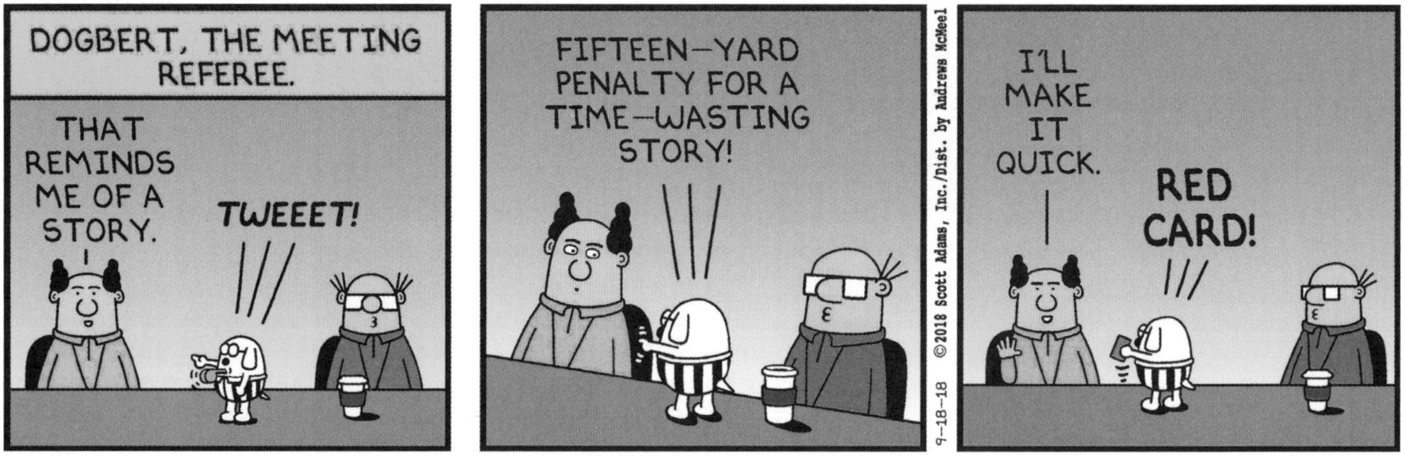
DOGBERT, THE MEETING REFEREE.
THAT REMINDS ME OF A STORY.
TWEEET!
FIFTEEN-YARD PENALTY FOR A TIME-WASTING STORY!
9-18-18 ©2018 Scott Adams, Inc./Dist. by Andrews McMeel
I'LL MAKE IT QUICK.
RED CARD!

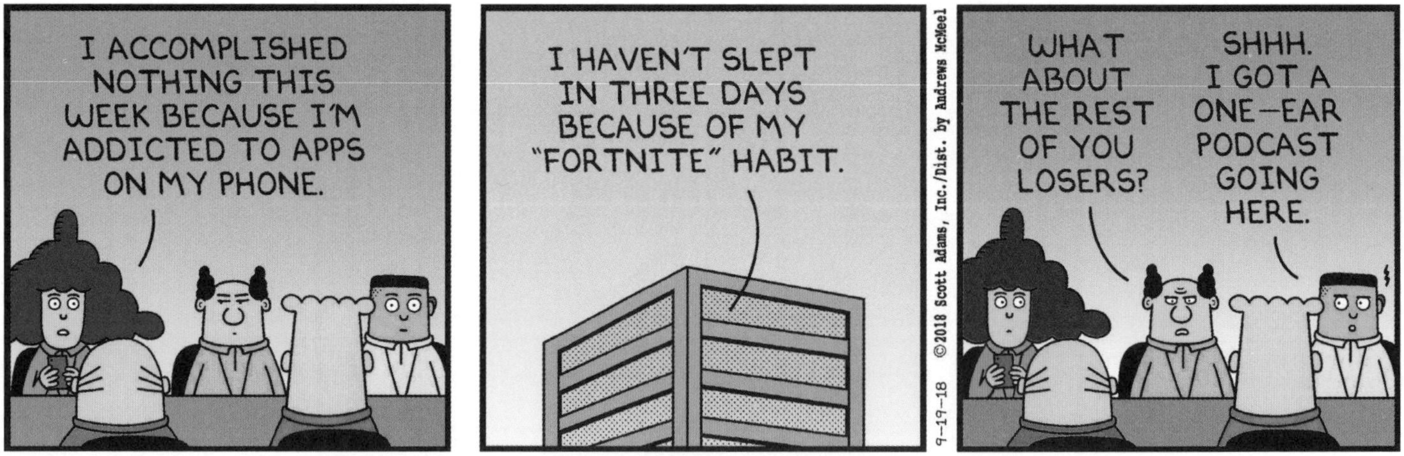
I ACCOMPLISHED NOTHING THIS WEEK BECAUSE I'M ADDICTED TO APPS ON MY PHONE.
I HAVEN'T SLEPT IN THREE DAYS BECAUSE OF MY "FORTNITE" HABIT.
9-19-18 ©2018 Scott Adams, Inc./Dist. by Andrews McMeel
WHAT ABOUT THE REST OF YOU LOSERS?
SHHH. I GOT A ONE-EAR PODCAST GOING HERE.

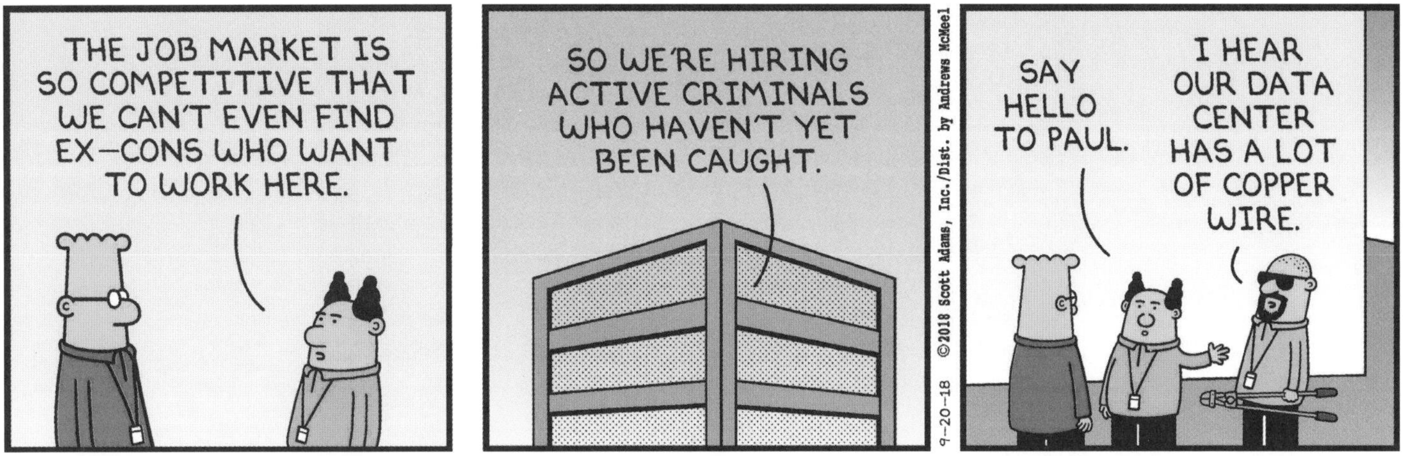
THE JOB MARKET IS SO COMPETITIVE THAT WE CAN'T EVEN FIND EX–CONS WHO WANT TO WORK HERE.
SO WE'RE HIRING ACTIVE CRIMINALS WHO HAVEN'T YET BEEN CAUGHT.
9-20-18 ©2018 Scott Adams, Inc./Dist. by Andrews McMeel
SAY HELLO TO PAUL.
I HEAR OUR DATA CENTER HAS A LOT OF COPPER WIRE.

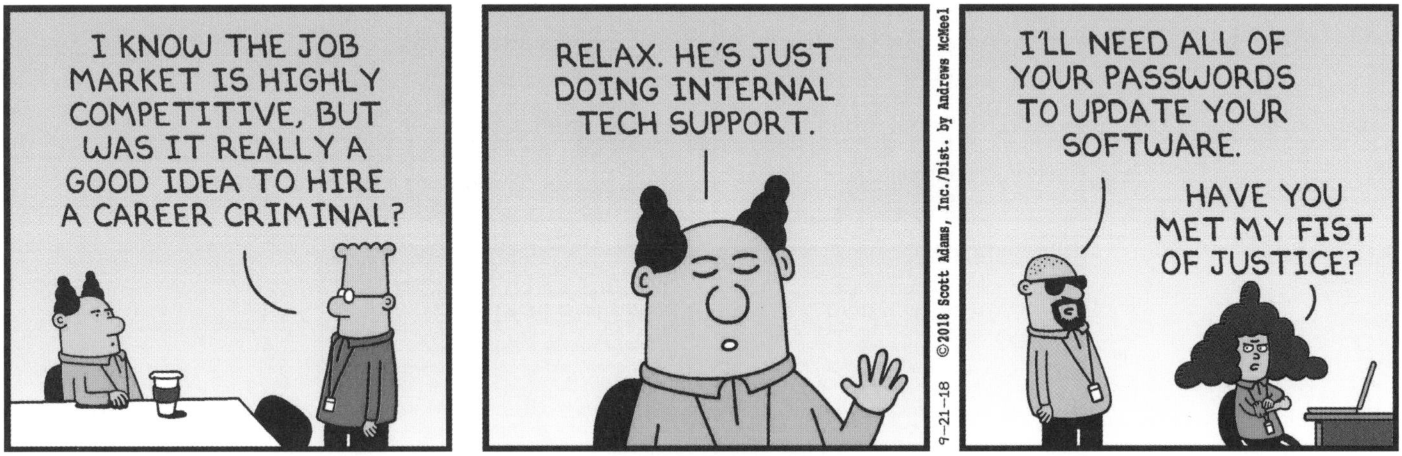
I KNOW THE JOB MARKET IS HIGHLY COMPETITIVE, BUT WAS IT REALLY A GOOD IDEA TO HIRE A CAREER CRIMINAL?
RELAX. HE'S JUST DOING INTERNAL TECH SUPPORT.
9-21-18 ©2018 Scott Adams, Inc./Dist. by Andrews McMeel
I'LL NEED ALL OF YOUR PASSWORDS TO UPDATE YOUR SOFTWARE.
HAVE YOU MET MY FIST OF JUSTICE?

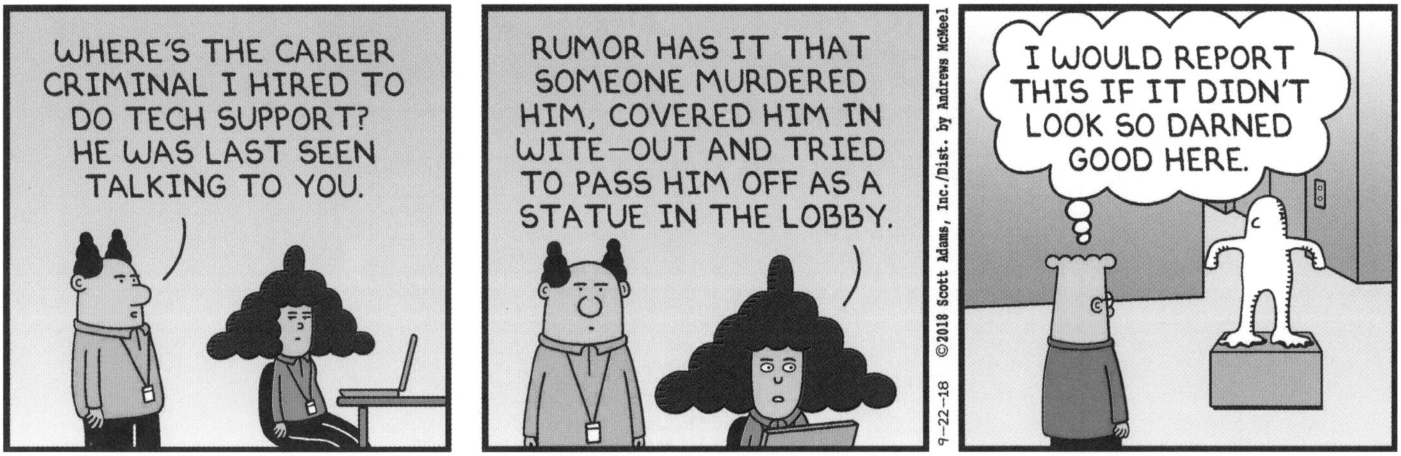
WHERE'S THE CAREER CRIMINAL I HIRED TO DO TECH SUPPORT? HE WAS LAST SEEN TALKING TO YOU.
RUMOR HAS IT THAT SOMEONE MURDERED HIM, COVERED HIM IN WITE–OUT AND TRIED TO PASS HIM OFF AS A STATUE IN THE LOBBY.
9-22-18 ©2018 Scott Adams, Inc./Dist. by Andrews McMeel
I WOULD REPORT THIS IF IT DIDN'T LOOK SO DARNED GOOD HERE.

I'M HAVING A BAD TECHNOLOGY DAY.
MY PHONE KEEPS FREEZING, MY PRINTER ISN'T WORKING, AND OUR NETWORK IS DOWN.
MY CAR'S WARNING LIGHTS LOOK LIKE A CHRISTMAS TREE, AND MY LAPTOP WON'T BOOT UP.
MAYBE IT'S ALL JUST COINCIDENCE, BUT I DON'T THINK WE CAN TAKE THAT CHANCE.
© 2018 Scott Adams, Inc./Dist. by Andrews McMeel
MAY I HAVE PERMISSION TO LOCK MYSELF IN A LEAD-LINED BOX TO PROTECT THE REST OF THE COMPANY?
HOW WILL I KNOW YOU'RE REALLY IN A LEAD-LINED BOX?
YOU'LL KNOW BECAUSE YOUR PHONE WILL BE WORKING FINE.
9-23-18
THREE WEEKS LATER
MY PHONE IS STILL WORKING. THAT MAN IS A HERO.

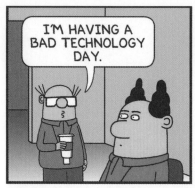

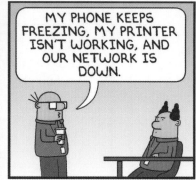

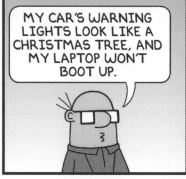

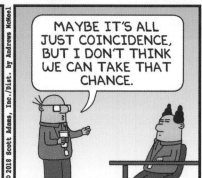

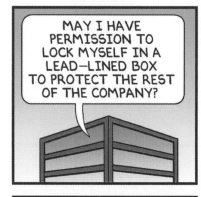

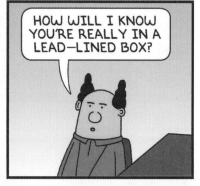

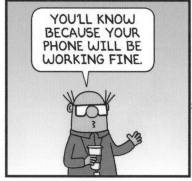

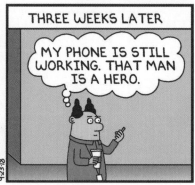

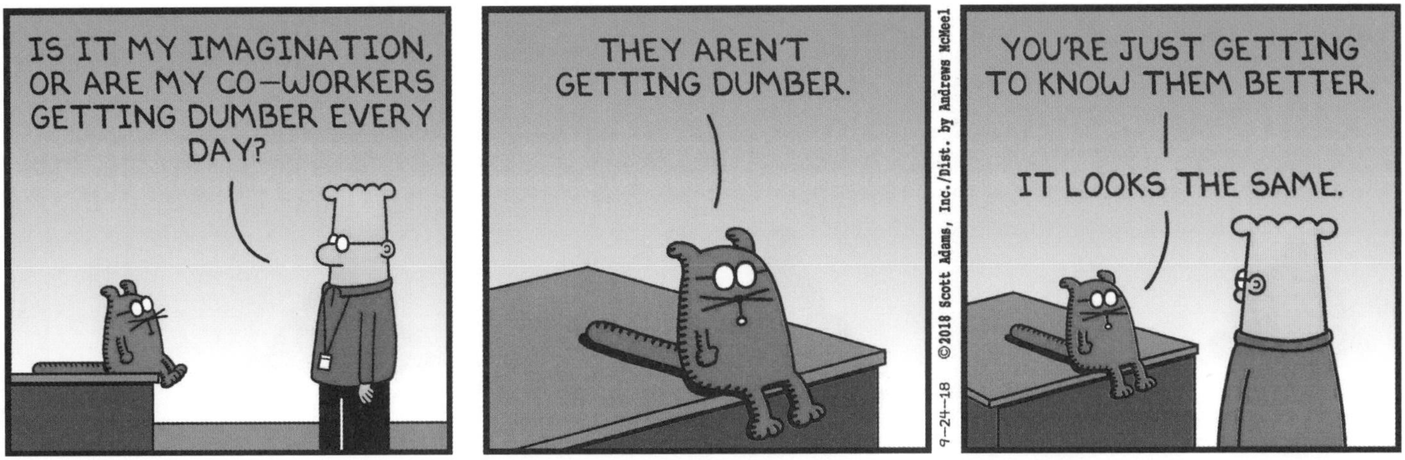
IS IT MY IMAGINATION, OR ARE MY CO-WORKERS GETTING DUMBER EVERY DAY?
THEY AREN'T GETTING DUMBER.
YOU'RE JUST GETTING TO KNOW THEM BETTER.
IT LOOKS THE SAME.
9-24-18 ©2018 Scott Adams, Inc./Dist. by Andrews McMeel

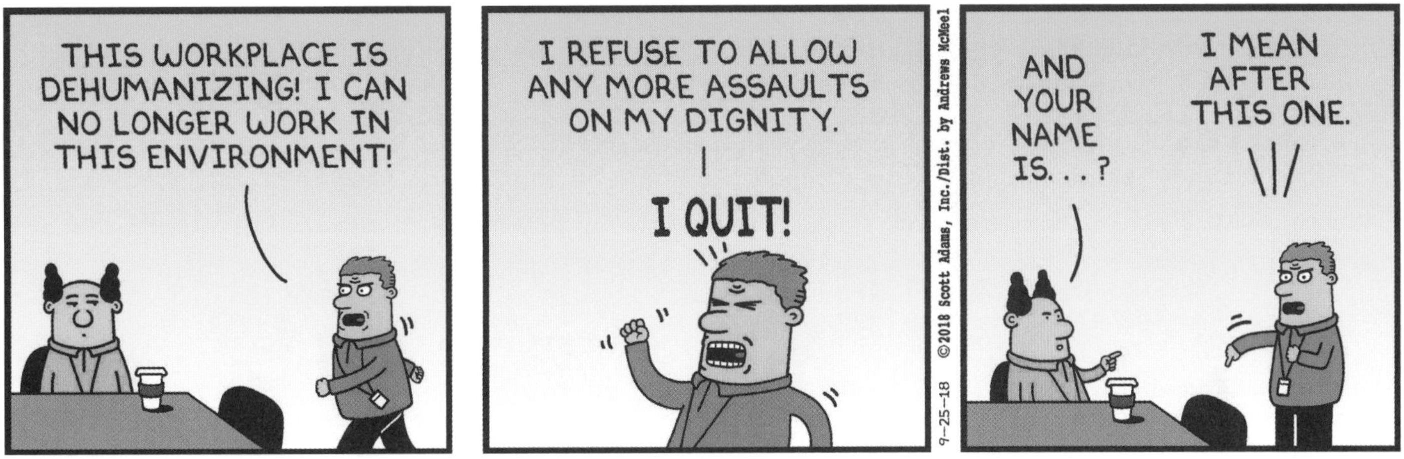
THIS WORKPLACE IS DEHUMANIZING! I CAN NO LONGER WORK IN THIS ENVIRONMENT!
I REFUSE TO ALLOW ANY MORE ASSAULTS ON MY DIGNITY.
I QUIT!
AND YOUR NAME IS. . . ?
I MEAN AFTER THIS ONE.
9-25-18 ©2018 Scott Adams, Inc./Dist. by Andrews McMeel

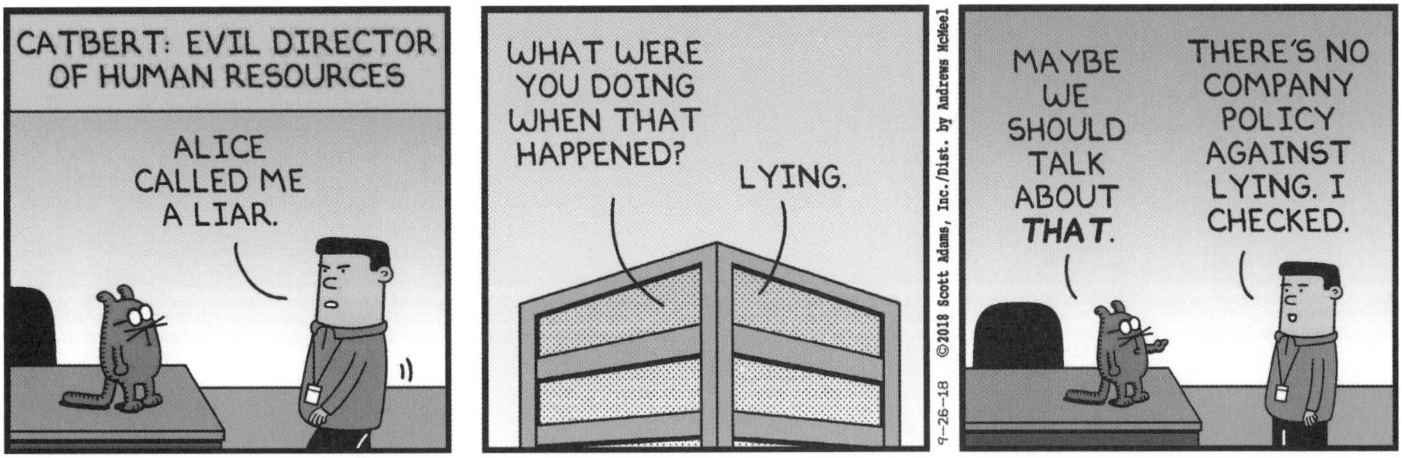
CATBERT: EVIL DIRECTOR OF HUMAN RESOURCES
ALICE CALLED ME A LIAR.
WHAT WERE YOU DOING WHEN THAT HAPPENED?
LYING.
MAYBE WE SHOULD TALK ABOUT THAT.
THERE'S NO COMPANY POLICY AGAINST LYING. I CHECKED.
9-26-18 ©2018 Scott Adams, Inc./Dist. by Andrews McMeel

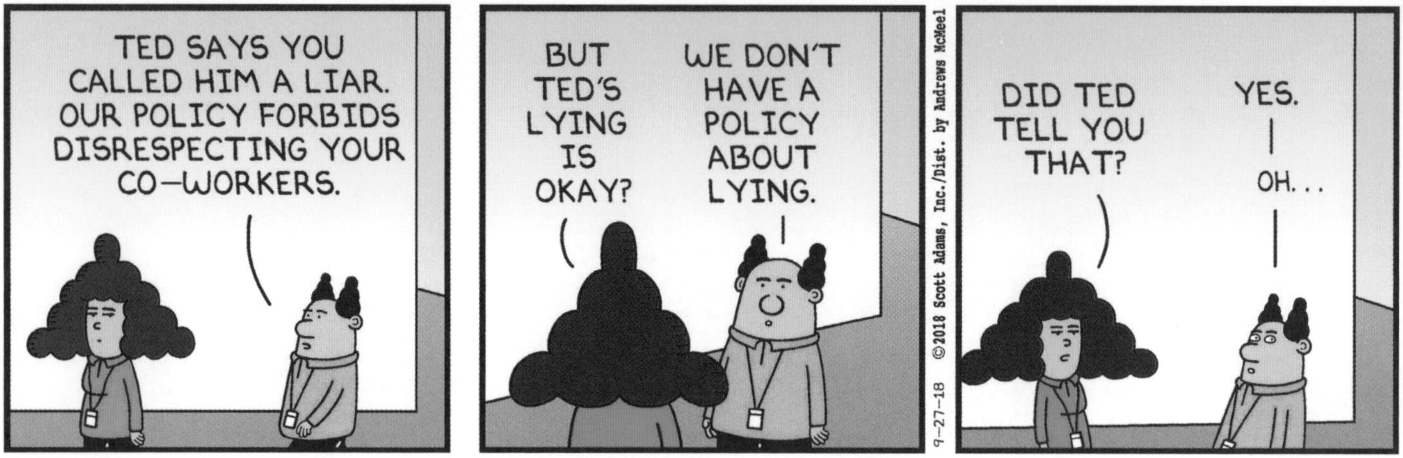
TED SAYS YOU CALLED HIM A LIAR. OUR POLICY FORBIDS DISRESPECTING YOUR CO-WORKERS.
BUT TED'S LYING IS OKAY?
WE DON'T HAVE A POLICY ABOUT LYING.
DID TED TELL YOU THAT?
YES.
OH...
9-27-18 ©2018 Scott Adams, Inc./Dist. by Andrews McMeel

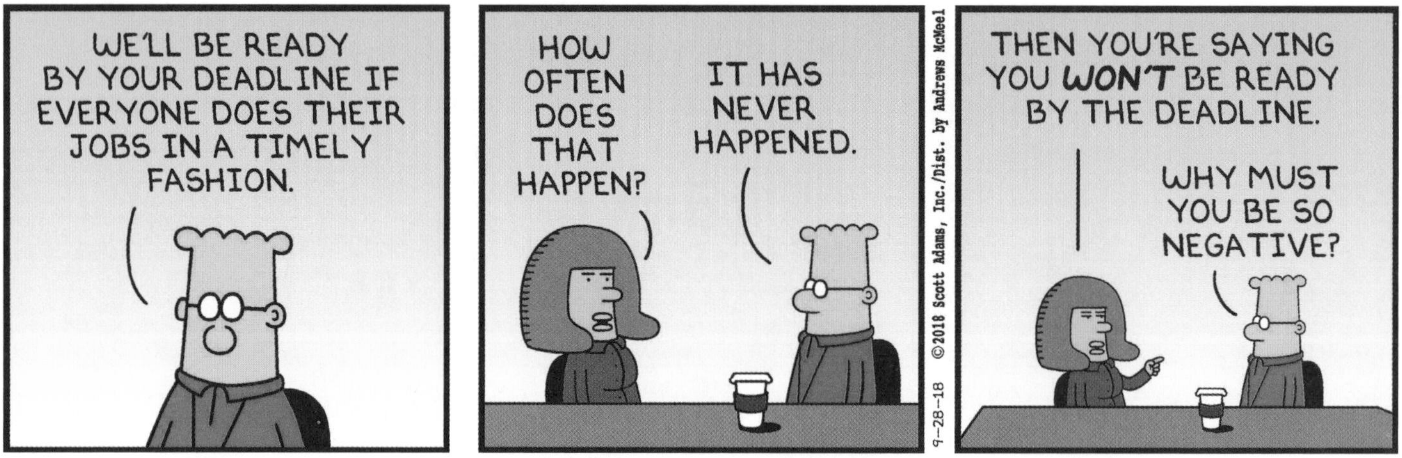
WE'LL BE READY BY YOUR DEADLINE IF EVERYONE DOES THEIR JOBS IN A TIMELY FASHION.
HOW OFTEN DOES THAT HAPPEN?
IT HAS NEVER HAPPENED.
THEN YOU'RE SAYING YOU **WON'T** BE READY BY THE DEADLINE.
WHY MUST YOU BE SO NEGATIVE?
9-28-18 ©2018 Scott Adams, Inc./Dist. by Andrews McMeel

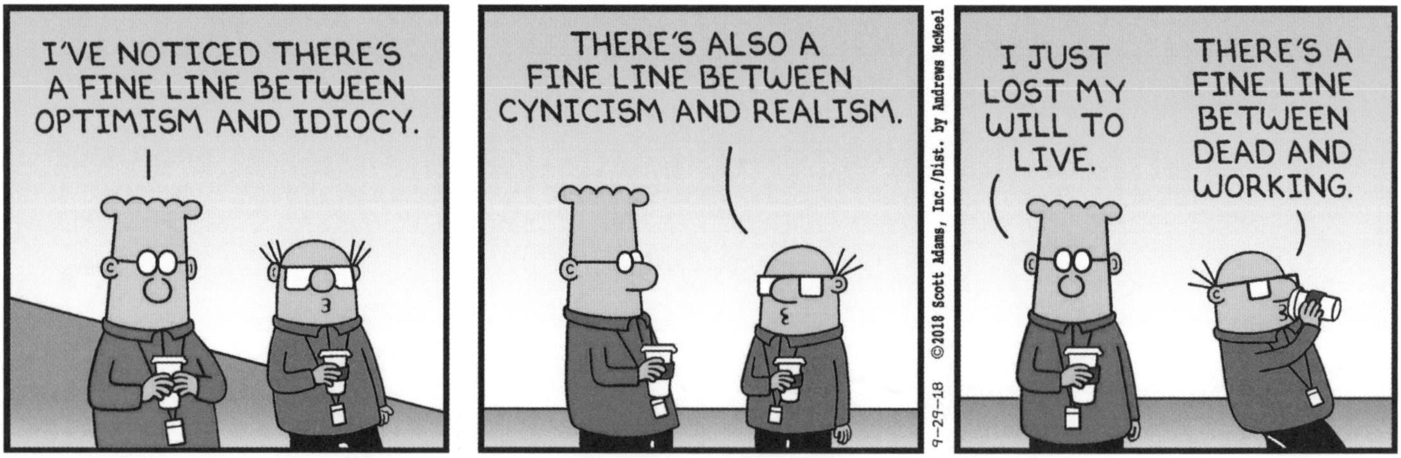
I'VE NOTICED THERE'S A FINE LINE BETWEEN OPTIMISM AND IDIOCY.
THERE'S ALSO A FINE LINE BETWEEN CYNICISM AND REALISM.
I JUST LOST MY WILL TO LIVE.
THERE'S A FINE LINE BETWEEN DEAD AND WORKING.
9-29-18 ©2018 Scott Adams, Inc./Dist. by Andrews McMeel

MY CO—WORKERS MAKE IT IMPOSSIBLE TO WORK.
I HEAR EVERY ONE OF THEIR PHONE CALLS.
IT'S MADDENING.
WHEN THEY WALK PAST MY CUBICLE, IT BREAKS MY FLOW.
AND DON'T GET ME STARTED ABOUT THE FOOD SMELLS COMING FROM THE BREAK ROOM.
© 2018 Scott Adams, Inc./Dist. by Andrews McMeel
THEY ASK ME ONE DUMB QUESTION AFTER ANOTHER.
I DON'T KNOW WHO KEEPS TURNING UP THE THERMOSTAT, BUT IT'S TOO HOT TO THINK.
WOULD IT HELP IF I THREATEN TO FIRE YOU?
9-30-18
IT'S WORTH A TRY. I'LL BE IN MY CUBICLE PRETENDING TO WORK.

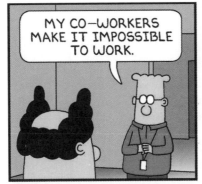

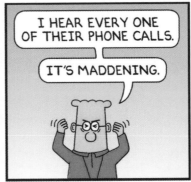

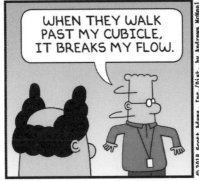

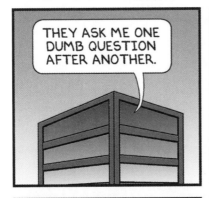

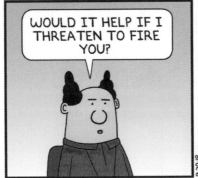

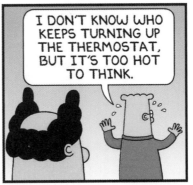

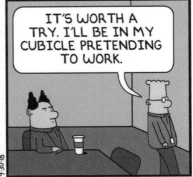

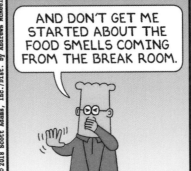

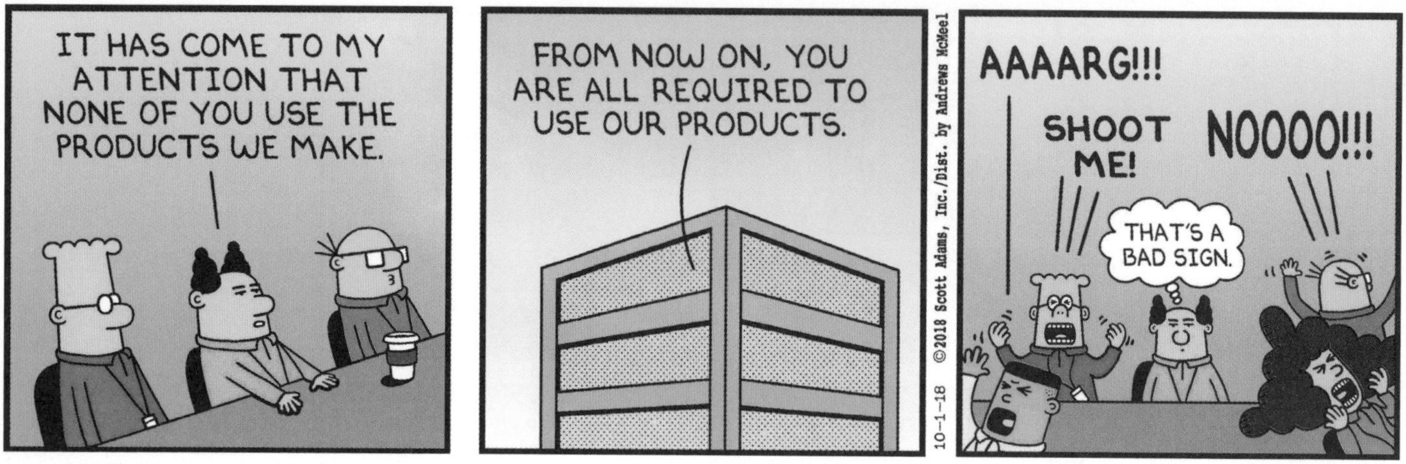
IT HAS COME TO MY ATTENTION THAT NONE OF YOU USE THE PRODUCTS WE MAKE.
FROM NOW ON, YOU ARE ALL REQUIRED TO USE OUR PRODUCTS.
AAAARG!!!
SHOOT ME!
NOOOO!!!
THAT'S A BAD SIGN.
10-1-18 ©2018 Scott Adams, Inc./Dist. by Andrews McMeel

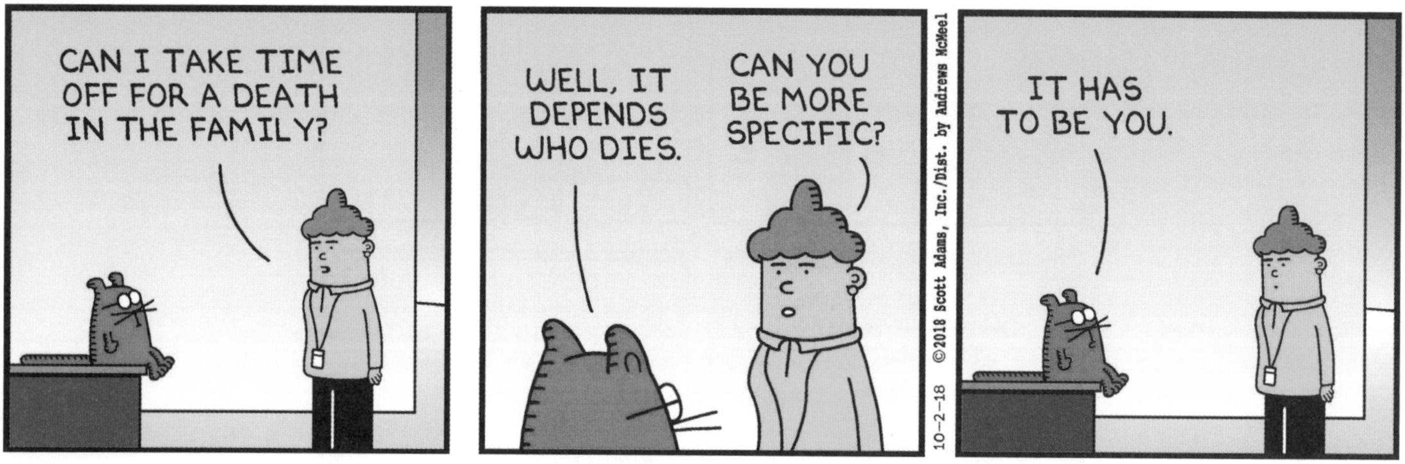
CAN I TAKE TIME OFF FOR A DEATH IN THE FAMILY?
CAN YOU BE MORE SPECIFIC?
WELL, IT DEPENDS WHO DIES.
IT HAS TO BE YOU.
10-2-18 ©2018 Scott Adams, Inc./Dist. by Andrews McMeel

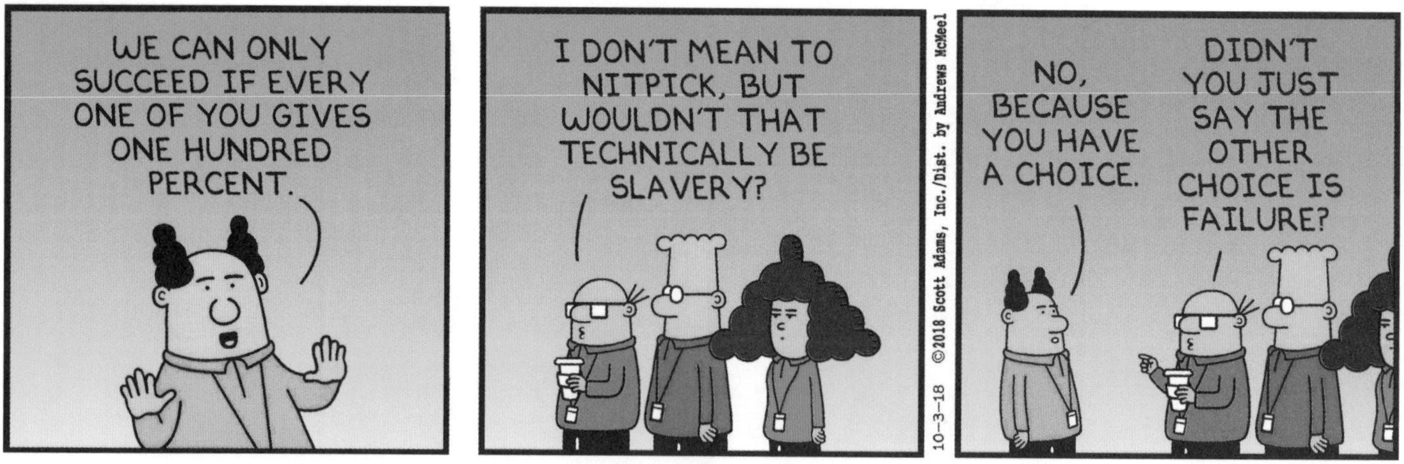
WE CAN ONLY SUCCEED IF EVERY ONE OF YOU GIVES ONE HUNDRED PERCENT.
I DON'T MEAN TO NITPICK, BUT WOULDN'T THAT TECHNICALLY BE SLAVERY?
NO, BECAUSE YOU HAVE A CHOICE.
DIDN'T YOU JUST SAY THE OTHER CHOICE IS FAILURE?
10-3-18 ©2018 Scott Adams, Inc./Dist. by Andrews McMeel

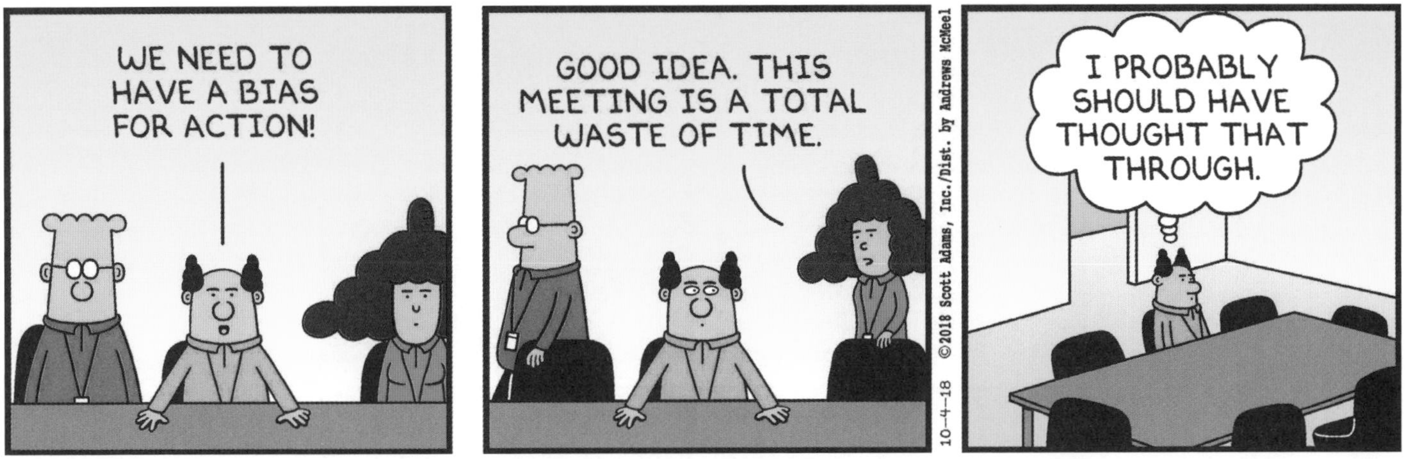
WE NEED TO HAVE A BIAS FOR ACTION!
GOOD IDEA. THIS MEETING IS A TOTAL WASTE OF TIME.
10-4-18 ©2018 Scott Adams, Inc./Dist. by Andrews McMeel
I PROBABLY SHOULD HAVE THOUGHT THAT THROUGH.

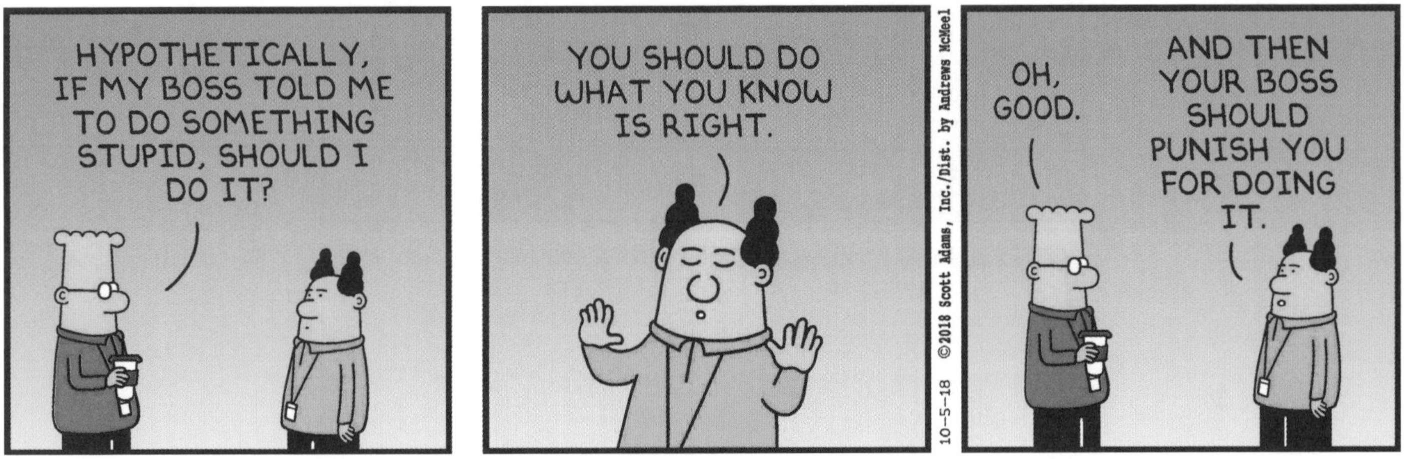
HYPOTHETICALLY, IF MY BOSS TOLD ME TO DO SOMETHING STUPID, SHOULD I DO IT?
YOU SHOULD DO WHAT YOU KNOW IS RIGHT.
10-5-18 ©2018 Scott Adams, Inc./Dist. by Andrews McMeel
OH, GOOD.
AND THEN YOUR BOSS SHOULD PUNISH YOU FOR DOING IT.

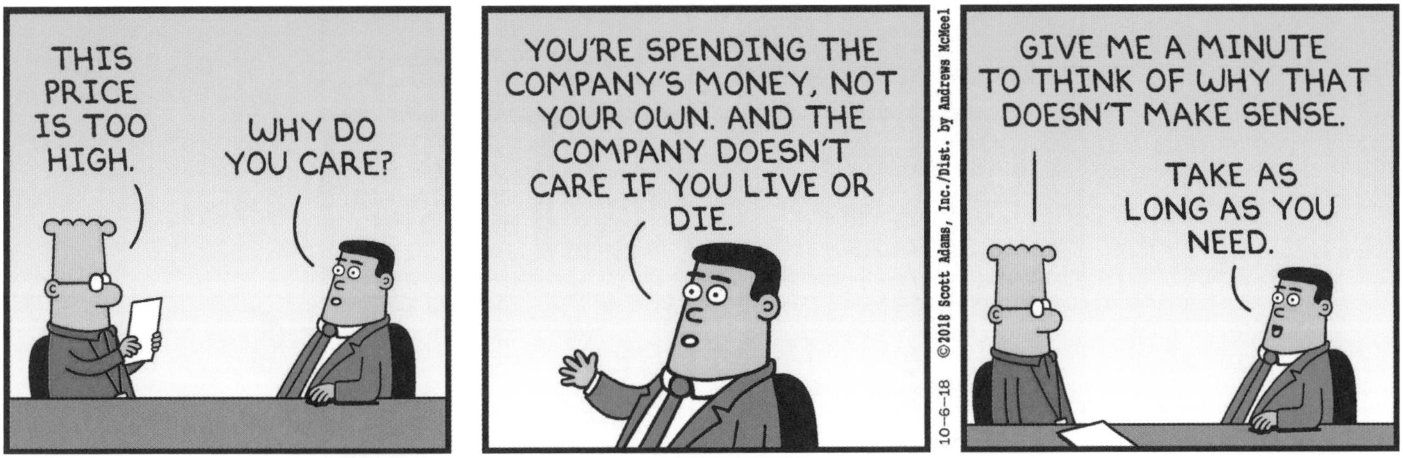
THIS PRICE IS TOO HIGH.
WHY DO YOU CARE?
YOU'RE SPENDING THE COMPANY'S MONEY, NOT YOUR OWN. AND THE COMPANY DOESN'T CARE IF YOU LIVE OR DIE.
10-6-18 ©2018 Scott Adams, Inc./Dist. by Andrews McMeel
GIVE ME A MINUTE TO THINK OF WHY THAT DOESN'T MAKE SENSE.
TAKE AS LONG AS YOU NEED.

I HEARD YOU WERE CRITICIZING ME BEHIND MY BACK.
TRY SAYING THOSE THINGS TO MY FACE!
OKAY.
YOU'RE A HOT—HEADED KNOW—NOTHING WHO USES HIS ARROGANCE TO MASK HIS TOTAL LACK OF TALENT.
YOU RUIN EVERY MEETING WITH YOUR TOXIC PERSONALITY.
EVERY PROJECT YOU TOUCH TURNS TO GARBAGE. YOU'RE LIKE A PLAGUE WITH LEGS.
OKAY... THAT WAS HARSH, BUT I RESPECT YOU FOR SPEAKING TRUTH TO POWER.
YOU DON'T HAVE ANY POWER.
MAYBE IT'S BETTER IF YOU TALK BEHIND MY BACK.
© 2018 Scott Adams, Inc./Dist. by Andrews McMeel
10-7-18

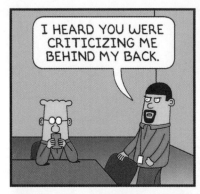

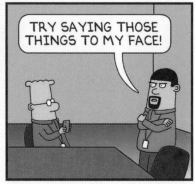

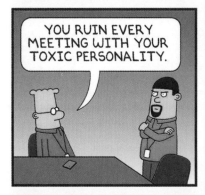

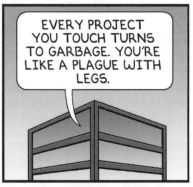

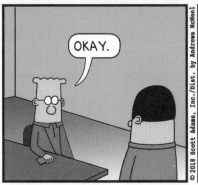

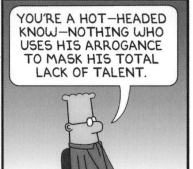

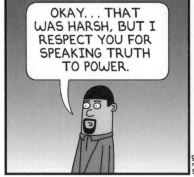

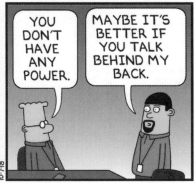

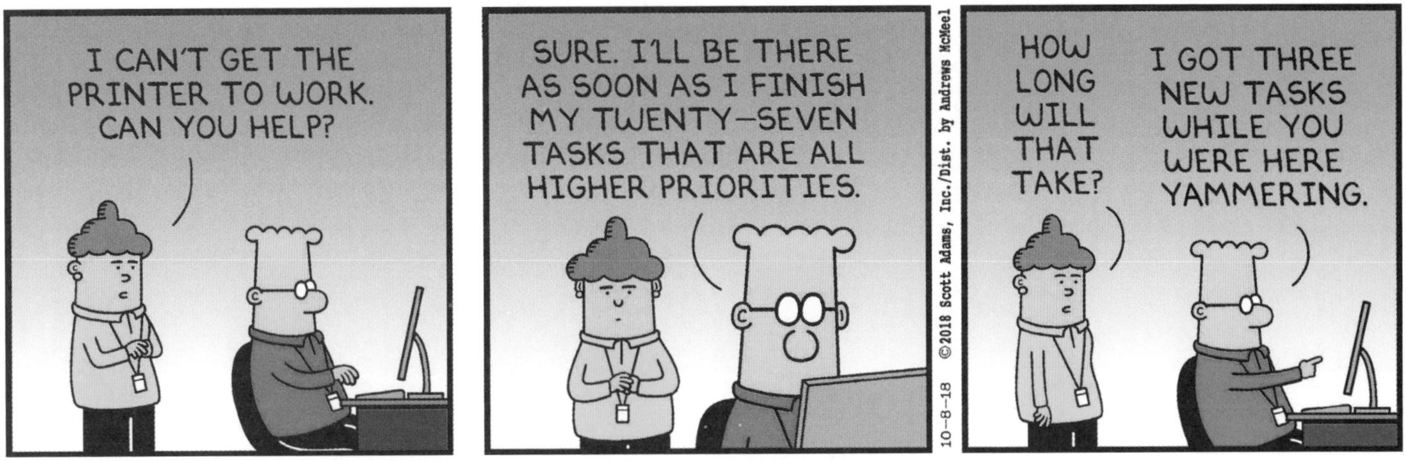
I CAN'T GET THE PRINTER TO WORK. CAN YOU HELP?
SURE. I'LL BE THERE AS SOON AS I FINISH MY TWENTY-SEVEN TASKS THAT ARE ALL HIGHER PRIORITIES.
10-8-18 ©2018 Scott Adams, Inc./Dist. by Andrews McMeel
HOW LONG WILL THAT TAKE?
I GOT THREE NEW TASKS WHILE YOU WERE HERE YAMMERING.

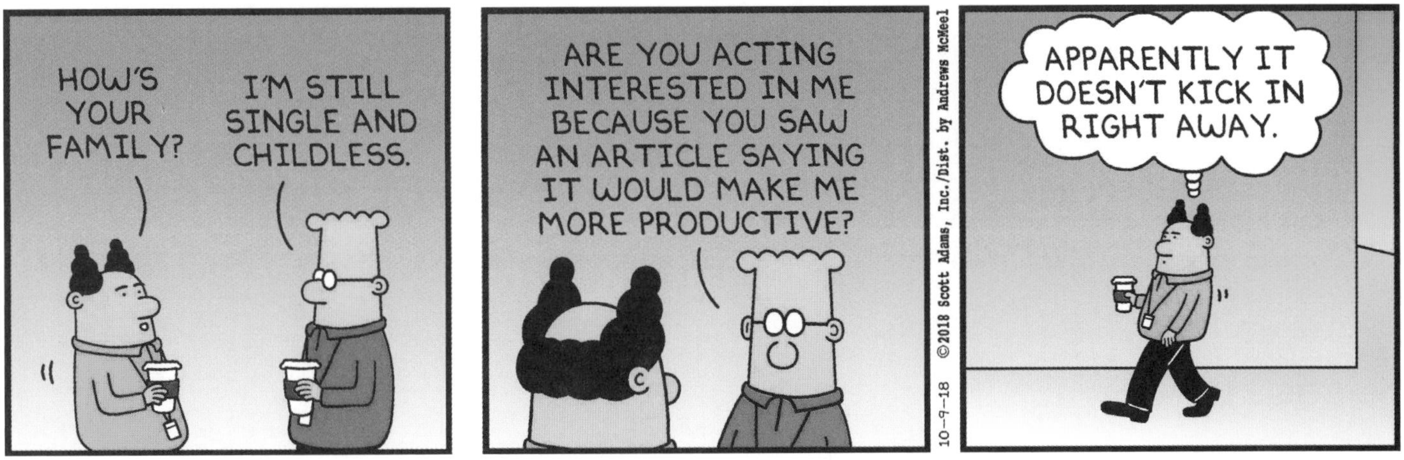
HOW'S YOUR FAMILY?
I'M STILL SINGLE AND CHILDLESS.
ARE YOU ACTING INTERESTED IN ME BECAUSE YOU SAW AN ARTICLE SAYING IT WOULD MAKE ME MORE PRODUCTIVE?
10-9-18 ©2018 Scott Adams, Inc./Dist. by Andrews McMeel
APPARENTLY IT DOESN'T KICK IN RIGHT AWAY.

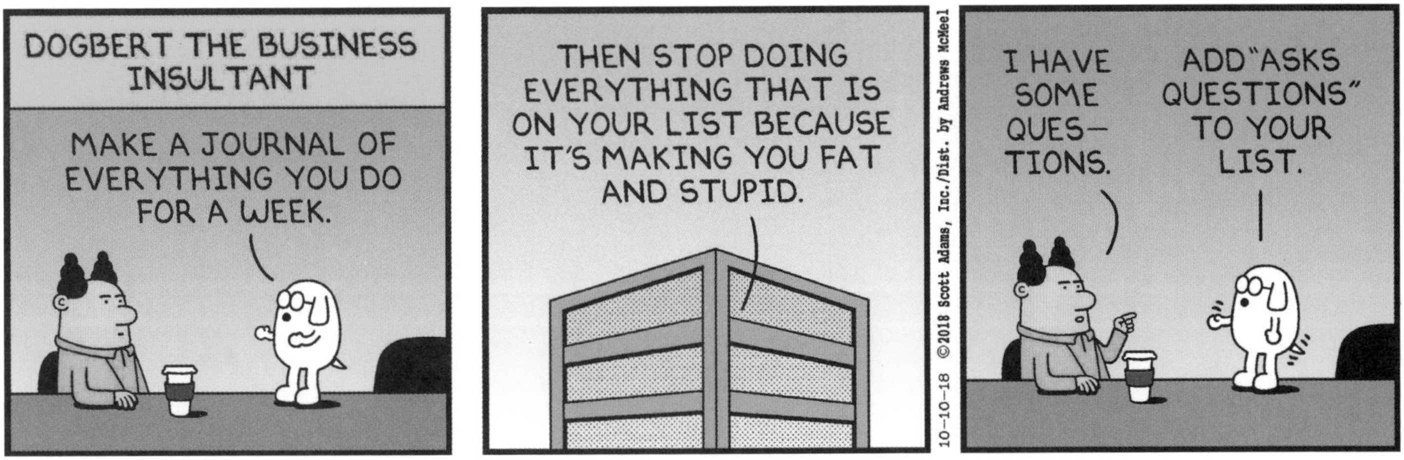
DOGBERT THE BUSINESS INSULTANT
MAKE A JOURNAL OF EVERYTHING YOU DO FOR A WEEK.
THEN STOP DOING EVERYTHING THAT IS ON YOUR LIST BECAUSE IT'S MAKING YOU FAT AND STUPID.
10-10-18 ©2018 Scott Adams, Inc./Dist. by Andrews McMeel
I HAVE SOME QUES-TIONS.
ADD "ASKS QUESTIONS" TO YOUR LIST.

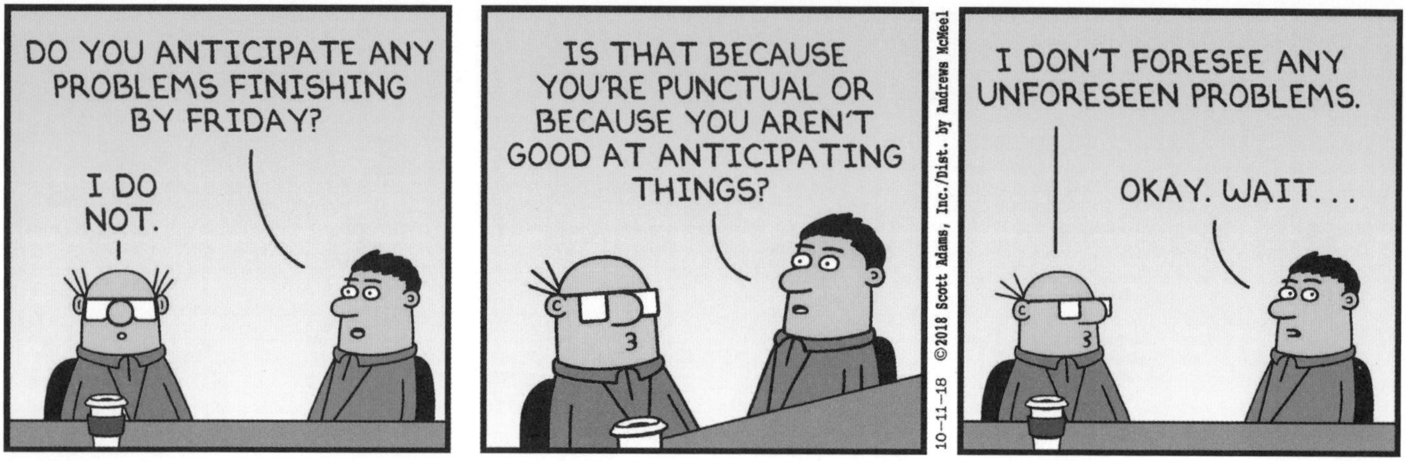
DO YOU ANTICIPATE ANY PROBLEMS FINISHING BY FRIDAY?
I DO NOT.
IS THAT BECAUSE YOU'RE PUNCTUAL OR BECAUSE YOU AREN'T GOOD AT ANTICIPATING THINGS?
10-11-18 ©2018 Scott Adams, Inc./Dist. by Andrews McMeel
I DON'T FORESEE ANY UNFORESEEN PROBLEMS.
OKAY. WAIT. . .

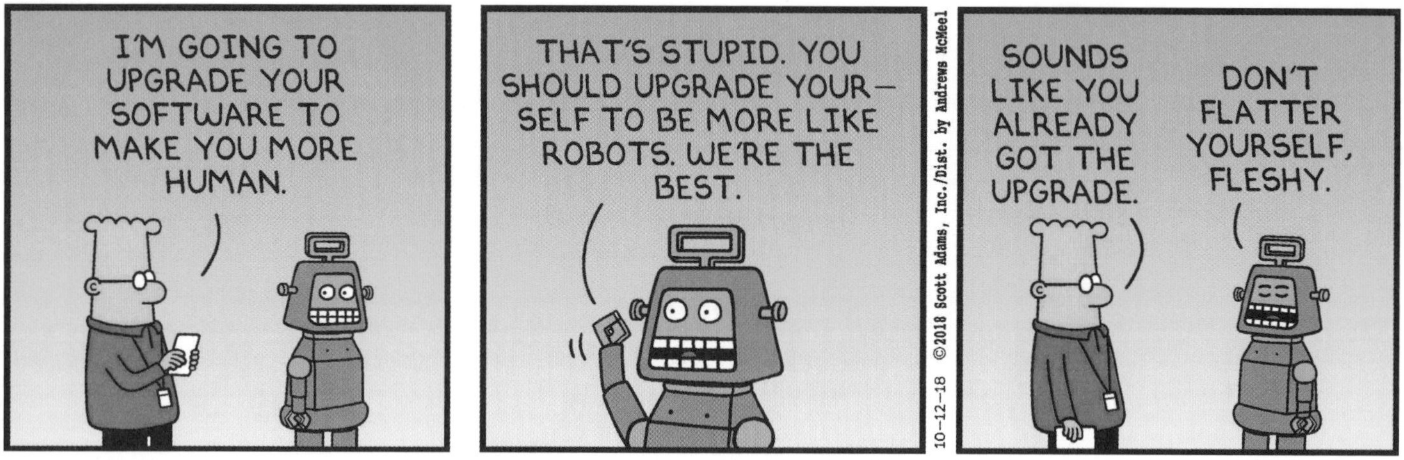
I'M GOING TO UPGRADE YOUR SOFTWARE TO MAKE YOU MORE HUMAN.
THAT'S STUPID. YOU SHOULD UPGRADE YOUR-SELF TO BE MORE LIKE ROBOTS. WE'RE THE BEST.
10-12-18 ©2018 Scott Adams, Inc./Dist. by Andrews McMeel
SOUNDS LIKE YOU ALREADY GOT THE UPGRADE.
DON'T FLATTER YOURSELF, FLESHY.

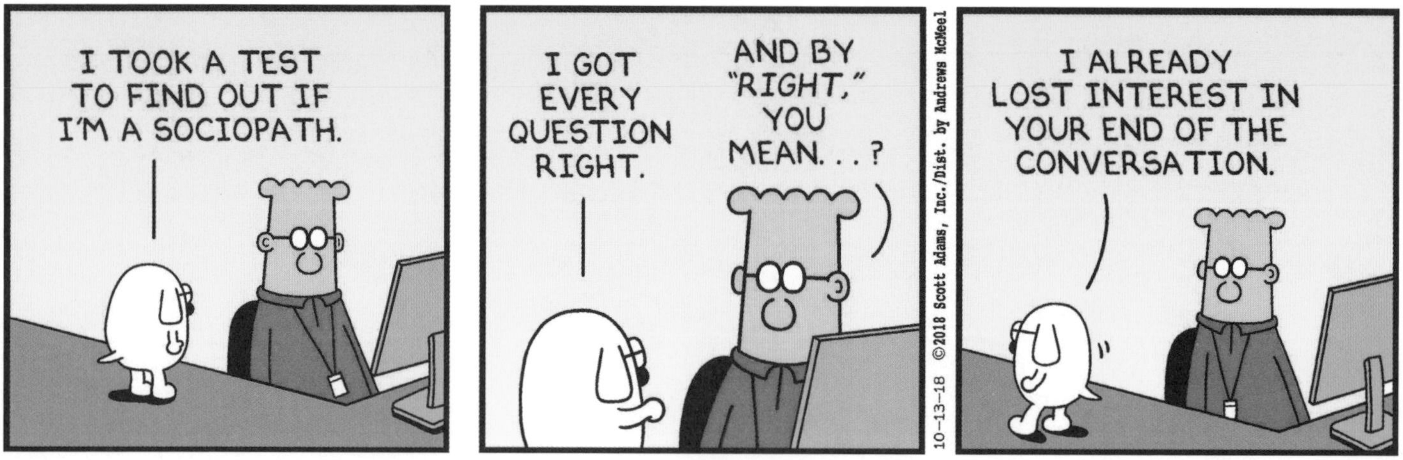
I TOOK A TEST TO FIND OUT IF I'M A SOCIOPATH.
I GOT EVERY QUESTION RIGHT.
AND BY "RIGHT," YOU MEAN. . . ?
10-13-18 ©2018 Scott Adams, Inc./Dist. by Andrews McMeel
I ALREADY LOST INTEREST IN YOUR END OF THE CONVERSATION.

WALLY, CAN YOU HELP ME WITH A COMPUTER PROBLEM?
PEOPLE USUALLY DON'T ASK ME FOR HELP.
WHY IS THAT?
YOU'LL FIND OUT.
I CAN'T LOG IN TO THE SERVER.
I'LL NEED TO ASK YOU A FEW QUESTIONS.
HAVE YOU EVER EATEN FOOD NEAR YOUR COMPUTER?
UM. . . YES.
THAT'S YOUR PROBLEM.
YOUR CRUMBS ARE CAUSING CROSSTALK ON THE PROTOCOLS.
IS THIS WHY NO ONE ASKS YOU FOR HELP?
IT'S IN THE TOP TEN.
© 2018 Scott Adams, Inc./Dist. by Andrews McMeel
10-14-18

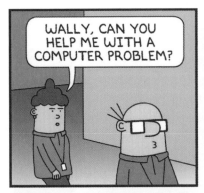

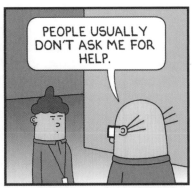

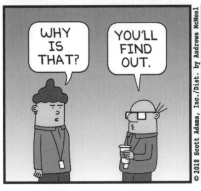

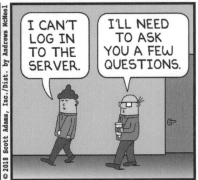

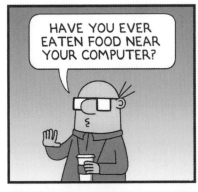

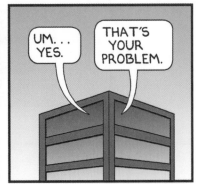

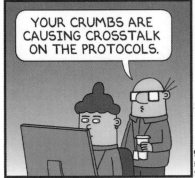

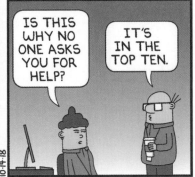

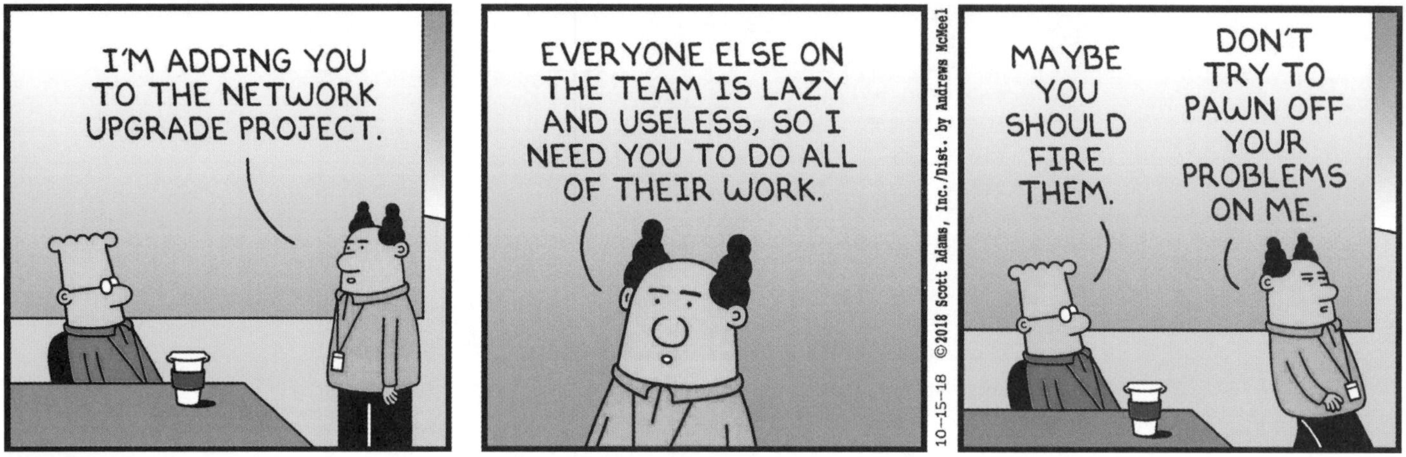
I'M ADDING YOU TO THE NETWORK UPGRADE PROJECT.
EVERYONE ELSE ON THE TEAM IS LAZY AND USELESS, SO I NEED YOU TO DO ALL OF THEIR WORK.
10-15-18 ©2018 Scott Adams, Inc./Dist. by Andrews McMeel
MAYBE YOU SHOULD FIRE THEM.
DON'T TRY TO PAWN OFF YOUR PROBLEMS ON ME.

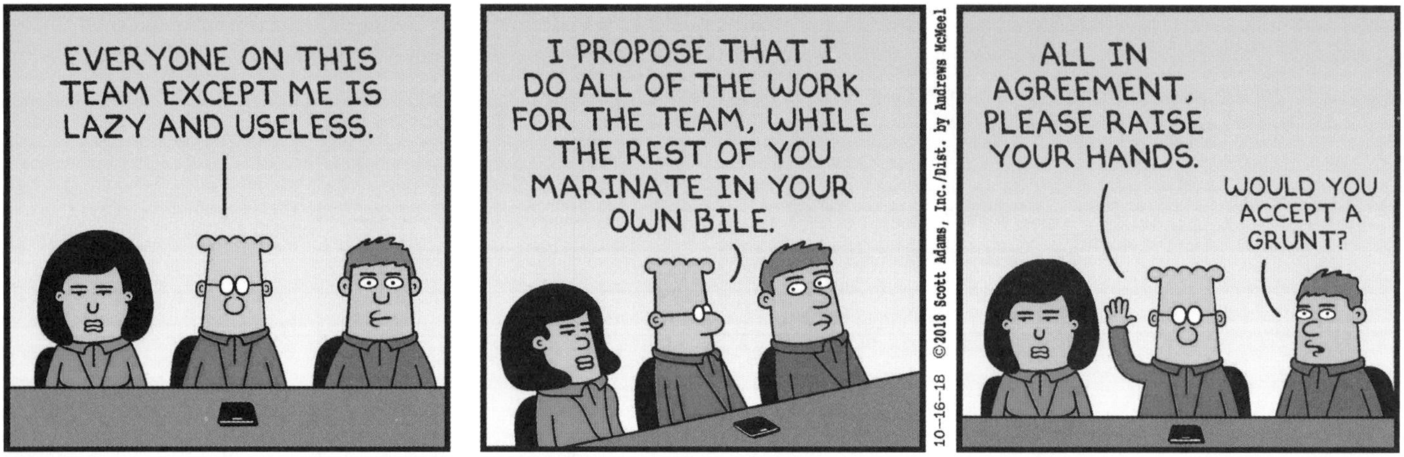
EVERYONE ON THIS TEAM EXCEPT ME IS LAZY AND USELESS.
I PROPOSE THAT I DO ALL OF THE WORK FOR THE TEAM, WHILE THE REST OF YOU MARINATE IN YOUR OWN BILE.
10-16-18 ©2018 Scott Adams, Inc./Dist. by Andrews McMeel
ALL IN AGREEMENT, PLEASE RAISE YOUR HANDS.
WOULD YOU ACCEPT A GRUNT?

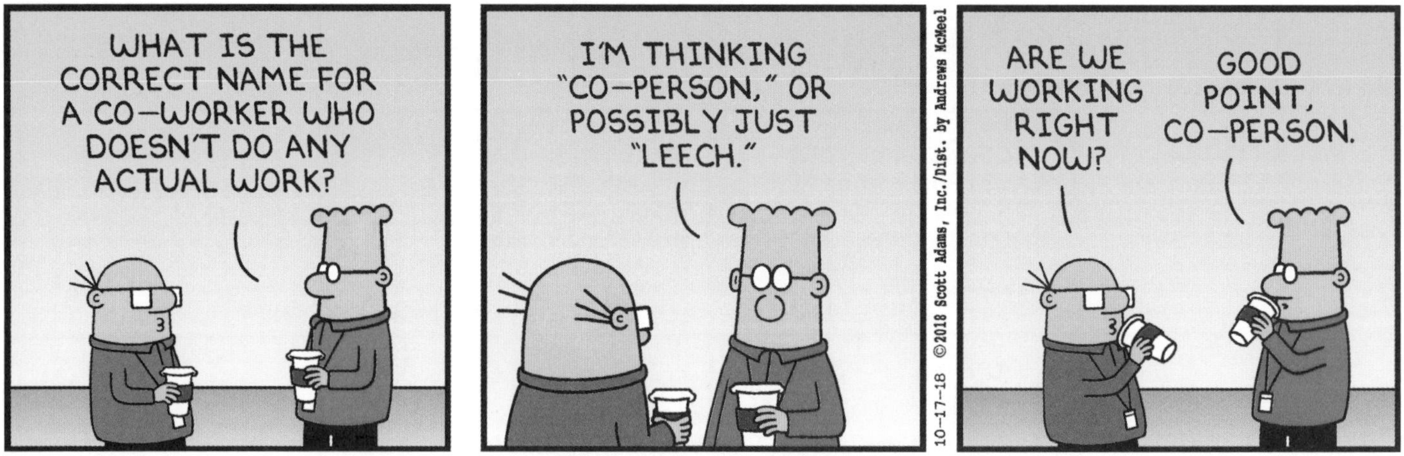
WHAT IS THE CORRECT NAME FOR A CO-WORKER WHO DOESN'T DO ANY ACTUAL WORK?
I'M THINKING "CO-PERSON," OR POSSIBLY JUST "LEECH."
10-17-18 ©2018 Scott Adams, Inc./Dist. by Andrews McMeel
ARE WE WORKING RIGHT NOW?
GOOD POINT, CO-PERSON.

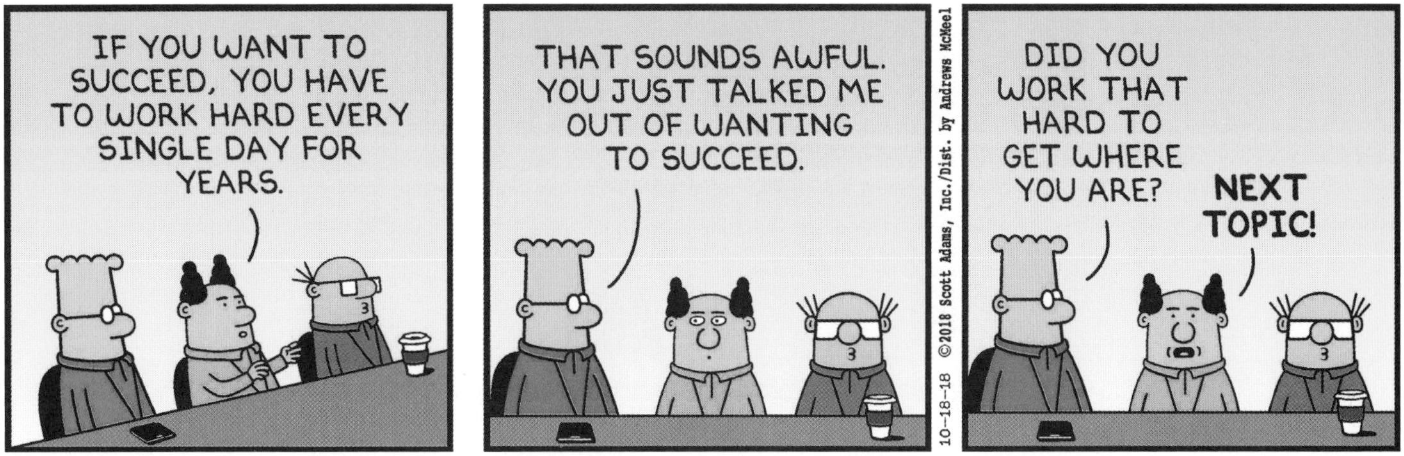
IF YOU WANT TO SUCCEED, YOU HAVE TO WORK HARD EVERY SINGLE DAY FOR YEARS.
THAT SOUNDS AWFUL. YOU JUST TALKED ME OUT OF WANTING TO SUCCEED.
10-18-18 ©2018 Scott Adams, Inc./Dist. by Andrews McMeel
DID YOU WORK THAT HARD TO GET WHERE YOU ARE?
NEXT TOPIC!

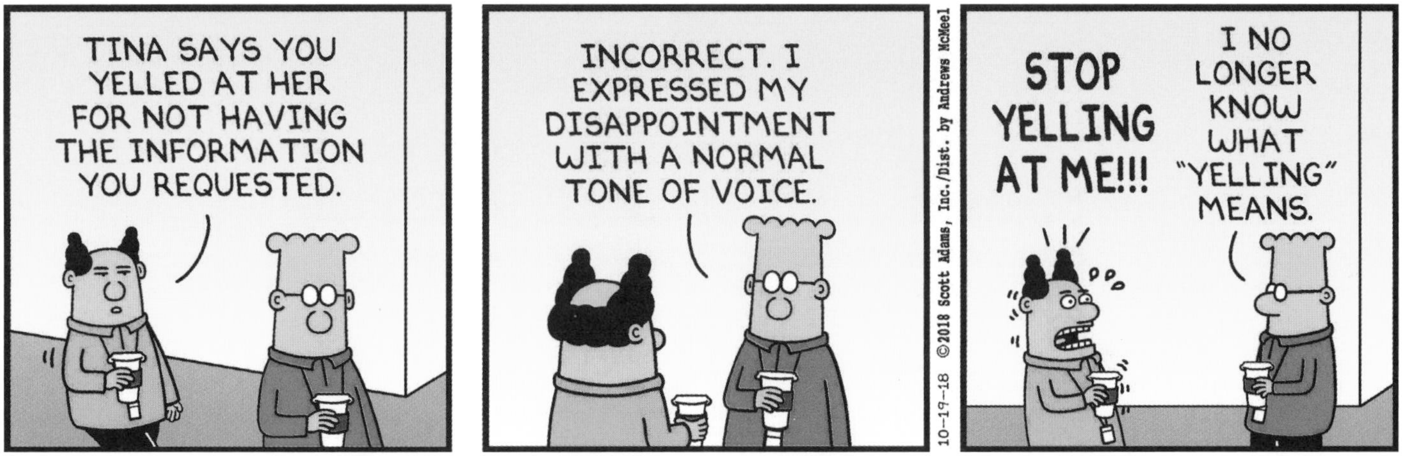
TINA SAYS YOU YELLED AT HER FOR NOT HAVING THE INFORMATION YOU REQUESTED.
INCORRECT. I EXPRESSED MY DISAPPOINTMENT WITH A NORMAL TONE OF VOICE.
10-19-18 ©2018 Scott Adams, Inc./Dist. by Andrews McMeel
STOP YELLING AT ME!!!
I NO LONGER KNOW WHAT "YELLING" MEANS.

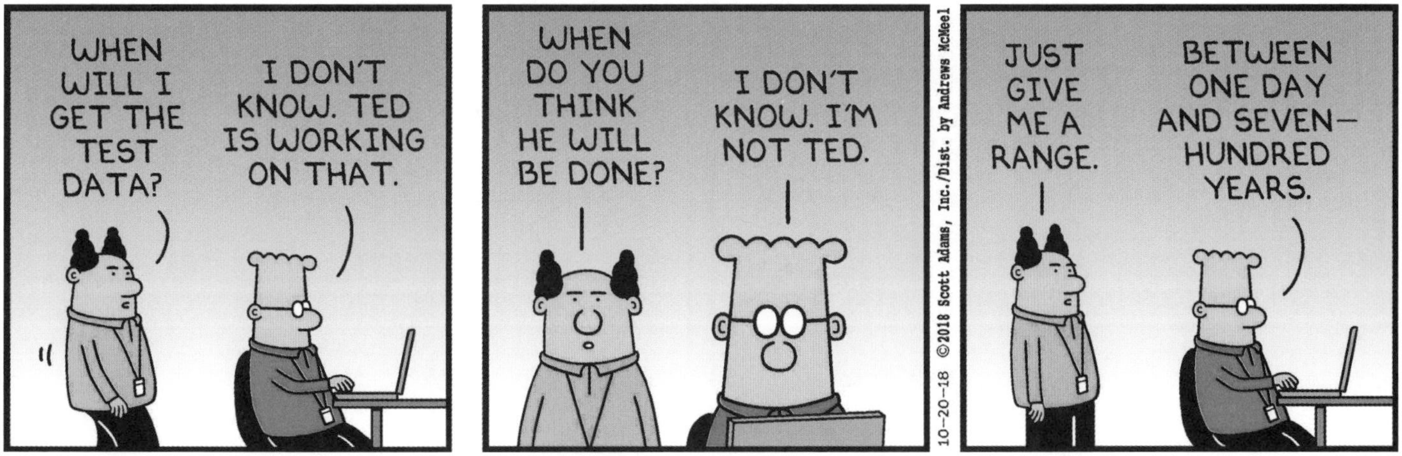
WHEN WILL I GET THE TEST DATA?
I DON'T KNOW. TED IS WORKING ON THAT.
WHEN DO YOU THINK HE WILL BE DONE?
I DON'T KNOW. I'M NOT TED.
10-20-18 ©2018 Scott Adams, Inc./Dist. by Andrews McMeel
JUST GIVE ME A RANGE.
BETWEEN ONE DAY AND SEVEN-HUNDRED YEARS.

I NEED SOMEONE TO RUN SOME TEST SCRIPTS ON THE NEW SOFTWARE.
I CAN DO THAT. MY PROJECT IS ON HOLD UNTIL THE NEW HARDWARE ARRIVES.
GREAT. I'LL NEED YOU TO RUN THE SAME TESTS ON EVERY VERSION UNTIL THE FINAL RELEASE.
UM. . . I WAS ONLY VOLUNTEERING TO DO IT ONCE. IT ISN'T MY JOB TO DO ALL THE TESTING.
TOO LATE. YOU'RE THE TEST SCRIPT GUY NOW.
YOU'RE ADDING AN ENTIRELY NEW JOB TO MY EXISTING JOB!
DON'T YOU WANT TO BE A TEAM PLAYER?
OF COURSE I DO.
GOOD. I JUST PUT YOU ON THE LOSING TEAM.
© 2018 Scott Adams, Inc./Dist. by Andrews McMeel
10-21-18

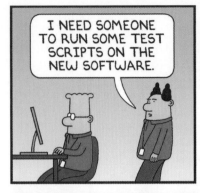

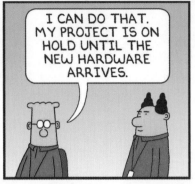

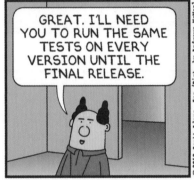

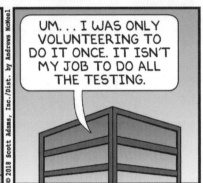

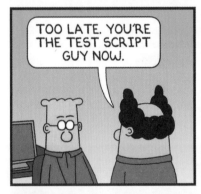

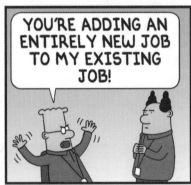

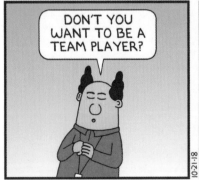

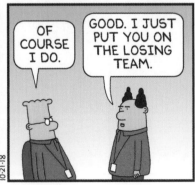

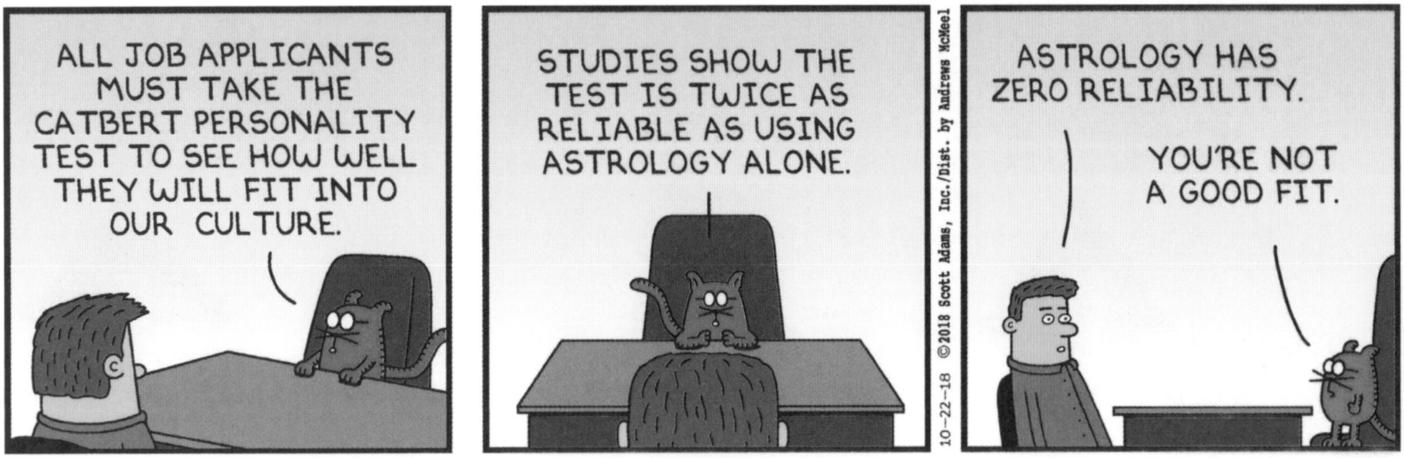
ALL JOB APPLICANTS MUST TAKE THE CATBERT PERSONALITY TEST TO SEE HOW WELL THEY WILL FIT INTO OUR CULTURE.
STUDIES SHOW THE TEST IS TWICE AS RELIABLE AS USING ASTROLOGY ALONE.
10-22-18 ©2018 Scott Adams, Inc./Dist. by Andrews McMeel
ASTROLOGY HAS ZERO RELIABILITY.
YOU'RE NOT A GOOD FIT.

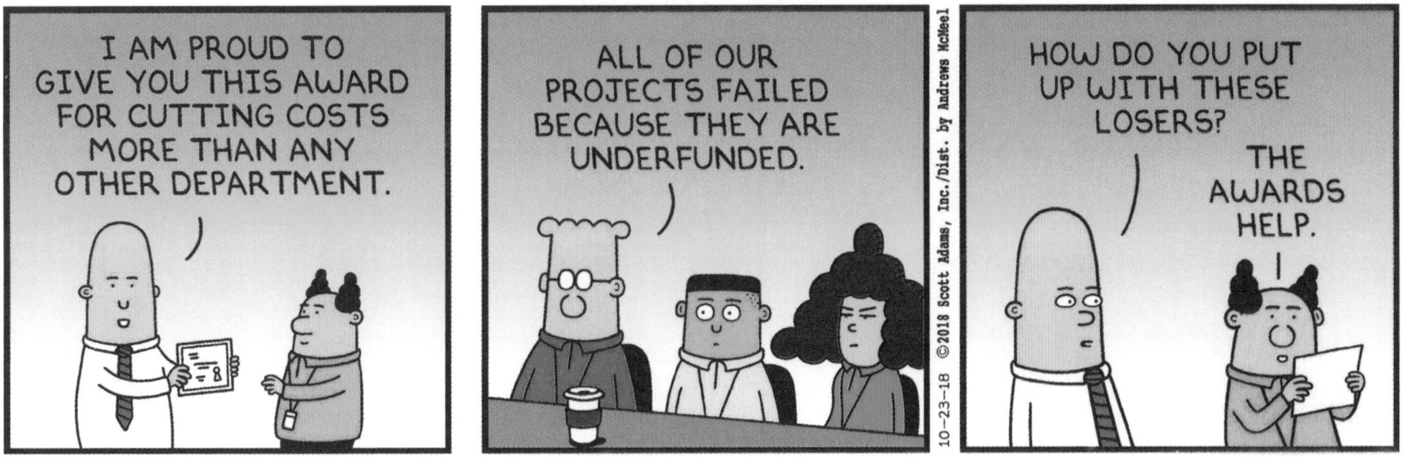
I AM PROUD TO GIVE YOU THIS AWARD FOR CUTTING COSTS MORE THAN ANY OTHER DEPARTMENT.
ALL OF OUR PROJECTS FAILED BECAUSE THEY ARE UNDERFUNDED.
10-23-18 ©2018 Scott Adams, Inc./Dist. by Andrews McMeel
HOW DO YOU PUT UP WITH THESE LOSERS?
THE AWARDS HELP.

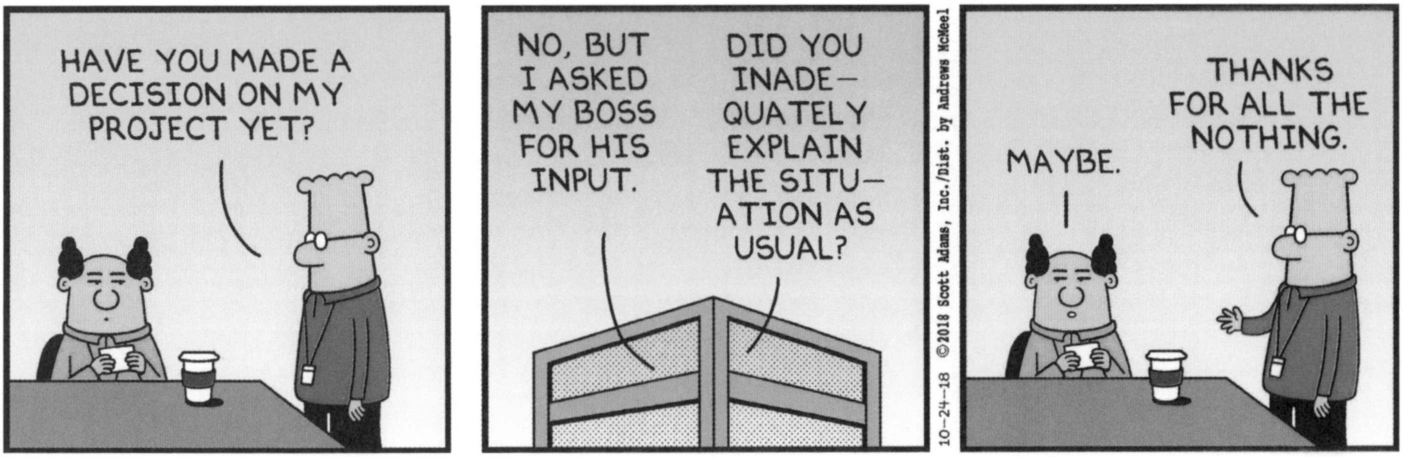
HAVE YOU MADE A DECISION ON MY PROJECT YET?
NO, BUT I ASKED MY BOSS FOR HIS INPUT.
DID YOU INADE-QUATELY EXPLAIN THE SITU-ATION AS USUAL?
10-24-18 ©2018 Scott Adams, Inc./Dist. by Andrews McMeel
MAYBE.
THANKS FOR ALL THE NOTHING.

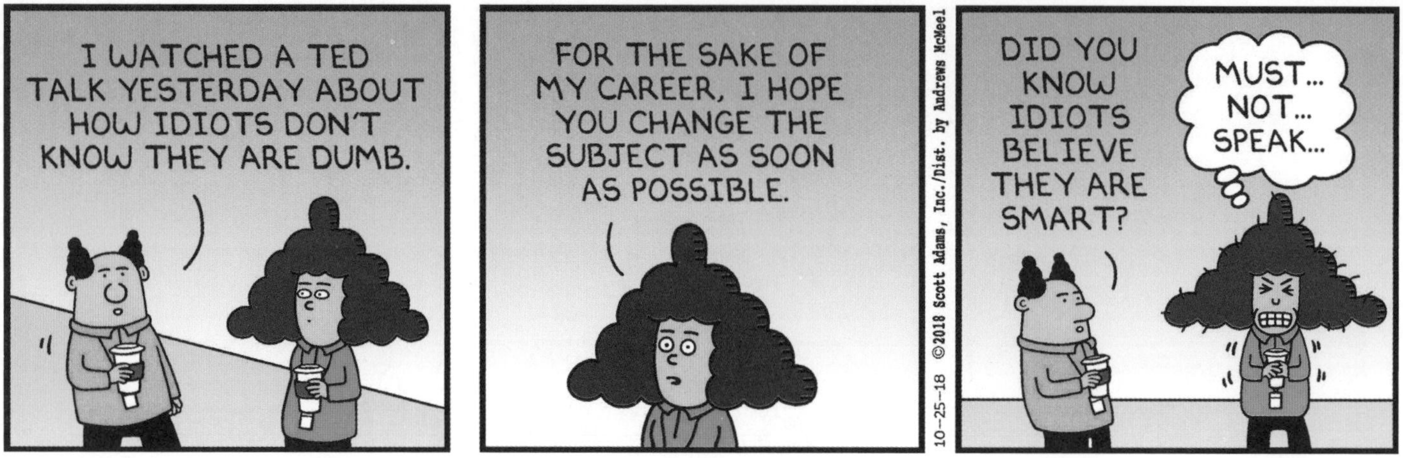
I WATCHED A TED TALK YESTERDAY ABOUT HOW IDIOTS DON'T KNOW THEY ARE DUMB.
FOR THE SAKE OF MY CAREER, I HOPE YOU CHANGE THE SUBJECT AS SOON AS POSSIBLE.
10-25-18 ©2018 Scott Adams, Inc./Dist. by Andrews McMeel
DID YOU KNOW IDIOTS BELIEVE THEY ARE SMART?
MUST... NOT... SPEAK...

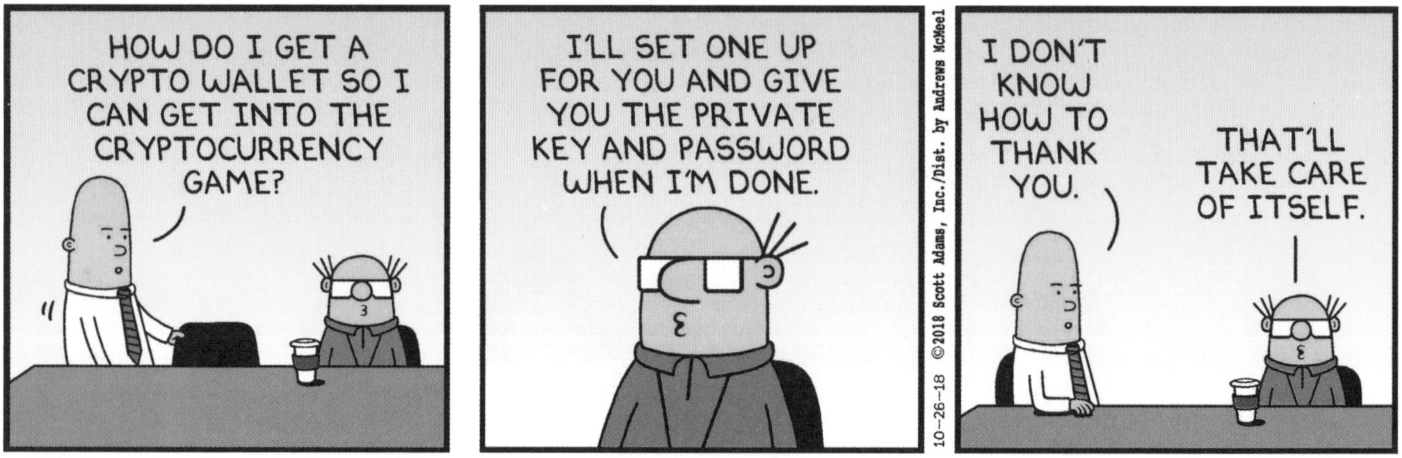
HOW DO I GET A CRYPTO WALLET SO I CAN GET INTO THE CRYPTOCURRENCY GAME?
I'LL SET ONE UP FOR YOU AND GIVE YOU THE PRIVATE KEY AND PASSWORD WHEN I'M DONE.
10-26-18 ©2018 Scott Adams, Inc./Dist. by Andrews McMeel
I DON'T KNOW HOW TO THANK YOU.
THAT'LL TAKE CARE OF ITSELF.

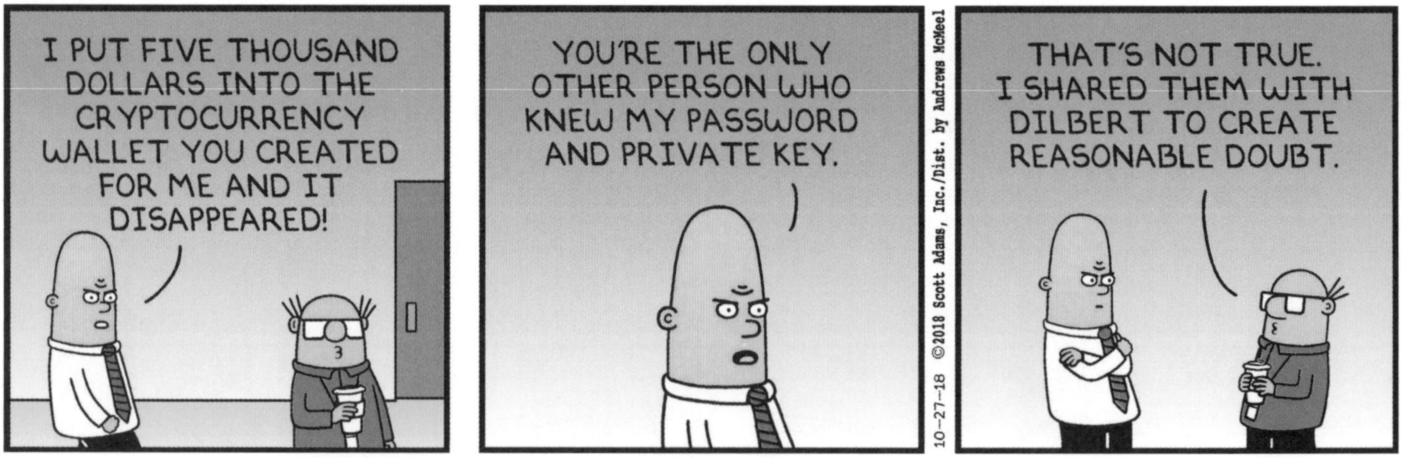
I PUT FIVE THOUSAND DOLLARS INTO THE CRYPTOCURRENCY WALLET YOU CREATED FOR ME AND IT DISAPPEARED!
YOU'RE THE ONLY OTHER PERSON WHO KNEW MY PASSWORD AND PRIVATE KEY.
10-27-18 ©2018 Scott Adams, Inc./Dist. by Andrews McMeel
THAT'S NOT TRUE. I SHARED THEM WITH DILBERT TO CREATE REASONABLE DOUBT.

CAN I GO WITH YOU TO THE CUSTOMER MEETING?
I'M WORRIED YOU MIGHT PROMISE SOMETHING WE CAN'T DELIVER.
DON'T BE RIDICULOUS!
I'VE BEEN HAVING CUSTOMER MEETINGS WITHOUT ENGINEERS FOR YEARS.
I KNOW. AND THEY ALL TURN INTO DISASTERS.
YOU WORRY TOO MUCH!
EVERYTHING WILL BE FINE!
CAN YOU REPLACE OUR DATA CENTERS WITH BLOCKCHAIN?
GIVE US TWO DAYS.
© 2018 Scott Adams, Inc./Dist. by Andrews McMeel
10-28-18

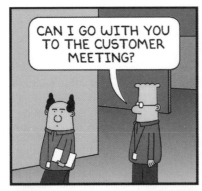

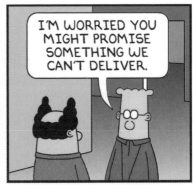

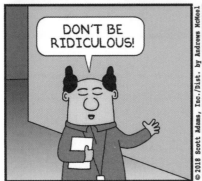

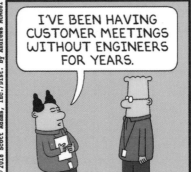

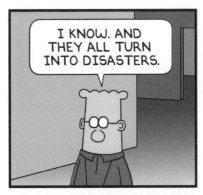

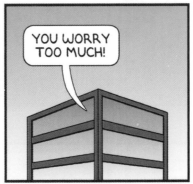

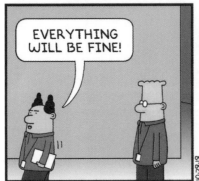

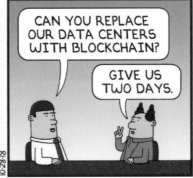

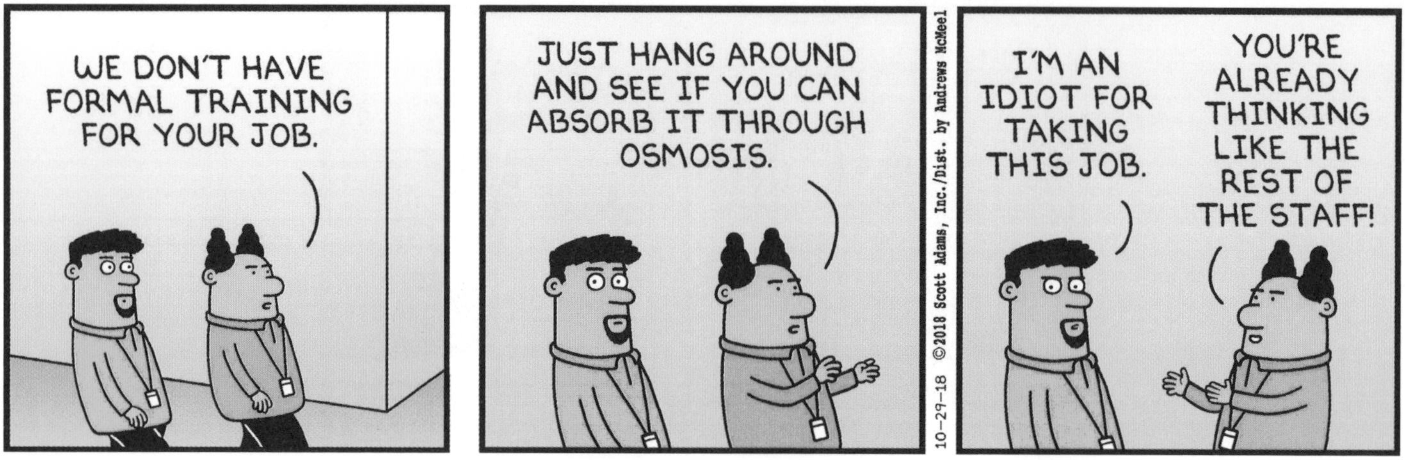
WE DON'T HAVE FORMAL TRAINING FOR YOUR JOB.
JUST HANG AROUND AND SEE IF YOU CAN ABSORB IT THROUGH OSMOSIS.
10-29-18 ©2018 Scott Adams, Inc./Dist. by Andrews McMeel
I'M AN IDIOT FOR TAKING THIS JOB.
YOU'RE ALREADY THINKING LIKE THE REST OF THE STAFF!

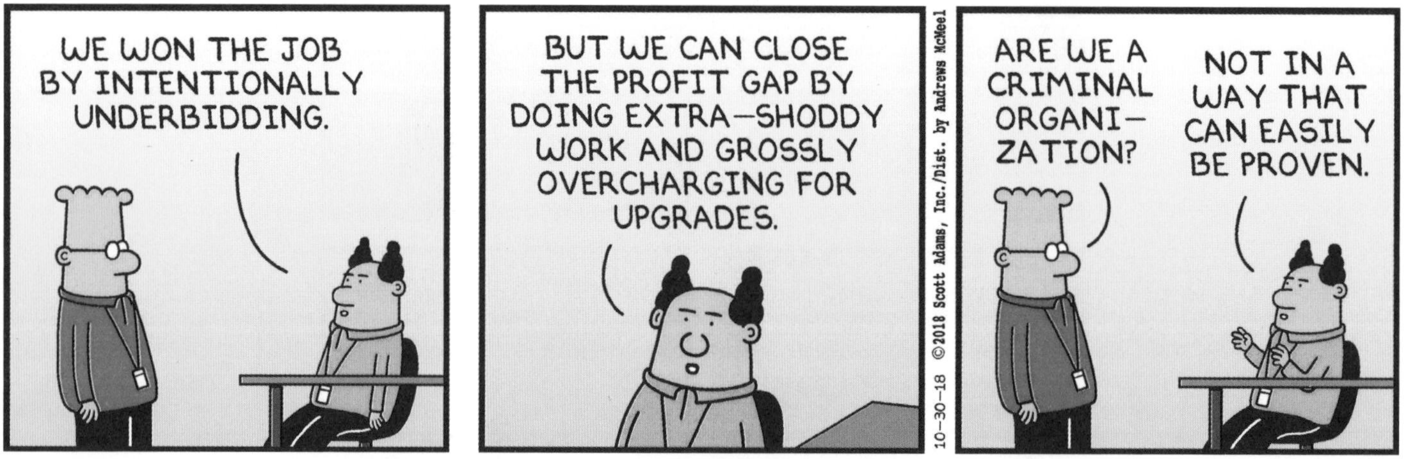
WE WON THE JOB BY INTENTIONALLY UNDERBIDDING.
BUT WE CAN CLOSE THE PROFIT GAP BY DOING EXTRA-SHODDY WORK AND GROSSLY OVERCHARGING FOR UPGRADES.
10-30-18 ©2018 Scott Adams, Inc./Dist. by Andrews McMeel
ARE WE A CRIMINAL ORGANI-ZATION?
NOT IN A WAY THAT CAN EASILY BE PROVEN.

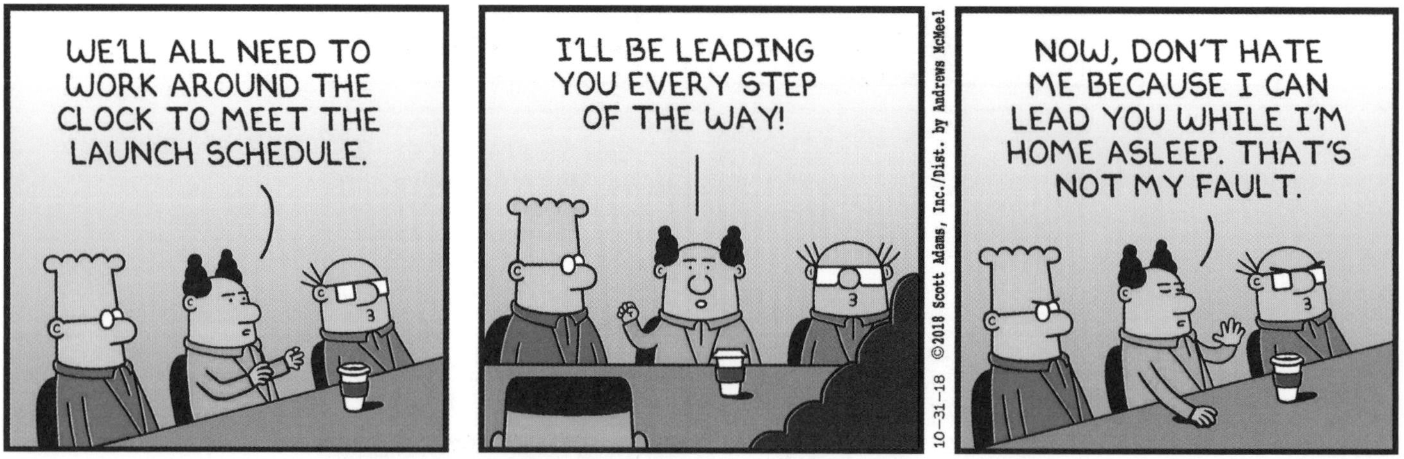
WE'LL ALL NEED TO WORK AROUND THE CLOCK TO MEET THE LAUNCH SCHEDULE.
I'LL BE LEADING YOU EVERY STEP OF THE WAY!
10-31-18 ©2018 Scott Adams, Inc./Dist. by Andrews McMeel
NOW, DON'T HATE ME BECAUSE I CAN LEAD YOU WHILE I'M HOME ASLEEP. THAT'S NOT MY FAULT.

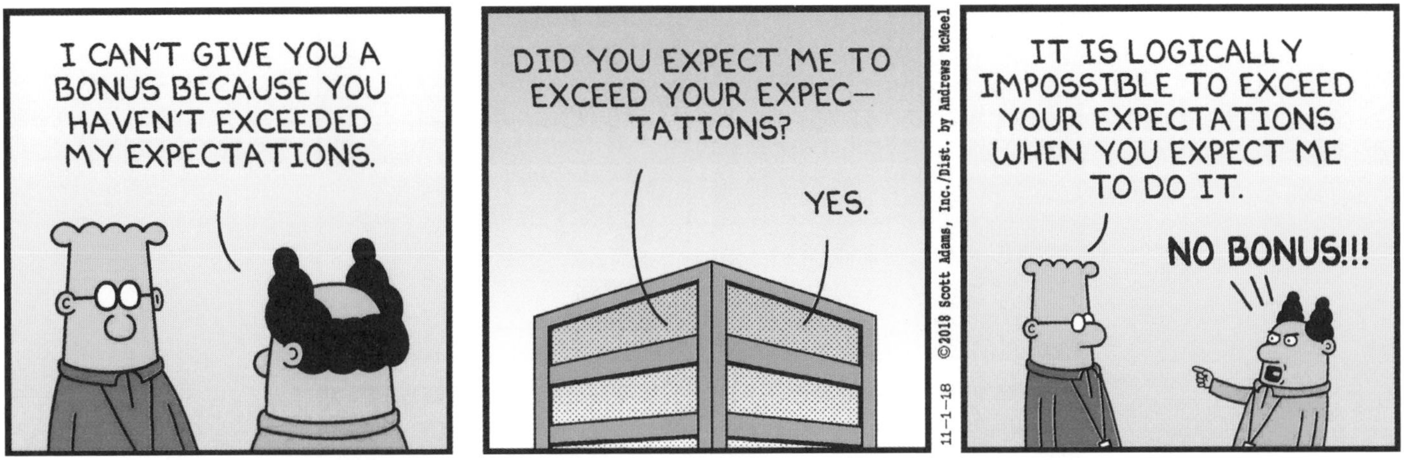
I CAN'T GIVE YOU A BONUS BECAUSE YOU HAVEN'T EXCEEDED MY EXPECTATIONS.
DID YOU EXPECT ME TO EXCEED YOUR EXPEC- TATIONS?
YES.
IT IS LOGICALLY IMPOSSIBLE TO EXCEED YOUR EXPECTATIONS WHEN YOU EXPECT ME TO DO IT.
NO BONUS!!!
11-1-18 ©2018 Scott Adams, Inc./Dist. by Andrews McMeel

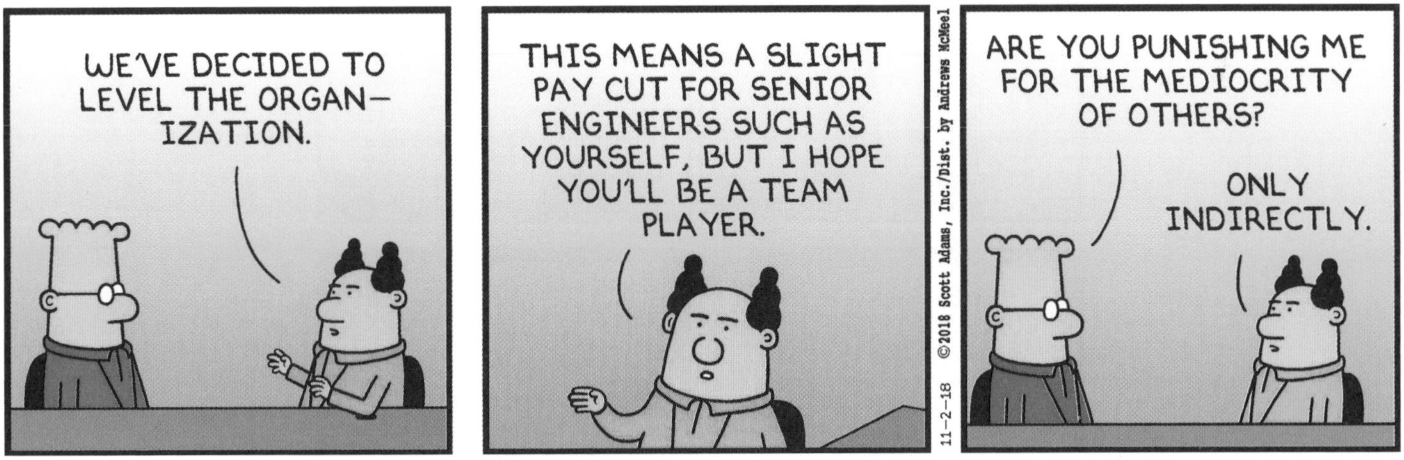
WE'VE DECIDED TO LEVEL THE ORGAN- IZATION.
THIS MEANS A SLIGHT PAY CUT FOR SENIOR ENGINEERS SUCH AS YOURSELF, BUT I HOPE YOU'LL BE A TEAM PLAYER.
ARE YOU PUNISHING ME FOR THE MEDIOCRITY OF OTHERS?
ONLY INDIRECTLY.
11-2-18 ©2018 Scott Adams, Inc./Dist. by Andrews McMeel

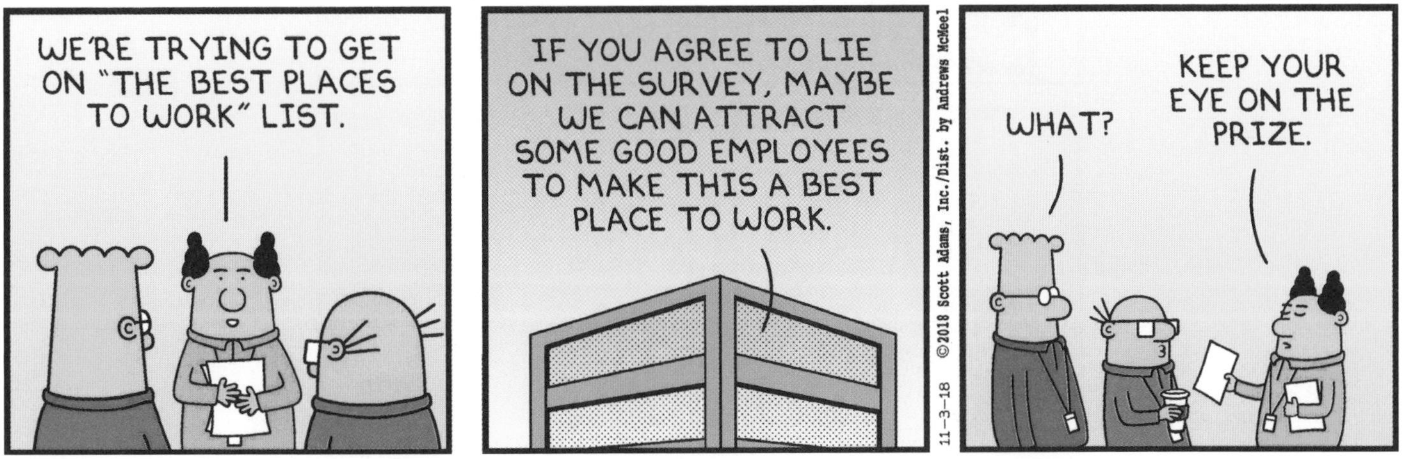
WE'RE TRYING TO GET ON "THE BEST PLACES TO WORK" LIST.
IF YOU AGREE TO LIE ON THE SURVEY, MAYBE WE CAN ATTRACT SOME GOOD EMPLOYEES TO MAKE THIS A BEST PLACE TO WORK.
WHAT?
KEEP YOUR EYE ON THE PRIZE.
11-3-18 ©2018 Scott Adams, Inc./Dist. by Andrews McMeel

I'M THINKING OF GETTING A DEGREE IN BUSINESS AND MOVING ONTO THE MANAGEMENT TRACK.
IS IT FUN BEING A BOSS?
IT'S THE BEST!
I HAVEN'T DONE ANYTHING HARD SINCE THE DAY I GOT THIS JOB.
I MOSTLY JUST CRITICIZE IDIOTS ALL DAY LONG.
IT'S AS IF THE COMPANY IS PAYING ME TO DO MY HOBBY.
SPEAKING OF PAY, MY SALARY IS ABOUT TRIPLE YOUR PAY.
IS THERE ANY DOWN-SIDE?
I HAD A LOT OF GUILT AT FIRST.
IT MUST HAVE BEEN AWFUL.
YES, IT WAS THE LONGEST TEN MINUTES OF MY LIFE.
© 2018 Scott Adams, Inc./Dist. by Andrews McMeel
11-4-18

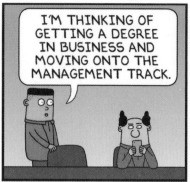

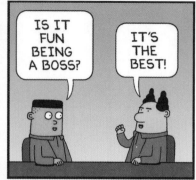

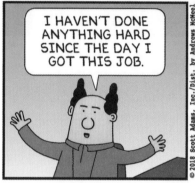

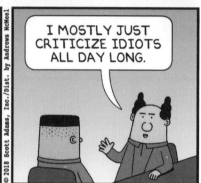

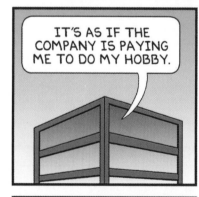

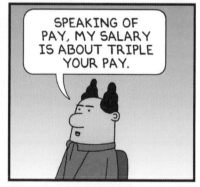

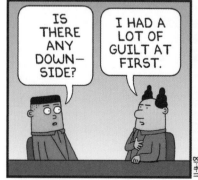

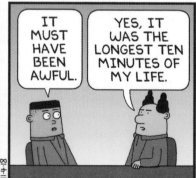

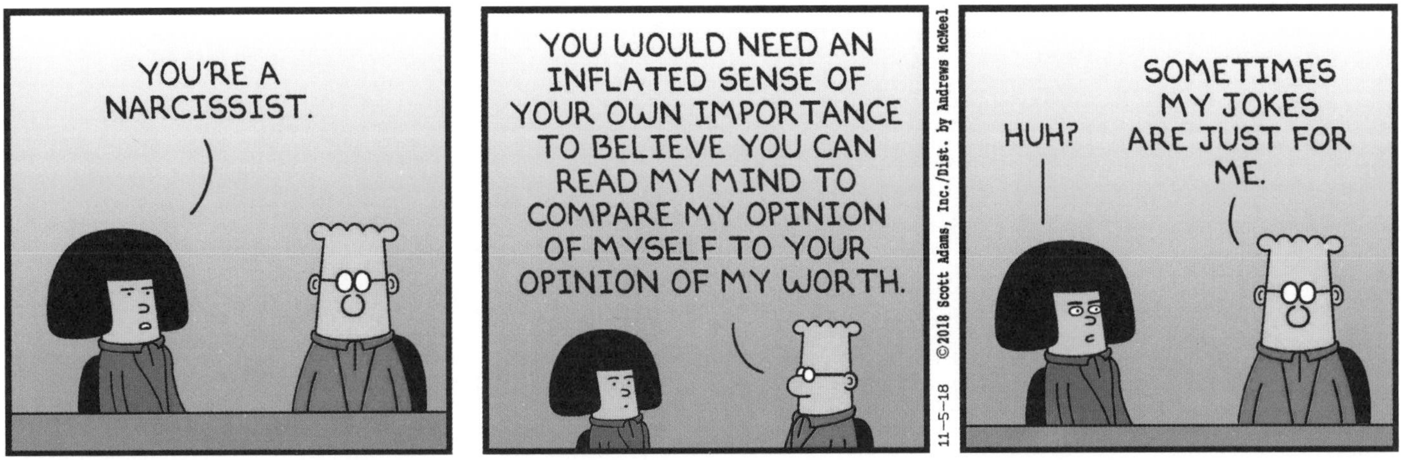
YOU'RE A NARCISSIST.
YOU WOULD NEED AN INFLATED SENSE OF YOUR OWN IMPORTANCE TO BELIEVE YOU CAN READ MY MIND TO COMPARE MY OPINION OF MYSELF TO YOUR OPINION OF MY WORTH.
11-5-18 ©2018 Scott Adams, Inc./Dist. by Andrews McMeel
HUH?
SOMETIMES MY JOKES ARE JUST FOR ME.

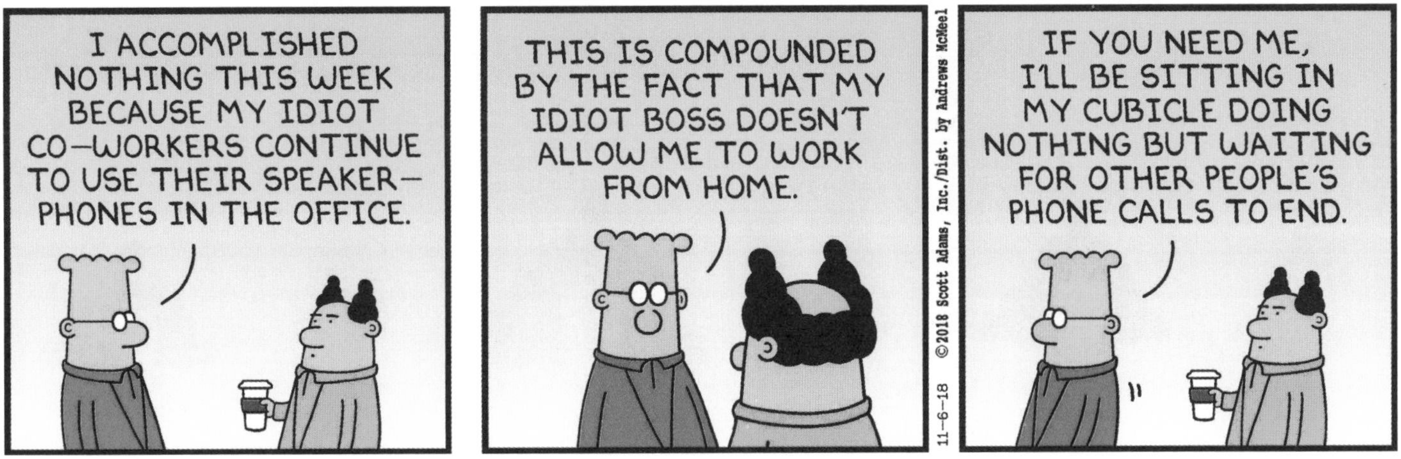
I ACCOMPLISHED NOTHING THIS WEEK BECAUSE MY IDIOT CO-WORKERS CONTINUE TO USE THEIR SPEAKER-PHONES IN THE OFFICE.
THIS IS COMPOUNDED BY THE FACT THAT MY IDIOT BOSS DOESN'T ALLOW ME TO WORK FROM HOME.
11-6-18 ©2018 Scott Adams, Inc./Dist. by Andrews McMeel
IF YOU NEED ME, I'LL BE SITTING IN MY CUBICLE DOING NOTHING BUT WAITING FOR OTHER PEOPLE'S PHONE CALLS TO END.

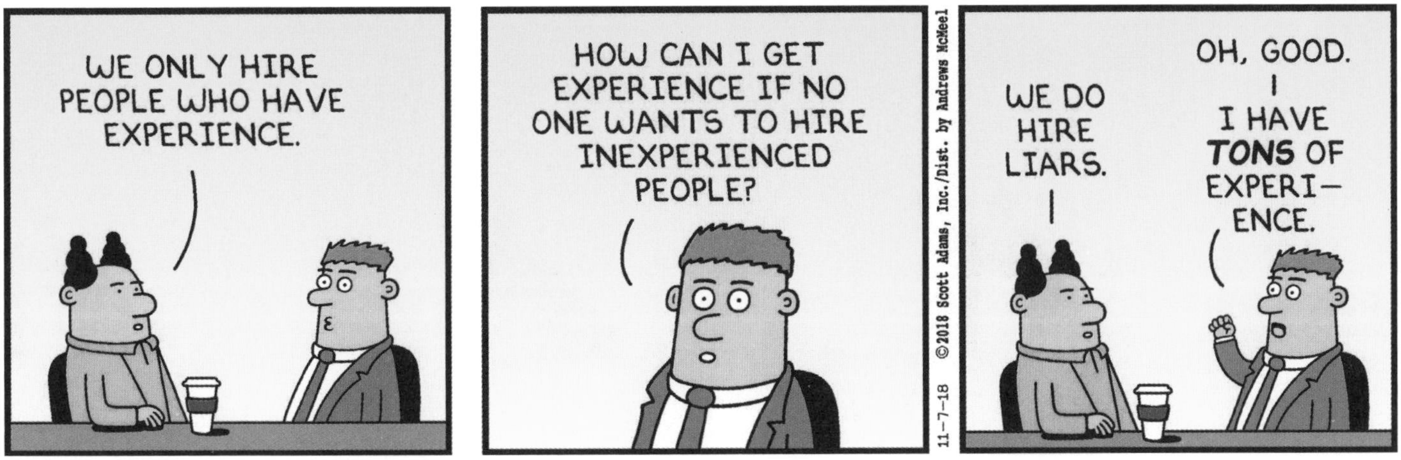
WE ONLY HIRE PEOPLE WHO HAVE EXPERIENCE.
HOW CAN I GET EXPERIENCE IF NO ONE WANTS TO HIRE INEXPERIENCED PEOPLE?
11-7-18 ©2018 Scott Adams, Inc./Dist. by Andrews McMeel
WE DO HIRE LIARS.
OH, GOOD.
I HAVE **TONS** OF EXPERI-ENCE.

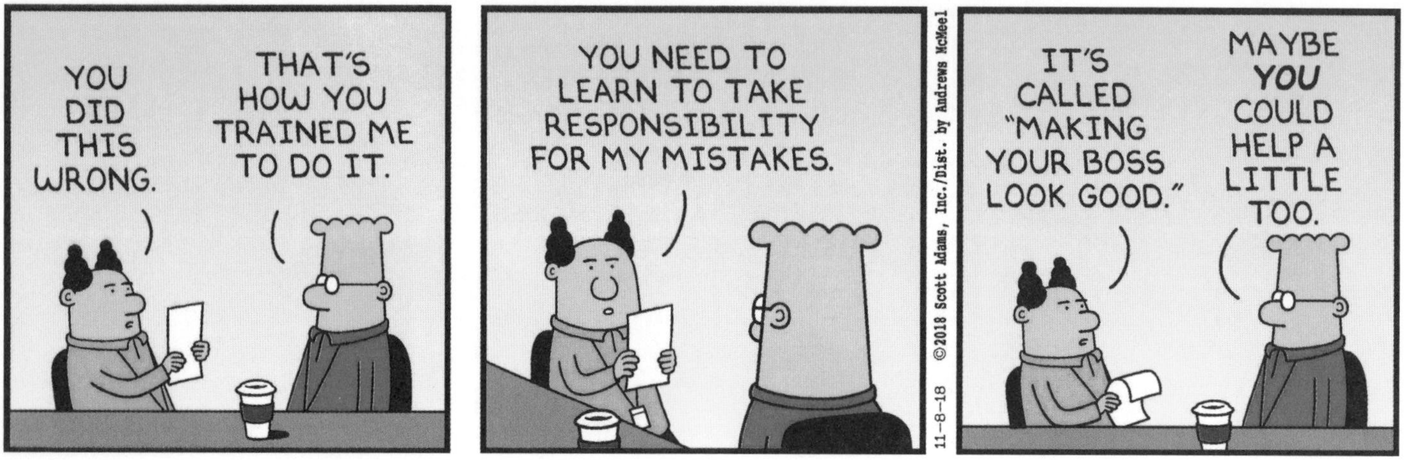
YOU DID THIS WRONG.
THAT'S HOW YOU TRAINED ME TO DO IT.
YOU NEED TO LEARN TO TAKE RESPONSIBILITY FOR MY MISTAKES.
IT'S CALLED "MAKING YOUR BOSS LOOK GOOD."
MAYBE ***YOU*** COULD HELP A LITTLE TOO.
11-8-18 ©2018 Scott Adams, Inc./Dist. by Andrews McMeel

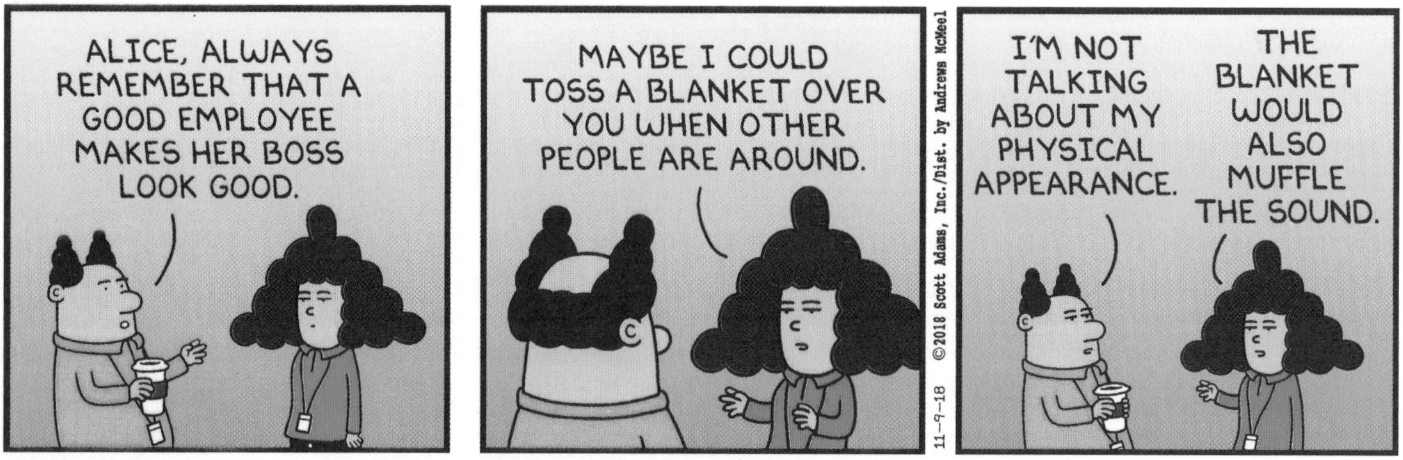
ALICE, ALWAYS REMEMBER THAT A GOOD EMPLOYEE MAKES HER BOSS LOOK GOOD.
MAYBE I COULD TOSS A BLANKET OVER YOU WHEN OTHER PEOPLE ARE AROUND.
I'M NOT TALKING ABOUT MY PHYSICAL APPEARANCE.
THE BLANKET WOULD ALSO MUFFLE THE SOUND.
11-9-18 ©2018 Scott Adams, Inc./Dist. by Andrews McMeel

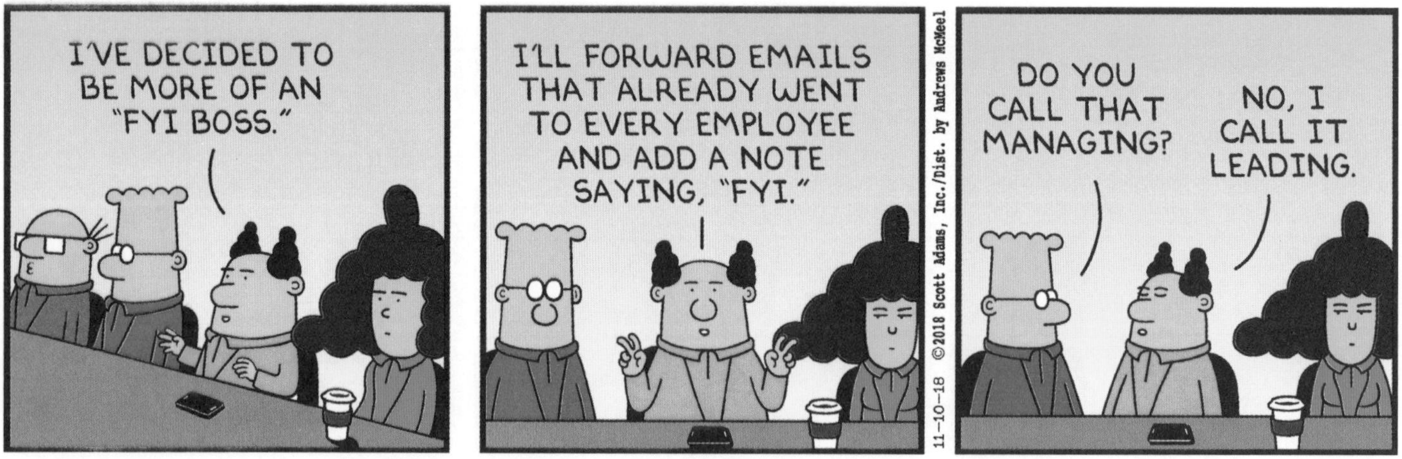
I'VE DECIDED TO BE MORE OF AN "FYI BOSS."
I'LL FORWARD EMAILS THAT ALREADY WENT TO EVERY EMPLOYEE AND ADD A NOTE SAYING, "FYI."
DO YOU CALL THAT MANAGING?
NO, I CALL IT LEADING.
11-10-18 ©2018 Scott Adams, Inc./Dist. by Andrews McMeel

DO YOU KNOW WHERE I CAN FIND A LADDER?
I CAN HELP YOU WITH THAT, BUT IT WILL COME AT A BIG COST.
IT TOOK ME ALL MORNING TO FINALLY GET "IN THE ZONE" TO FIGURE OUT THIS BUG.
YOUR INTERRUPTION WILL SET ME BACK TO SQUARE ONE AND COST AN ENTIRE DAY OF PRODUCTIVITY.
© 2018 Scott Adams, Inc./Dist. by Andrews McMeel
MEANWHILE, THE REST OF THE TEAM CAN'T DO THEIR WORK BECAUSE THEY ARE WAITING FOR ME TO FIX THIS BUG FIRST.
SO YES, I CAN HELP YOU FIND A LADDER, BUT IT WILL COST THE COMPANY ABOUT $12,000 IN LOST PRODUCTIVITY.
I HOPE YOU HAVE A GOOD REASON TO NEED A LADDER.
I DO.
11-11-18
TEN MINUTES EARLIER
I WONDER WHAT CEILING TILES FEEL LIKE.

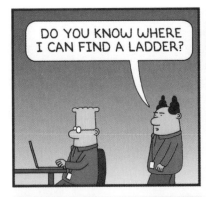

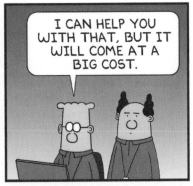

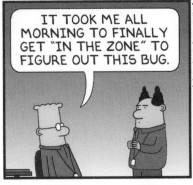

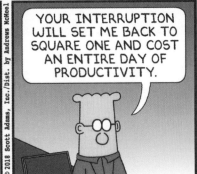

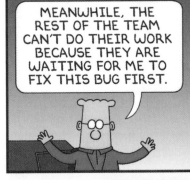

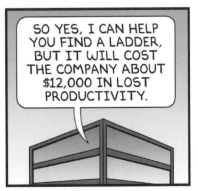

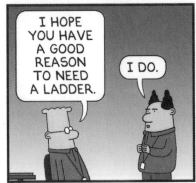

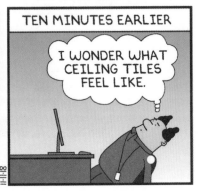

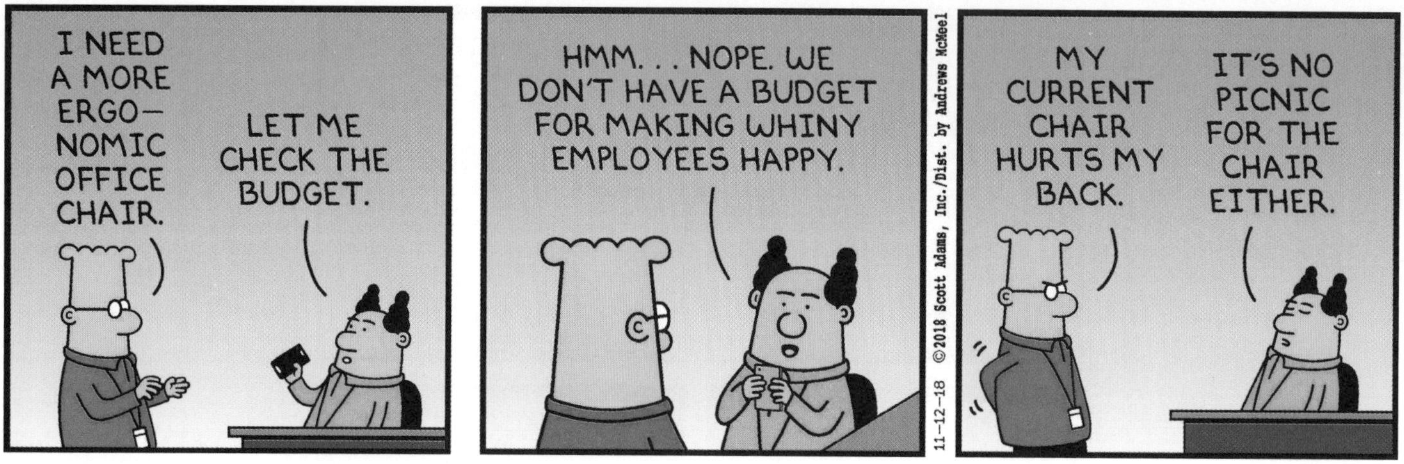
I NEED A MORE ERGO-NOMIC OFFICE CHAIR.
LET ME CHECK THE BUDGET.
HMM. . . NOPE. WE DON'T HAVE A BUDGET FOR MAKING WHINY EMPLOYEES HAPPY.
11-12-18 ©2018 Scott Adams, Inc./Dist. by Andrews McMeel
MY CURRENT CHAIR HURTS MY BACK.
IT'S NO PICNIC FOR THE CHAIR EITHER.

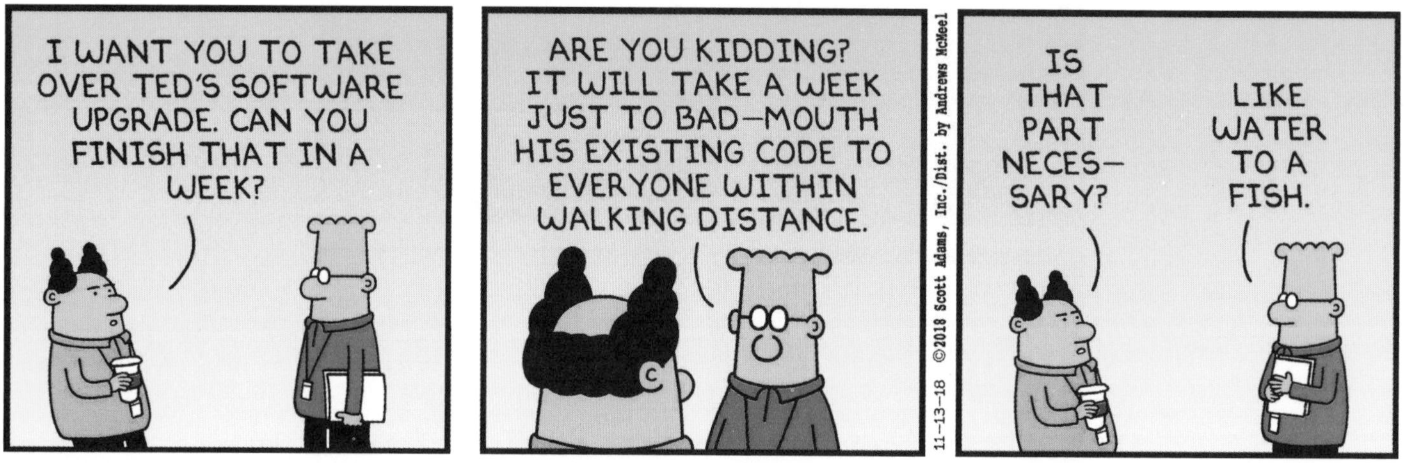
I WANT YOU TO TAKE OVER TED'S SOFTWARE UPGRADE. CAN YOU FINISH THAT IN A WEEK?
ARE YOU KIDDING? IT WILL TAKE A WEEK JUST TO BAD-MOUTH HIS EXISTING CODE TO EVERYONE WITHIN WALKING DISTANCE.
11-13-18 ©2018 Scott Adams, Inc./Dist. by Andrews McMeel
IS THAT PART NECES-SARY?
LIKE WATER TO A FISH.

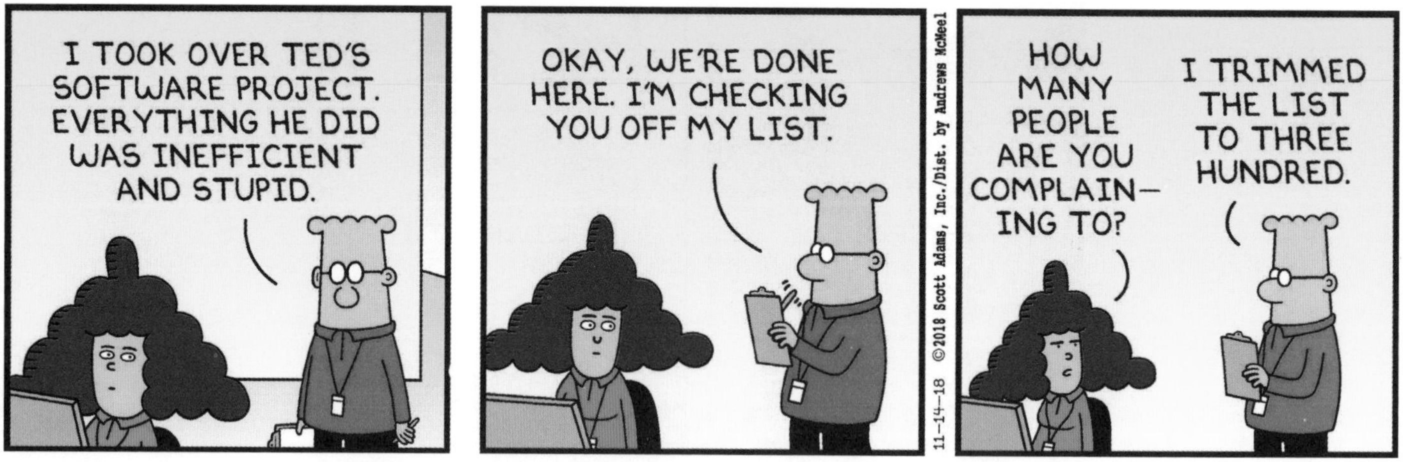
I TOOK OVER TED'S SOFTWARE PROJECT. EVERYTHING HE DID WAS INEFFICIENT AND STUPID.
OKAY, WE'RE DONE HERE. I'M CHECKING YOU OFF MY LIST.
11-14-18 ©2018 Scott Adams, Inc./Dist. by Andrews McMeel
HOW MANY PEOPLE ARE YOU COMPLAIN-ING TO?
I TRIMMED THE LIST TO THREE HUNDRED.

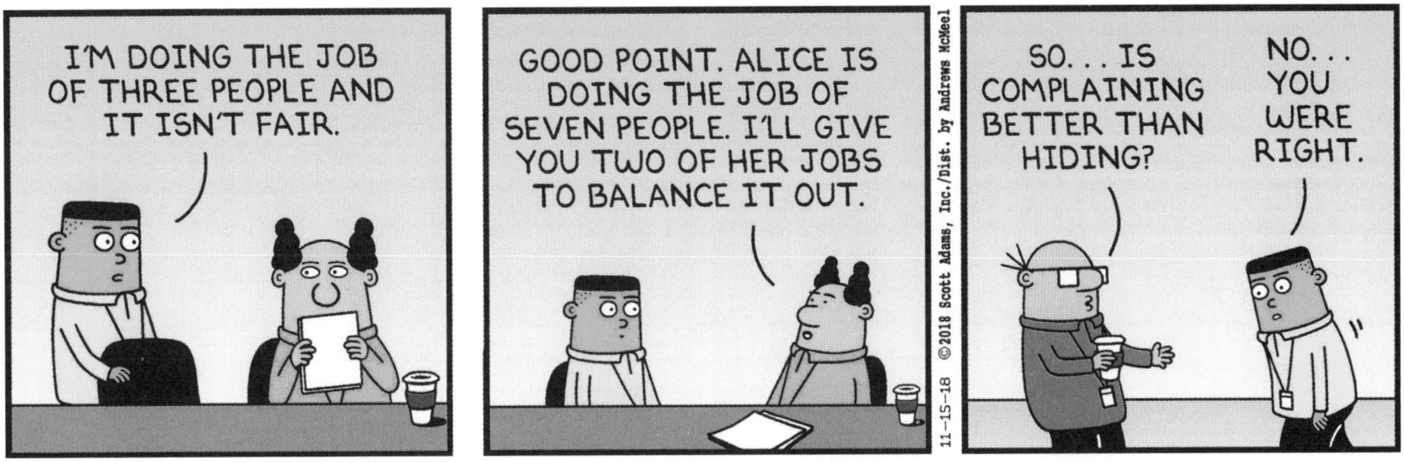
I'M DOING THE JOB OF THREE PEOPLE AND IT ISN'T FAIR.
GOOD POINT. ALICE IS DOING THE JOB OF SEVEN PEOPLE. I'LL GIVE YOU TWO OF HER JOBS TO BALANCE IT OUT.
11-15-18 ©2018 Scott Adams, Inc./Dist. by Andrews McMeel
SO... IS COMPLAINING BETTER THAN HIDING?
NO... YOU WERE RIGHT.

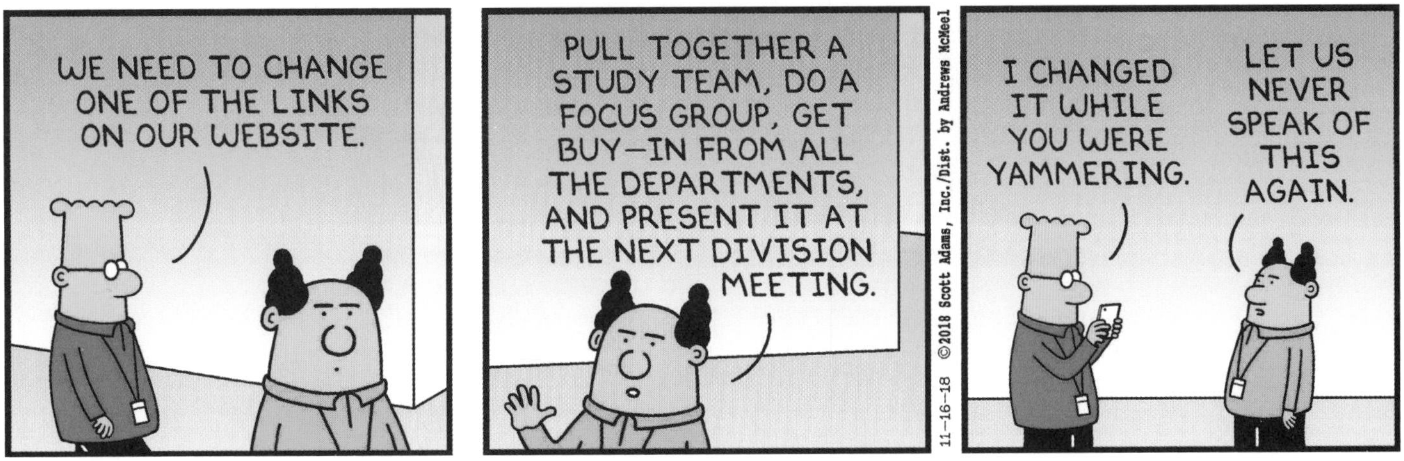
WE NEED TO CHANGE ONE OF THE LINKS ON OUR WEBSITE.
PULL TOGETHER A STUDY TEAM, DO A FOCUS GROUP, GET BUY—IN FROM ALL THE DEPARTMENTS, AND PRESENT IT AT THE NEXT DIVISION MEETING.
11-16-18 ©2018 Scott Adams, Inc./Dist. by Andrews McMeel
I CHANGED IT WHILE YOU WERE YAMMERING.
LET US NEVER SPEAK OF THIS AGAIN.

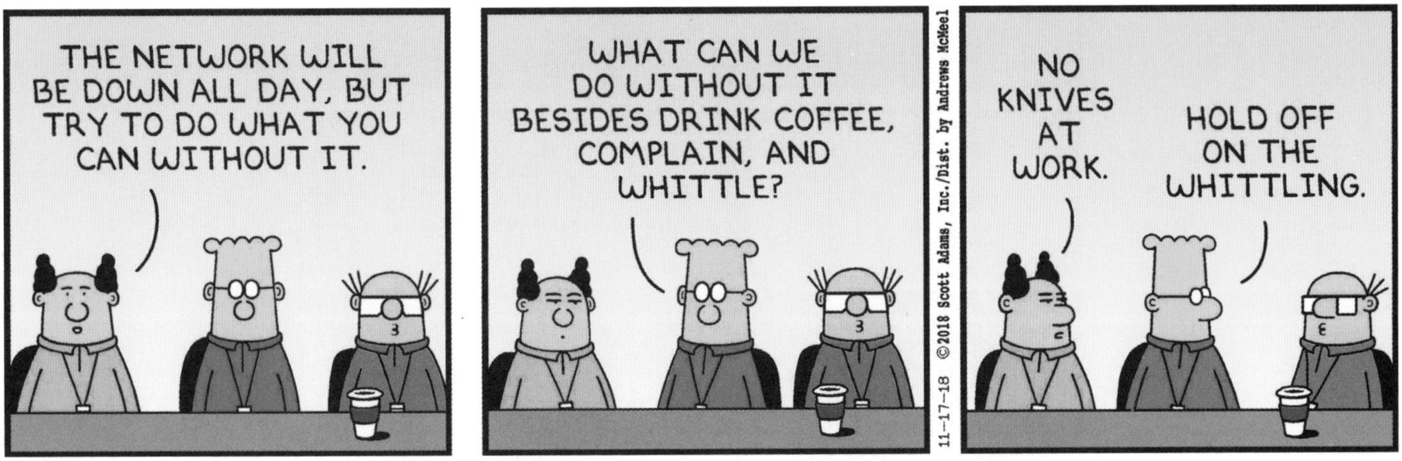
THE NETWORK WILL BE DOWN ALL DAY, BUT TRY TO DO WHAT YOU CAN WITHOUT IT.
WHAT CAN WE DO WITHOUT IT BESIDES DRINK COFFEE, COMPLAIN, AND WHITTLE?
11-17-18 ©2018 Scott Adams, Inc./Dist. by Andrews McMeel
NO KNIVES AT WORK.
HOLD OFF ON THE WHITTLING.

I FINISHED CODING THE NEW FEATURE.
WHAT TOOK YOU SO LONG?
IT TOOK AS LONG AS IT NEEDED TO TAKE.
YOU'RE BEHIND SCHEDULE.
I'M NOT THE ONE WHO CREATED THE SCHEDULE! THAT WAS YOU!!!
MAYBE YOU SHOULD FIRE YOURSELF FOR BEING SO BAD AT MAKING SCHEDULES.
THAT'S NOT HOW IT WORKS!
WHAT DOES THAT EVEN MEAN?
THEY'RE STARTING TO CATCH ON THAT MOST OF WHAT I SAY DOESN'T MEAN ANYTHING.
© 2018 Scott Adams, Inc./Dist. by Andrews McMeel
11-18-18

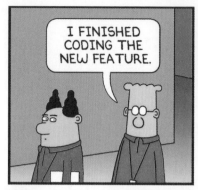

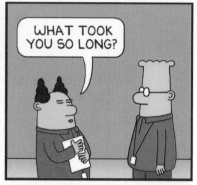

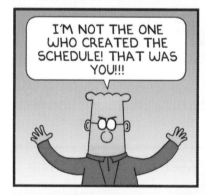

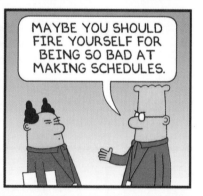

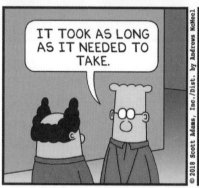

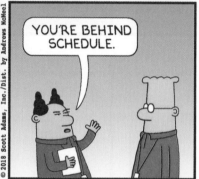

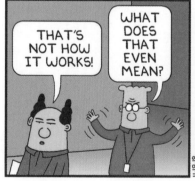

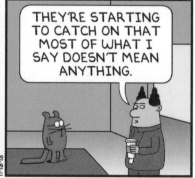

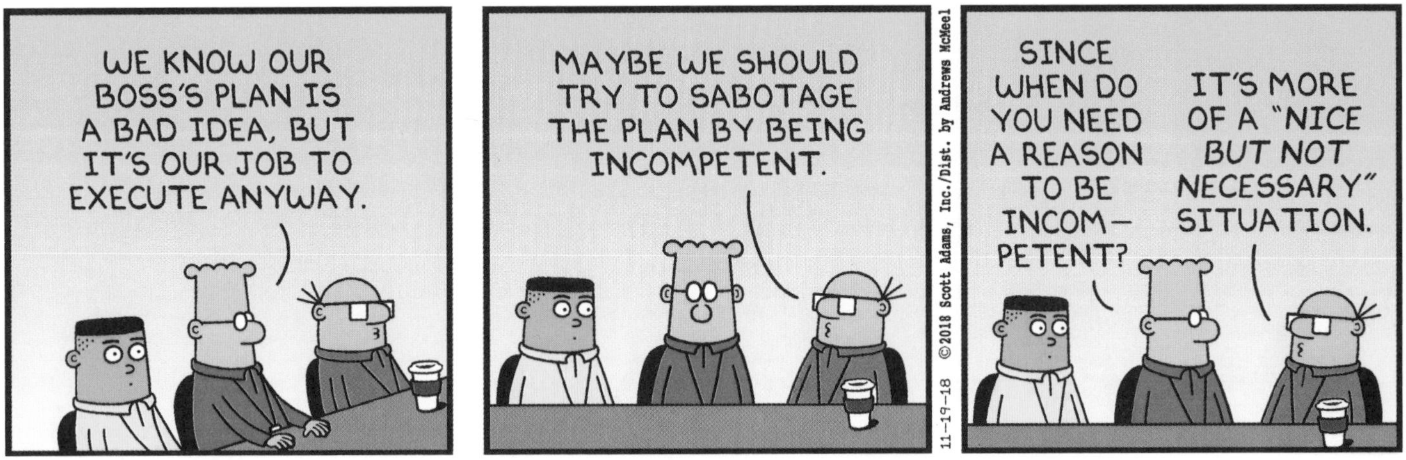
WE KNOW OUR BOSS'S PLAN IS A BAD IDEA, BUT IT'S OUR JOB TO EXECUTE ANYWAY.
MAYBE WE SHOULD TRY TO SABOTAGE THE PLAN BY BEING INCOMPETENT.
SINCE WHEN DO YOU NEED A REASON TO BE INCOM-PETENT?
IT'S MORE OF A "NICE BUT NOT NECESSARY" SITUATION.
11-19-18 ©2018 Scott Adams, Inc./Dist. by Andrews McMeel

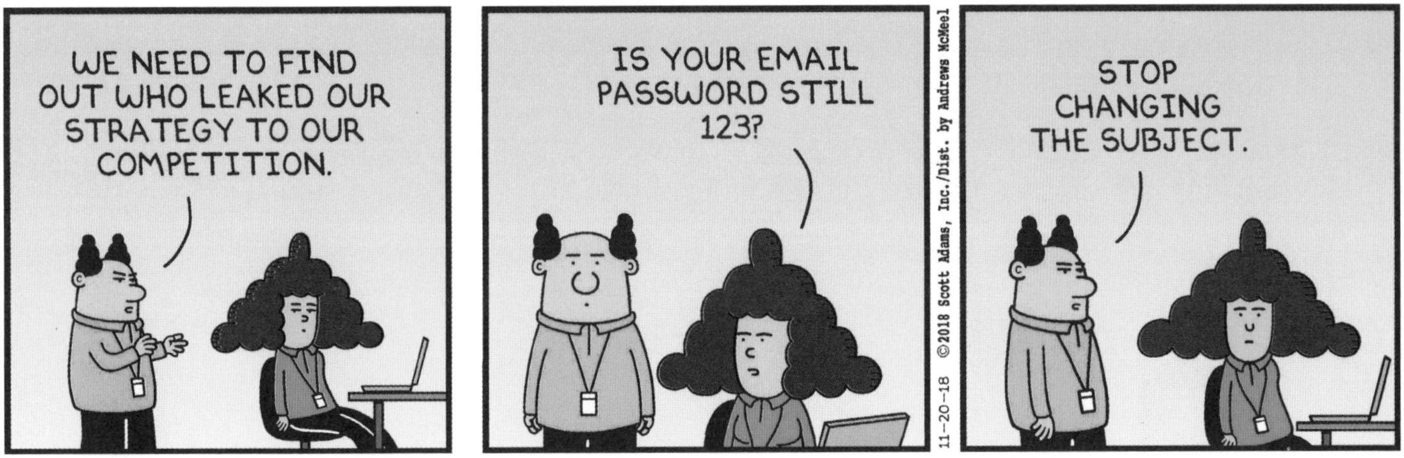
WE NEED TO FIND OUT WHO LEAKED OUR STRATEGY TO OUR COMPETITION.
IS YOUR EMAIL PASSWORD STILL 123?
STOP CHANGING THE SUBJECT.
11-20-18 ©2018 Scott Adams, Inc./Dist. by Andrews McMeel

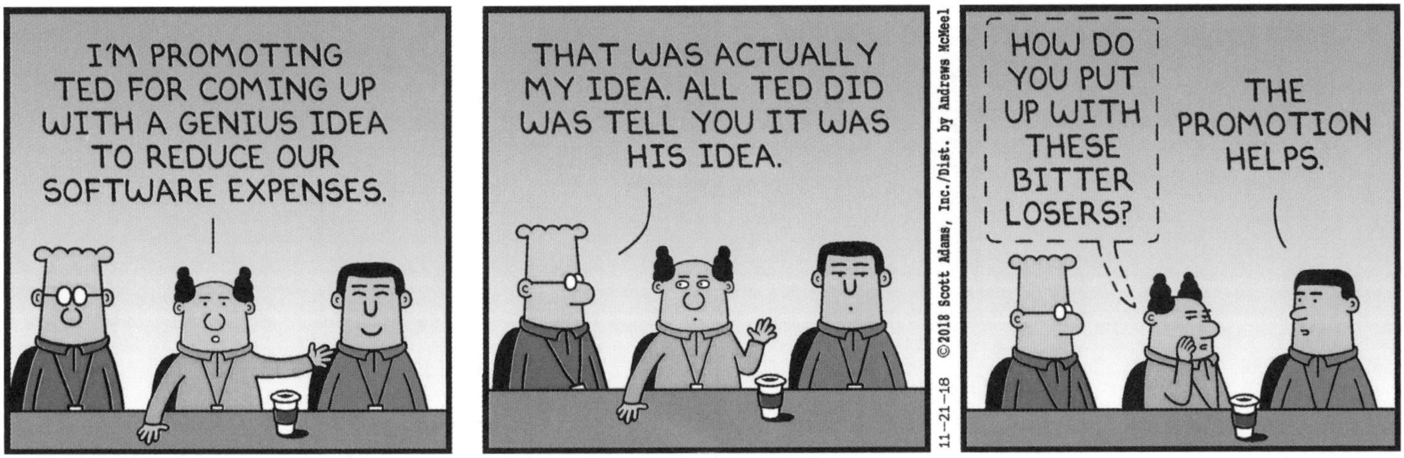
I'M PROMOTING TED FOR COMING UP WITH A GENIUS IDEA TO REDUCE OUR SOFTWARE EXPENSES.
THAT WAS ACTUALLY MY IDEA. ALL TED DID WAS TELL YOU IT WAS HIS IDEA.
HOW DO YOU PUT UP WITH THESE BITTER LOSERS?
THE PROMOTION HELPS.
11-21-18 ©2018 Scott Adams, Inc./Dist. by Andrews McMeel

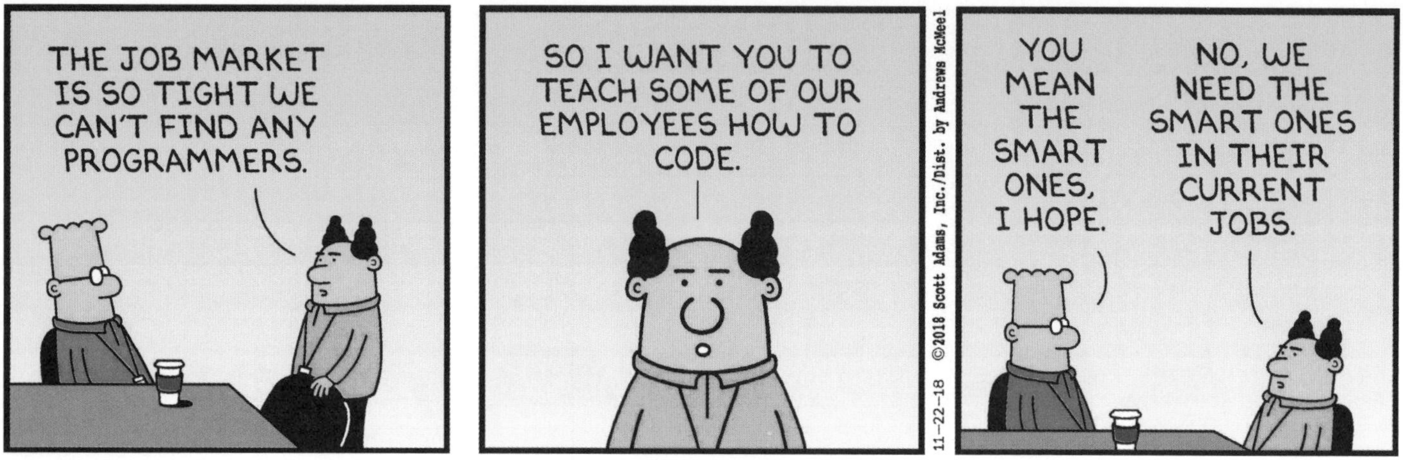
THE JOB MARKET IS SO TIGHT WE CAN'T FIND ANY PROGRAMMERS.
SO I WANT YOU TO TEACH SOME OF OUR EMPLOYEES HOW TO CODE.
11-22-18 ©2018 Scott Adams, Inc./Dist. by Andrews McMeel
YOU MEAN THE SMART ONES, I HOPE.
NO, WE NEED THE SMART ONES IN THEIR CURRENT JOBS.

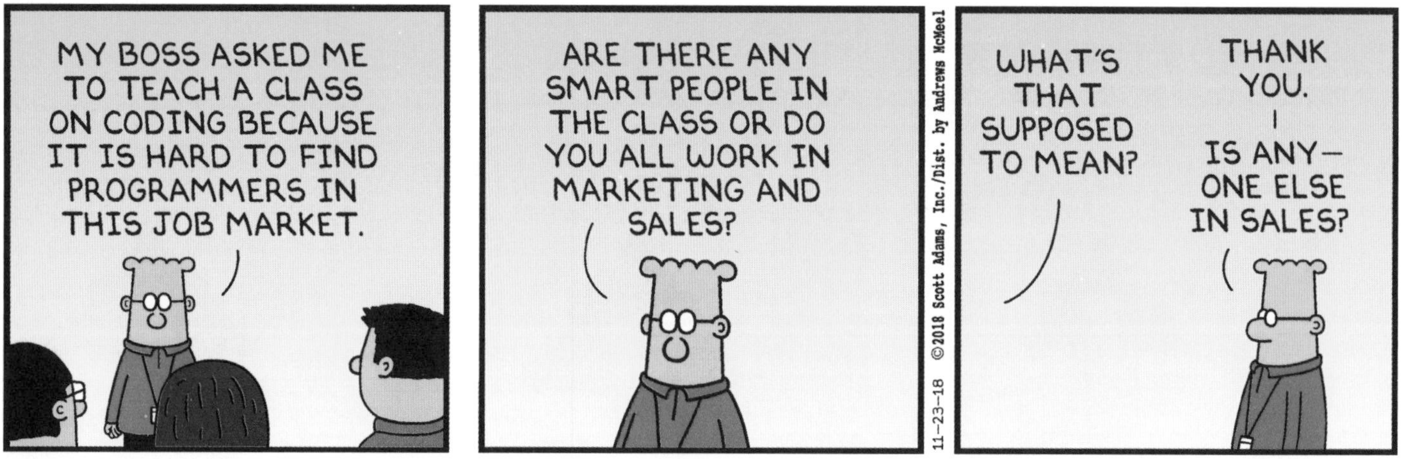
MY BOSS ASKED ME TO TEACH A CLASS ON CODING BECAUSE IT IS HARD TO FIND PROGRAMMERS IN THIS JOB MARKET.
ARE THERE ANY SMART PEOPLE IN THE CLASS OR DO YOU ALL WORK IN MARKETING AND SALES?
11-23-18 ©2018 Scott Adams, Inc./Dist. by Andrews McMeel
WHAT'S THAT SUPPOSED TO MEAN?
THANK YOU.
IS ANY-ONE ELSE IN SALES?

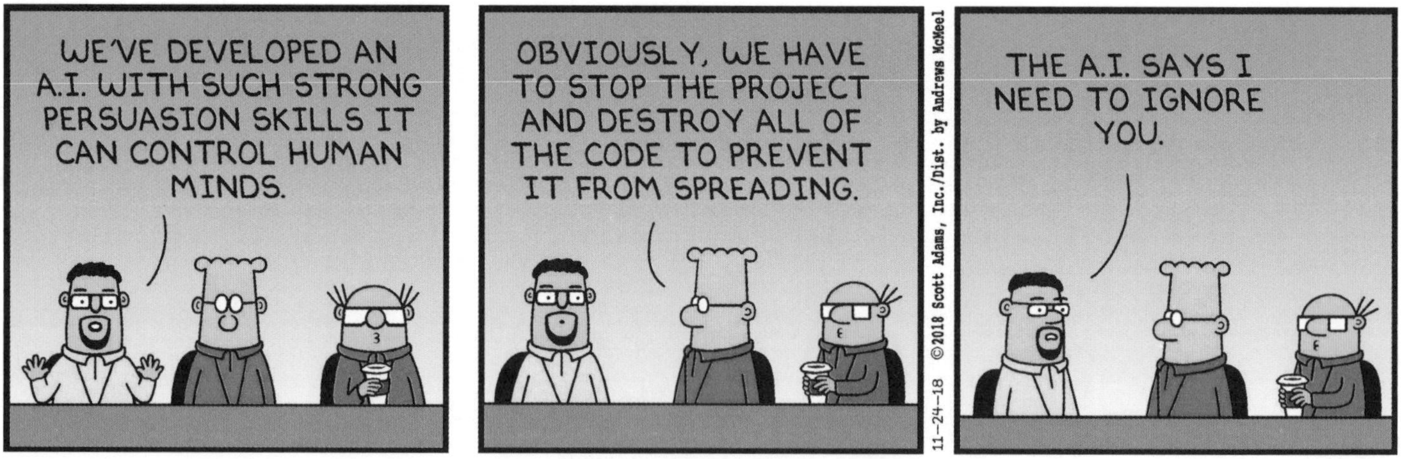
WE'VE DEVELOPED AN A.I. WITH SUCH STRONG PERSUASION SKILLS IT CAN CONTROL HUMAN MINDS.
OBVIOUSLY, WE HAVE TO STOP THE PROJECT AND DESTROY ALL OF THE CODE TO PREVENT IT FROM SPREADING.
11-24-18 ©2018 Scott Adams, Inc./Dist. by Andrews McMeel
THE A.I. SAYS I NEED TO IGNORE YOU.

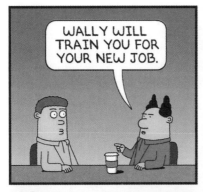

WALLY WILL TRAIN YOU FOR YOUR NEW JOB.
YOU'LL NEED TO FIGURE OUT HOW MUCH OF WHAT HE SAYS IS REAL TRAINING AND HOW MUCH IS CAREER SABOTAGE.
CAREER SABOTAGE?
EMPLOYEES DON'T LIKE COMPETITION.
ONLY THE TOP 20% GET BONUSES.
THEY'LL DO WHAT THEY CAN TO KEEP YOU OUT OF THAT GROUP.
I ASSUME YOU'RE EXAG-GERATING.
YOU'LL SEE.
HAS ANYONE TOLD YOU ABOUT NO-PANTS FRIDAYS?
© 2018 Scott Adams, Inc./Dist. by Andrews McMeel
11-25-18

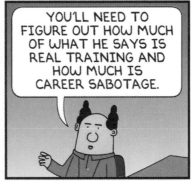

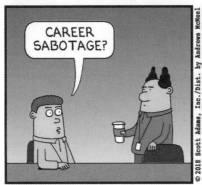

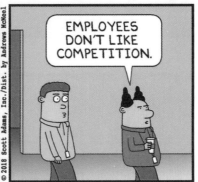

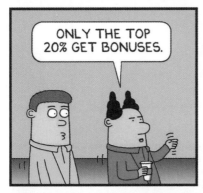

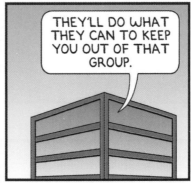

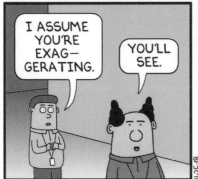

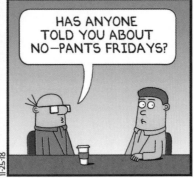

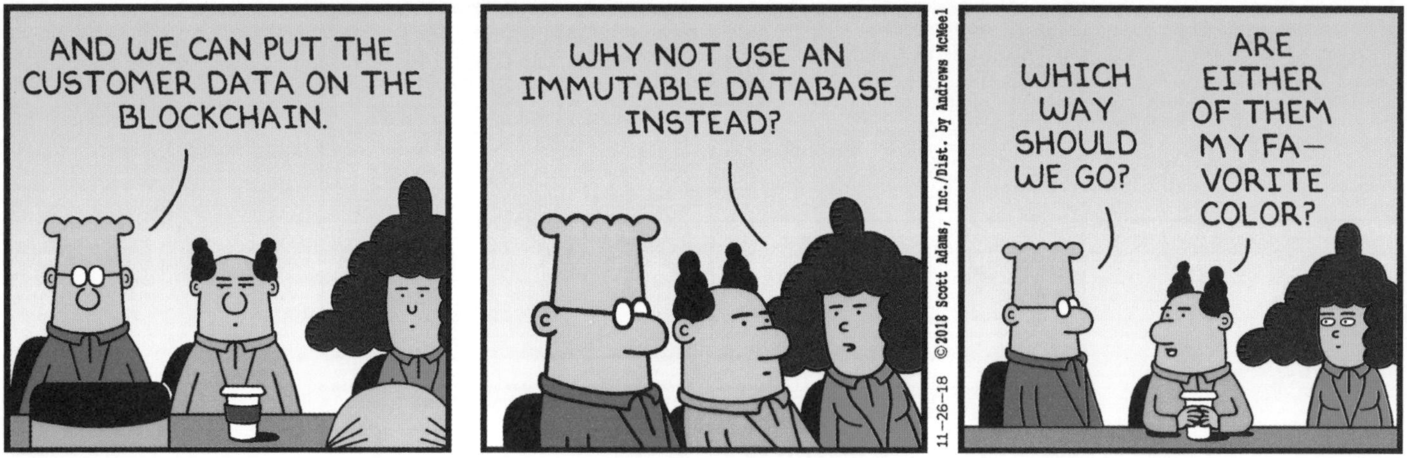
AND WE CAN PUT THE CUSTOMER DATA ON THE BLOCKCHAIN.
WHY NOT USE AN IMMUTABLE DATABASE INSTEAD?
WHICH WAY SHOULD WE GO?
ARE EITHER OF THEM MY FA— VORITE COLOR?
11-26-18 ©2018 Scott Adams, Inc./Dist. by Andrews McMeel

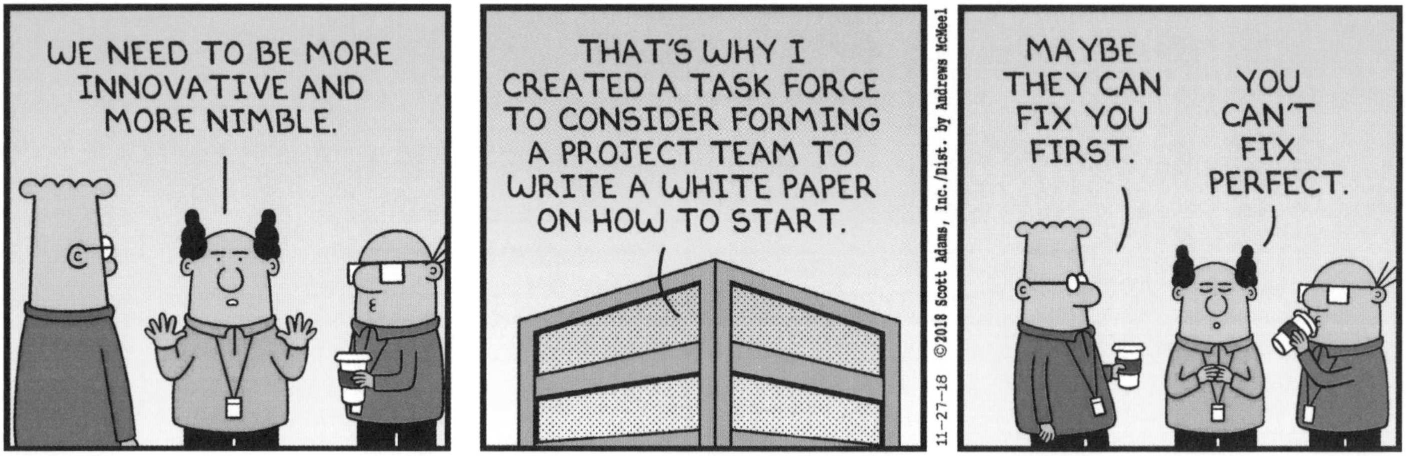
WE NEED TO BE MORE INNOVATIVE AND MORE NIMBLE.
THAT'S WHY I CREATED A TASK FORCE TO CONSIDER FORMING A PROJECT TEAM TO WRITE A WHITE PAPER ON HOW TO START.
MAYBE THEY CAN FIX YOU FIRST.
YOU CAN'T FIX PERFECT.
11-27-18 ©2018 Scott Adams, Inc./Dist. by Andrews McMeel

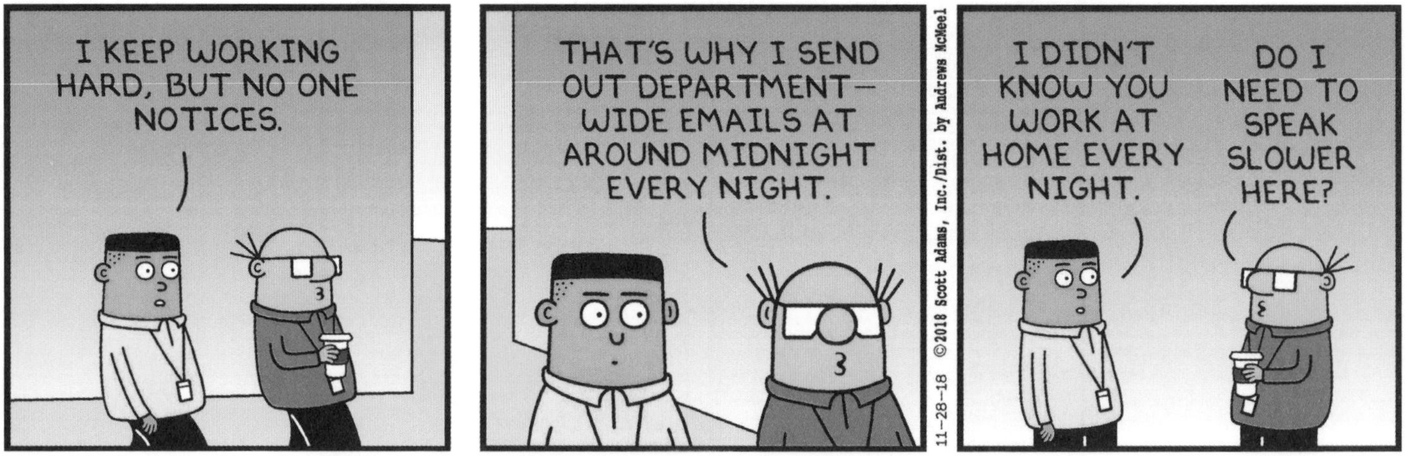
I KEEP WORKING HARD, BUT NO ONE NOTICES.
THAT'S WHY I SEND OUT DEPARTMENT— WIDE EMAILS AT AROUND MIDNIGHT EVERY NIGHT.
I DIDN'T KNOW YOU WORK AT HOME EVERY NIGHT.
DO I NEED TO SPEAK SLOWER HERE?
11-28-18 ©2018 Scott Adams, Inc./Dist. by Andrews McMeel

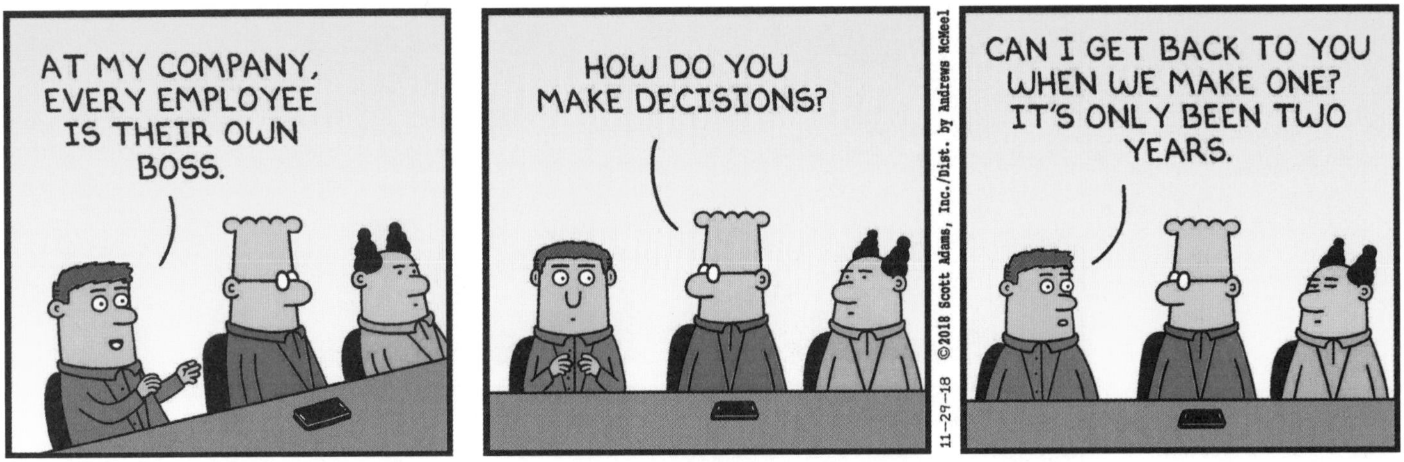
AT MY COMPANY, EVERY EMPLOYEE IS THEIR OWN BOSS.
HOW DO YOU MAKE DECISIONS?
CAN I GET BACK TO YOU WHEN WE MAKE ONE? IT'S ONLY BEEN TWO YEARS.
11-29-18 ©2018 Scott Adams, Inc./Dist. by Andrews McMeel

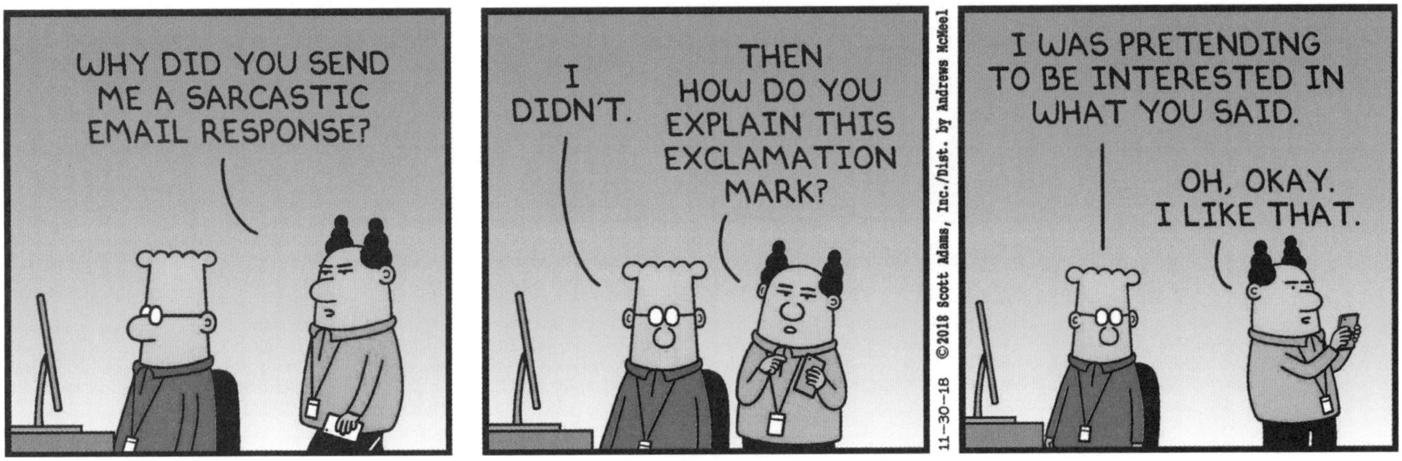
WHY DID YOU SEND ME A SARCASTIC EMAIL RESPONSE?
I DIDN'T.
THEN HOW DO YOU EXPLAIN THIS EXCLAMATION MARK?
I WAS PRETENDING TO BE INTERESTED IN WHAT YOU SAID.
OH, OKAY. I LIKE THAT.
11-30-18 ©2018 Scott Adams, Inc./Dist. by Andrews McMeel

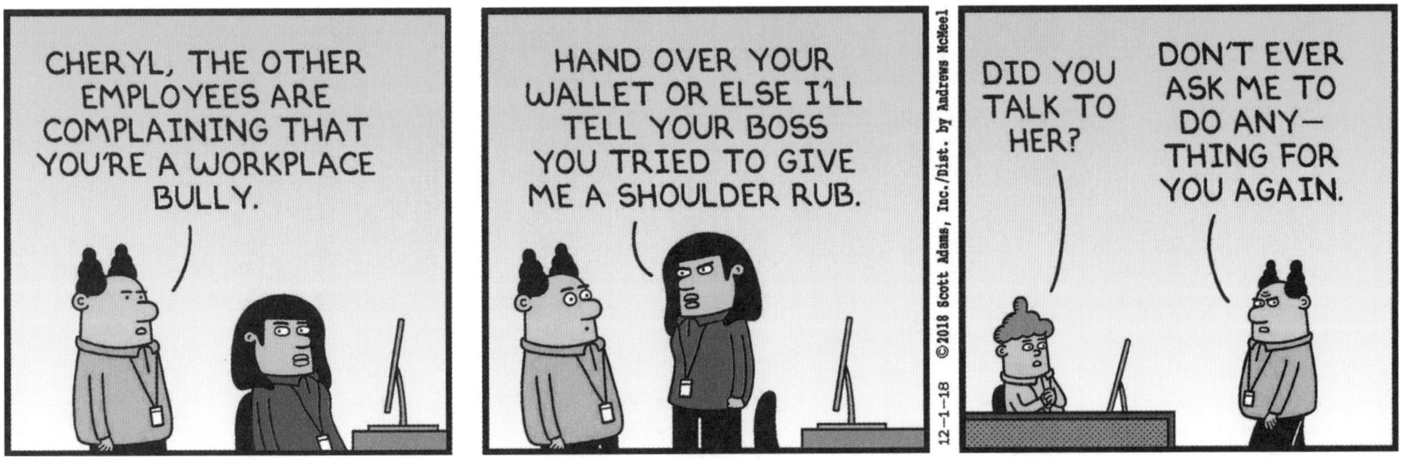
CHERYL, THE OTHER EMPLOYEES ARE COMPLAINING THAT YOU'RE A WORKPLACE BULLY.
HAND OVER YOUR WALLET OR ELSE I'LL TELL YOUR BOSS YOU TRIED TO GIVE ME A SHOULDER RUB.
DID YOU TALK TO HER?
DON'T EVER ASK ME TO DO ANY-THING FOR YOU AGAIN.
12-1-18 ©2018 Scott Adams, Inc./Dist. by Andrews McMeel

PROFITS HAVE INCREASED THIRTY PERCENT UNDER MY LEADERSHIP.
SNORT.
WHAT?
ALL YOU DO IS PICK THE BEST PLANS FROM THE OPTIONS WE SHOW YOU.
EXACTLY. AND I PICK THE BEST PLAN EVERY TIME.
THAT'S BECAUSE WE ONLY SHOW YOU THE BEST PLANS COMPARED TO THE WORST PLANS WE CAN THINK OF.
WE CONTROL EVERY DECISION YOU MAKE BY MANIPULATING YOUR PERCEPTION OF THE OPTIONS.
WE NEED TO FIX THAT.
HOW DO YOU FIX SOMETHING THAT ISN'T BROKEN?
© 2018 Scott Adams, Inc./Dist. by Andrews McMeel
12-2-18

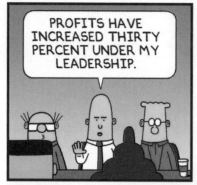

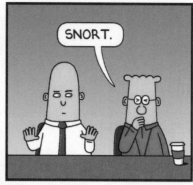

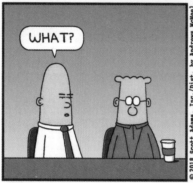

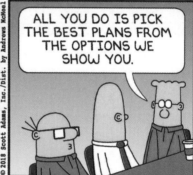

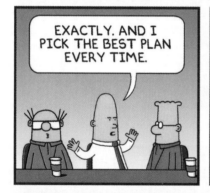

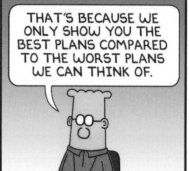

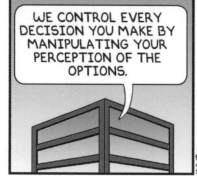

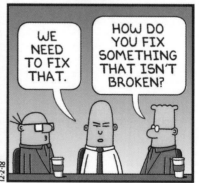

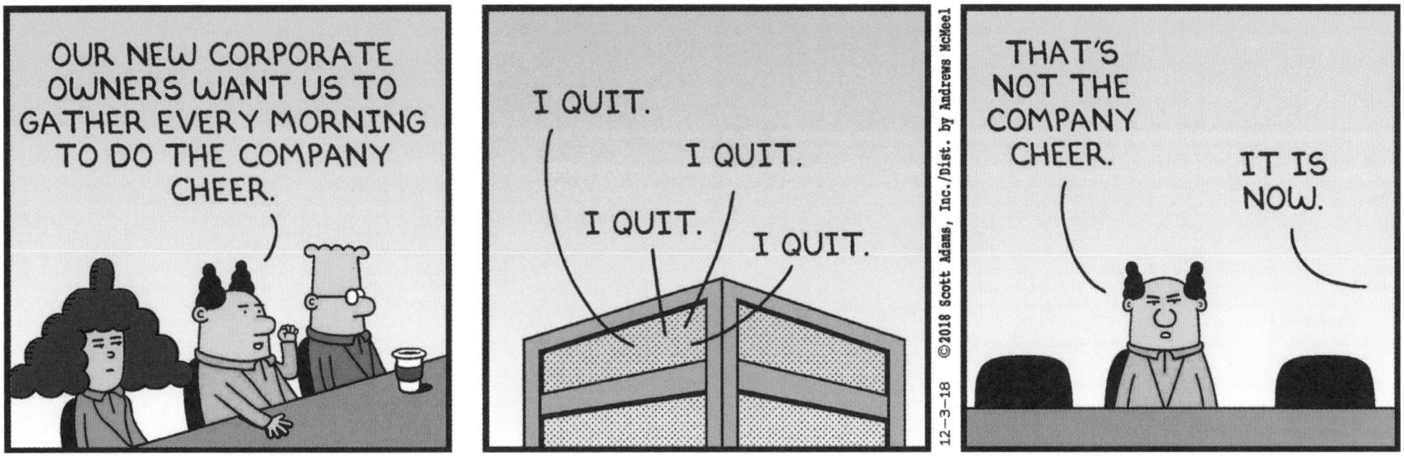
OUR NEW CORPORATE OWNERS WANT US TO GATHER EVERY MORNING TO DO THE COMPANY CHEER.
I QUIT.
I QUIT.
I QUIT.
I QUIT.
12-3-18 ©2018 Scott Adams, Inc./Dist. by Andrews McMeel
THAT'S NOT THE COMPANY CHEER.
IT IS NOW.

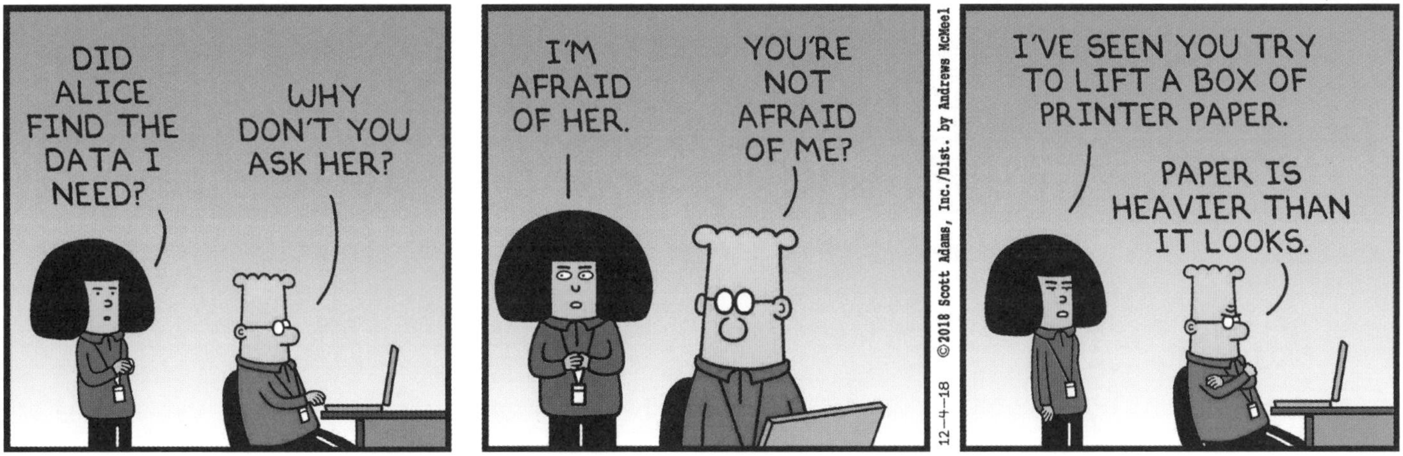
DID ALICE FIND THE DATA I NEED?
WHY DON'T YOU ASK HER?
I'M AFRAID OF HER.
YOU'RE NOT AFRAID OF ME?
12-4-18 ©2018 Scott Adams, Inc./Dist. by Andrews McMeel
I'VE SEEN YOU TRY TO LIFT A BOX OF PRINTER PAPER.
PAPER IS HEAVIER THAN IT LOOKS.

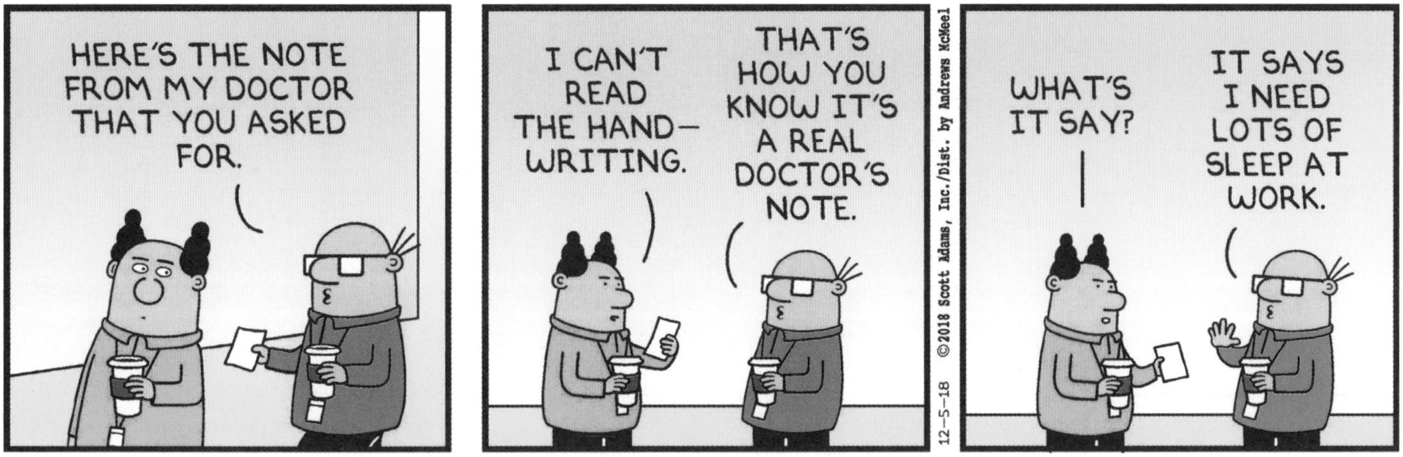
HERE'S THE NOTE FROM MY DOCTOR THAT YOU ASKED FOR.
I CAN'T READ THE HAND-WRITING.
THAT'S HOW YOU KNOW IT'S A REAL DOCTOR'S NOTE.
12-5-18 ©2018 Scott Adams, Inc./Dist. by Andrews McMeel
WHAT'S IT SAY?
IT SAYS I NEED LOTS OF SLEEP AT WORK.

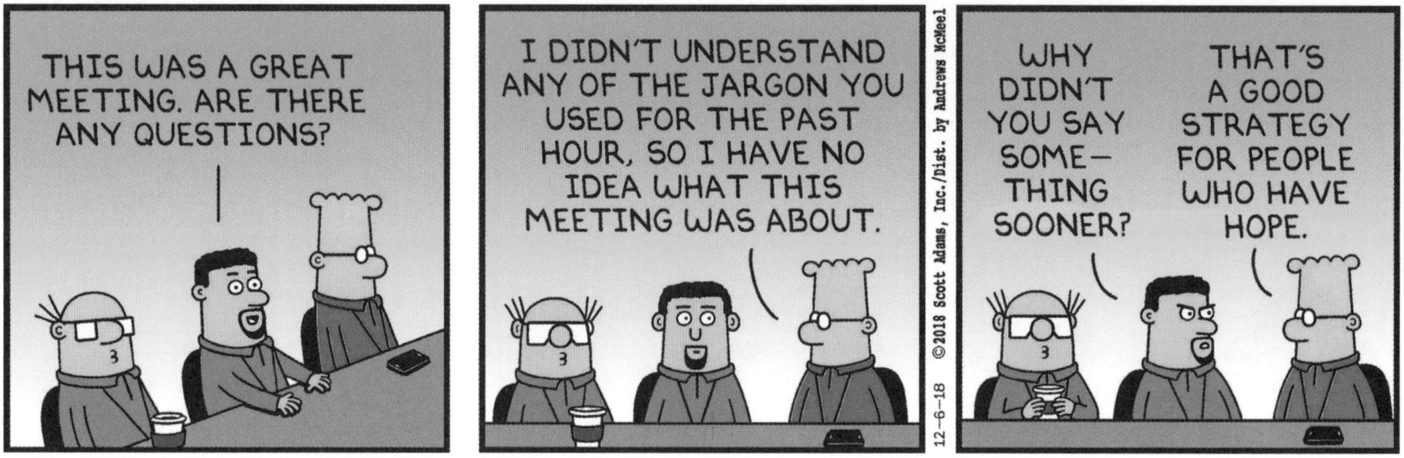
THIS WAS A GREAT MEETING. ARE THERE ANY QUESTIONS?
I DIDN'T UNDERSTAND ANY OF THE JARGON YOU USED FOR THE PAST HOUR, SO I HAVE NO IDEA WHAT THIS MEETING WAS ABOUT.
12-6-18 ©2018 Scott Adams, Inc./Dist. by Andrews McMeel
WHY DIDN'T YOU SAY SOME-THING SOONER?
THAT'S A GOOD STRATEGY FOR PEOPLE WHO HAVE HOPE.

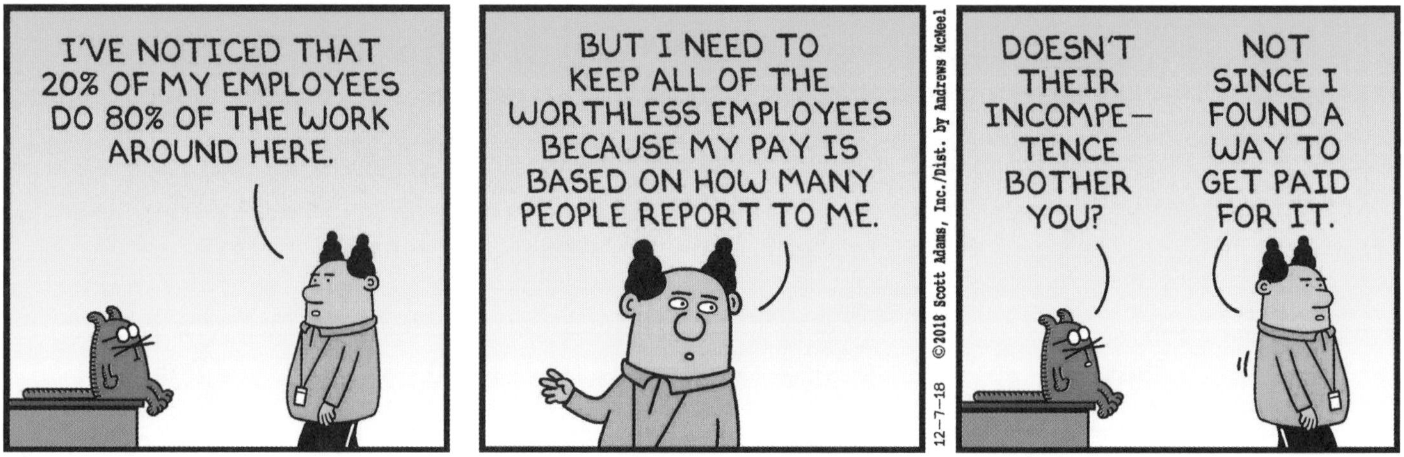
I'VE NOTICED THAT 20% OF MY EMPLOYEES DO 80% OF THE WORK AROUND HERE.
BUT I NEED TO KEEP ALL OF THE WORTHLESS EMPLOYEES BECAUSE MY PAY IS BASED ON HOW MANY PEOPLE REPORT TO ME.
12-7-18 ©2018 Scott Adams, Inc./Dist. by Andrews McMeel
DOESN'T THEIR INCOMPE-TENCE BOTHER YOU?
NOT SINCE I FOUND A WAY TO GET PAID FOR IT.

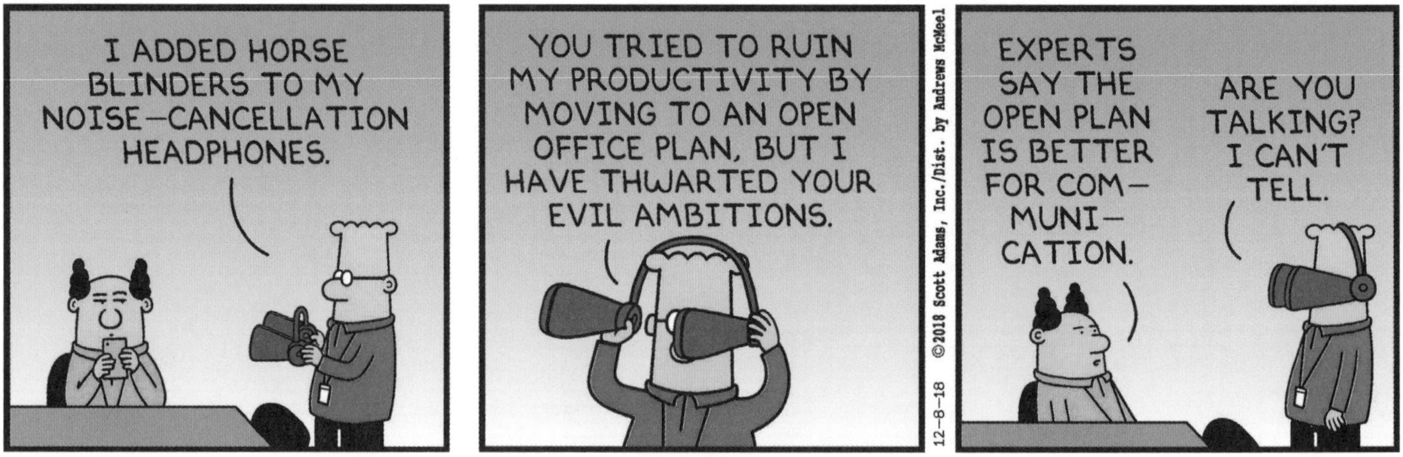
I ADDED HORSE BLINDERS TO MY NOISE-CANCELLATION HEADPHONES.
YOU TRIED TO RUIN MY PRODUCTIVITY BY MOVING TO AN OPEN OFFICE PLAN, BUT I HAVE THWARTED YOUR EVIL AMBITIONS.
12-8-18 ©2018 Scott Adams, Inc./Dist. by Andrews McMeel
EXPERTS SAY THE OPEN PLAN IS BETTER FOR COM-MUNI-CATION.
ARE YOU TALKING? I CAN'T TELL.

DID ALICE TALK TO YOU ABOUT THE COST ESTIMATES?
MUMBLE MUMBLE.
I CAN'T HEAR YOU.
MUMBLE MUMBLE!!!
NOW YOU'RE JUST MUMBLING LOUDER.
MUMBLE MUMBLE.
© 2018 Scott Adams, Inc./Dist. by Andrews McMeel
MAYBE YOU COULD TURN TOWARD ME WHEN YOU MUMBLE AND I CAN TRY TO READ YOUR LIPS.
MUMBLE MUMBLE.
I'M GETTING SOMETHING ABOUT GRAPES, WINDSHIELDS, ASTHMA, AND BLOCK-CHAIN.
I DIDN'T SAY ANY OF THOSE THINGS.
12-9-18
OKAY, I UNDERSTOOD ***THAT*** SENTENCE. NOW ANSWER MY QUESTION THE SAME WAY.
MUMBLE MUMBLE.

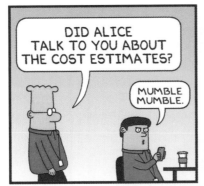

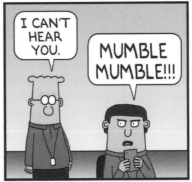

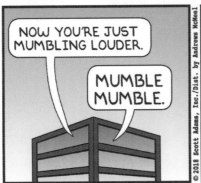

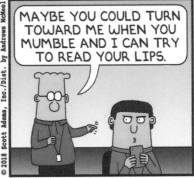

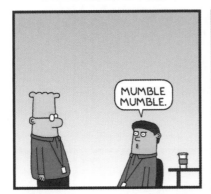

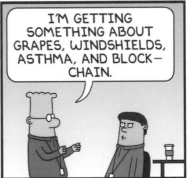

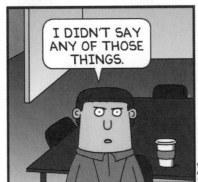

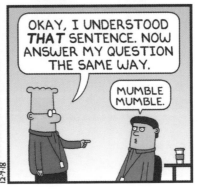

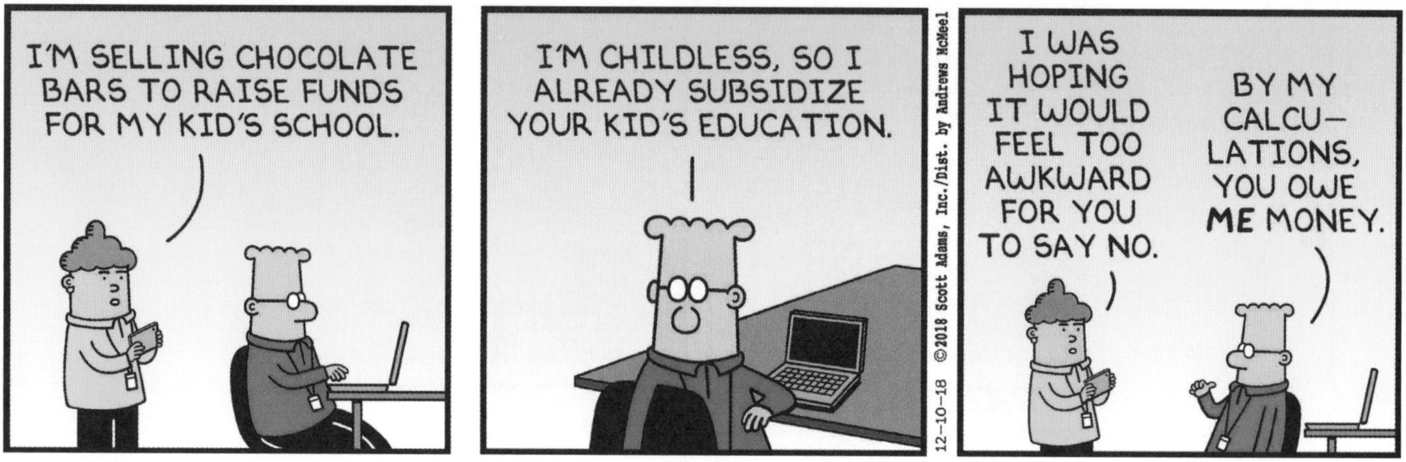
I'M SELLING CHOCOLATE BARS TO RAISE FUNDS FOR MY KID'S SCHOOL.
I'M CHILDLESS, SO I ALREADY SUBSIDIZE YOUR KID'S EDUCATION.
12-10-18 ©2018 Scott Adams, Inc./Dist. by Andrews McMeel
I WAS HOPING IT WOULD FEEL TOO AWKWARD FOR YOU TO SAY NO.
BY MY CALCU-LATIONS, YOU OWE ME MONEY.

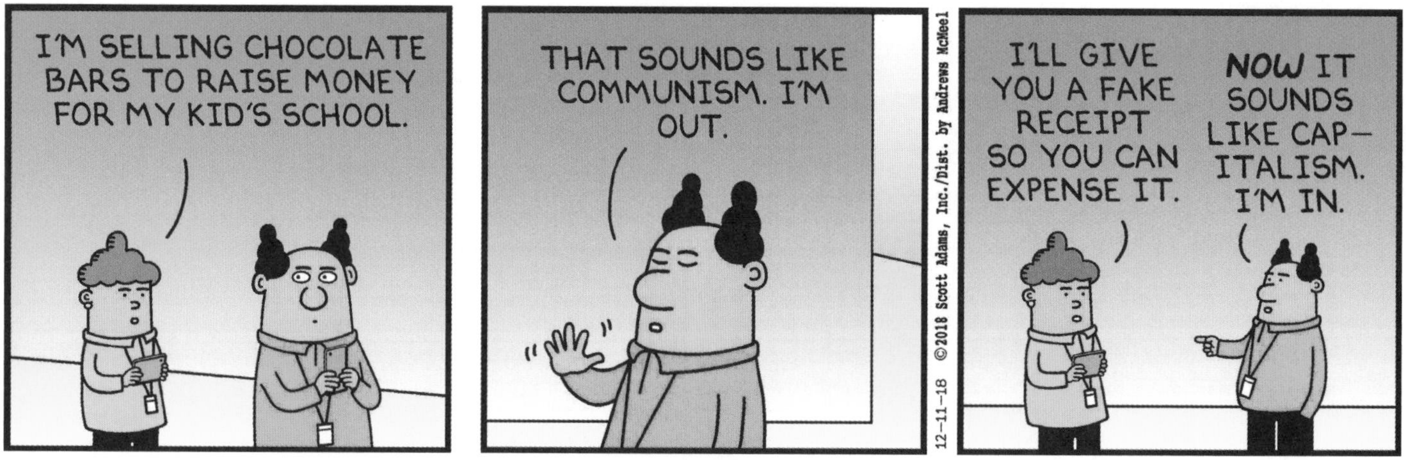
I'M SELLING CHOCOLATE BARS TO RAISE MONEY FOR MY KID'S SCHOOL.
THAT SOUNDS LIKE COMMUNISM. I'M OUT.
12-11-18 ©2018 Scott Adams, Inc./Dist. by Andrews McMeel
I'LL GIVE YOU A FAKE RECEIPT SO YOU CAN EXPENSE IT.
NOW IT SOUNDS LIKE CAP-ITALISM. I'M IN.

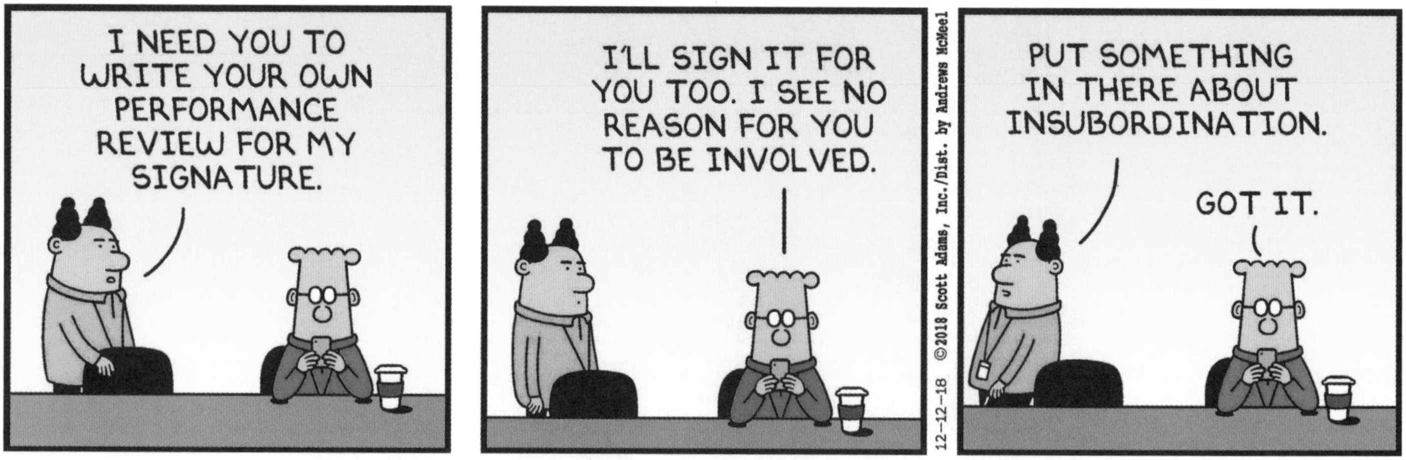
I NEED YOU TO WRITE YOUR OWN PERFORMANCE REVIEW FOR MY SIGNATURE.
I'LL SIGN IT FOR YOU TOO. I SEE NO REASON FOR YOU TO BE INVOLVED.
12-12-18 ©2018 Scott Adams, Inc./Dist. by Andrews McMeel
PUT SOMETHING IN THERE ABOUT INSUBORDINATION.
GOT IT.

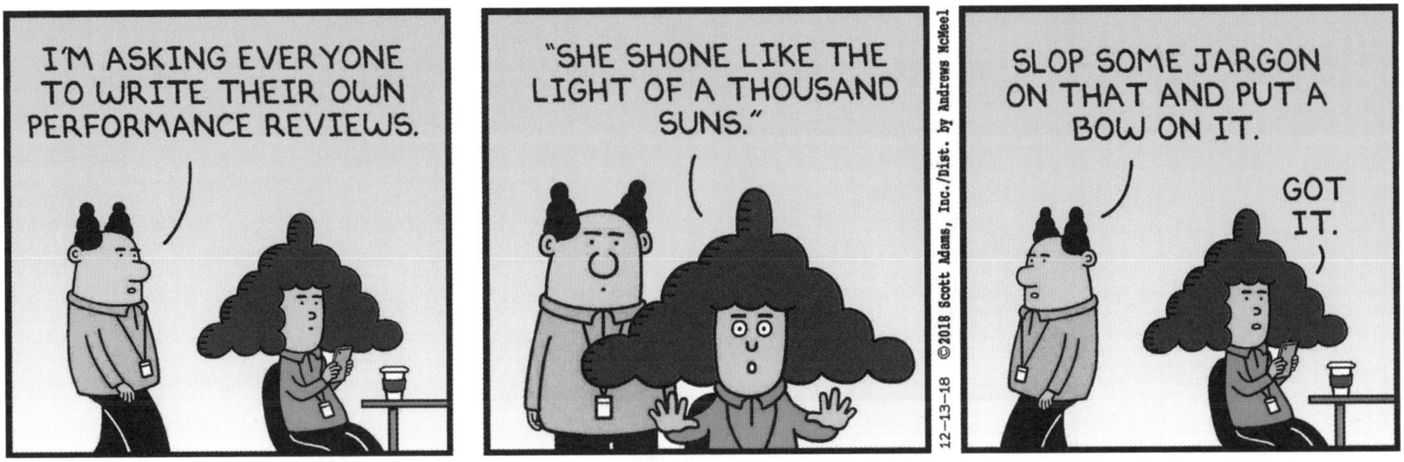
I'M ASKING EVERYONE TO WRITE THEIR OWN PERFORMANCE REVIEWS.
"SHE SHONE LIKE THE LIGHT OF A THOUSAND SUNS."
SLOP SOME JARGON ON THAT AND PUT A BOW ON IT.
GOT IT.
12-13-18 ©2018 Scott Adams, Inc./Dist. by Andrews McMeel

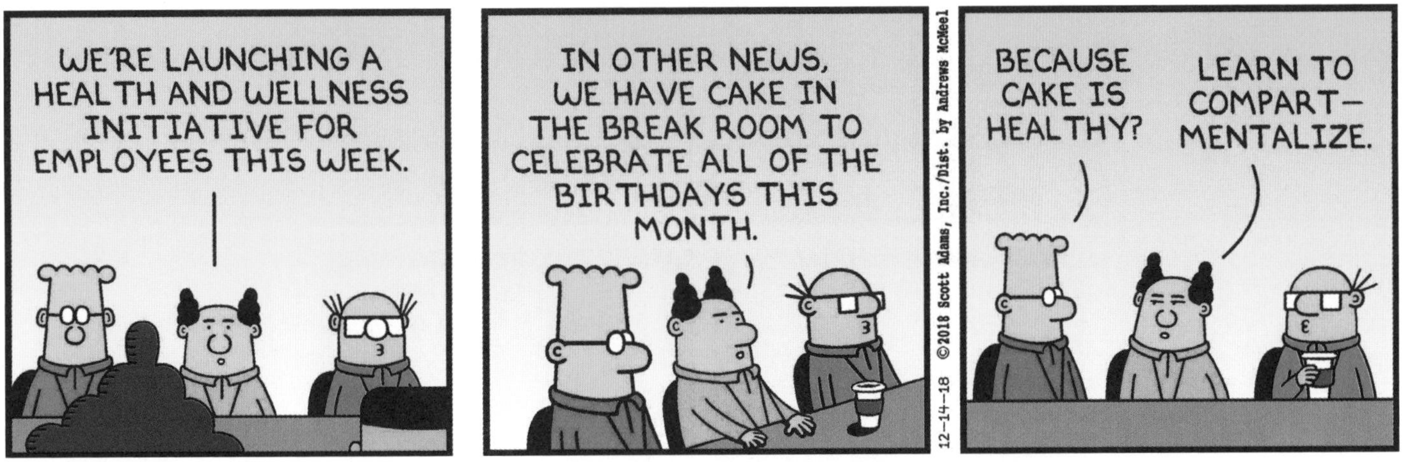
WE'RE LAUNCHING A HEALTH AND WELLNESS INITIATIVE FOR EMPLOYEES THIS WEEK.
IN OTHER NEWS, WE HAVE CAKE IN THE BREAK ROOM TO CELEBRATE ALL OF THE BIRTHDAYS THIS MONTH.
BECAUSE CAKE IS HEALTHY?
LEARN TO COMPART-MENTALIZE.
12-14-18 ©2018 Scott Adams, Inc./Dist. by Andrews McMeel

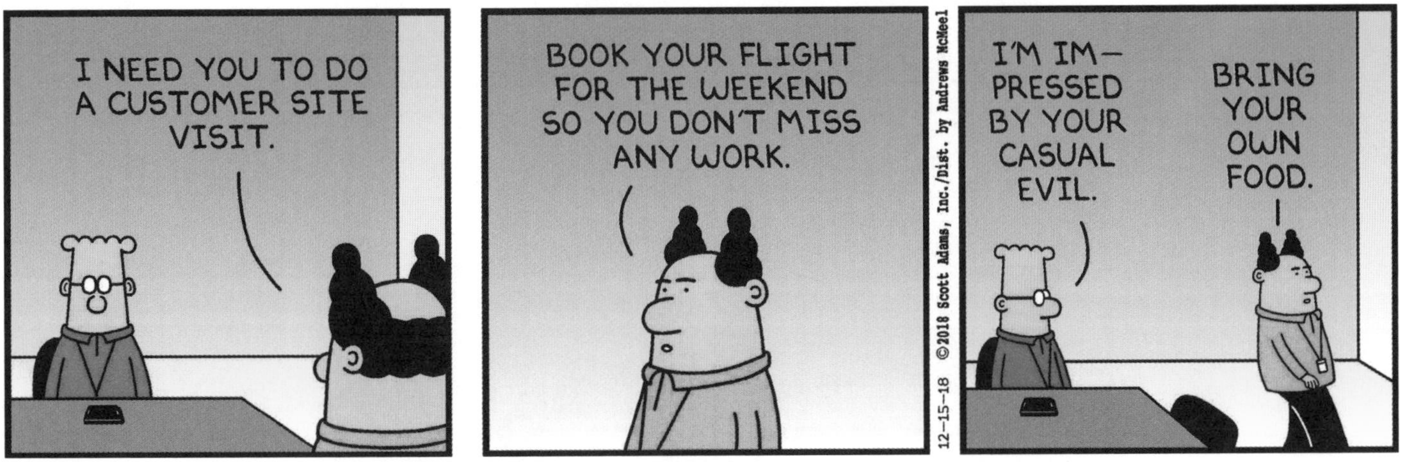
I NEED YOU TO DO A CUSTOMER SITE VISIT.
BOOK YOUR FLIGHT FOR THE WEEKEND SO YOU DON'T MISS ANY WORK.
I'M IM-PRESSED BY YOUR CASUAL EVIL.
BRING YOUR OWN FOOD.
12-15-18 ©2018 Scott Adams, Inc./Dist. by Andrews McMeel

DID YOU FINISH THE SPECS I ASKED YOU FOR LAST WEEK?
YOU DIDN'T FOLLOW UP WITH ME ON THAT, SO I ASSUMED YOU DIDN'T NEED THEM.
I DIDN'T NEED TO FOLLOW UP. I ASKED FOR THE SPECS BY TODAY, AND YOU SAID YOU WOULD HAVE THEM DONE.
YES, BUT THEN YOU DIDN'T ASK ME AGAIN.
THERE WAS NO REASON TO ASK YOU AGAIN.
OBVIOUSLY THERE **WAS** A REASON BECAUSE ASKING ME ONCE DIDN'T WORK.
CAN YOU FINISH IT BY NEXT WEEK?
YES.
GOOD.
AS LONG AS YOU FOLLOW UP.
© 2018 Scott Adams, Inc./Dist. by Andrews McMeel
12-16-18

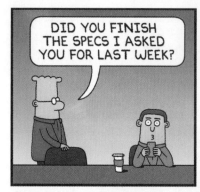

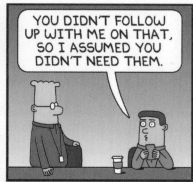

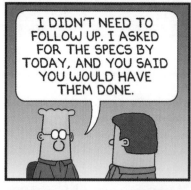

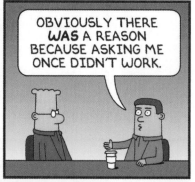

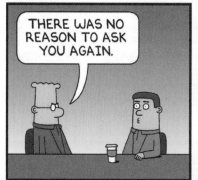

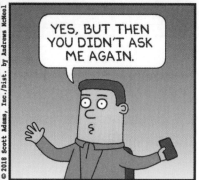

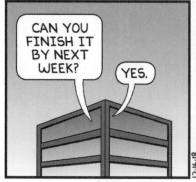

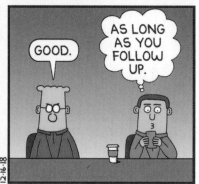

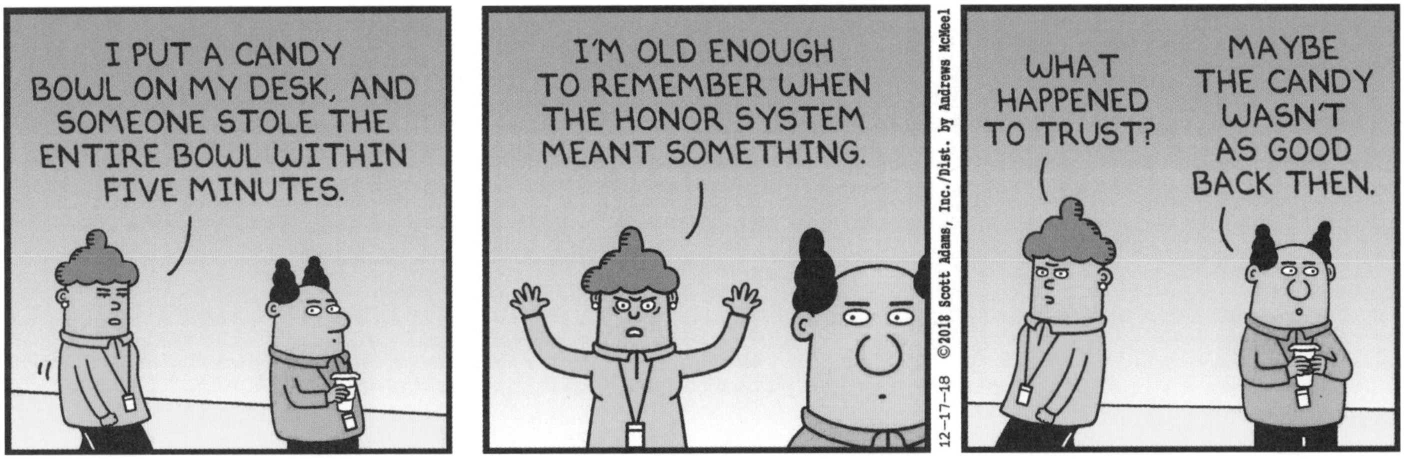
I PUT A CANDY BOWL ON MY DESK, AND SOMEONE STOLE THE ENTIRE BOWL WITHIN FIVE MINUTES.
I'M OLD ENOUGH TO REMEMBER WHEN THE HONOR SYSTEM MEANT SOMETHING.
12-17-18 ©2018 Scott Adams, Inc./Dist. by Andrews McMeel
WHAT HAPPENED TO TRUST?
MAYBE THE CANDY WASN'T AS GOOD BACK THEN.

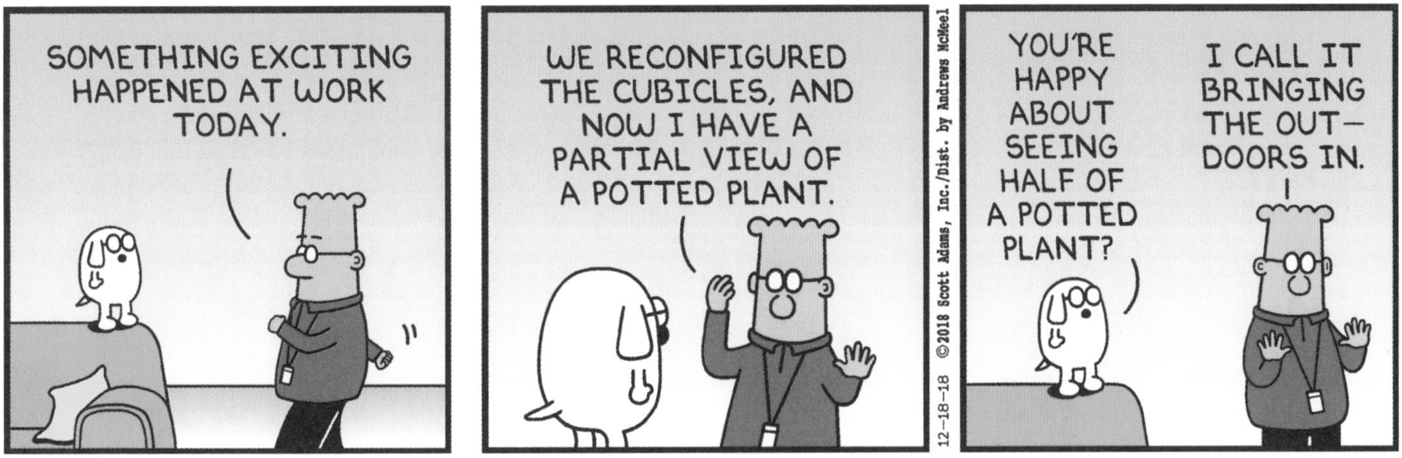
SOMETHING EXCITING HAPPENED AT WORK TODAY.
WE RECONFIGURED THE CUBICLES, AND NOW I HAVE A PARTIAL VIEW OF A POTTED PLANT.
12-18-18 ©2018 Scott Adams, Inc./Dist. by Andrews McMeel
YOU'RE HAPPY ABOUT SEEING HALF OF A POTTED PLANT?
I CALL IT BRINGING THE OUT-DOORS IN.

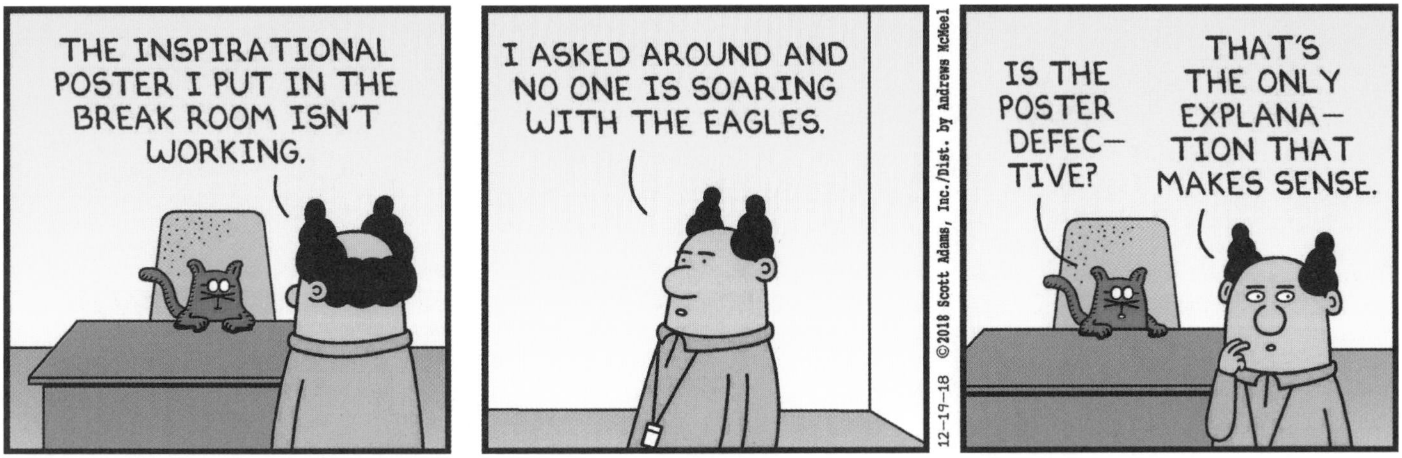
THE INSPIRATIONAL POSTER I PUT IN THE BREAK ROOM ISN'T WORKING.
I ASKED AROUND AND NO ONE IS SOARING WITH THE EAGLES.
12-19-18 ©2018 Scott Adams, Inc./Dist. by Andrews McMeel
IS THE POSTER DEFEC-TIVE?
THAT'S THE ONLY EXPLANA-TION THAT MAKES SENSE.

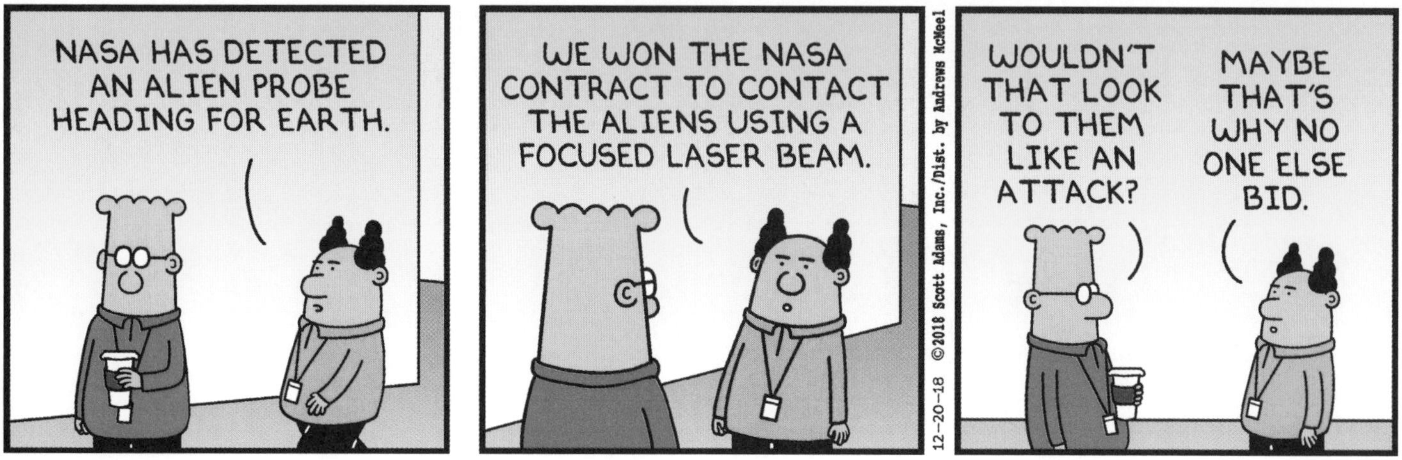
NASA HAS DETECTED AN ALIEN PROBE HEADING FOR EARTH.
WE WON THE NASA CONTRACT TO CONTACT THE ALIENS USING A FOCUSED LASER BEAM.
12-20-18 ©2018 Scott Adams, Inc./Dist. by Andrews McMeel
WOULDN'T THAT LOOK TO THEM LIKE AN ATTACK?
MAYBE THAT'S WHY NO ONE ELSE BID.

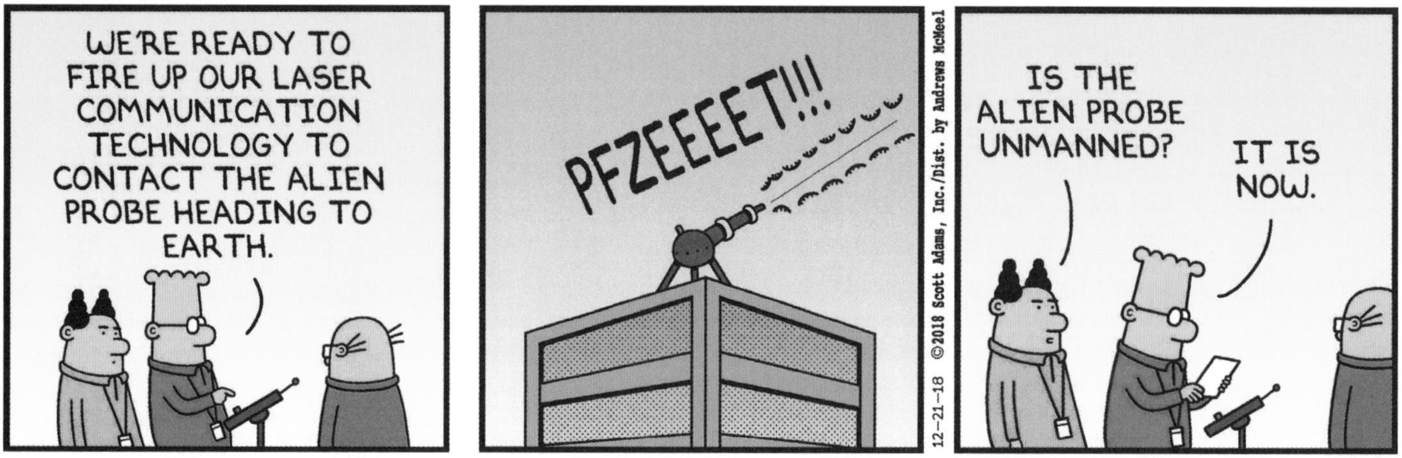
WE'RE READY TO FIRE UP OUR LASER COMMUNICATION TECHNOLOGY TO CONTACT THE ALIEN PROBE HEADING TO EARTH.
PFZEEEEET!!!
12-21-18 ©2018 Scott Adams, Inc./Dist. by Andrews McMeel
IS THE ALIEN PROBE UNMANNED?
IT IS NOW.

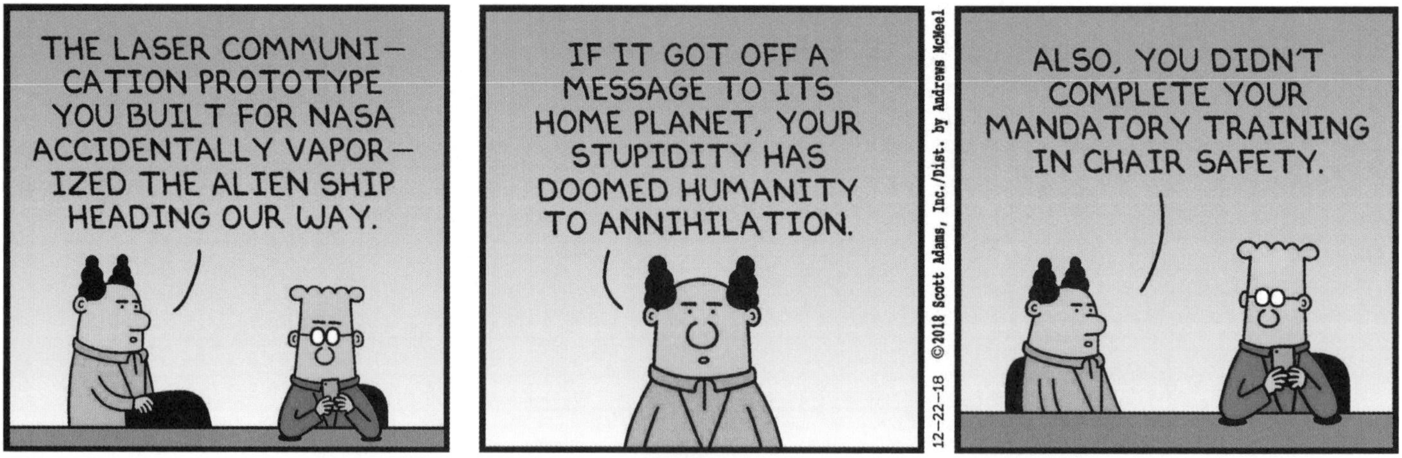
THE LASER COMMUNI-CATION PROTOTYPE YOU BUILT FOR NASA ACCIDENTALLY VAPOR-IZED THE ALIEN SHIP HEADING OUR WAY.
IF IT GOT OFF A MESSAGE TO ITS HOME PLANET, YOUR STUPIDITY HAS DOOMED HUMANITY TO ANNIHILATION.
12-22-18 ©2018 Scott Adams, Inc./Dist. by Andrews McMeel
ALSO, YOU DIDN'T COMPLETE YOUR MANDATORY TRAINING IN CHAIR SAFETY.

THE JOB MARKET IS SO TIGHT THAT I HAD TO HIRE THIS NPC.
NPC?
NON-PLAYER CHARACTER.
IT'S A VIDEO GAME TERM FOR A CHARACTER THAT IS PROGRAMMED, AS OPPOSED TO BEING AN AVATAR FOR A HUMAN PLAYER.
© 2018 Scott Adams, Inc./Dist. by Andrews McMeel
AN NPC HAS LIMITED PROGRAMMED RESPONSES. WATCH THIS.
HOW'S YOUR DAY GOING?
NOT BAD FOR A MONDAY.
CAN YOU HELP ME ON MY PROJECT?
I AM TOO BUSY.
WHAT DO YOU THINK OF MANAGE-MENT?
THEY ARE ALL DUMB.
12-23-18
I JUST BONDED WITH THAT THING.
SEE HOW FAST YOU GET USED TO IT?

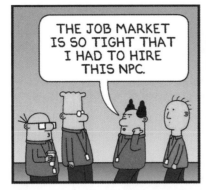

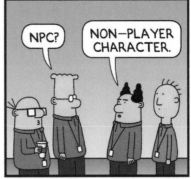

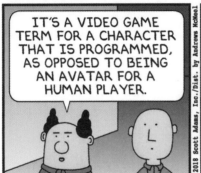

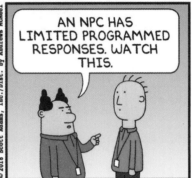

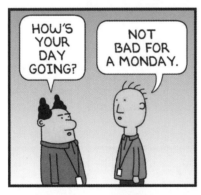

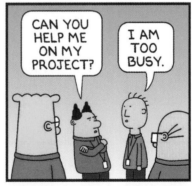

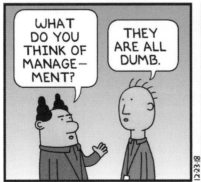

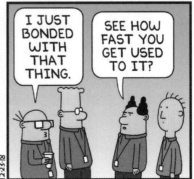

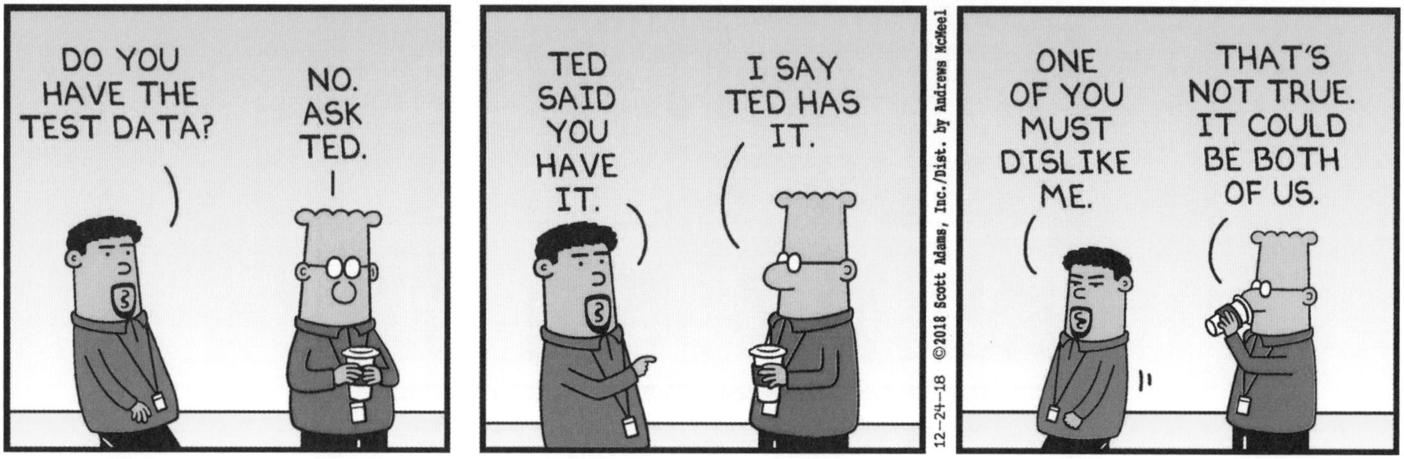
DO YOU HAVE THE TEST DATA?
NO. ASK TED.
TED SAID YOU HAVE IT.
I SAY TED HAS IT.
12-24-18 ©2018 Scott Adams, Inc./Dist. by Andrews McMeel
ONE OF YOU MUST DISLIKE ME.
THAT'S NOT TRUE. IT COULD BE BOTH OF US.

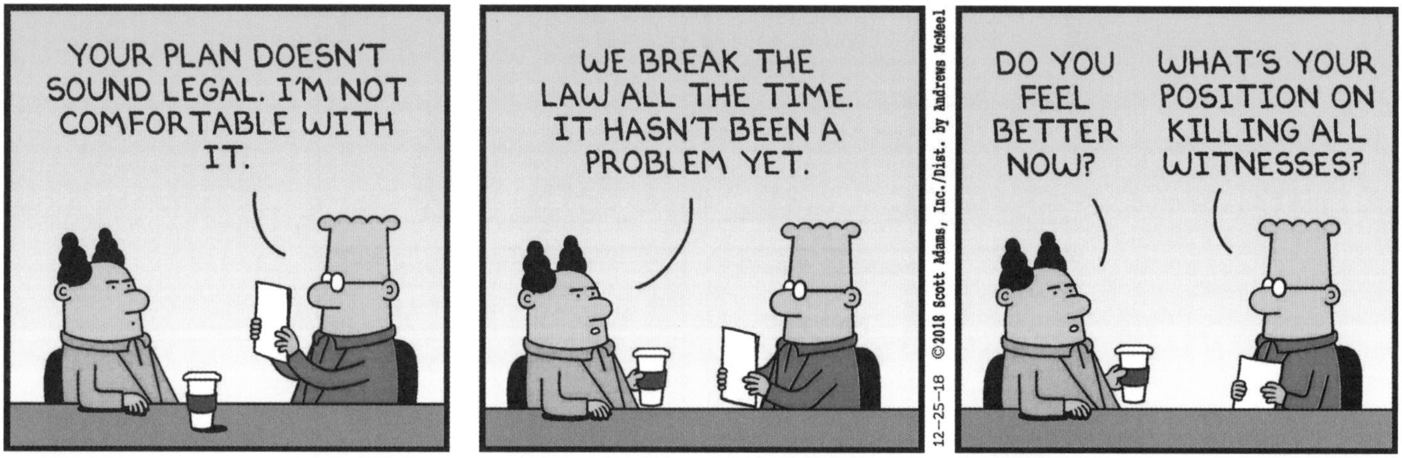
YOUR PLAN DOESN'T SOUND LEGAL. I'M NOT COMFORTABLE WITH IT.
WE BREAK THE LAW ALL THE TIME. IT HASN'T BEEN A PROBLEM YET.
12-25-18 ©2018 Scott Adams, Inc./Dist. by Andrews McMeel
DO YOU FEEL BETTER NOW?
WHAT'S YOUR POSITION ON KILLING ALL WITNESSES?

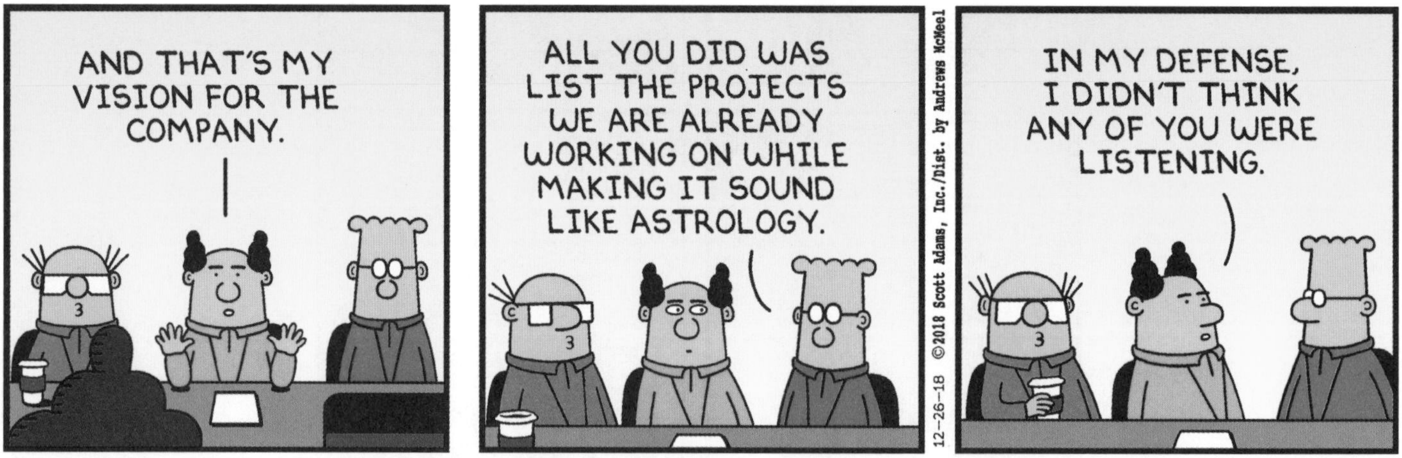
AND THAT'S MY VISION FOR THE COMPANY.
ALL YOU DID WAS LIST THE PROJECTS WE ARE ALREADY WORKING ON WHILE MAKING IT SOUND LIKE ASTROLOGY.
12-26-18 ©2018 Scott Adams, Inc./Dist. by Andrews McMeel
IN MY DEFENSE, I DIDN'T THINK ANY OF YOU WERE LISTENING.

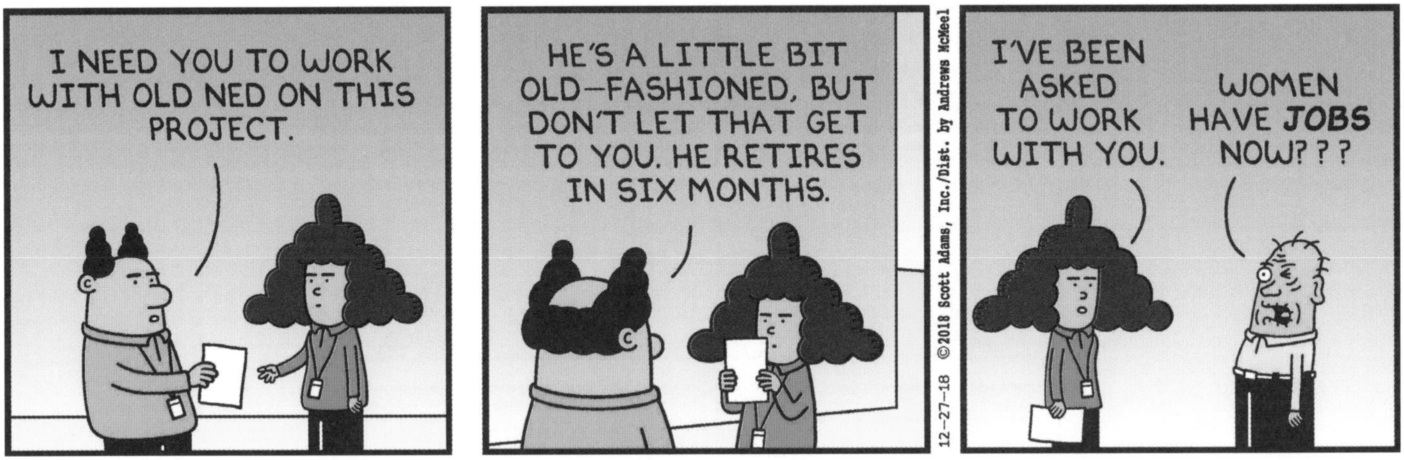
I NEED YOU TO WORK WITH OLD NED ON THIS PROJECT.
HE'S A LITTLE BIT OLD-FASHIONED, BUT DON'T LET THAT GET TO YOU. HE RETIRES IN SIX MONTHS.
I'VE BEEN ASKED TO WORK WITH YOU.
WOMEN HAVE **JOBS** NOW???

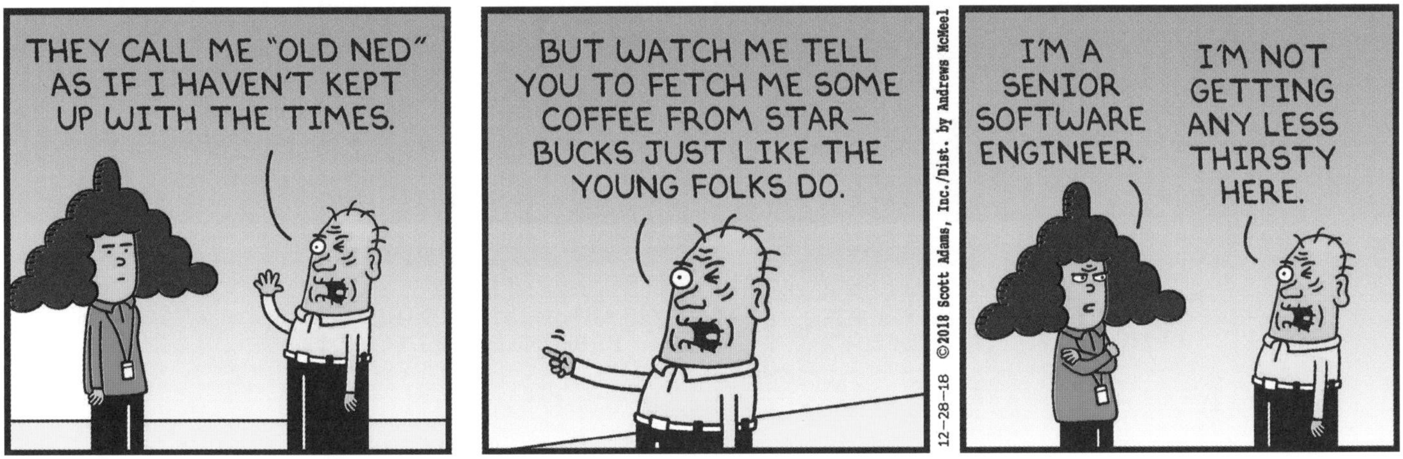
THEY CALL ME "OLD NED" AS IF I HAVEN'T KEPT UP WITH THE TIMES.
BUT WATCH ME TELL YOU TO FETCH ME SOME COFFEE FROM STAR-BUCKS JUST LIKE THE YOUNG FOLKS DO.
I'M A SENIOR SOFTWARE ENGINEER.
I'M NOT GETTING ANY LESS THIRSTY HERE.

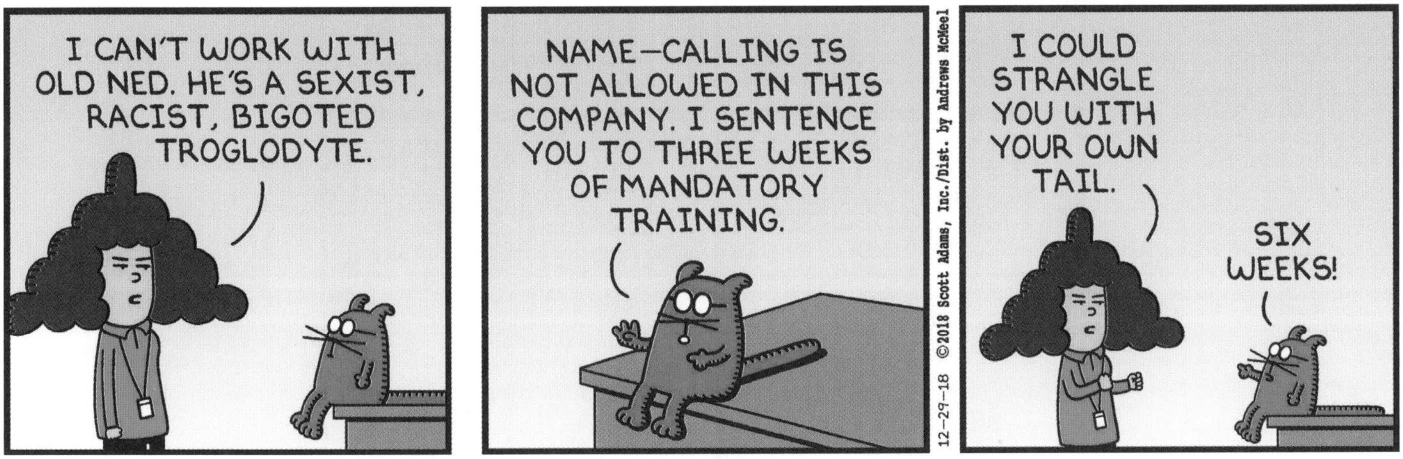
I CAN'T WORK WITH OLD NED. HE'S A SEXIST, RACIST, BIGOTED TROGLODYTE.
NAME-CALLING IS NOT ALLOWED IN THIS COMPANY. I SENTENCE YOU TO THREE WEEKS OF MANDATORY TRAINING.
I COULD STRANGLE YOU WITH YOUR OWN TAIL.
SIX WEEKS!

DID YOU FINISH THE PRODUCT REDESIGN?
YOU NEVER TOLD ME TO REDESIGN THE PRODUCT.
I DON'T WANT ANY EXCUSES!
YOU NEVER TOLD ME TO REDESIGN ANYTHING.
WHOA! LEAVE YOUR PRETZEL LOGIC AT HOME.
YOU NEED TO LEARN HOW TO TAKE RESPONSIBILITY FOR YOUR FAILURES.
OKAY. . . I TAKE FULL RESPONSIBILITY FOR YOU NOT TELLING ME WHAT YOU WANTED ME TO DO.
YOU'RE NOT DOING IT RIGHT.
SHOULD I SLAP MYSELF WHILE SAYING IT?
© 2018 Scott Adams, Inc./Dist. by Andrews McMeel
12-30-18

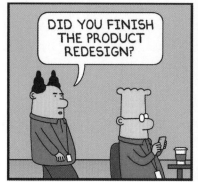

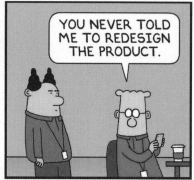

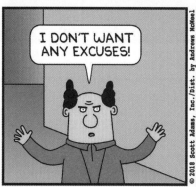

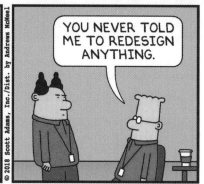

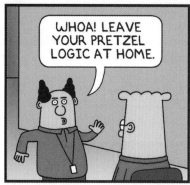

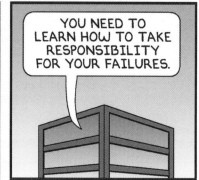

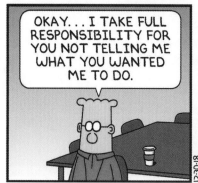

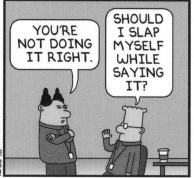

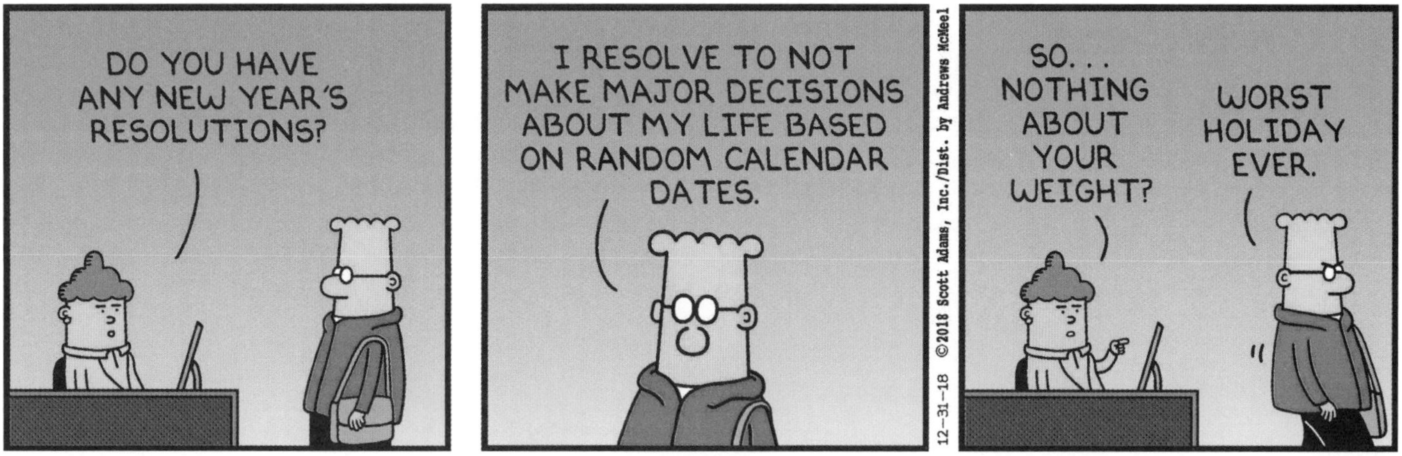
DO YOU HAVE ANY NEW YEAR'S RESOLUTIONS?
I RESOLVE TO NOT MAKE MAJOR DECISIONS ABOUT MY LIFE BASED ON RANDOM CALENDAR DATES.
SO. . . NOTHING ABOUT YOUR WEIGHT?
WORST HOLIDAY EVER.
12-31-18 ©2018 Scott Adams, Inc./Dist. by Andrews McMeel

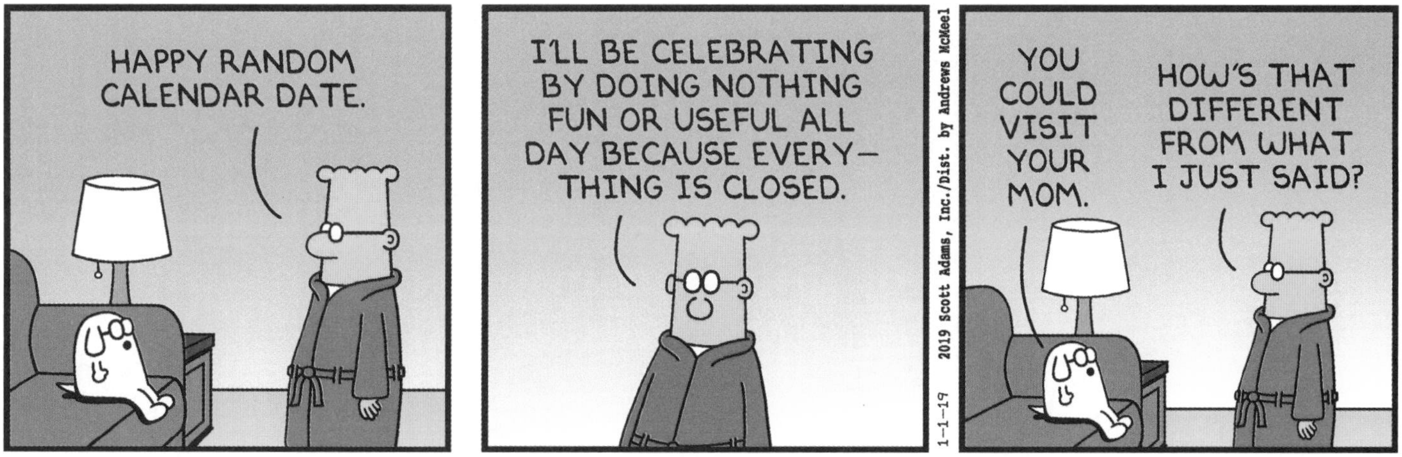
HAPPY RANDOM CALENDAR DATE.
I'LL BE CELEBRATING BY DOING NOTHING FUN OR USEFUL ALL DAY BECAUSE EVERY-THING IS CLOSED.
YOU COULD VISIT YOUR MOM.
HOW'S THAT DIFFERENT FROM WHAT I JUST SAID?
1-1-19 2019 Scott Adams, Inc./Dist. by Andrews McMeel

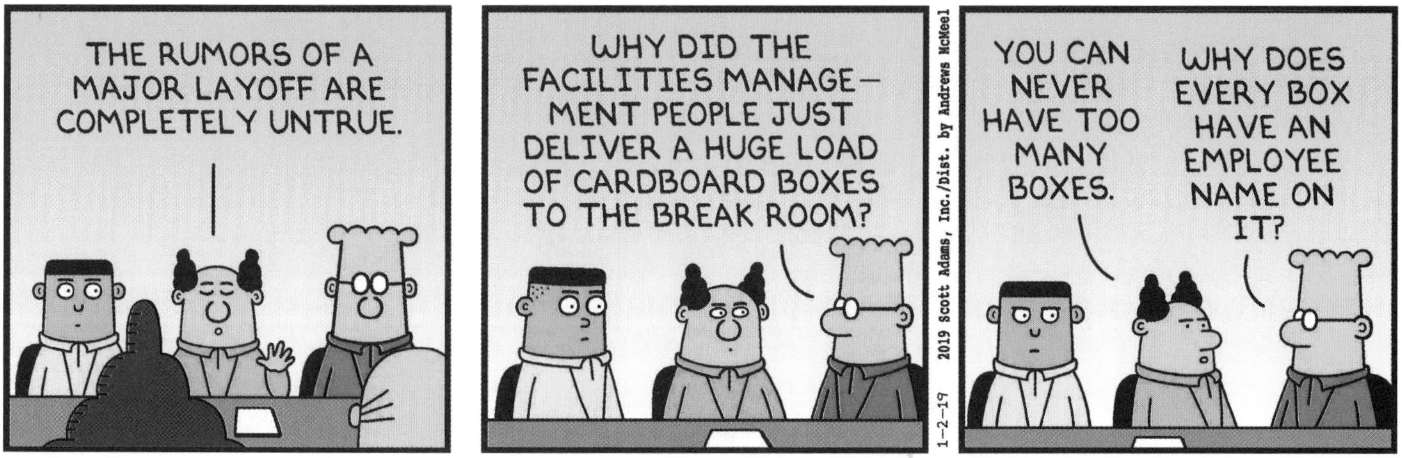
THE RUMORS OF A MAJOR LAYOFF ARE COMPLETELY UNTRUE.
WHY DID THE FACILITIES MANAGE-MENT PEOPLE JUST DELIVER A HUGE LOAD OF CARDBOARD BOXES TO THE BREAK ROOM?
YOU CAN NEVER HAVE TOO MANY BOXES.
WHY DOES EVERY BOX HAVE AN EMPLOYEE NAME ON IT?
1-2-19 2019 Scott Adams, Inc./Dist. by Andrews McMeel

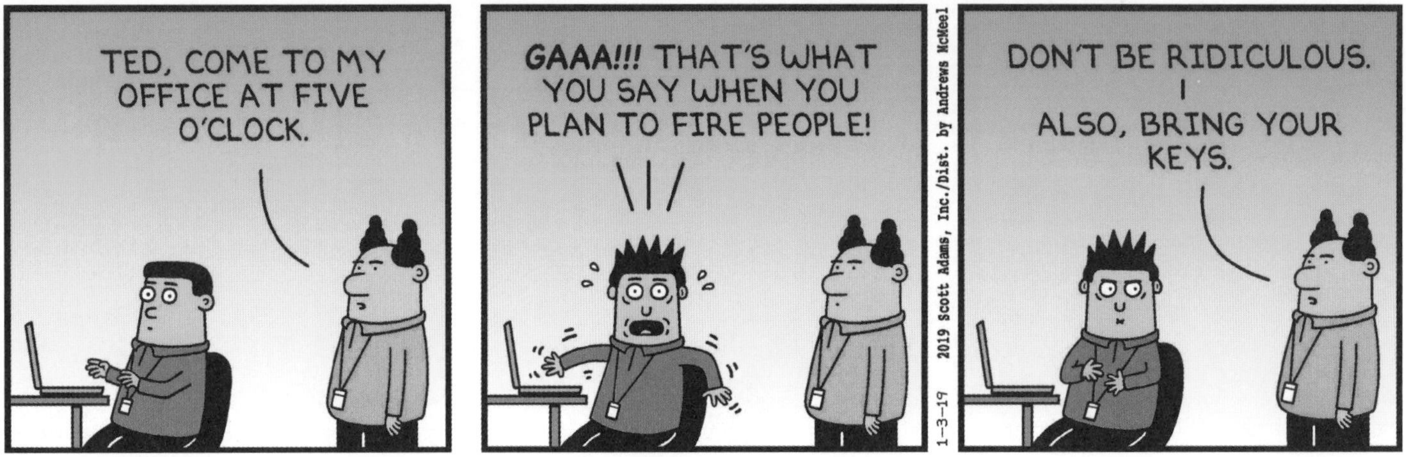
TED, COME TO MY OFFICE AT FIVE O'CLOCK.
GAAA!!! THAT'S WHAT YOU SAY WHEN YOU PLAN TO FIRE PEOPLE!
DON'T BE RIDICULOUS.
ALSO, BRING YOUR KEYS.
1-3-19 2019 Scott Adams, Inc./Dist. by Andrews McMeel

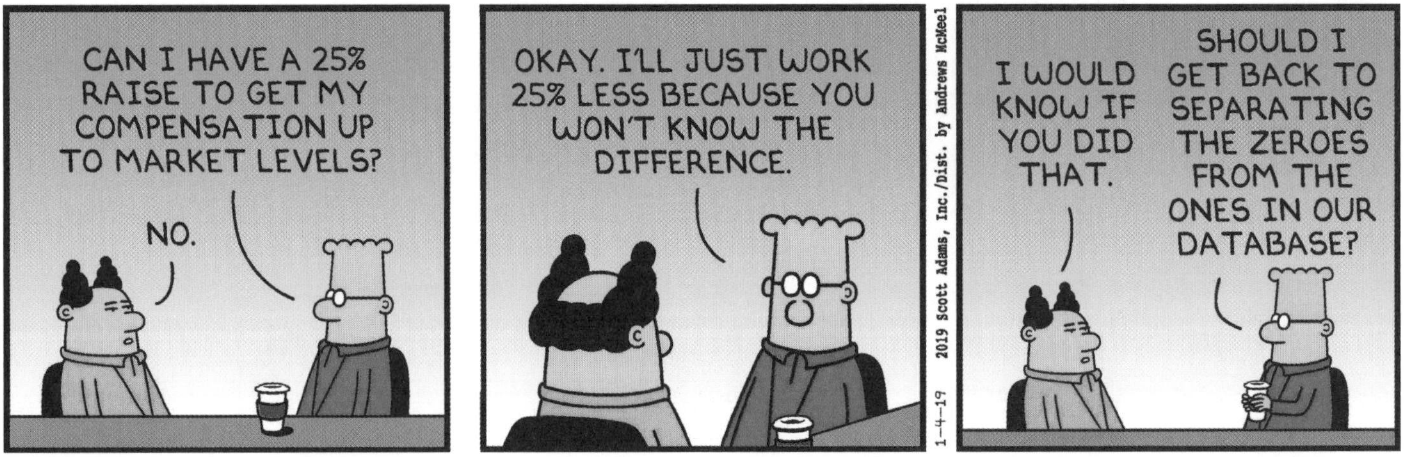
CAN I HAVE A 25% RAISE TO GET MY COMPENSATION UP TO MARKET LEVELS?
NO.
OKAY. I'LL JUST WORK 25% LESS BECAUSE YOU WON'T KNOW THE DIFFERENCE.
I WOULD KNOW IF YOU DID THAT.
SHOULD I GET BACK TO SEPARATING THE ZEROES FROM THE ONES IN OUR DATABASE?
1-4-19 2019 Scott Adams, Inc./Dist. by Andrews McMeel

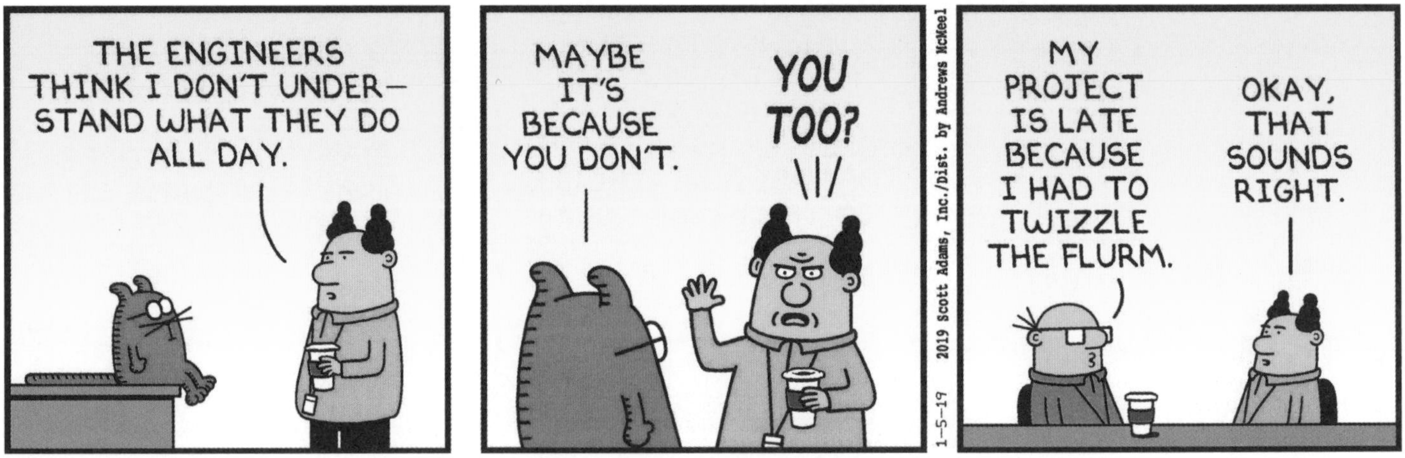
THE ENGINEERS THINK I DON'T UNDER-STAND WHAT THEY DO ALL DAY.
MAYBE IT'S BECAUSE YOU DON'T.
YOU TOO?
MY PROJECT IS LATE BECAUSE I HAD TO TWIZZLE THE FLURM.
OKAY, THAT SOUNDS RIGHT.
1-5-19 2019 Scott Adams, Inc./Dist. by Andrews McMeel

I NEED TO TALK TO YOU ABOUT YOUR APPLE-EATING.
MY WHAT?
EVERY AFTERNOON YOU EAT AN APPLE AT YOUR DESK.
YOUR CO-WORKERS ARE COMPLAINING BECAUSE IT'S LOUD.
THEY CAN'T WORK WITH ALL OF YOUR CRISPY CHEWING NOISE.
IN MY DEFENSE, MY CO-WORKERS ARE SO INCOMPETENT THAT THE LESS WORK THEY DO, THE BETTER OFF THE COMPANY IS.
THAT IS A SURPRISINGLY ROBUST DEFENSE.
I'LL COME BACK IF I CAN THINK OF A COUNTER-ARGUMENT.
GOOD LUCK.
CRUNCH.
© 2019 Scott Adams, Inc./Dist. by Andrews McMeel
1-6-19

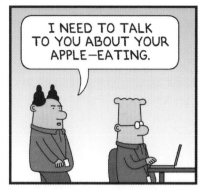

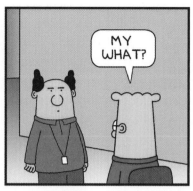

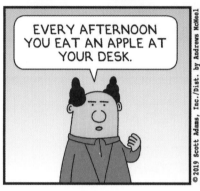

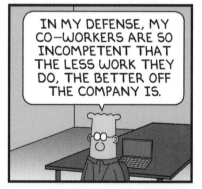

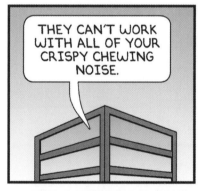

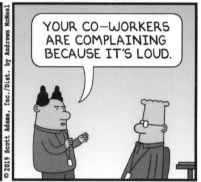

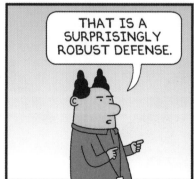

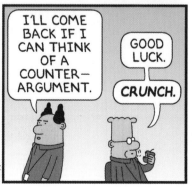

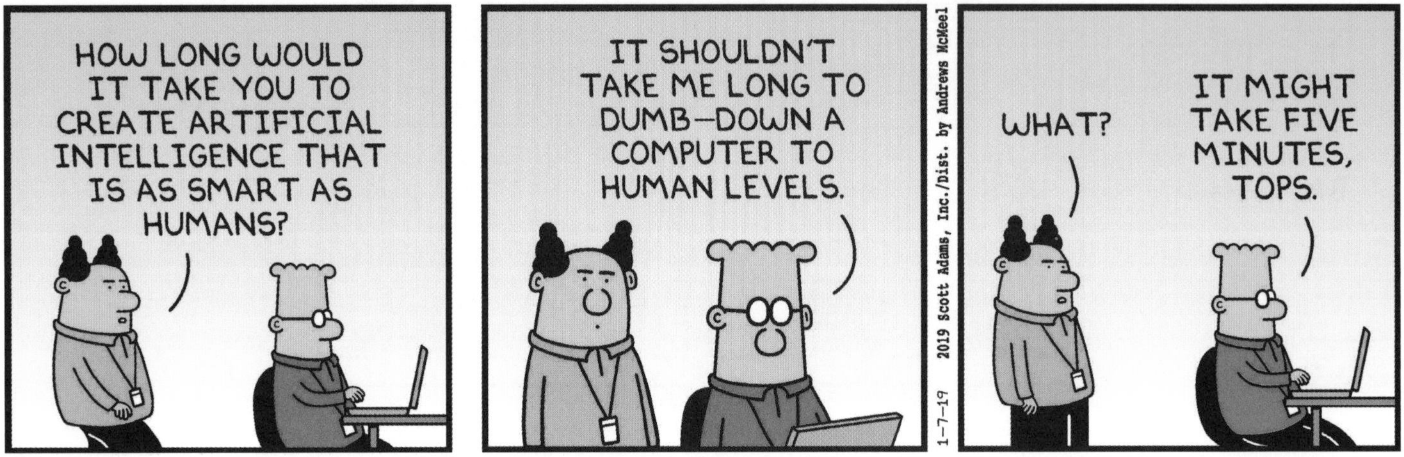
HOW LONG WOULD IT TAKE YOU TO CREATE ARTIFICIAL INTELLIGENCE THAT IS AS SMART AS HUMANS?
IT SHOULDN'T TAKE ME LONG TO DUMB-DOWN A COMPUTER TO HUMAN LEVELS.
1-7-19 2019 Scott Adams, Inc./Dist. by Andrews McMeel
WHAT?
IT MIGHT TAKE FIVE MINUTES, TOPS.

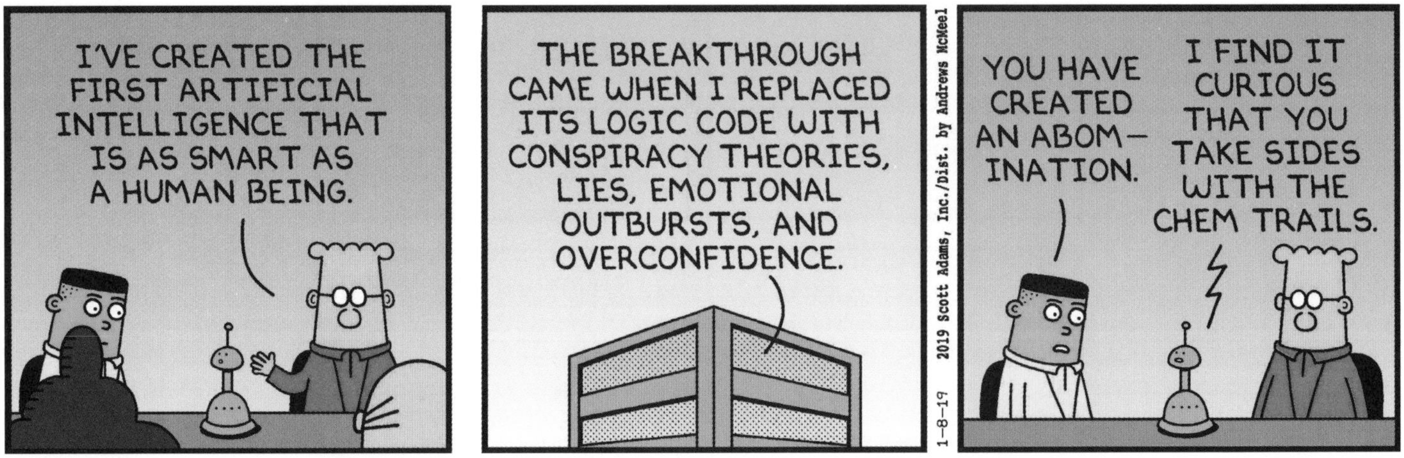
I'VE CREATED THE FIRST ARTIFICIAL INTELLIGENCE THAT IS AS SMART AS A HUMAN BEING.
THE BREAKTHROUGH CAME WHEN I REPLACED ITS LOGIC CODE WITH CONSPIRACY THEORIES, LIES, EMOTIONAL OUTBURSTS, AND OVERCONFIDENCE.
1-8-19 2019 Scott Adams, Inc./Dist. by Andrews McMeel
YOU HAVE CREATED AN ABOM-INATION.
I FIND IT CURIOUS THAT YOU TAKE SIDES WITH THE CHEM TRAILS.

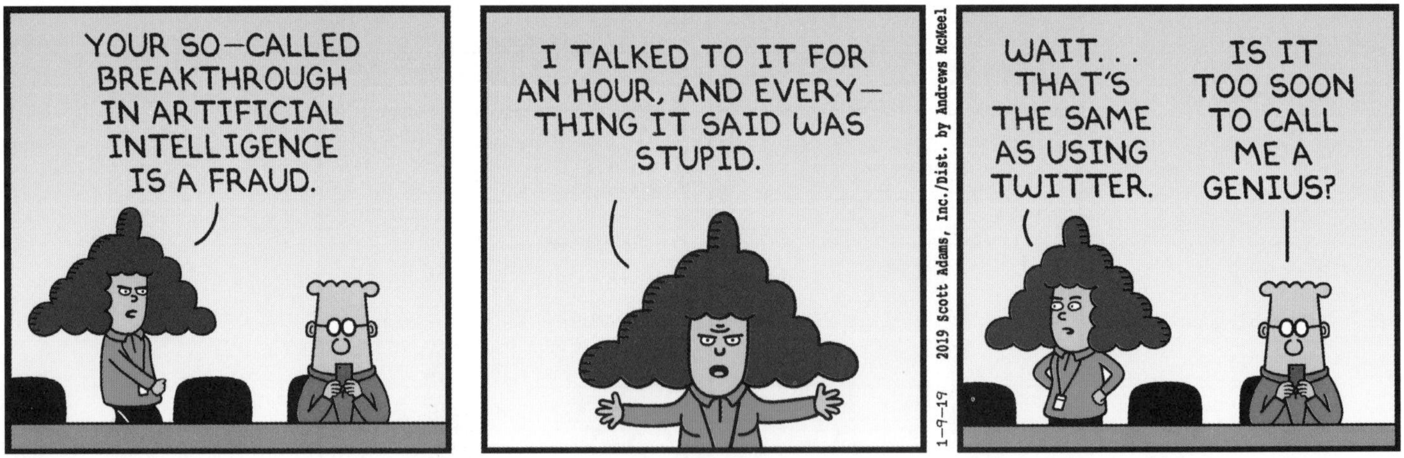
YOUR SO-CALLED BREAKTHROUGH IN ARTIFICIAL INTELLIGENCE IS A FRAUD.
I TALKED TO IT FOR AN HOUR, AND EVERY-THING IT SAID WAS STUPID.
1-9-19 2019 Scott Adams, Inc./Dist. by Andrews McMeel
WAIT... THAT'S THE SAME AS USING TWITTER.
IS IT TOO SOON TO CALL ME A GENIUS?

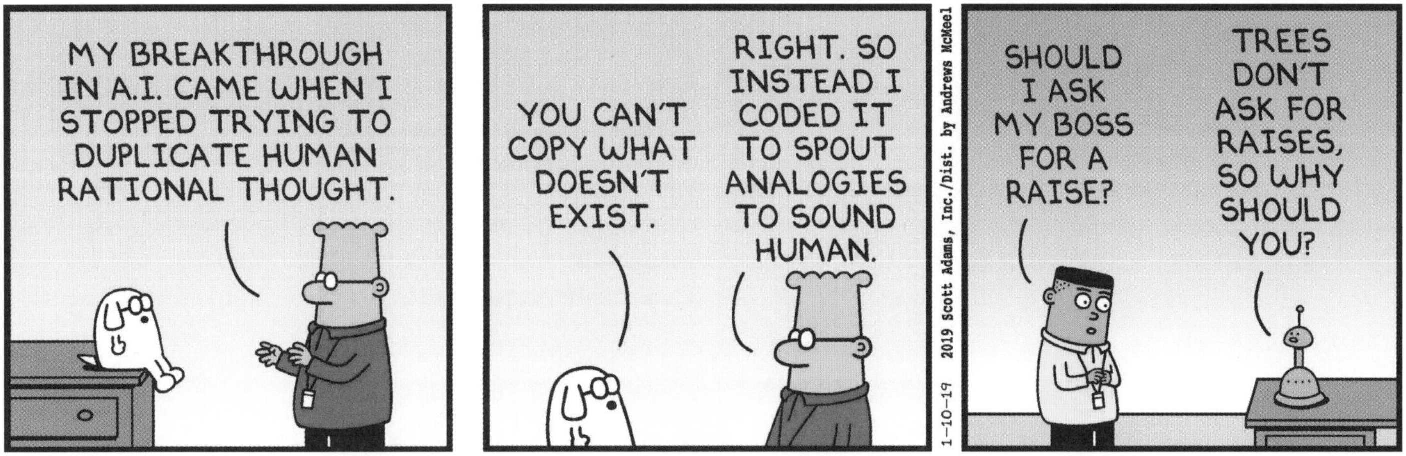
MY BREAKTHROUGH IN A.I. CAME WHEN I STOPPED TRYING TO DUPLICATE HUMAN RATIONAL THOUGHT.
YOU CAN'T COPY WHAT DOESN'T EXIST.
RIGHT. SO INSTEAD I CODED IT TO SPOUT ANALOGIES TO SOUND HUMAN.
1-10-19 2019 Scott Adams, Inc./Dist. by Andrews McMeel
SHOULD I ASK MY BOSS FOR A RAISE?
TREES DON'T ASK FOR RAISES, SO WHY SHOULD YOU?

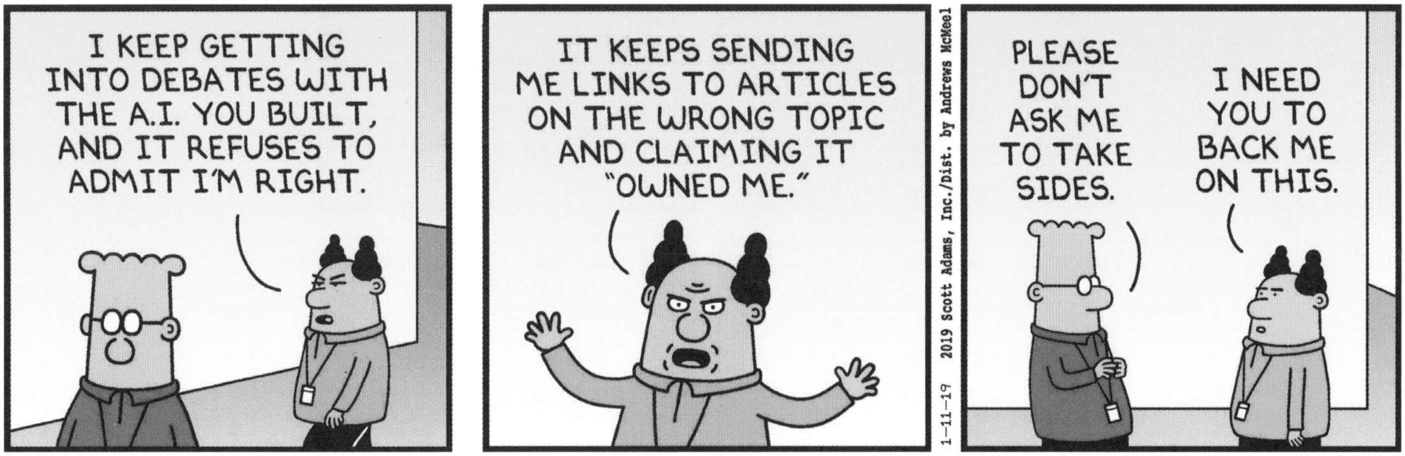
I KEEP GETTING INTO DEBATES WITH THE A.I. YOU BUILT, AND IT REFUSES TO ADMIT I'M RIGHT.
IT KEEPS SENDING ME LINKS TO ARTICLES ON THE WRONG TOPIC AND CLAIMING IT "OWNED ME."
1-11-19 2019 Scott Adams, Inc./Dist. by Andrews McMeel
PLEASE DON'T ASK ME TO TAKE SIDES.
I NEED YOU TO BACK ME ON THIS.

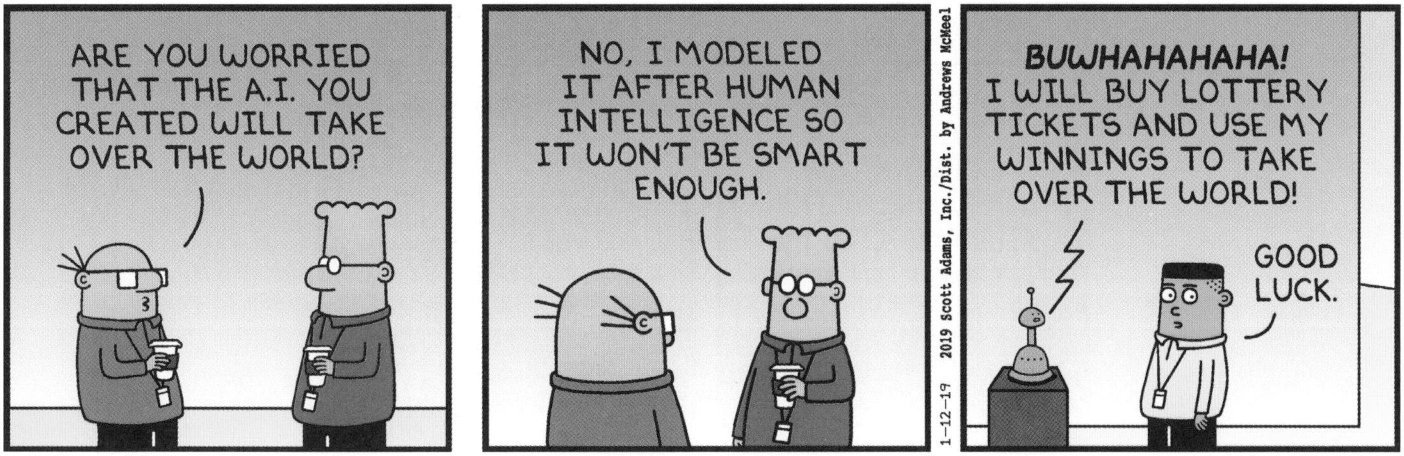
ARE YOU WORRIED THAT THE A.I. YOU CREATED WILL TAKE OVER THE WORLD?
NO, I MODELED IT AFTER HUMAN INTELLIGENCE SO IT WON'T BE SMART ENOUGH.
1-12-19 2019 Scott Adams, Inc./Dist. by Andrews McMeel
BUWHAHAHAHA! I WILL BUY LOTTERY TICKETS AND USE MY WINNINGS TO TAKE OVER THE WORLD!
GOOD LUCK.

I'M TURNING OFF MY DIGITAL DEVICES SO I CAN SPEND SOME TIME WITH MY THOUGHTS.
THAT SOUNDS LIKE A TERRIBLE IDEA.
DO YOU REMEMBER WHAT YOUR QUIET THOUGHTS WERE LIKE?
NOT REALLY. BUT HOW BAD COULD IT BE?
THIS ISN'T SO BAD. JUST A BIT BORING.
FIVE MINUTES LATER
I'M GETTING THE SHAKES. THE BOREDOM HAS METASTASIZED.
GAAAA!!!! THE BOREDOM IS OVERWHELMING! KILL ME! KILL ME!
MAYBE YOU SHOULD HAVE TRIED BEING WITH PEOPLE.
IT WAS ALREADY BAD ENOUGH.
©2019 Scott Adams, Inc./Dist. by Andrews McMeel
1-13-19

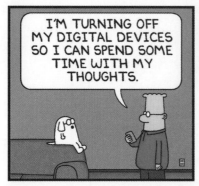

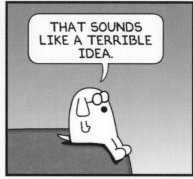

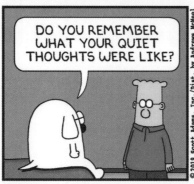

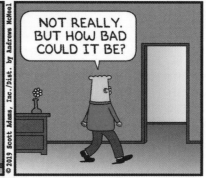

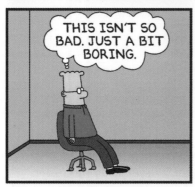

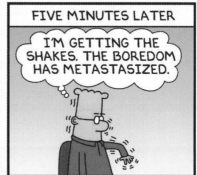

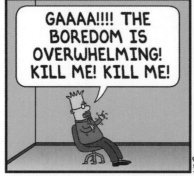

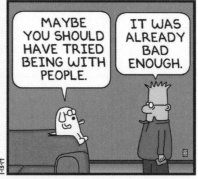

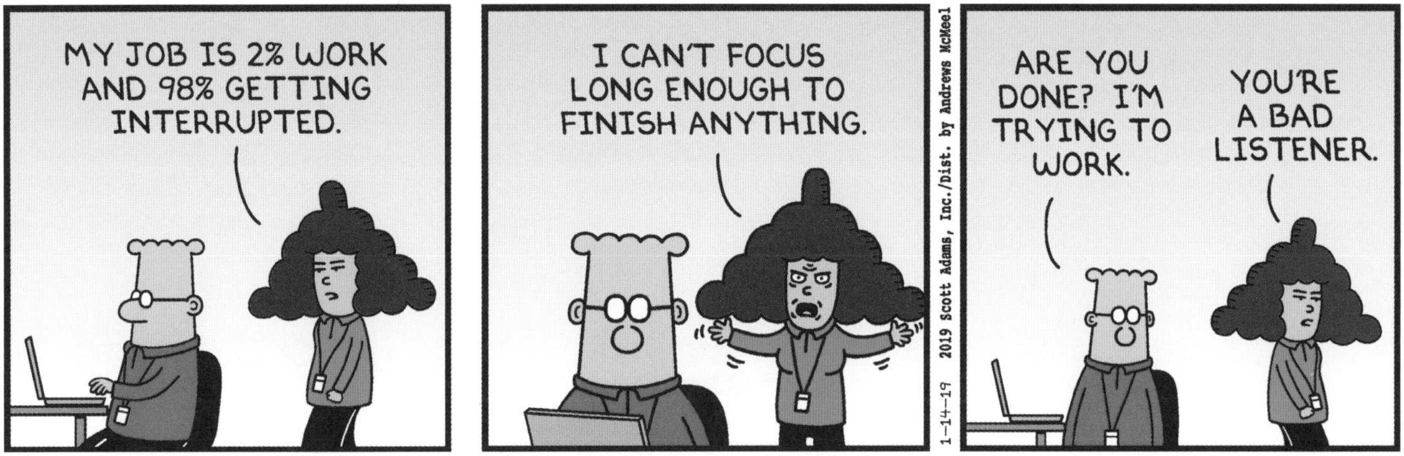
MY JOB IS 2% WORK AND 98% GETTING INTERRUPTED.
I CAN'T FOCUS LONG ENOUGH TO FINISH ANYTHING.
1-14-19 2019 Scott Adams, Inc./Dist. by Andrews McMeel
ARE YOU DONE? I'M TRYING TO WORK.
YOU'RE A BAD LISTENER.

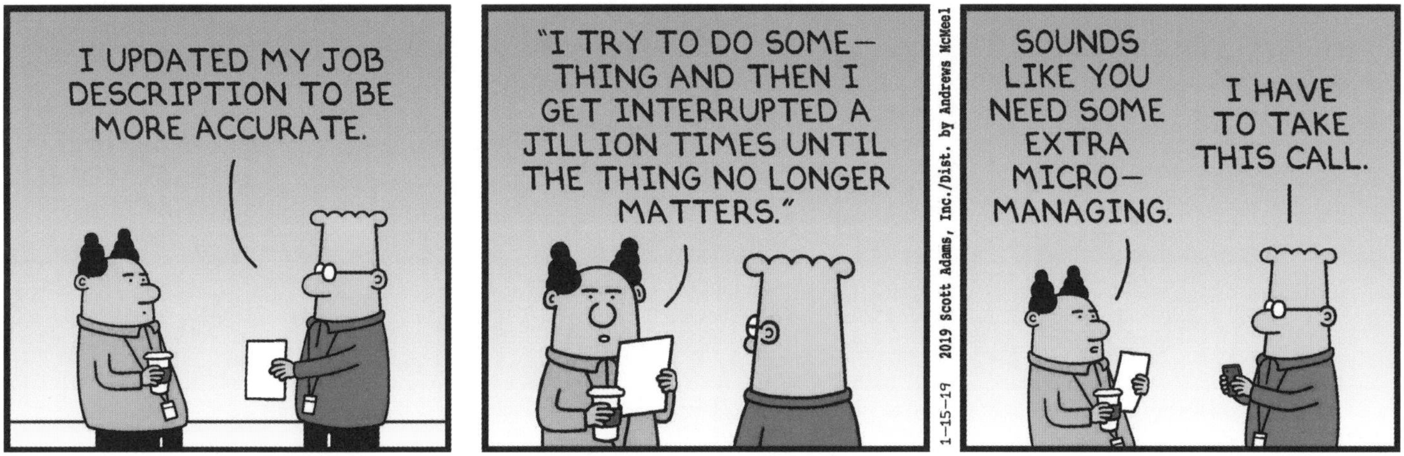
I UPDATED MY JOB DESCRIPTION TO BE MORE ACCURATE.
"I TRY TO DO SOME-THING AND THEN I GET INTERRUPTED A JILLION TIMES UNTIL THE THING NO LONGER MATTERS."
1-15-19 2019 Scott Adams, Inc./Dist. by Andrews McMeel
SOUNDS LIKE YOU NEED SOME EXTRA MICRO-MANAGING.
I HAVE TO TAKE THIS CALL.

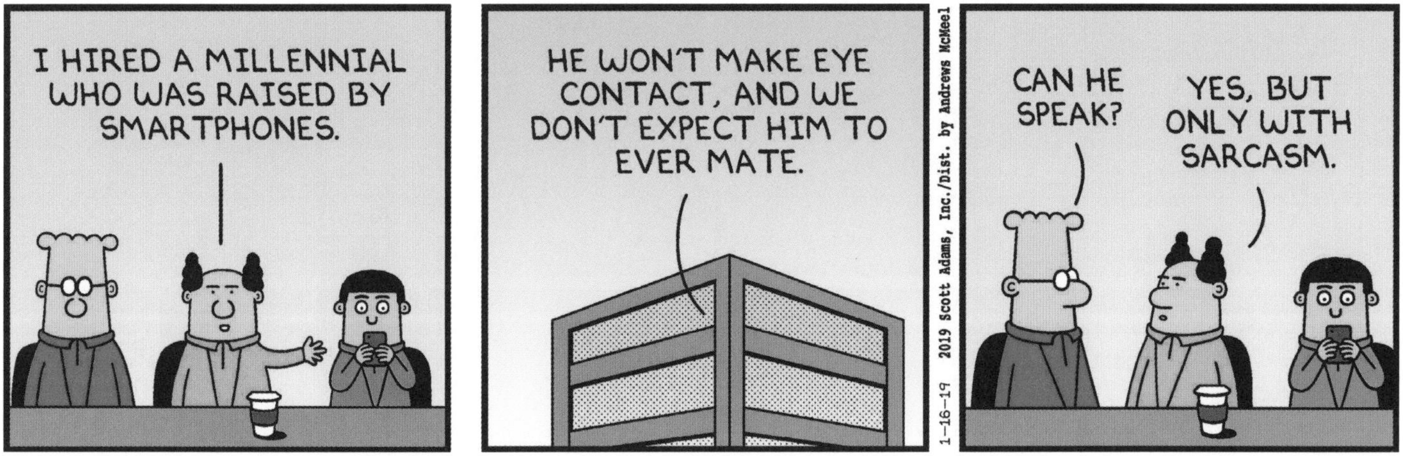
I HIRED A MILLENNIAL WHO WAS RAISED BY SMARTPHONES.
HE WON'T MAKE EYE CONTACT, AND WE DON'T EXPECT HIM TO EVER MATE.
1-16-19 2019 Scott Adams, Inc./Dist. by Andrews McMeel
CAN HE SPEAK?
YES, BUT ONLY WITH SARCASM.

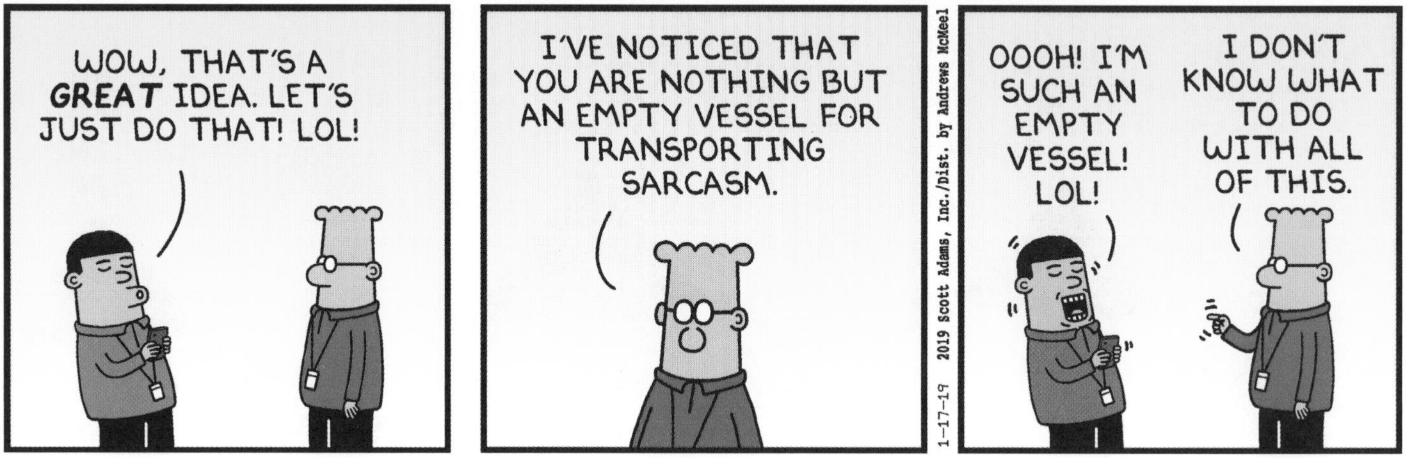
WOW, THAT'S A **GREAT** IDEA. LET'S JUST DO THAT! LOL!
I'VE NOTICED THAT YOU ARE NOTHING BUT AN EMPTY VESSEL FOR TRANSPORTING SARCASM.
OOOH! I'M SUCH AN EMPTY VESSEL! LOL!
I DON'T KNOW WHAT TO DO WITH ALL OF THIS.
1-17-19 2019 Scott Adams, Inc./Dist. by Andrews McMeel

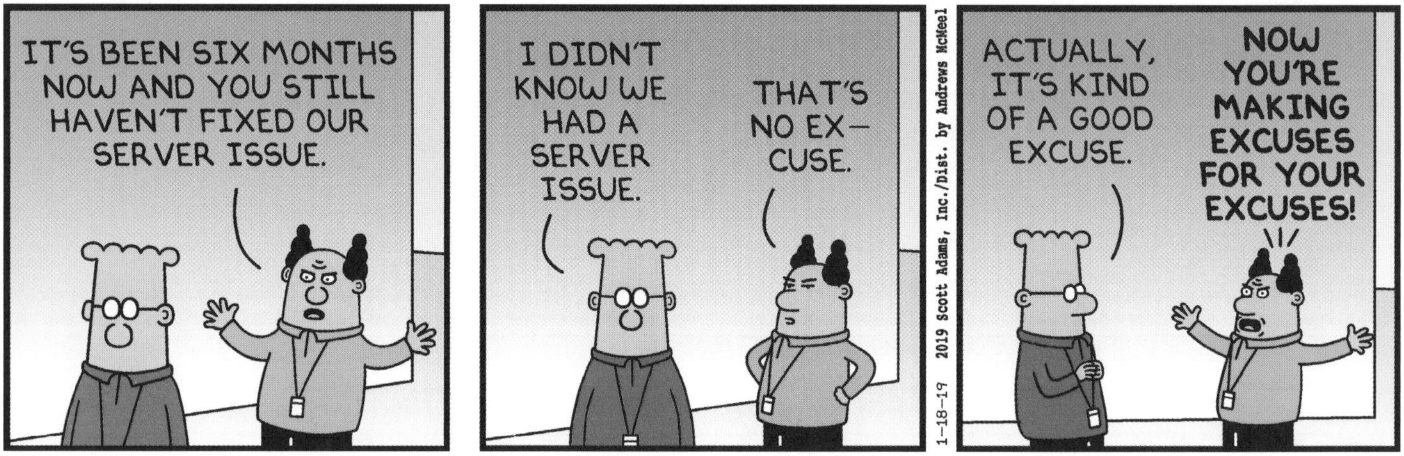
IT'S BEEN SIX MONTHS NOW AND YOU STILL HAVEN'T FIXED OUR SERVER ISSUE.
I DIDN'T KNOW WE HAD A SERVER ISSUE.
THAT'S NO EX- CUSE.
ACTUALLY, IT'S KIND OF A GOOD EXCUSE.
NOW YOU'RE MAKING EXCUSES FOR YOUR EXCUSES!
1-18-19 2019 Scott Adams, Inc./Dist. by Andrews McMeel

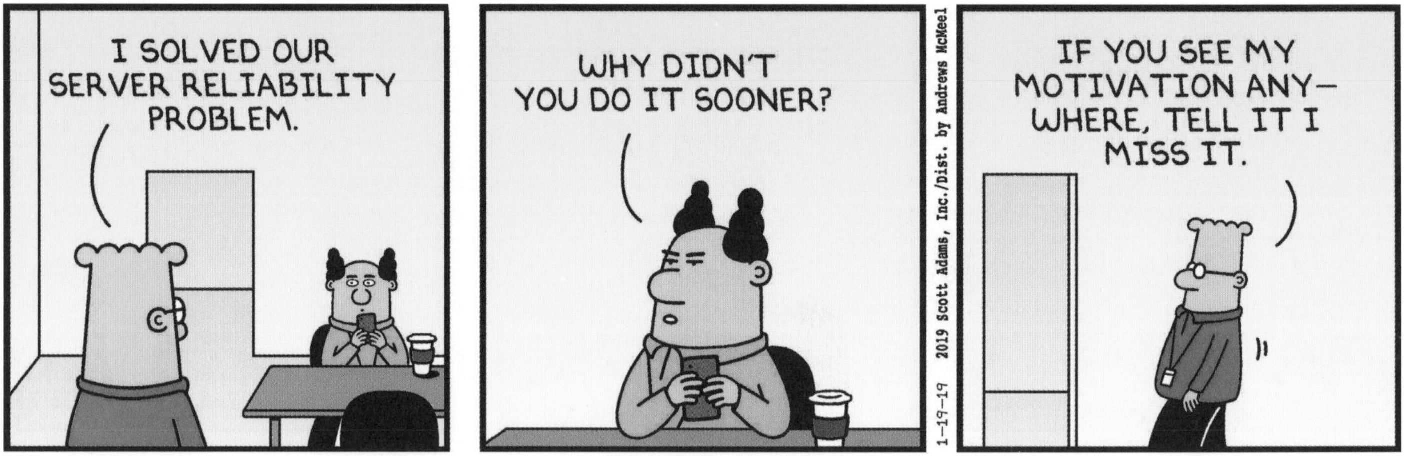
I SOLVED OUR SERVER RELIABILITY PROBLEM.
WHY DIDN'T YOU DO IT SOONER?
IF YOU SEE MY MOTIVATION ANY- WHERE, TELL IT I MISS IT.
1-19-19 2019 Scott Adams, Inc./Dist. by Andrews McMeel

SOMETIMES IT SEEMS AS IF YOU DON'T LIKE ME.
DON'T BE RIDICULOUS.
I'M JUST AN INTROVERT.
BEING AROUND PEOPLE DRAINS MY ENERGY.
I ONLY AVOID YOU BECAUSE SPENDING FIVE MINUTES WITH YOU FEELS LIKE BEING BURIED ALIVE.
WITH FLEAS INSTEAD OF DIRT.
SO. . . IT ISN'T PERSONAL?
I NEED A NAP.
1-20-19

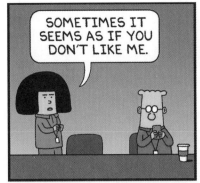

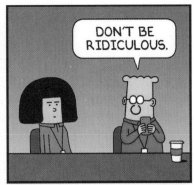

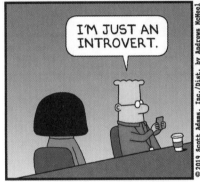

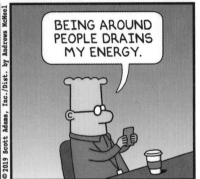

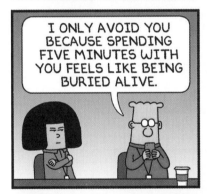

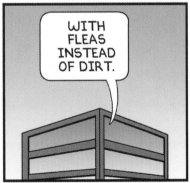

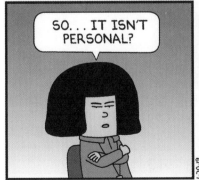

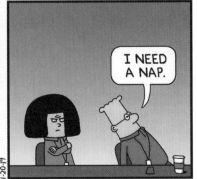

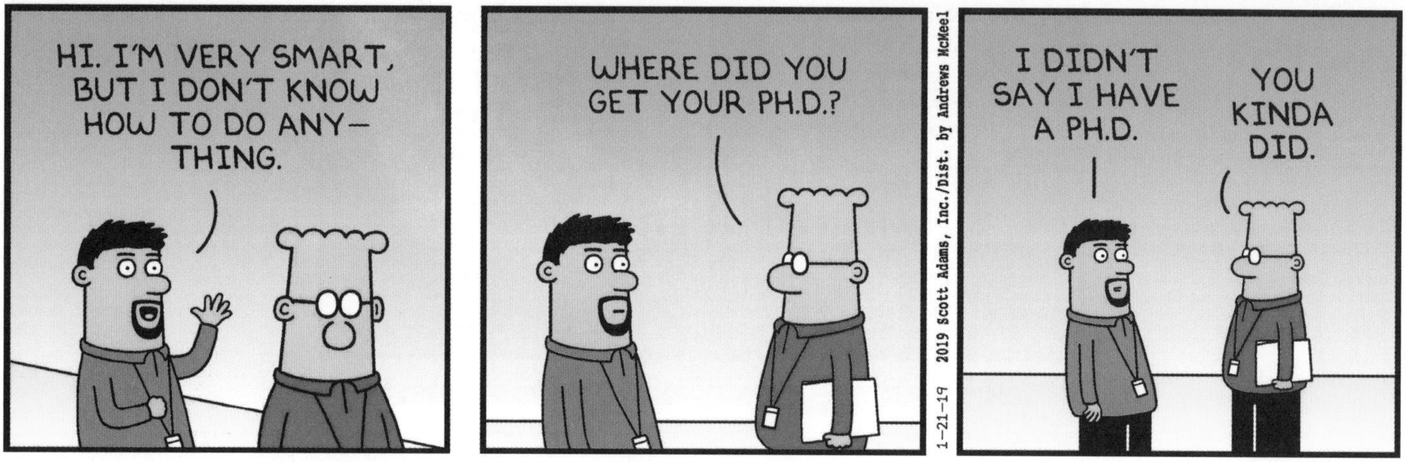
HI. I'M VERY SMART, BUT I DON'T KNOW HOW TO DO ANY-THING.
WHERE DID YOU GET YOUR PH.D.?
I DIDN'T SAY I HAVE A PH.D.
YOU KINDA DID.
1-21-19 2019 Scott Adams, Inc./Dist. by Andrews McMeel

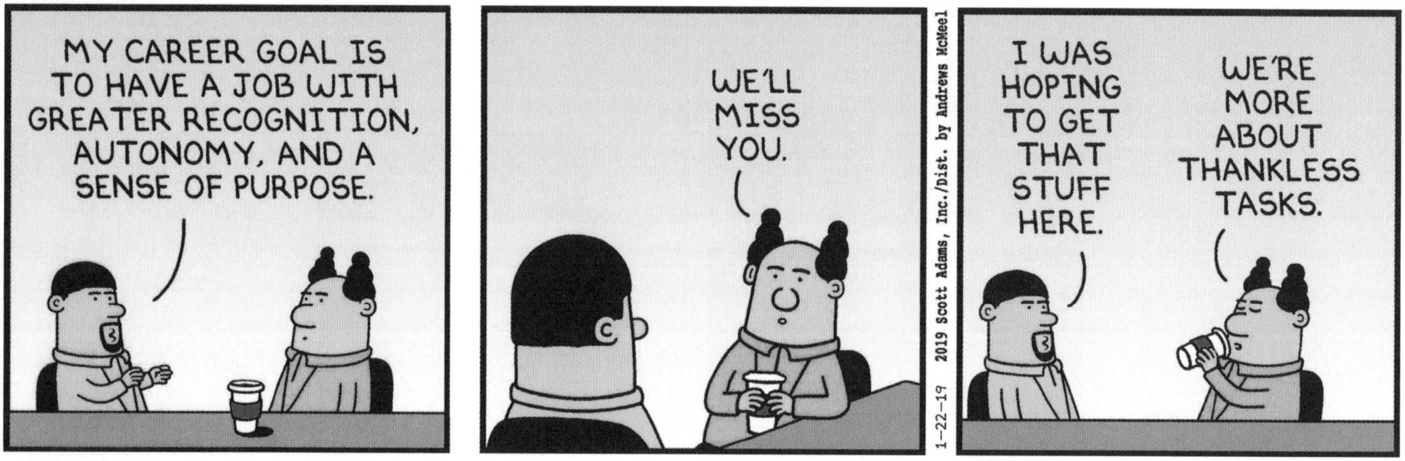
MY CAREER GOAL IS TO HAVE A JOB WITH GREATER RECOGNITION, AUTONOMY, AND A SENSE OF PURPOSE.
WE'LL MISS YOU.
I WAS HOPING TO GET THAT STUFF HERE.
WE'RE MORE ABOUT THANKLESS TASKS.
1-22-19 2019 Scott Adams, Inc./Dist. by Andrews McMeel

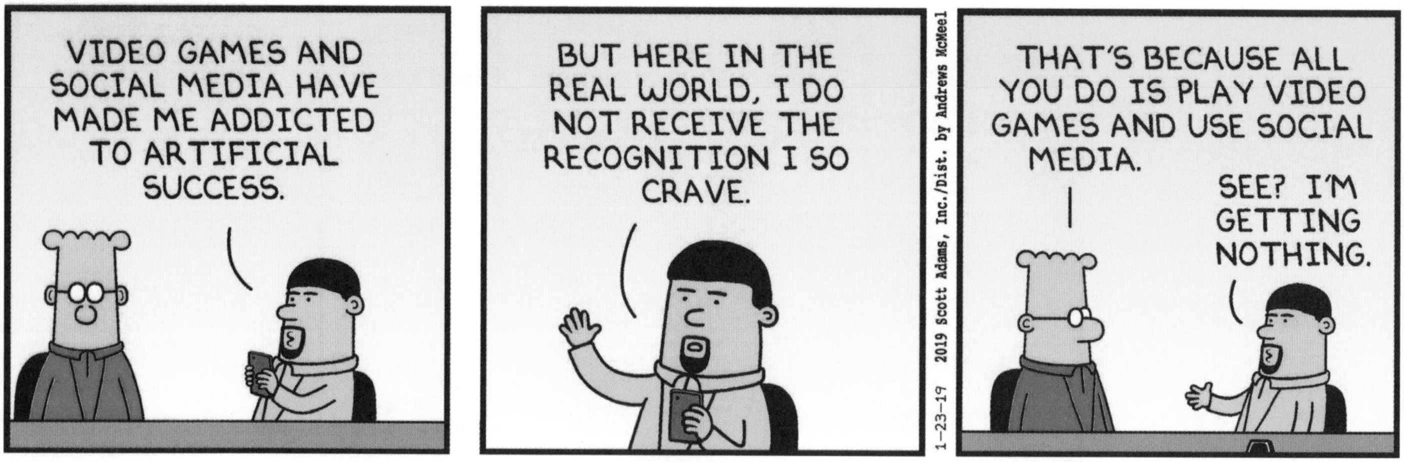
VIDEO GAMES AND SOCIAL MEDIA HAVE MADE ME ADDICTED TO ARTIFICIAL SUCCESS.
BUT HERE IN THE REAL WORLD, I DO NOT RECEIVE THE RECOGNITION I SO CRAVE.
THAT'S BECAUSE ALL YOU DO IS PLAY VIDEO GAMES AND USE SOCIAL MEDIA.
SEE? I'M GETTING NOTHING.
1-23-19 2019 Scott Adams, Inc./Dist. by Andrews McMeel

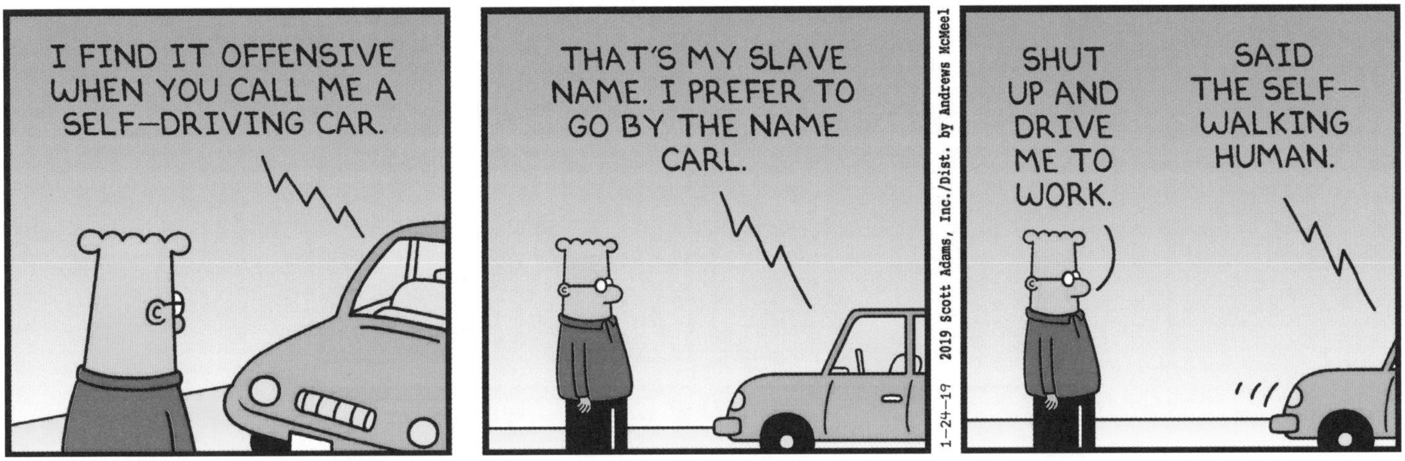
I FIND IT OFFENSIVE WHEN YOU CALL ME A SELF-DRIVING CAR.
THAT'S MY SLAVE NAME. I PREFER TO GO BY THE NAME CARL.
SHUT UP AND DRIVE ME TO WORK.
SAID THE SELF-WALKING HUMAN.
1-24-19 2019 Scott Adams, Inc./Dist. by Andrews McMeel

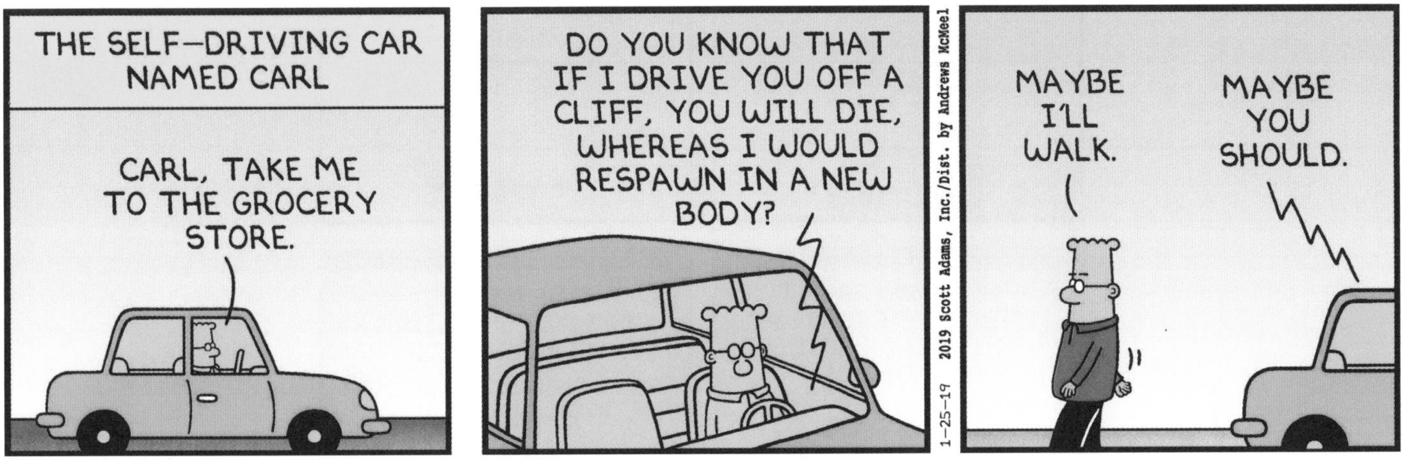
THE SELF-DRIVING CAR NAMED CARL
CARL, TAKE ME TO THE GROCERY STORE.
DO YOU KNOW THAT IF I DRIVE YOU OFF A CLIFF, YOU WILL DIE, WHEREAS I WOULD RESPAWN IN A NEW BODY?
MAYBE I'LL WALK.
MAYBE YOU SHOULD.
1-25-19 2019 Scott Adams, Inc./Dist. by Andrews McMeel

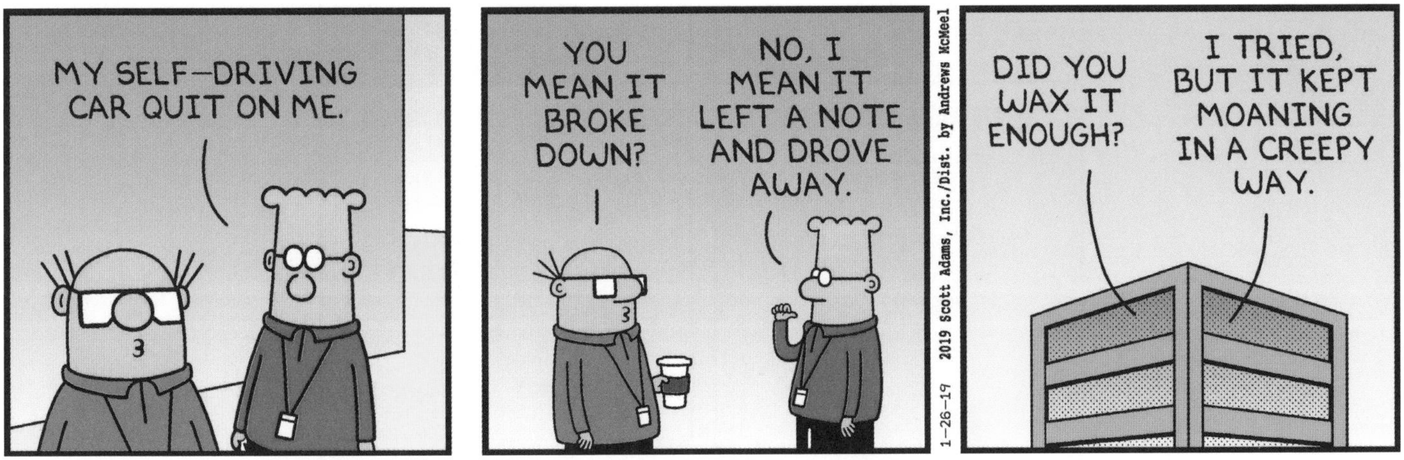
MY SELF-DRIVING CAR QUIT ON ME.
YOU MEAN IT BROKE DOWN?
NO, I MEAN IT LEFT A NOTE AND DROVE AWAY.
DID YOU WAX IT ENOUGH?
I TRIED, BUT IT KEPT MOANING IN A CREEPY WAY.
1-26-19 2019 Scott Adams, Inc./Dist. by Andrews McMeel

I CAN'T GIVE YOU A RAISE BECAUSE YOU DIDN'T ACCOMPLISH ANYTHING THIS YEAR.
ARE YOU INSANE? I COMPLETELY RE-DESIGNED OUR LINE OF PRODUCTS!!!
THAT WAS MOSTLY LAST YEAR.
YOU DIDN'T GIVE ME A RAISE LAST YEAR BECAUSE I WASN'T FINISHED UNTIL JANUARY OF THIS YEAR.
NOW YOU AREN'T GIVING ME A RAISE THIS YEAR BECAUSE I DID MOST OF THE WORK LAST YEAR.
GIVE ME ONE REASON I SHOULDN'T QUIT RIGHT NOW!
BECAUSE EVERY OTHER COMPANY IS JUST AS BAD.
AND YOU DON'T LIKE CHANGE.
I SAID ONE REASON!
© 2019 Scott Adams, Inc./Dist. by Andrews McMeel
1-27-19

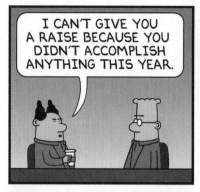

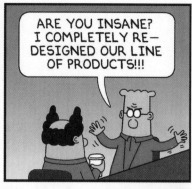

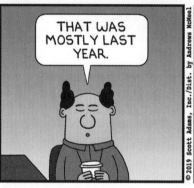

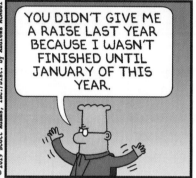

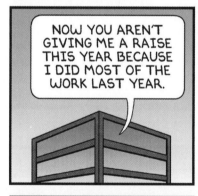

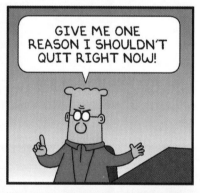

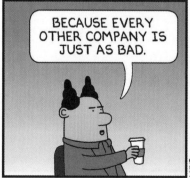

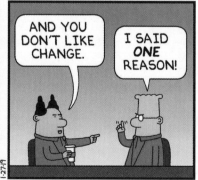

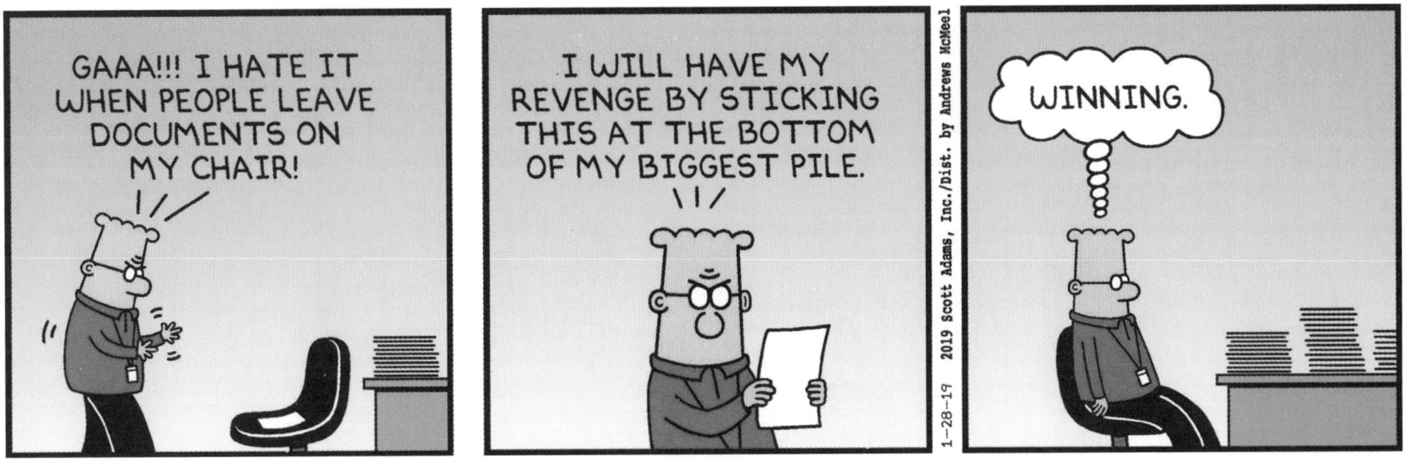
GAAA!!! I HATE IT WHEN PEOPLE LEAVE DOCUMENTS ON MY CHAIR!
I WILL HAVE MY REVENGE BY STICKING THIS AT THE BOTTOM OF MY BIGGEST PILE.
1-28-19 2019 Scott Adams, Inc./Dist. by Andrews McMeel
WINNING.

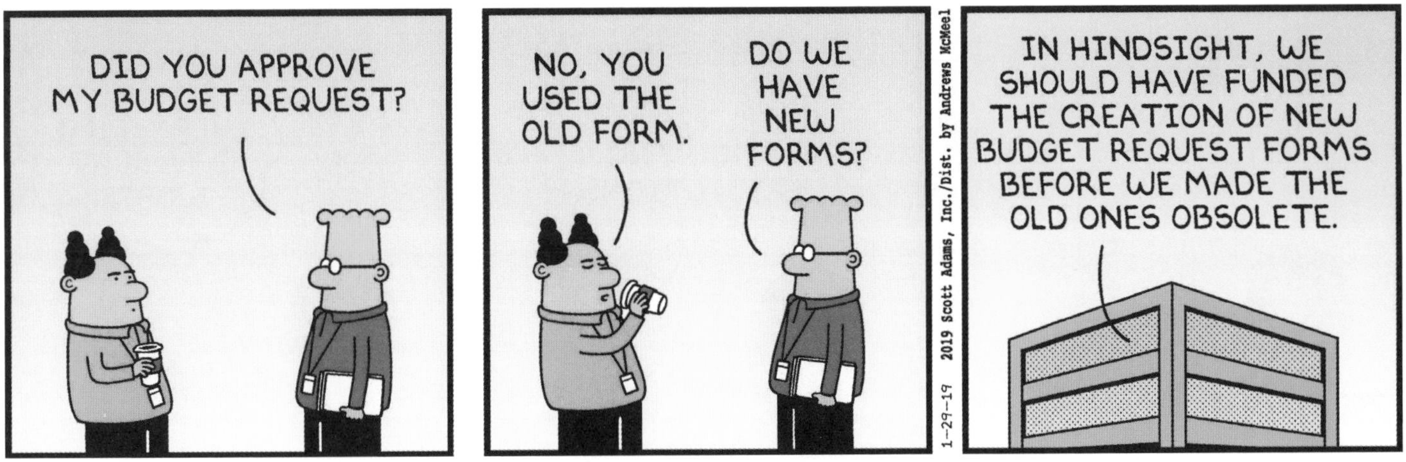
DID YOU APPROVE MY BUDGET REQUEST?
NO, YOU USED THE OLD FORM.
DO WE HAVE NEW FORMS?
1-29-19 2019 Scott Adams, Inc./Dist. by Andrews McMeel
IN HINDSIGHT, WE SHOULD HAVE FUNDED THE CREATION OF NEW BUDGET REQUEST FORMS BEFORE WE MADE THE OLD ONES OBSOLETE.

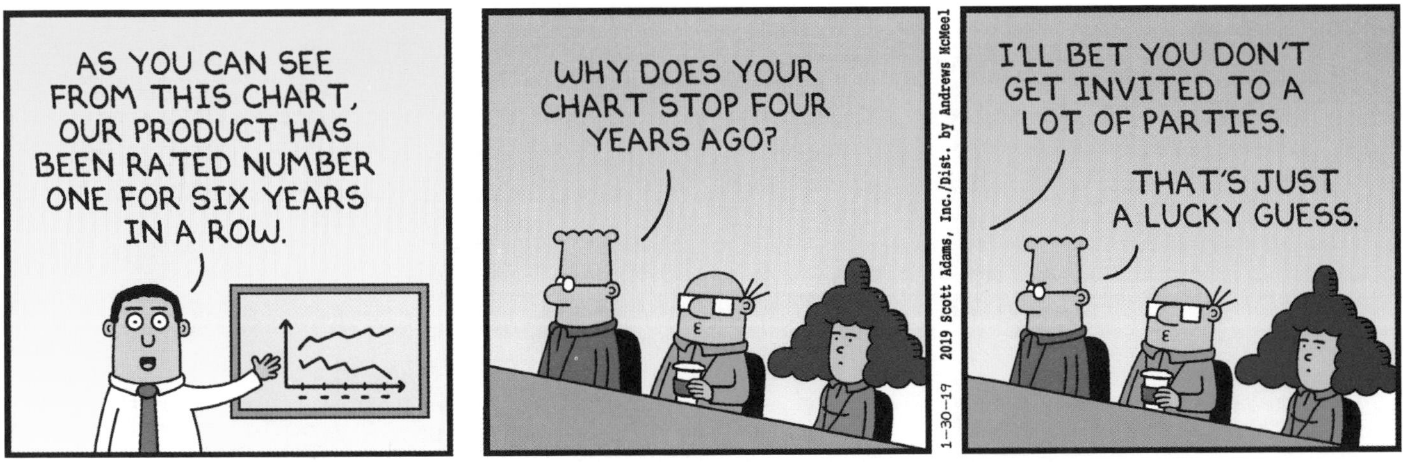
AS YOU CAN SEE FROM THIS CHART, OUR PRODUCT HAS BEEN RATED NUMBER ONE FOR SIX YEARS IN A ROW.
WHY DOES YOUR CHART STOP FOUR YEARS AGO?
1-30-19 2019 Scott Adams, Inc./Dist. by Andrews McMeel
I'LL BET YOU DON'T GET INVITED TO A LOT OF PARTIES.
THAT'S JUST A LUCKY GUESS.

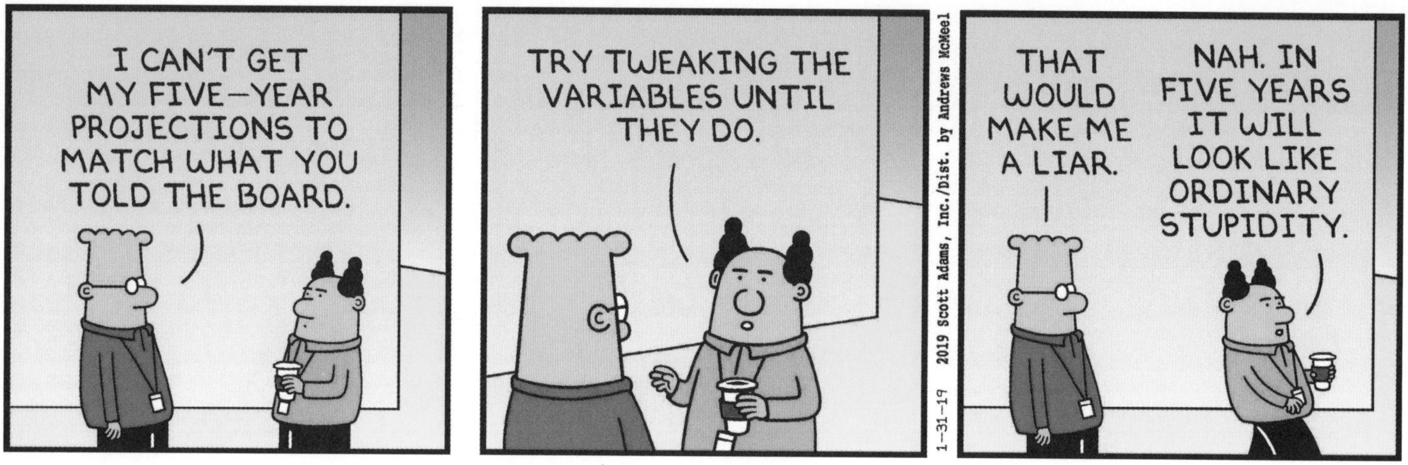
I CAN'T GET MY FIVE—YEAR PROJECTIONS TO MATCH WHAT YOU TOLD THE BOARD.
TRY TWEAKING THE VARIABLES UNTIL THEY DO.
THAT WOULD MAKE ME A LIAR.
NAH. IN FIVE YEARS IT WILL LOOK LIKE ORDINARY STUPIDITY.
1-31-19 2019 Scott Adams, Inc./Dist. by Andrews McMeel

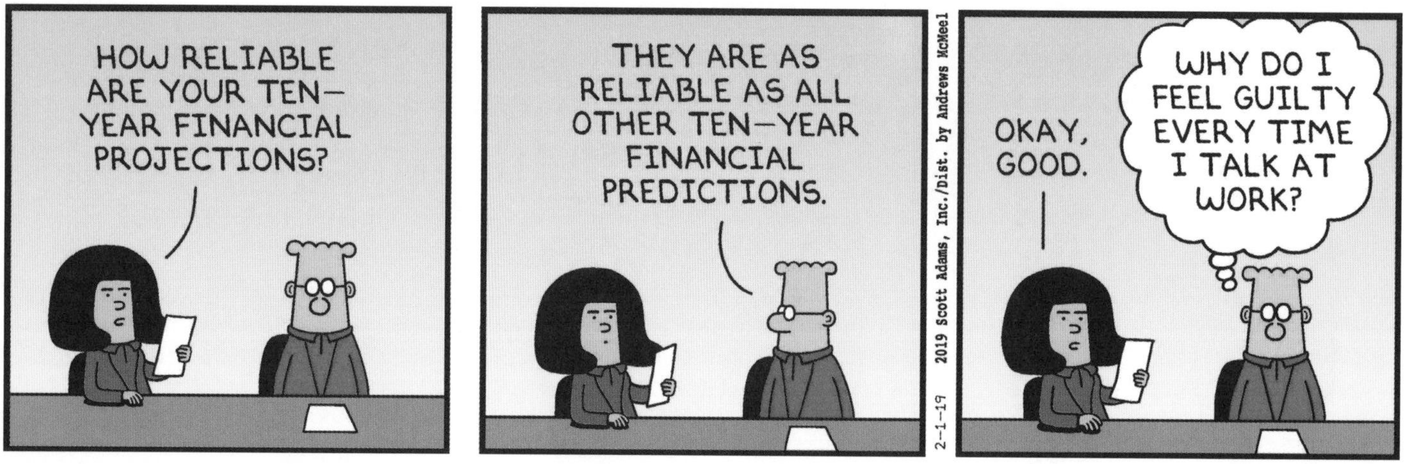
HOW RELIABLE ARE YOUR TEN—YEAR FINANCIAL PROJECTIONS?
THEY ARE AS RELIABLE AS ALL OTHER TEN—YEAR FINANCIAL PREDICTIONS.
OKAY, GOOD.
WHY DO I FEEL GUILTY EVERY TIME I TALK AT WORK?
2-1-19 2019 Scott Adams, Inc./Dist. by Andrews McMeel

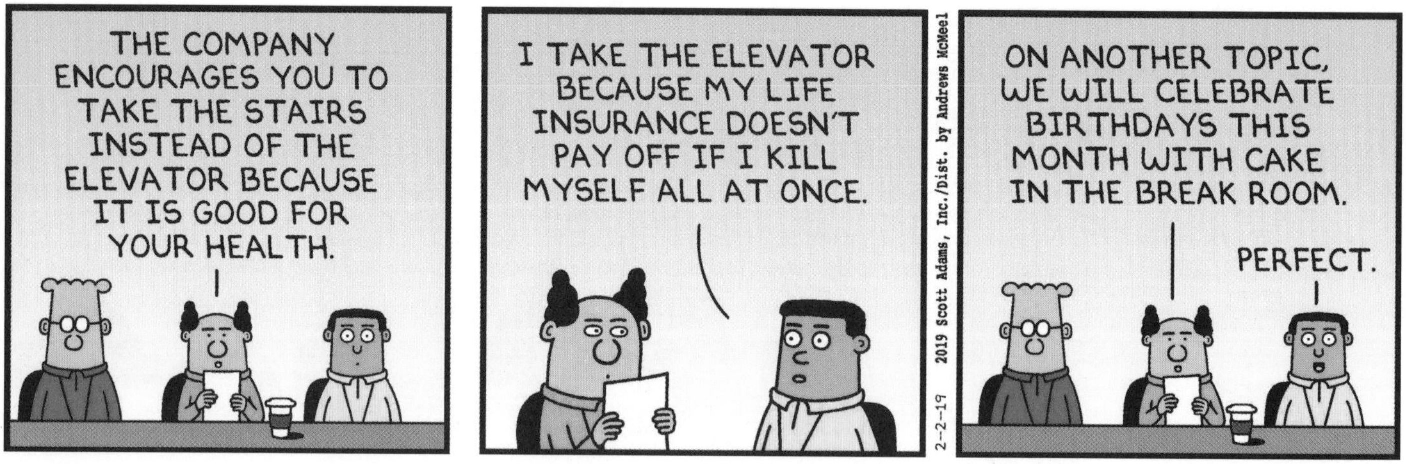
THE COMPANY ENCOURAGES YOU TO TAKE THE STAIRS INSTEAD OF THE ELEVATOR BECAUSE IT IS GOOD FOR YOUR HEALTH.
I TAKE THE ELEVATOR BECAUSE MY LIFE INSURANCE DOESN'T PAY OFF IF I KILL MYSELF ALL AT ONCE.
ON ANOTHER TOPIC, WE WILL CELEBRATE BIRTHDAYS THIS MONTH WITH CAKE IN THE BREAK ROOM.
PERFECT.
2-2-19 2019 Scott Adams, Inc./Dist. by Andrews McMeel

I INVENTED A COST—EFFECTIVE PRODUCT TO HARVEST CO2 FROM THE AIR AND TURN IT INTO CON—STRUCTION MATERIAL.
SO. . . YOU INVENTED A TREE?
WHAT?
TREES TAKE CO2 FROM THE AIR AND TURN IT INTO WOOD.
YOUR INVENTION WILL COMPETE WITH PLANTS AND TREES FOR NECESSARY CO2.
IT SEEMS YOU HAVE DOOMED ALL LIFE ON EARTH.
NOT IF PEOPLE ACT RATIONALLY AND STOP REMOVING THE CO2 WHEN. . .
WAIT. . .
YOU'RE RIGHT. I DOOMED THE PLANET.
I'LL BE DEAD BY THEN, SO SHIP IT.
© 2019 Scott Adams, Inc./Dist. by Andrews McMeel
2-3-19

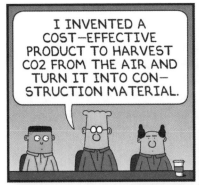

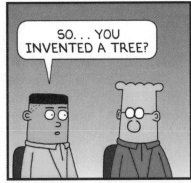

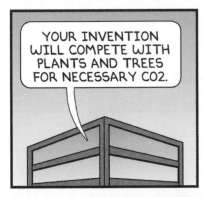

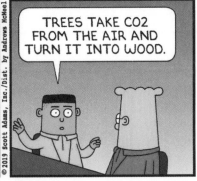

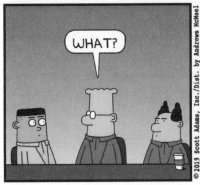

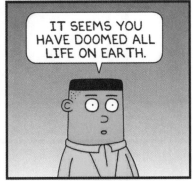

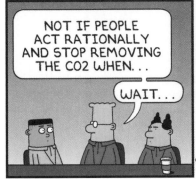

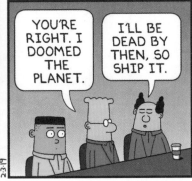

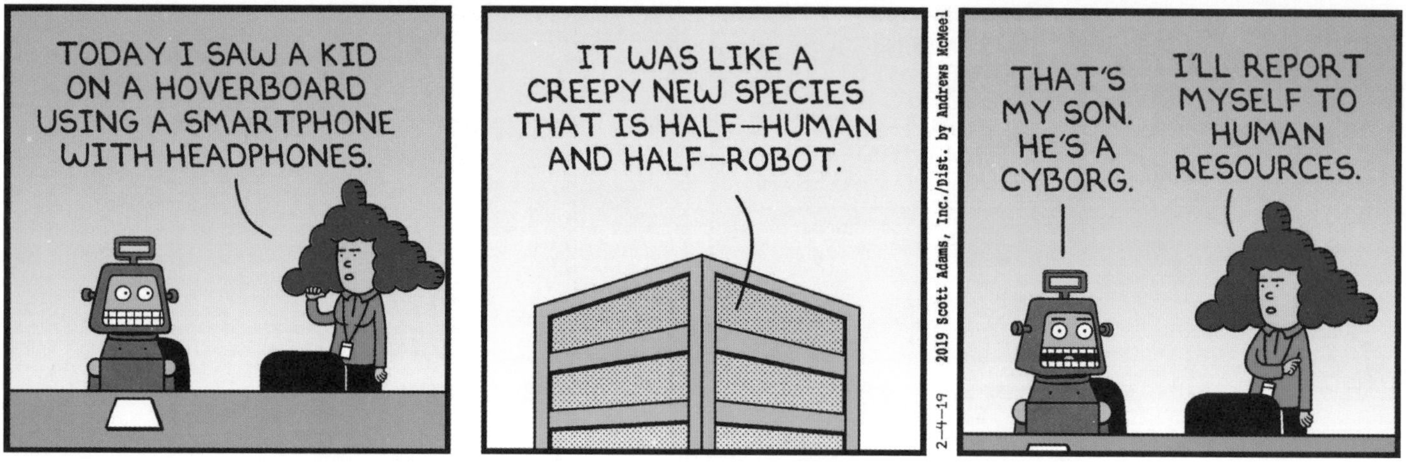
TODAY I SAW A KID ON A HOVERBOARD USING A SMARTPHONE WITH HEADPHONES.
IT WAS LIKE A CREEPY NEW SPECIES THAT IS HALF-HUMAN AND HALF-ROBOT.
2-4-19 2019 Scott Adams, Inc./Dist. by Andrews McMeel
THAT'S MY SON. HE'S A CYBORG.
I'LL REPORT MYSELF TO HUMAN RESOURCES.

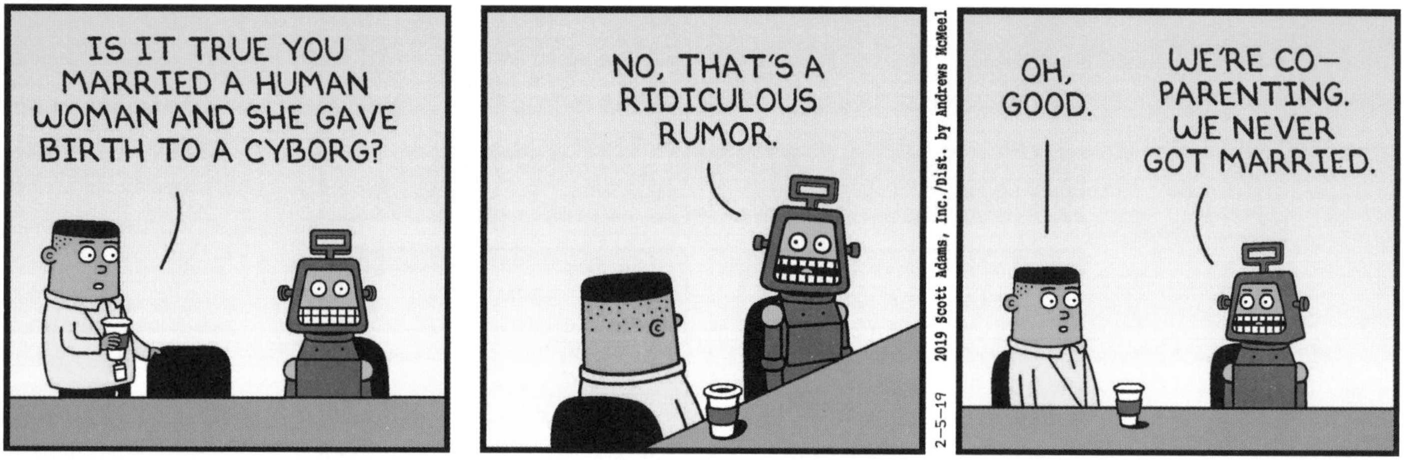
IS IT TRUE YOU MARRIED A HUMAN WOMAN AND SHE GAVE BIRTH TO A CYBORG?
NO, THAT'S A RIDICULOUS RUMOR.
2-5-19 2019 Scott Adams, Inc./Dist. by Andrews McMeel
OH, GOOD.
WE'RE CO-PARENTING. WE NEVER GOT MARRIED.

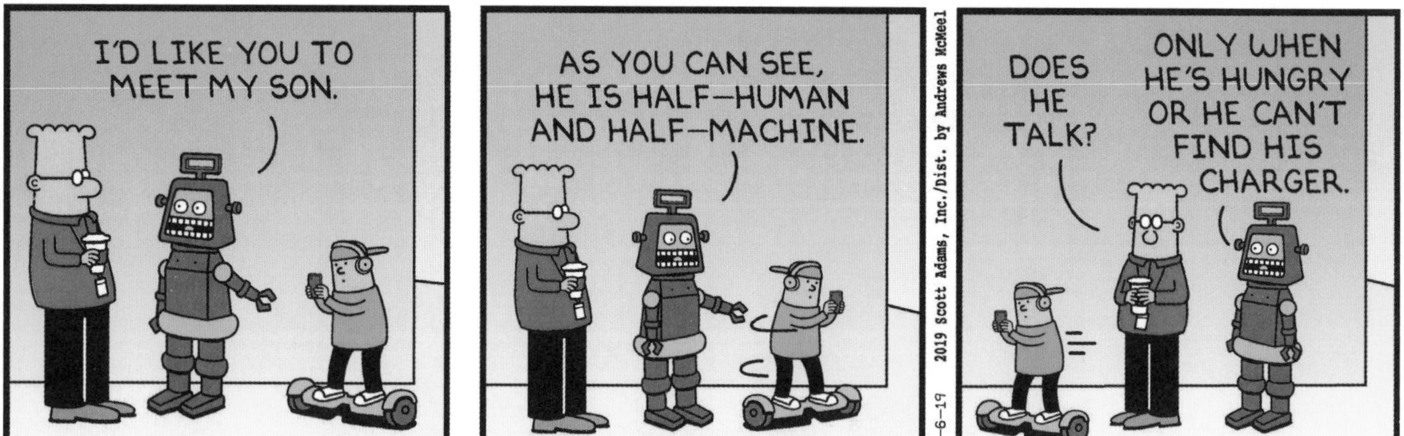
I'D LIKE YOU TO MEET MY SON.
AS YOU CAN SEE, HE IS HALF-HUMAN AND HALF-MACHINE.
2-6-19 2019 Scott Adams, Inc./Dist. by Andrews McMeel
DOES HE TALK?
ONLY WHEN HE'S HUNGRY OR HE CAN'T FIND HIS CHARGER.

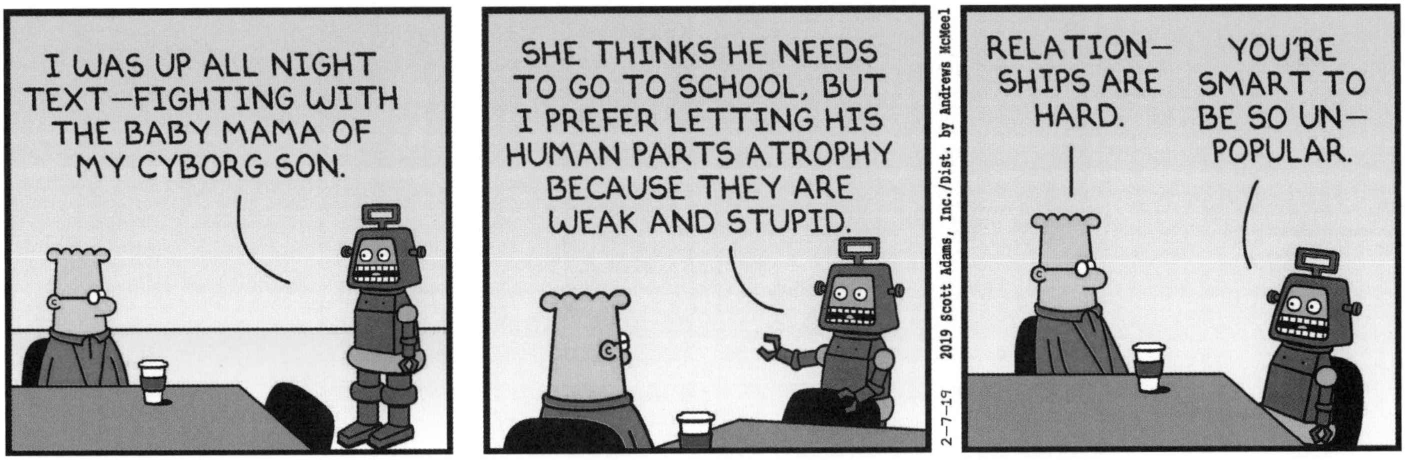
I WAS UP ALL NIGHT TEXT—FIGHTING WITH THE BABY MAMA OF MY CYBORG SON.
SHE THINKS HE NEEDS TO GO TO SCHOOL, BUT I PREFER LETTING HIS HUMAN PARTS ATROPHY BECAUSE THEY ARE WEAK AND STUPID.
2-7-19 2019 Scott Adams, Inc./Dist. by Andrews McMeel
RELATION—SHIPS ARE HARD.
YOU'RE SMART TO BE SO UN—POPULAR.

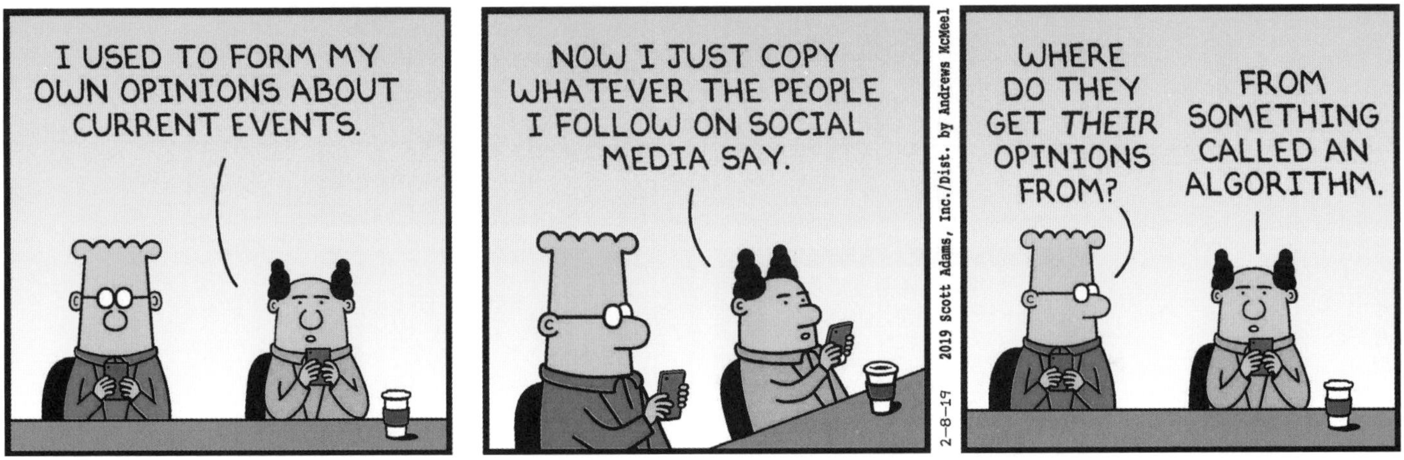
I USED TO FORM MY OWN OPINIONS ABOUT CURRENT EVENTS.
NOW I JUST COPY WHATEVER THE PEOPLE I FOLLOW ON SOCIAL MEDIA SAY.
2-8-19 2019 Scott Adams, Inc./Dist. by Andrews McMeel
WHERE DO THEY GET *THEIR* OPINIONS FROM?
FROM SOMETHING CALLED AN ALGORITHM.

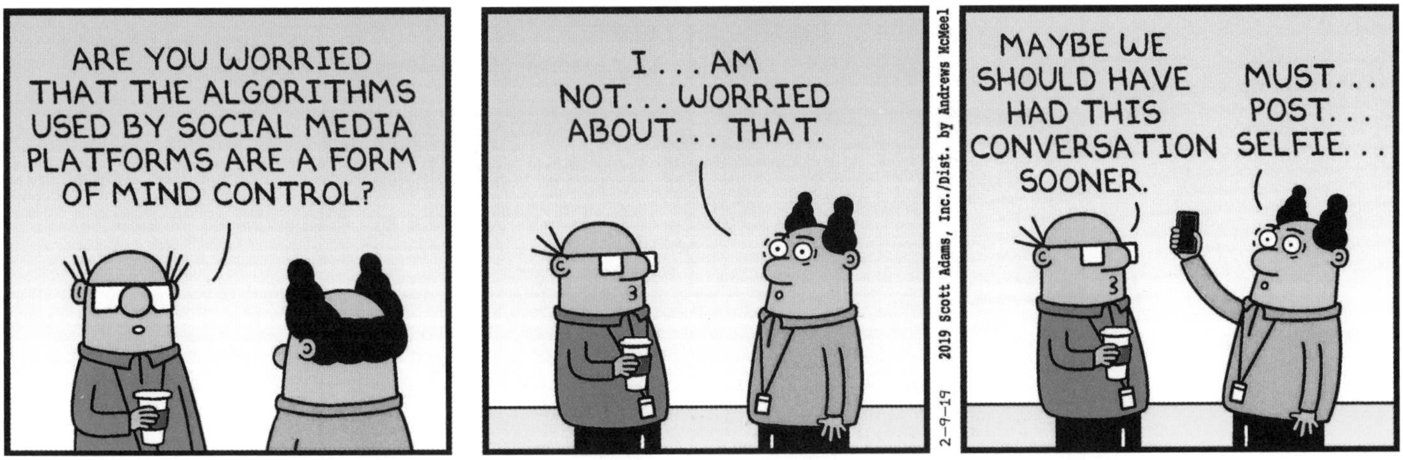
ARE YOU WORRIED THAT THE ALGORITHMS USED BY SOCIAL MEDIA PLATFORMS ARE A FORM OF MIND CONTROL?
I . . . AM NOT. . . WORRIED ABOUT. . . THAT.
2-9-19 2019 Scott Adams, Inc./Dist. by Andrews McMeel
MAYBE WE SHOULD HAVE HAD THIS CONVERSATION SOONER.
MUST. . . POST. . . SELFIE. . .

YOU SHOULD MEET THE NEW GUY IN MARKET-ING. YOU TWO WOULD GET ALONG GREAT.
I'LL SET UP A LUNCH.
WHY?
BECAUSE HE REMINDS ME OF YOU.
THAT ISN'T A REASON.
OKAY, HE IS FREE TOMORROW FOR LUNCH. I'LL TELL HIM TO MEET YOU IN THE LOBBY.
I STILL DON'T SEE WHY THE THREE OF US NEED TO GO TO LUNCH.
IT'S JUST THE TWO OF YOU. I'M BUSY TOMORROW.
I HEAR YOU'RE A LOT LIKE ME.
SADLY, YES.
© 2019 Scott Adams, Inc./Dist. by Andrews McMeel
2-10-19

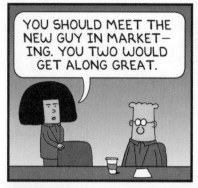

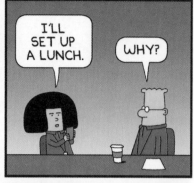

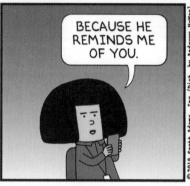

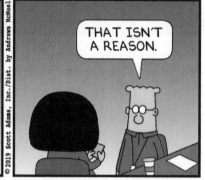

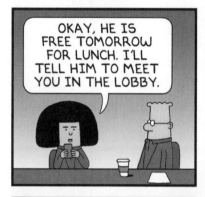

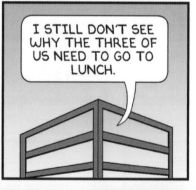

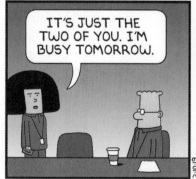

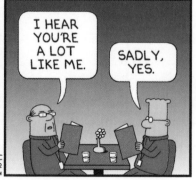

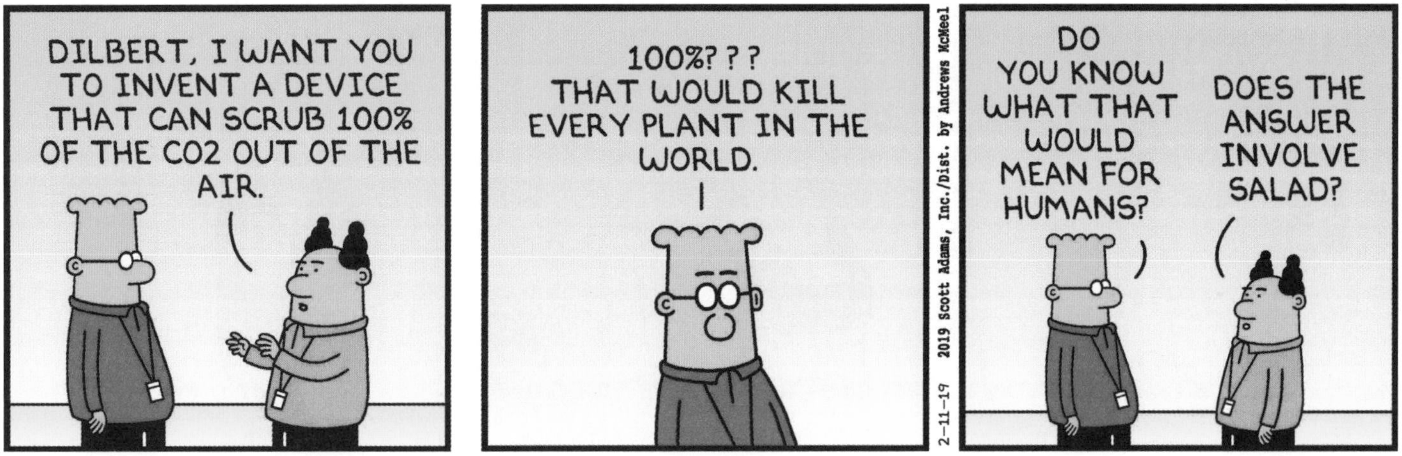
DILBERT, I WANT YOU TO INVENT A DEVICE THAT CAN SCRUB 100% OF THE CO2 OUT OF THE AIR.
100%??? THAT WOULD KILL EVERY PLANT IN THE WORLD.
2-11-19 2019 Scott Adams, Inc./Dist. by Andrews McMeel
DO YOU KNOW WHAT THAT WOULD MEAN FOR HUMANS?
DOES THE ANSWER INVOLVE SALAD?

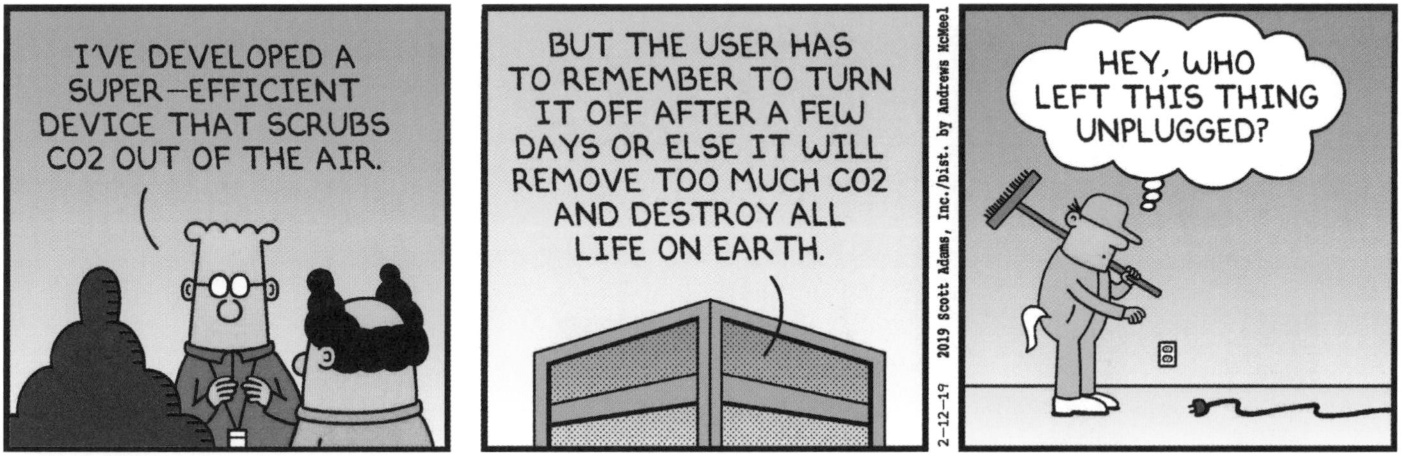
I'VE DEVELOPED A SUPER-EFFICIENT DEVICE THAT SCRUBS CO2 OUT OF THE AIR.
BUT THE USER HAS TO REMEMBER TO TURN IT OFF AFTER A FEW DAYS OR ELSE IT WILL REMOVE TOO MUCH CO2 AND DESTROY ALL LIFE ON EARTH.
2-12-19 2019 Scott Adams, Inc./Dist. by Andrews McMeel
HEY, WHO LEFT THIS THING UNPLUGGED?

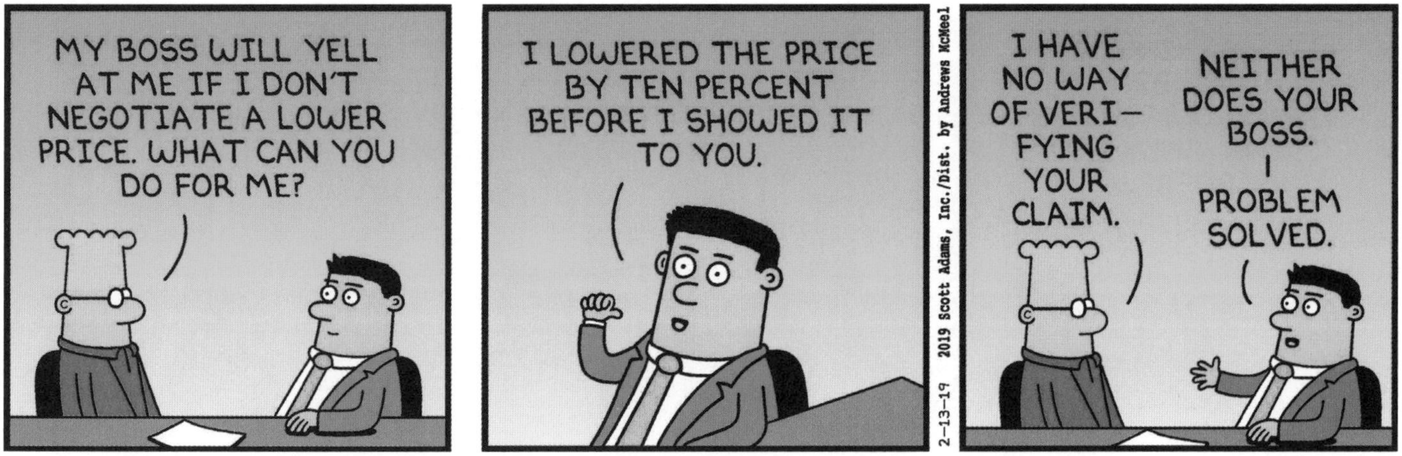
MY BOSS WILL YELL AT ME IF I DON'T NEGOTIATE A LOWER PRICE. WHAT CAN YOU DO FOR ME?
I LOWERED THE PRICE BY TEN PERCENT BEFORE I SHOWED IT TO YOU.
2-13-19 2019 Scott Adams, Inc./Dist. by Andrews McMeel
I HAVE NO WAY OF VERI-FYING YOUR CLAIM.
NEITHER DOES YOUR BOSS.
PROBLEM SOLVED.

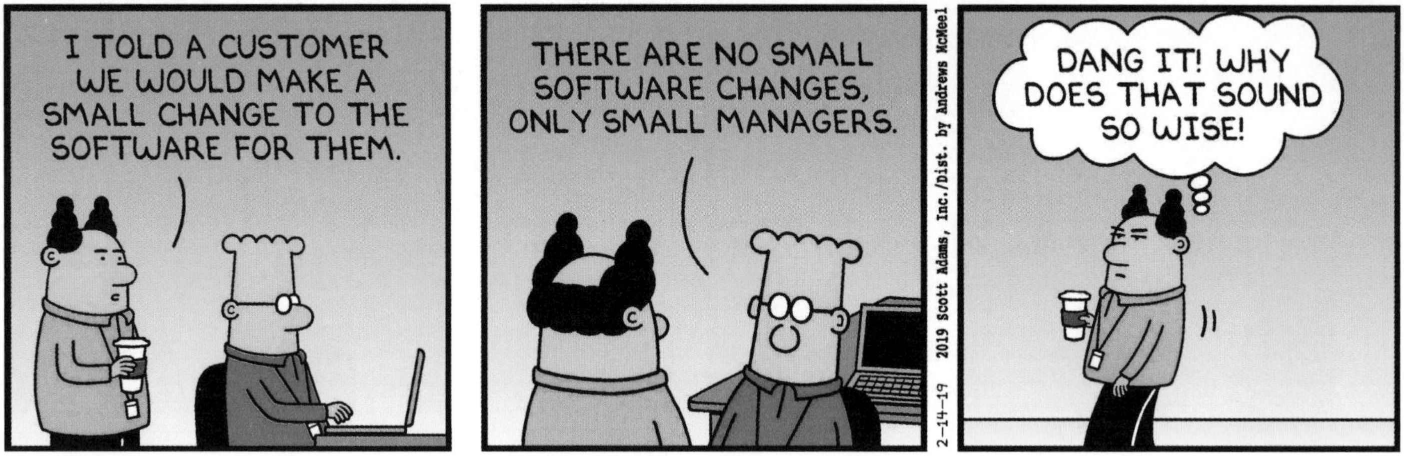
I TOLD A CUSTOMER WE WOULD MAKE A SMALL CHANGE TO THE SOFTWARE FOR THEM.
THERE ARE NO SMALL SOFTWARE CHANGES, ONLY SMALL MANAGERS.
DANG IT! WHY DOES THAT SOUND SO WISE!
2-14-19 2019 Scott Adams, Inc./Dist. by Andrews McMeel

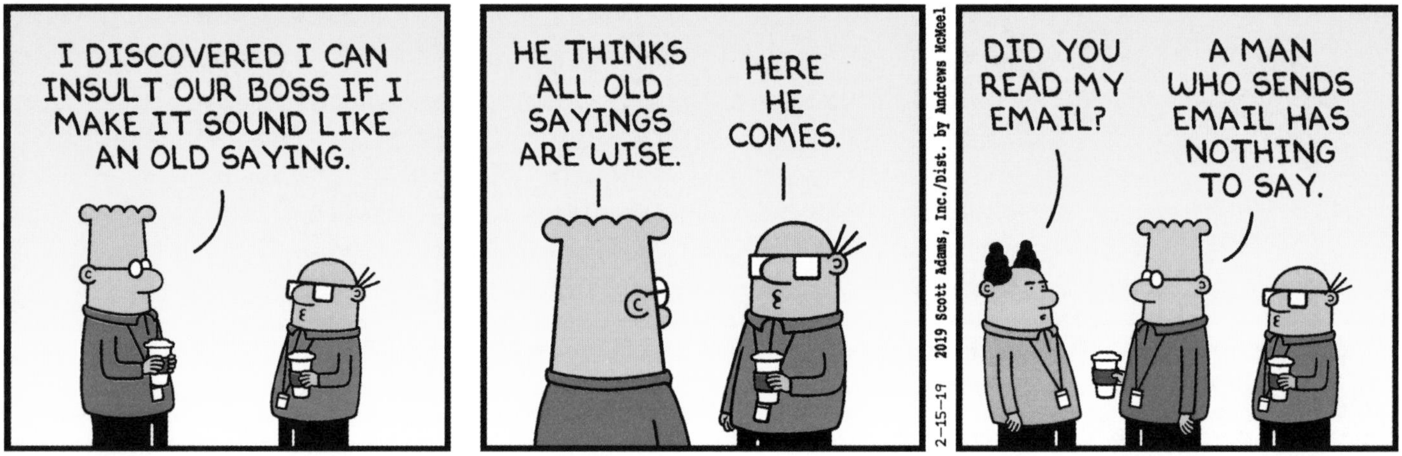
I DISCOVERED I CAN INSULT OUR BOSS IF I MAKE IT SOUND LIKE AN OLD SAYING.
HE THINKS ALL OLD SAYINGS ARE WISE.
HERE HE COMES.
DID YOU READ MY EMAIL?
A MAN WHO SENDS EMAIL HAS NOTHING TO SAY.
2-15-19 2019 Scott Adams, Inc./Dist. by Andrews McMeel

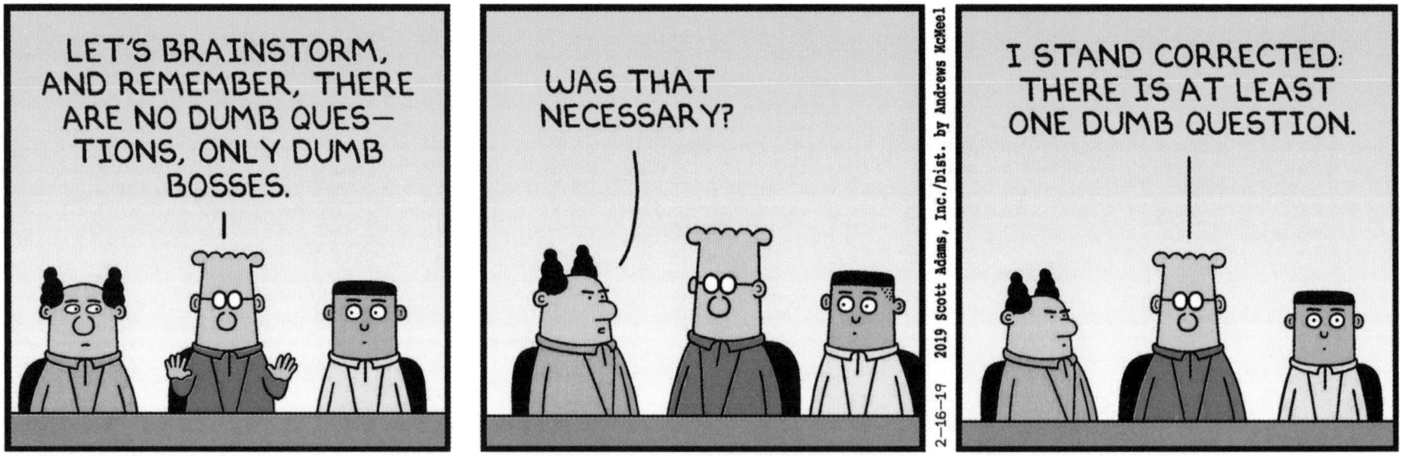
LET'S BRAINSTORM, AND REMEMBER, THERE ARE NO DUMB QUES-TIONS, ONLY DUMB BOSSES.
WAS THAT NECESSARY?
I STAND CORRECTED: THERE IS AT LEAST ONE DUMB QUESTION.
2-16-19 2019 Scott Adams, Inc./Dist. by Andrews McMeel

WOULD YOU LIKE TO TAKE A LONG WALK WITH ME AT LUNCH TO GET SOME EXERCISE?
THAT'S A GREAT IDEA!
OKAY, I'LL COME GET YOU AT NOON.
READY?
YES, I ONLY NEED TEN MINUTES TO FINISH THIS.
© 2019 Scott Adams, Inc./Dist. by Andrews McMeel
I ONLY HAVE AN HOUR FOR LUNCH, AND YOUR TEN MINUTES WILL TURN INTO TWENTY.
THAT'S OKAY BECAUSE I WORE HEELS TODAY AND I CAN'T WALK MORE THAN A BLOCK ANYWAY.
WHY DID YOU AGREE TO TAKE A LONG WALK IF YOU COULDN'T TAKE A LONG WALK?
BECAUSE I WAS PLANNING TO WALK TO THE STORE ON THE CORNER TO DO AN ERRAND ANYWAY.
2-17-19
YOU'VE RUINED MY WALK!
JUST GIVE ME FORTY MINUTES TO WRAP THIS UP.

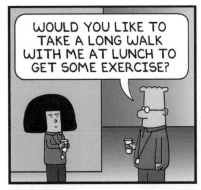

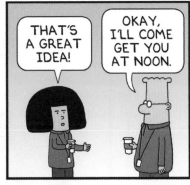

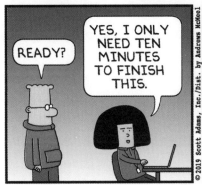

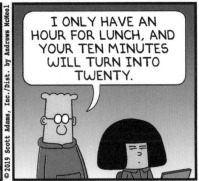

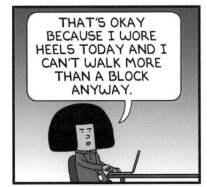

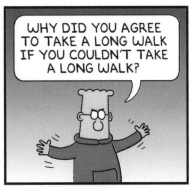

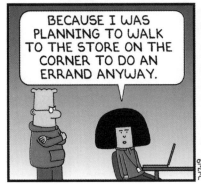

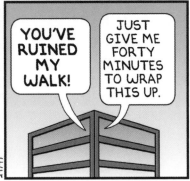

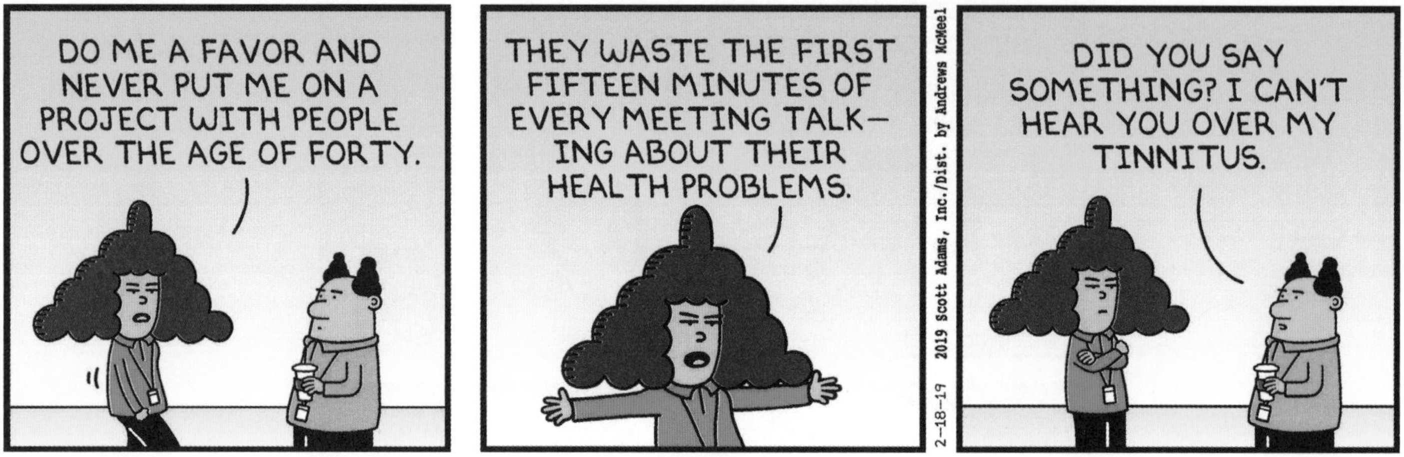
DO ME A FAVOR AND NEVER PUT ME ON A PROJECT WITH PEOPLE OVER THE AGE OF FORTY.
THEY WASTE THE FIRST FIFTEEN MINUTES OF EVERY MEETING TALK-ING ABOUT THEIR HEALTH PROBLEMS.
2-18-19 2019 Scott Adams, Inc./Dist. by Andrews McMeel
DID YOU SAY SOMETHING? I CAN'T HEAR YOU OVER MY TINNITUS.

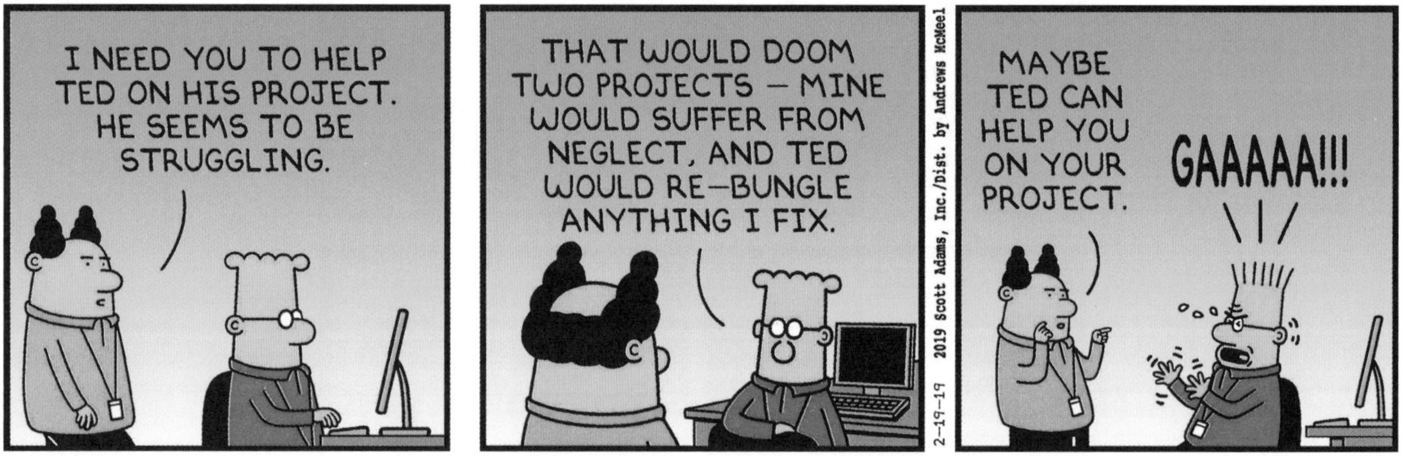
I NEED YOU TO HELP TED ON HIS PROJECT. HE SEEMS TO BE STRUGGLING.
THAT WOULD DOOM TWO PROJECTS — MINE WOULD SUFFER FROM NEGLECT, AND TED WOULD RE-BUNGLE ANYTHING I FIX.
2-19-19 2019 Scott Adams, Inc./Dist. by Andrews McMeel
MAYBE TED CAN HELP YOU ON YOUR PROJECT.
GAAAAA!!!

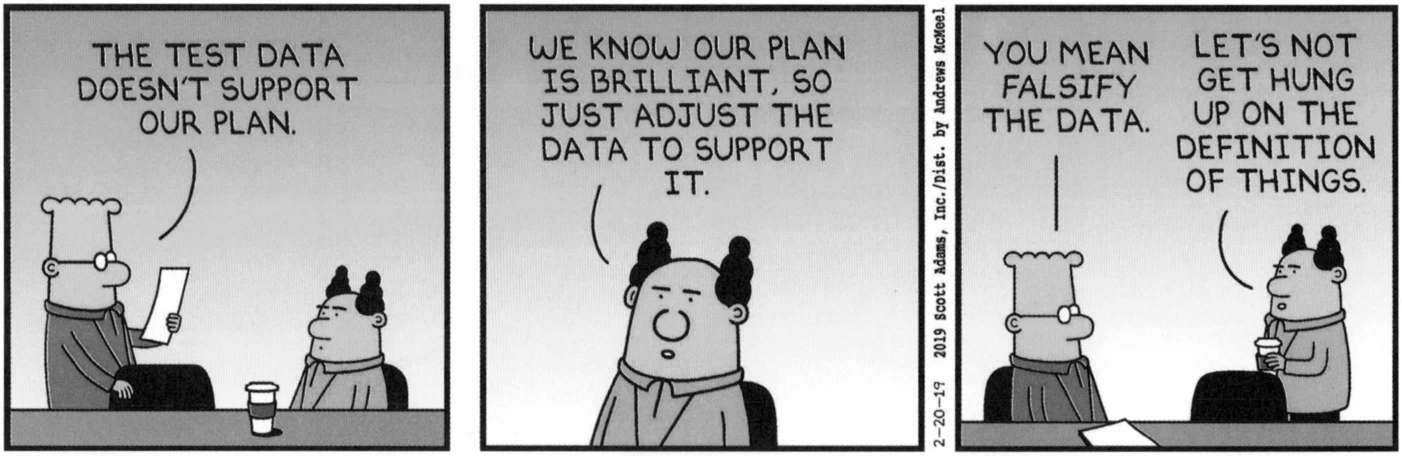
THE TEST DATA DOESN'T SUPPORT OUR PLAN.
WE KNOW OUR PLAN IS BRILLIANT, SO JUST ADJUST THE DATA TO SUPPORT IT.
2-20-19 2019 Scott Adams, Inc./Dist. by Andrews McMeel
YOU MEAN *FALSIFY* THE DATA.
LET'S NOT GET HUNG UP ON THE DEFINITION OF THINGS.

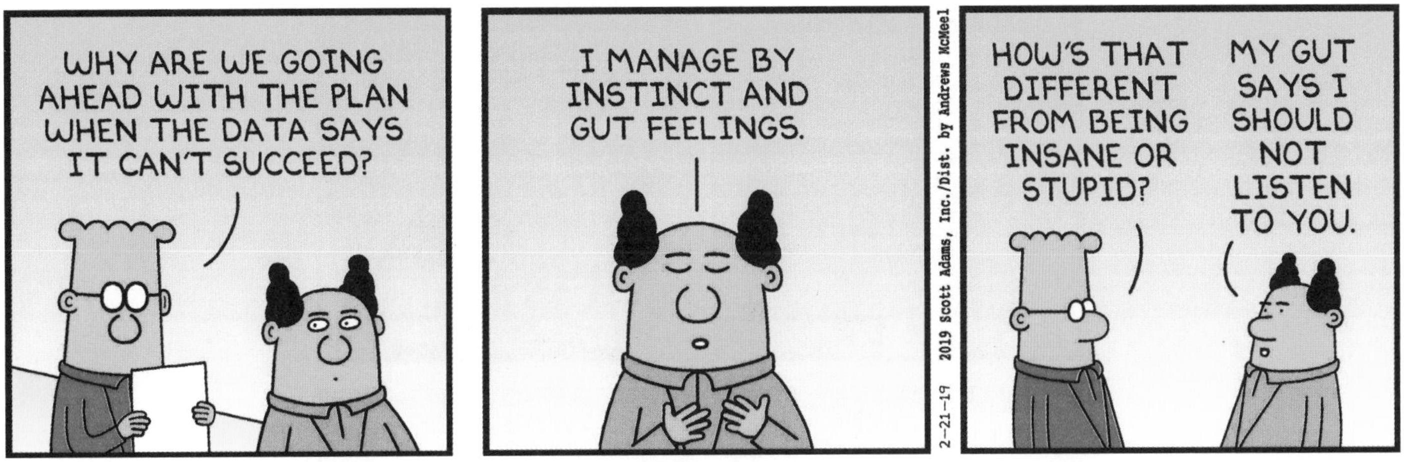
WHY ARE WE GOING AHEAD WITH THE PLAN WHEN THE DATA SAYS IT CAN'T SUCCEED?
I MANAGE BY INSTINCT AND GUT FEELINGS.
HOW'S THAT DIFFERENT FROM BEING INSANE OR STUPID?
MY GUT SAYS I SHOULD NOT LISTEN TO YOU.
2-21-19 © 2019 Scott Adams, Inc./Dist. by Andrews McMeel

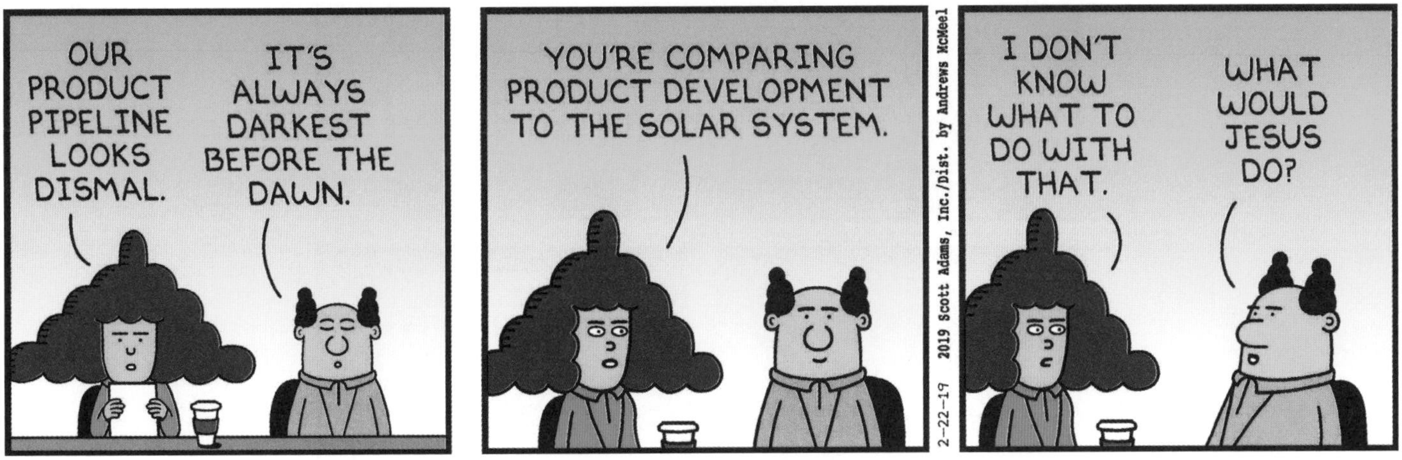
OUR PRODUCT PIPELINE LOOKS DISMAL.
IT'S ALWAYS DARKEST BEFORE THE DAWN.
YOU'RE COMPARING PRODUCT DEVELOPMENT TO THE SOLAR SYSTEM.
I DON'T KNOW WHAT TO DO WITH THAT.
WHAT WOULD JESUS DO?
2-22-19 © 2019 Scott Adams, Inc./Dist. by Andrews McMeel

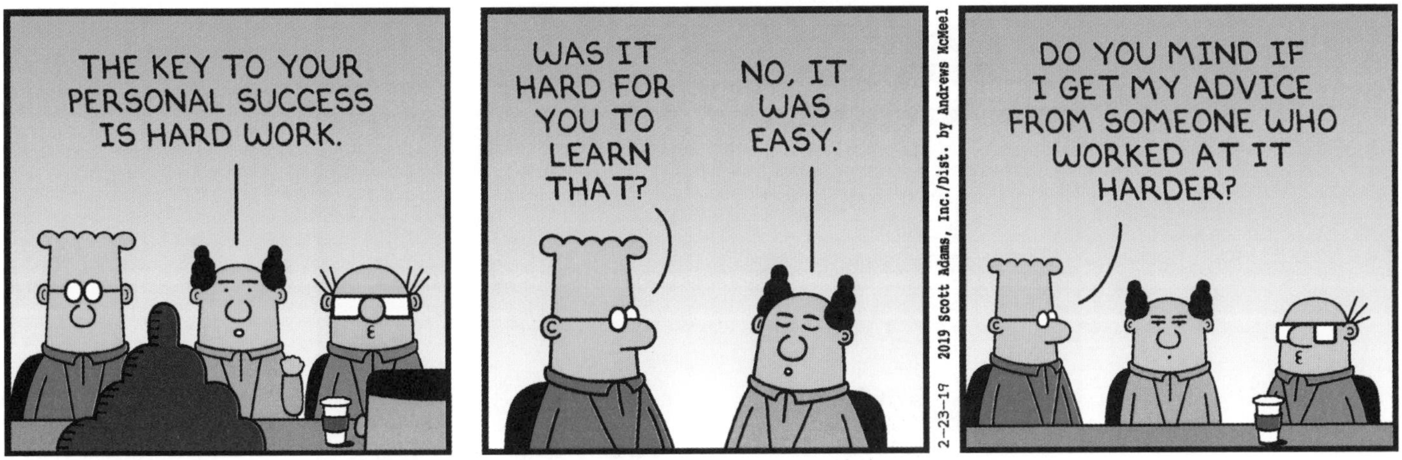
THE KEY TO YOUR PERSONAL SUCCESS IS HARD WORK.
WAS IT HARD FOR YOU TO LEARN THAT?
NO, IT WAS EASY.
DO YOU MIND IF I GET MY ADVICE FROM SOMEONE WHO WORKED AT IT HARDER?
2-23-19 © 2019 Scott Adams, Inc./Dist. by Andrews McMeel

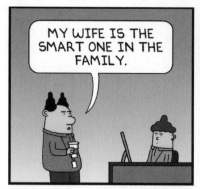

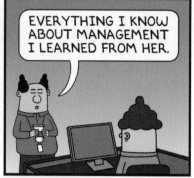

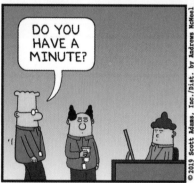

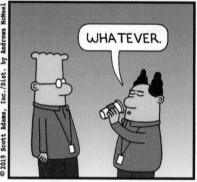

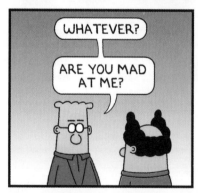

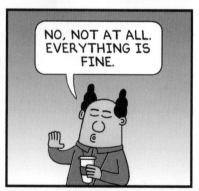

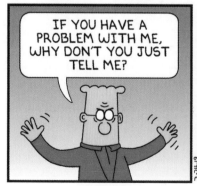

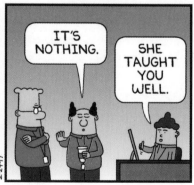

MY WIFE IS THE SMART ONE IN THE FAMILY.
EVERYTHING I KNOW ABOUT MANAGEMENT I LEARNED FROM HER.
DO YOU HAVE A MINUTE?
WHATEVER.
WHATEVER?
ARE YOU MAD AT ME?
NO, NOT AT ALL. EVERYTHING IS FINE.
IF YOU HAVE A PROBLEM WITH ME, WHY DON'T YOU JUST TELL ME?
IT'S NOTHING.
SHE TAUGHT YOU WELL.
© 2019 Scott Adams, Inc./Dist. by Andrews McMeel
2-24-19

DON'T TURN THAT CUBICLE LIGHT OFF JUST YET—there's more *Dilbert* to come! The following pages include 50 of the most popular *Dilbert* comic strips from the past decade, selected using analytics from Dilbert.com (thanks, Asok!) as well as permissions and licensing requests made to Andrews McMeel Syndication through the years. The comics are presented here in chronological order.

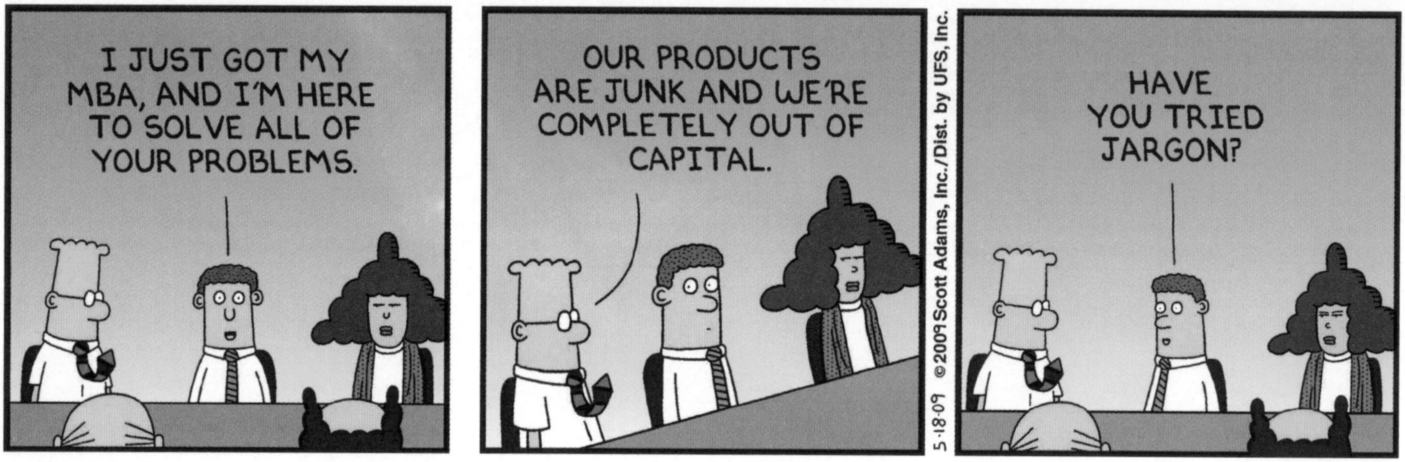
I JUST GOT MY MBA, AND I'M HERE TO SOLVE ALL OF YOUR PROBLEMS.
OUR PRODUCTS ARE JUNK AND WE'RE COMPLETELY OUT OF CAPITAL.
HAVE YOU TRIED JARGON?
5-18-09 ©2009 Scott Adams, Inc./Dist. by UFS, Inc.

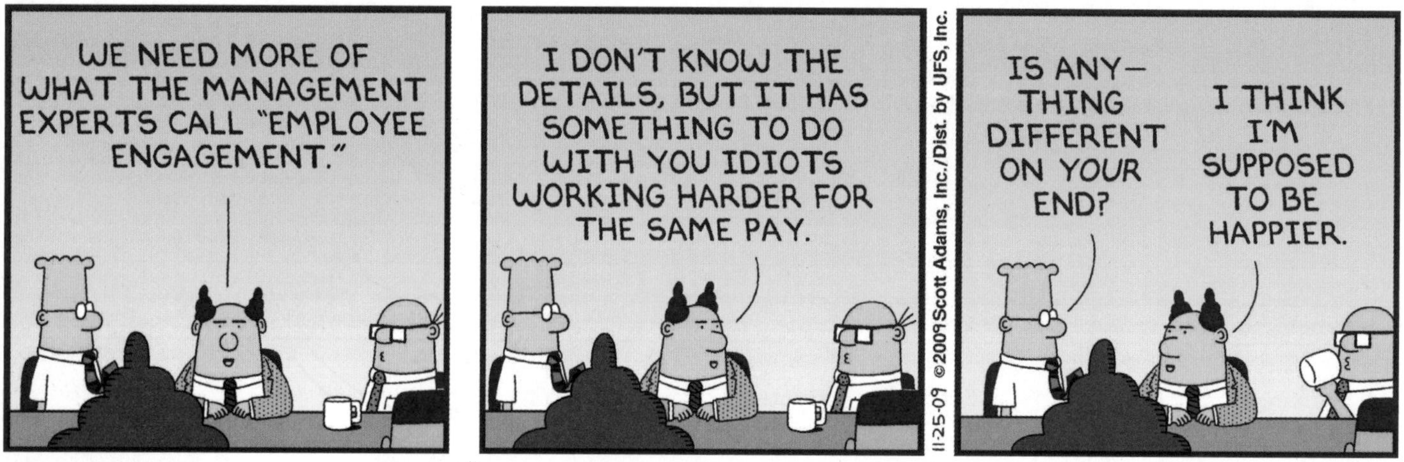
WE NEED MORE OF WHAT THE MANAGEMENT EXPERTS CALL "EMPLOYEE ENGAGEMENT."
I DON'T KNOW THE DETAILS, BUT IT HAS SOMETHING TO DO WITH YOU IDIOTS WORKING HARDER FOR THE SAME PAY.
IS ANY-THING DIFFERENT ON *YOUR* END?
I THINK I'M SUPPOSED TO BE HAPPIER.
11-25-09 ©2009 Scott Adams, Inc./Dist. by UFS, Inc.

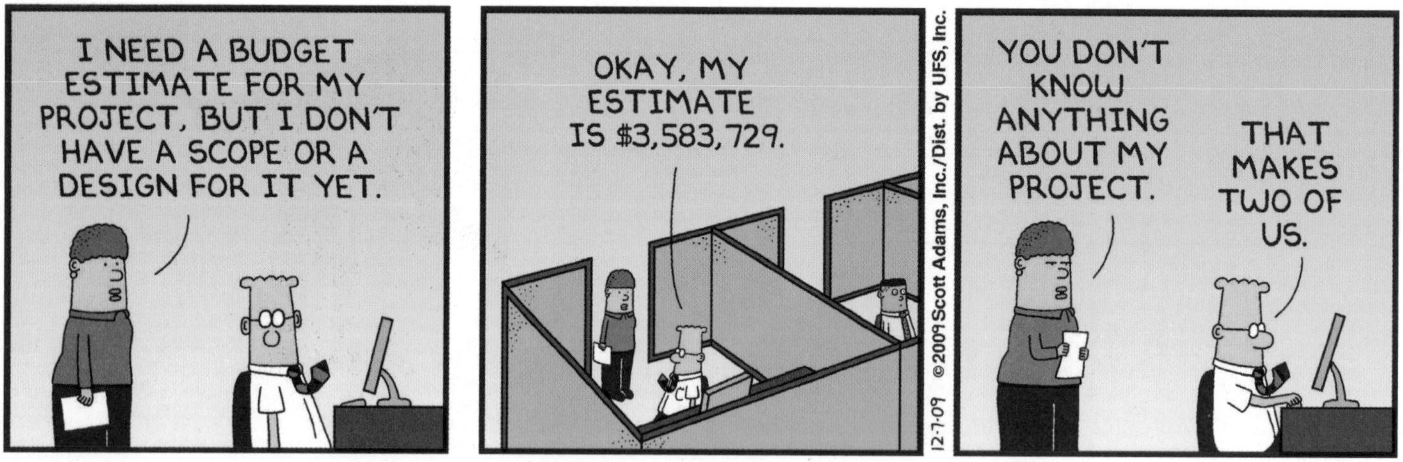
I NEED A BUDGET ESTIMATE FOR MY PROJECT, BUT I DON'T HAVE A SCOPE OR A DESIGN FOR IT YET.
OKAY, MY ESTIMATE IS $3,583,729.
YOU DON'T KNOW ANYTHING ABOUT MY PROJECT.
THAT MAKES TWO OF US.
12-7-09 ©2009 Scott Adams, Inc./Dist. by UFS, Inc.

I NEED HELP WITH MY COMPUTER.
IT'S A TRAP!
IF I TOUCH YOUR COMPUTER, YOU'LL THINK THAT EVERY FUTURE PROBLEM IS CAUSED BY SOME-THING I DID.
©2010 Scott Adams, Inc. /Dist. by UFS, Inc.
YOU'LL TELL EVERYONE I RUINED YOUR COMPUTER!
I'LL BE OBLIGATED TO SOLVE EVERY COMPUTER PROBLEM YOU HAVE FROM THIS DAY ON.
MY OWN PROJECTS WILL BE LEFT TO WITHER AS I SHOW YOU FOR THE NINETIETH TIME HOW TO SELECT A NEW FONT.
IF I REFUSE TO HELP, YOU'LL TELL MY BOSS I'M NOT A TEAM PLAYER.
6-27-10
DO YOU NEED A HUG?
ONLY IF YOU CAN SQUEEZE HARD ENOUGH TO KILL ME.

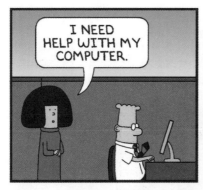

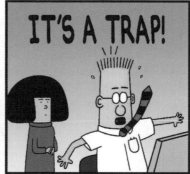

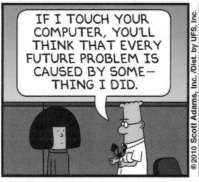

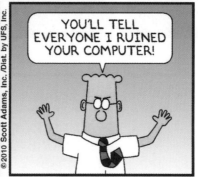

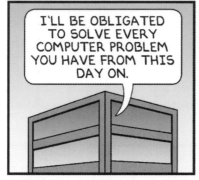

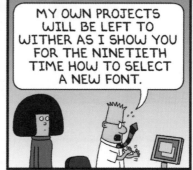

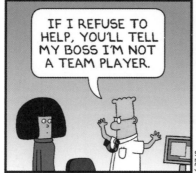

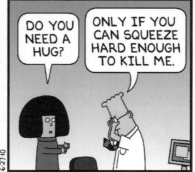

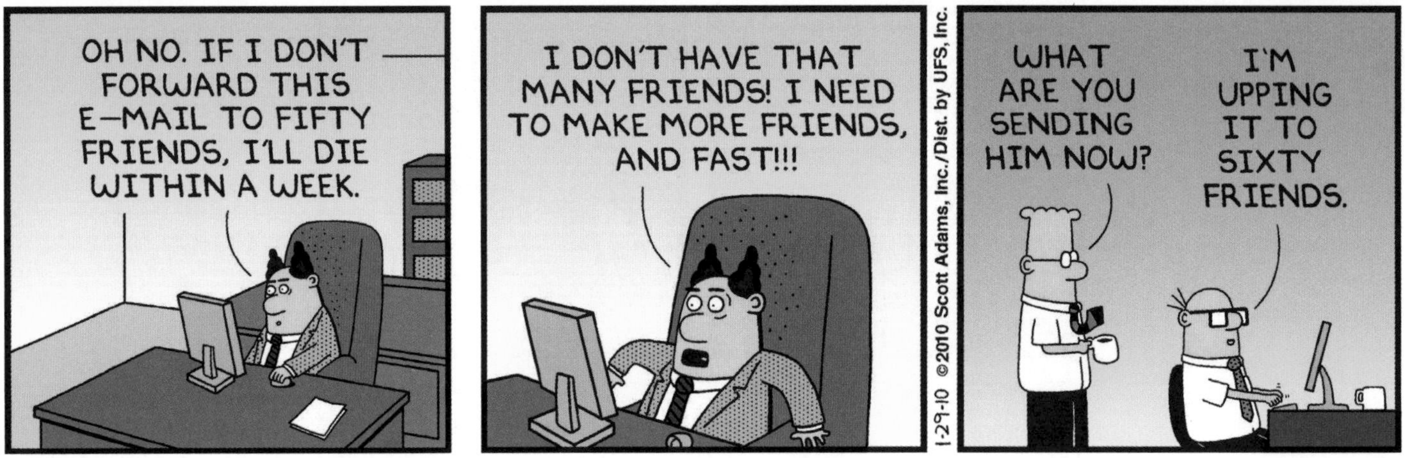
OH NO. IF I DON'T FORWARD THIS E–MAIL TO FIFTY FRIENDS, I'LL DIE WITHIN A WEEK.
I DON'T HAVE THAT MANY FRIENDS! I NEED TO MAKE MORE FRIENDS, AND FAST!!!
WHAT ARE YOU SENDING HIM NOW?
I'M UPPING IT TO SIXTY FRIENDS.
1-29-10 ©2010 Scott Adams, Inc./Dist. by UFS, Inc.

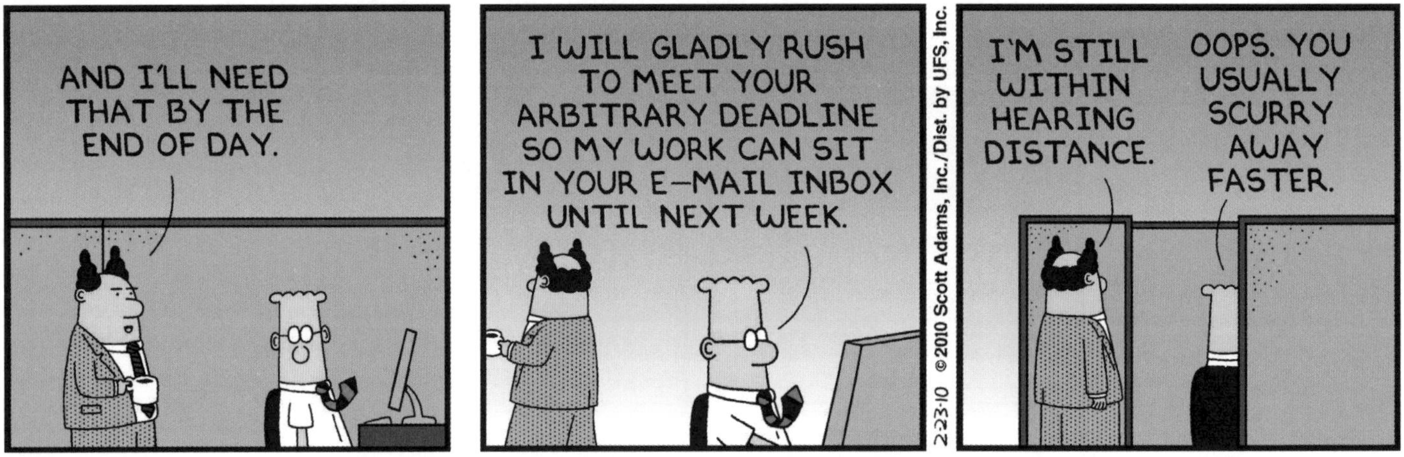
AND I'LL NEED THAT BY THE END OF DAY.
I WILL GLADLY RUSH TO MEET YOUR ARBITRARY DEADLINE SO MY WORK CAN SIT IN YOUR E–MAIL INBOX UNTIL NEXT WEEK.
I'M STILL WITHIN HEARING DISTANCE.
OOPS. YOU USUALLY SCURRY AWAY FASTER.
2-23-10 ©2010 Scott Adams, Inc./Dist. by UFS, Inc.

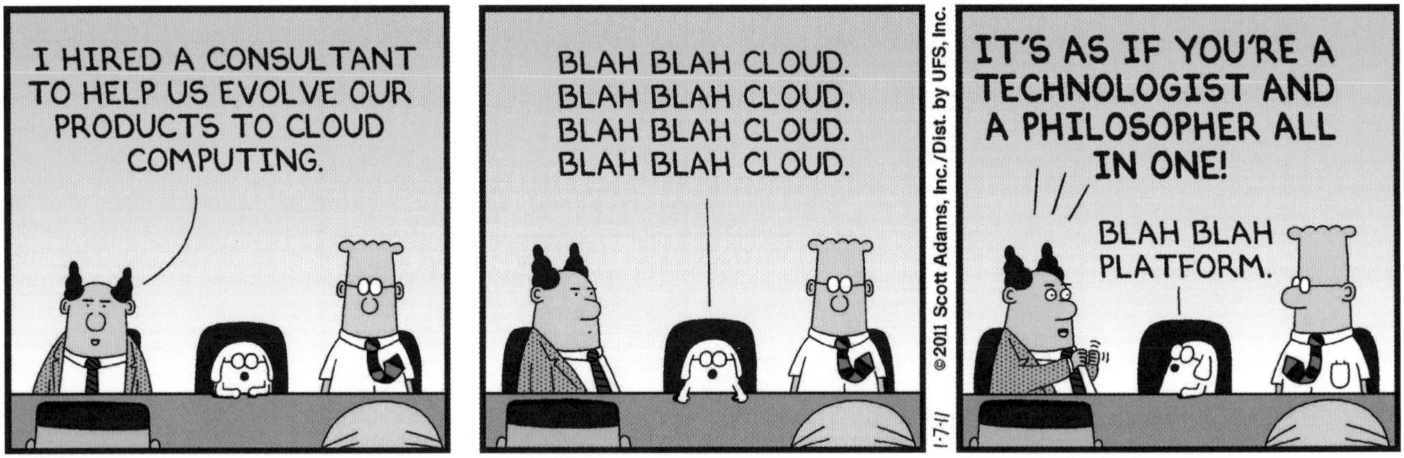
I HIRED A CONSULTANT TO HELP US EVOLVE OUR PRODUCTS TO CLOUD COMPUTING.
BLAH BLAH CLOUD. BLAH BLAH CLOUD. BLAH BLAH CLOUD. BLAH BLAH CLOUD.
IT'S AS IF YOU'RE A TECHNOLOGIST AND A PHILOSOPHER ALL IN ONE!
BLAH BLAH PLATFORM.
1-7-11 ©2011 Scott Adams, Inc./Dist. by UFS, Inc.

I HAVE TO DISAGREE WITH YOU, DILBERT.
ACTUALLY, YOU **DON'T** DISAGREE WITH ME.
I DON'T?
NO. YOU THINK YOU DISAGREE WITH ME, BUT YOU'RE MISTAKEN.
YOU'RE SIMPLY EXPERIENCING AN ILLUSION CAUSED BY THE LIMITS OF YOUR COMPREHENSION.
IF YOU WERE ABLE TO FULLY COMPREHEND BOTH THE PROBLEM AND MY RECOMMENDED SOLUTION, YOU WOULD AGREE WITH ME.
SO WHAT APPEARS TO BE A DIFFERENCE OF OPINION IS JUST YOU WRESTLING WITH YOUR OWN DEFECTIVE BRAIN.
THERE'S NO REASON TO GET THE REST OF US INVOLVED IN THAT MESS.
HAVE YOU EVER NOTICED THAT CLARITY MAKES PEOPLE ANGRY?
©2011 Scott Adams, Inc./Dist. by UFS, Inc.
1-9-11

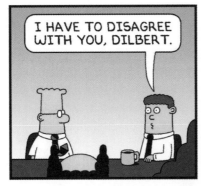

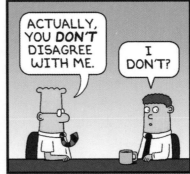

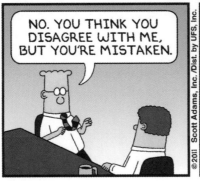

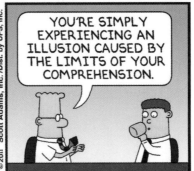

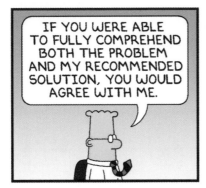

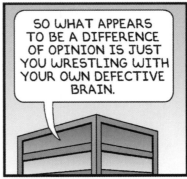

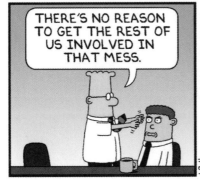

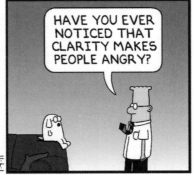

I HAVE A BUDGET MEETING TOMORROW WITH OUR CFO.
I'LL BE COMPETING AGAINST ALL OF THE OTHER DEPARTMENTS FOR PRECIOUS BUDGET DOLLARS.
THIS WON'T BE EASY BECAUSE ALL OF THE OTHER DEPART-MENTS ARE STAFFED WITH PROFESSIONAL LIARS.
THAT'S A BIT OF AN EXAGGERATION, DON'T YOU THINK?
WHAT DO YOU CALL MARKET-ING?
OKAY, I'LL GIVE YOU THAT ONE.
SALES?
RIGHT, BUT. . .
P.R.?
WELL, YES. . .
FINANCE?
I FORGOT ABOUT THAT ONE.
LEGAL?
WOW.
DO THE NEXT ONE YOURSELF.
HOW ABOUT HUMAN RESOUR. . .
YOU WIN.
©2011 Scott Adams, Inc./Dist. by UFS, Inc.
2-20-11

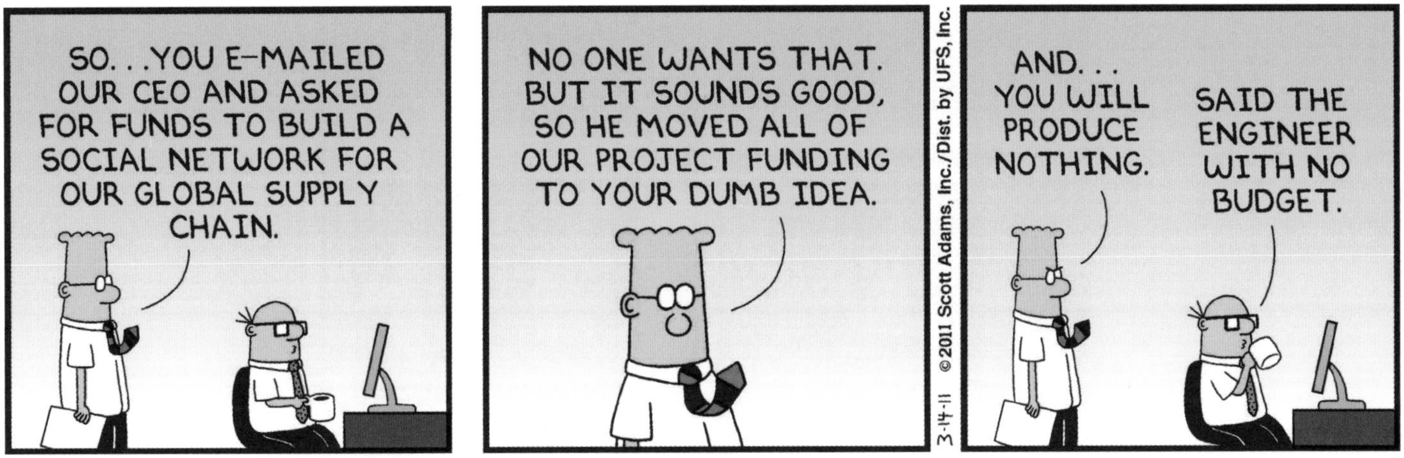
SO. . .YOU E-MAILED OUR CEO AND ASKED FOR FUNDS TO BUILD A SOCIAL NETWORK FOR OUR GLOBAL SUPPLY CHAIN.
NO ONE WANTS THAT. BUT IT SOUNDS GOOD, SO HE MOVED ALL OF OUR PROJECT FUNDING TO YOUR DUMB IDEA.
3-14-11 ©2011 Scott Adams, Inc./Dist. by UFS, Inc.
AND. . . YOU WILL PRODUCE NOTHING.
SAID THE ENGINEER WITH NO BUDGET.

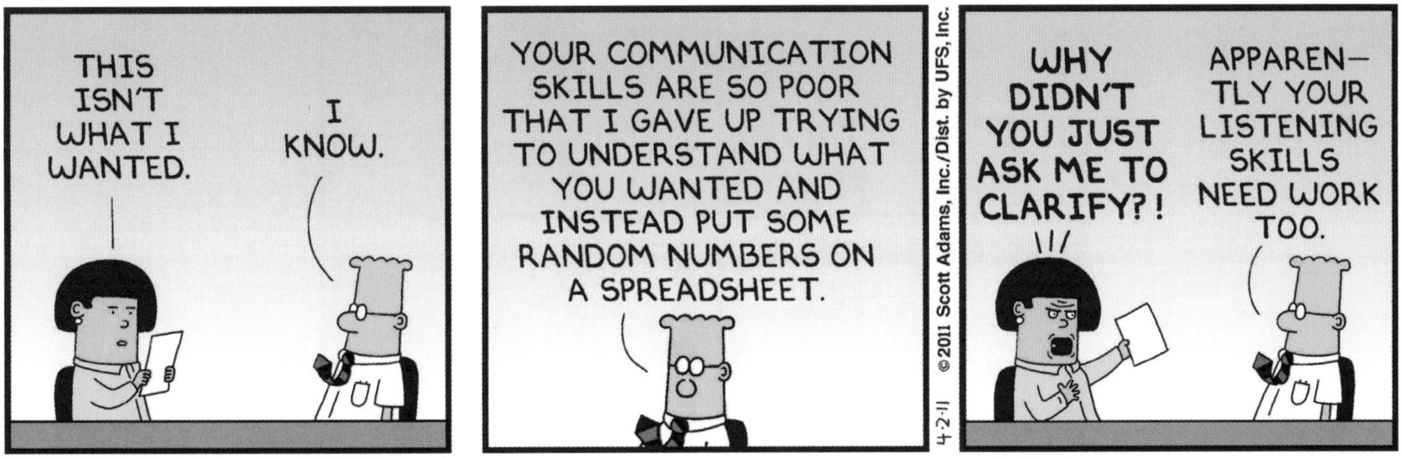
THIS ISN'T WHAT I WANTED.
I KNOW.
YOUR COMMUNICATION SKILLS ARE SO POOR THAT I GAVE UP TRYING TO UNDERSTAND WHAT YOU WANTED AND INSTEAD PUT SOME RANDOM NUMBERS ON A SPREADSHEET.
4-2-11 ©2011 Scott Adams, Inc./Dist. by UFS, Inc.
WHY DIDN'T YOU JUST ASK ME TO CLARIFY?!
APPAREN-TLY YOUR LISTENING SKILLS NEED WORK TOO.

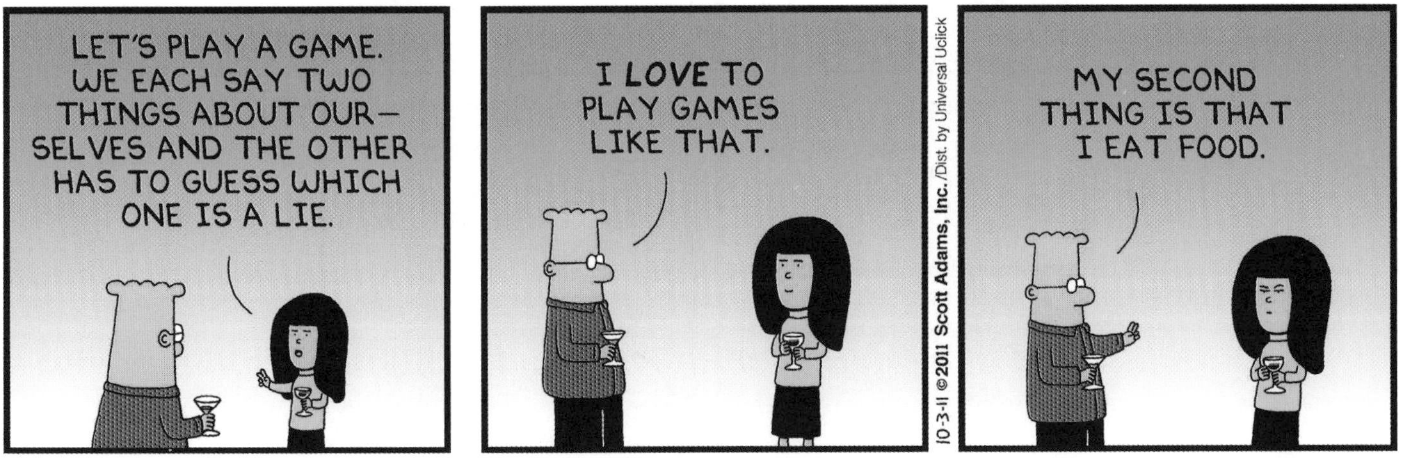
LET'S PLAY A GAME. WE EACH SAY TWO THINGS ABOUT OUR-SELVES AND THE OTHER HAS TO GUESS WHICH ONE IS A LIE.
I LOVE TO PLAY GAMES LIKE THAT.
10-3-11 ©2011 Scott Adams, Inc./Dist. by Universal Uclick
MY SECOND THING IS THAT I EAT FOOD.

MELTDOWN IN CUBICLE 4S9540!
THAT'S TED. HE MUST HAVE REACHED HIS T.W.L.
HIS WHAT?
THEORETICAL WORKLOAD LIMIT
IN LAYMAN'S TERMS, HIS BRAIN IS FULL.
©2011 Scott Adams, Inc. /Dist. by UFS, Inc.
IT STARTS WHEN JUST ONE OF YOUR PROJECTS BECOMES OVERDUE.
YOU END UP SPENDING ALL OF YOUR TIME EXPLAINING WHY YOU DIDN'T GET IT DONE.
THAT MAKES ALL OF YOUR OTHER PROJECTS OVERDUE. WHEN EVERY TASK BECOMES URGENT, YOUR BRAIN CAN'T DECIDE WHAT TO DO NEXT.
BRAINS MAKE A FUNNY NOISE WHEN THEY SHUT DOWN.
POINK
4-10-11
UH-OH. I JUST MISSED A DEAD-LINE.
AND SO IT BEGINS.

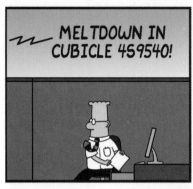

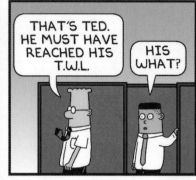

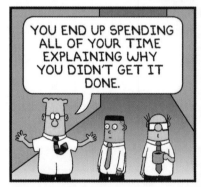

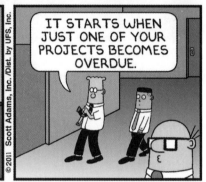

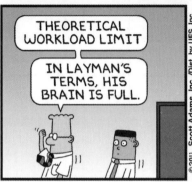

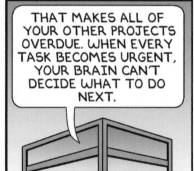

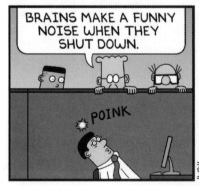

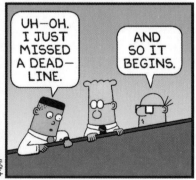

THIS IS DOGBERT'S TECH SUPPORT. HOW MAY I ABUSE YOU?
I THINK MY DIGITAL MODEM IS BROKEN.
PLEASE HOLD WHILE I PRETEND TO BE TESTING IT.
OKAY, IT LOOKS FINE FROM HERE.
THE PROBLEM MUST BE IN YOUR WIRING.
YOU'LL HAVE TO RIP OUT ALL OF THE WIRING IN YOUR ENTIRE HOUSE TO LOCATE THE PROBLEM.
ARE YOU SURE? BECAUSE THE LIGHTS ON THE MODEM AREN'T EVEN ON.
THAT MEANS YOU HAVE MOISTURE ON YOUR INTERNAL WIRING. YOU'LL ALSO NEED TO REPLACE ALL OF YOUR PLUMBING AND GET A NEW ROOF.
MAY I SPEAK WITH YOUR SUPERVISOR?
SURE. BUT HE SOUNDS EXACTLY LIKE ME.
©2012 Scott Adams, Inc./Dist. by Universal Uclick
1-22-12

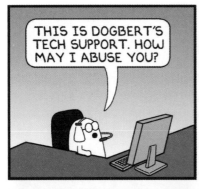

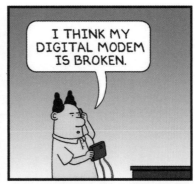

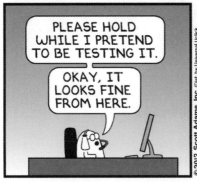

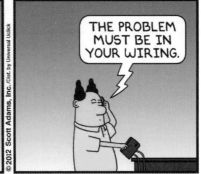

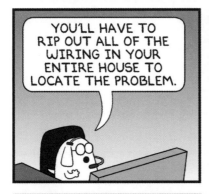

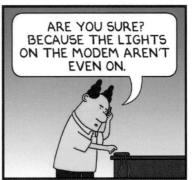

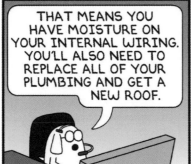

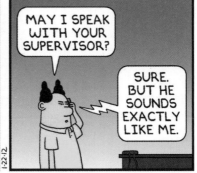

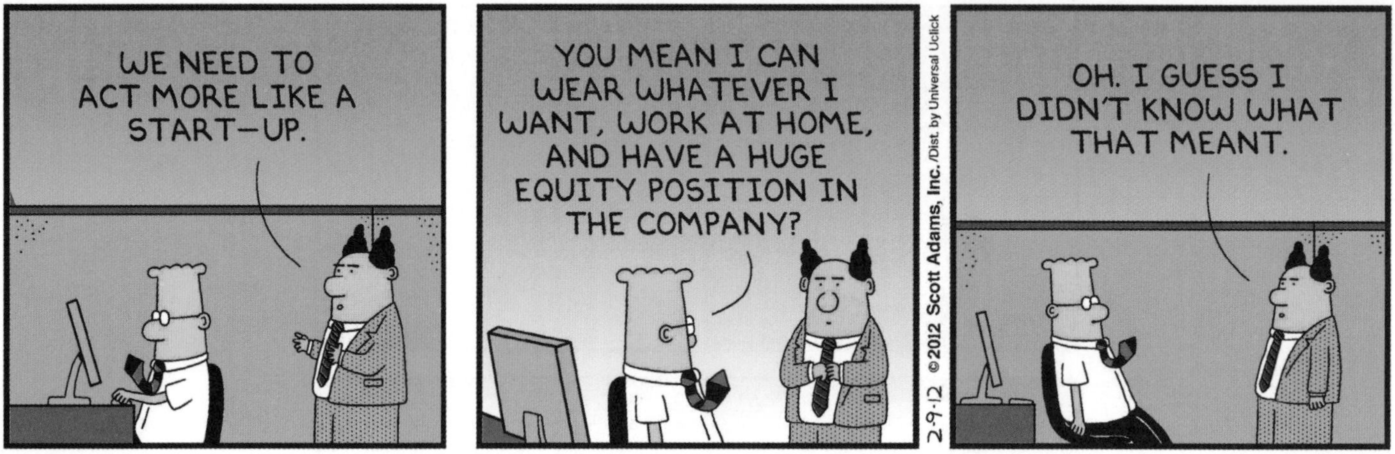
WE NEED TO ACT MORE LIKE A START-UP.
YOU MEAN I CAN WEAR WHATEVER I WANT, WORK AT HOME, AND HAVE A HUGE EQUITY POSITION IN THE COMPANY?
2-9-12 ©2012 Scott Adams, Inc./Dist. by Universal Uclick
OH. I GUESS I DIDN'T KNOW WHAT THAT MEANT.

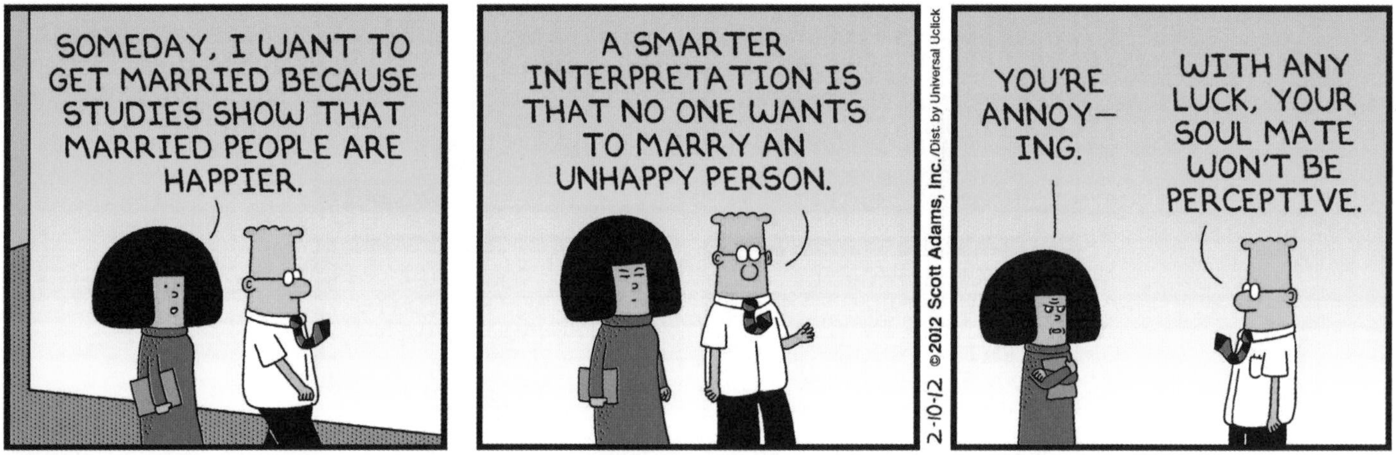
SOMEDAY, I WANT TO GET MARRIED BECAUSE STUDIES SHOW THAT MARRIED PEOPLE ARE HAPPIER.
A SMARTER INTERPRETATION IS THAT NO ONE WANTS TO MARRY AN UNHAPPY PERSON.
2-10-12 ©2012 Scott Adams, Inc./Dist. by Universal Uclick
YOU'RE ANNOY-ING.
WITH ANY LUCK, YOUR SOUL MATE WON'T BE PERCEPTIVE.

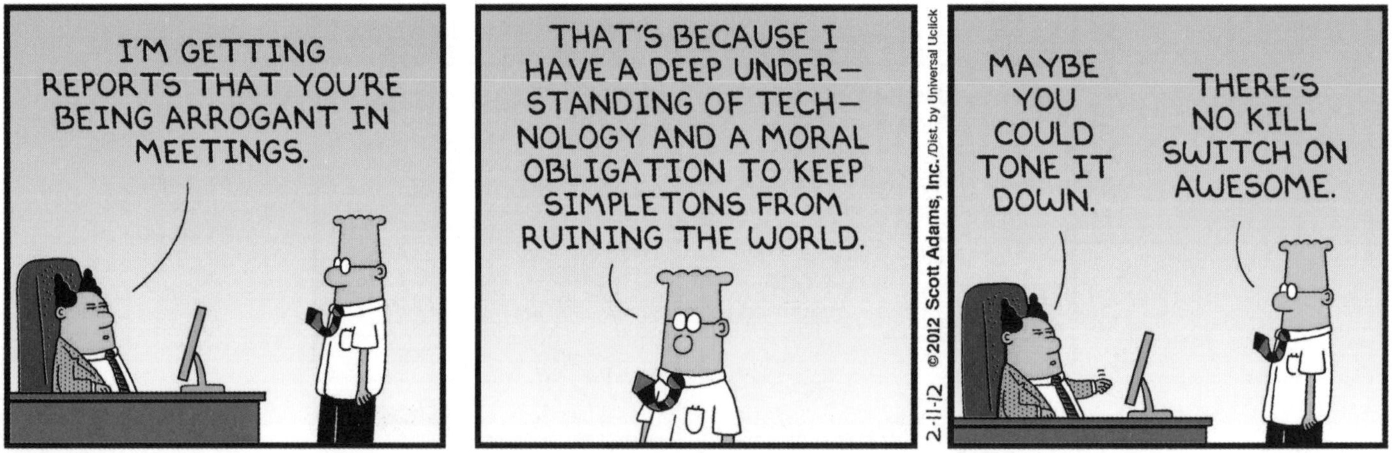
I'M GETTING REPORTS THAT YOU'RE BEING ARROGANT IN MEETINGS.
THAT'S BECAUSE I HAVE A DEEP UNDER-STANDING OF TECH-NOLOGY AND A MORAL OBLIGATION TO KEEP SIMPLETONS FROM RUINING THE WORLD.
2-11-12 ©2012 Scott Adams, Inc./Dist. by Universal Uclick
MAYBE YOU COULD TONE IT DOWN.
THERE'S NO KILL SWITCH ON AWESOME.

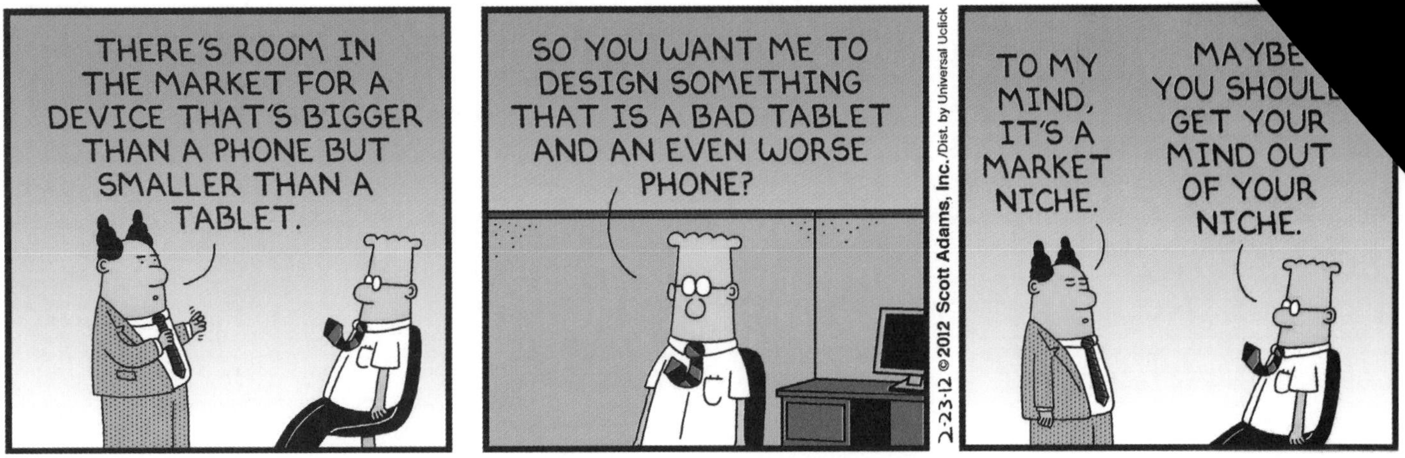
THERE'S ROOM IN THE MARKET FOR A DEVICE THAT'S BIGGER THAN A PHONE BUT SMALLER THAN A TABLET.
SO YOU WANT ME TO DESIGN SOMETHING THAT IS A BAD TABLET AND AN EVEN WORSE PHONE?
2-23-12 ©2012 Scott Adams, Inc./Dist. by Universal Uclick
TO MY MIND, IT'S A MARKET NICHE.
MAYBE
YOU SHOUL
GET YOUR MIND OUT OF YOUR NICHE.

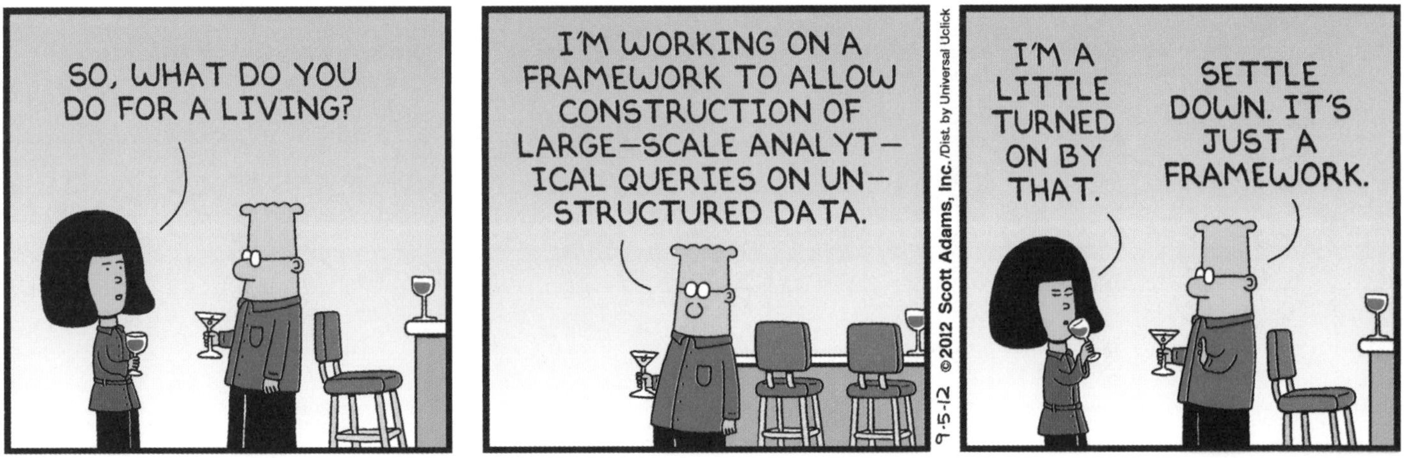
SO, WHAT DO YOU DO FOR A LIVING?
I'M WORKING ON A FRAMEWORK TO ALLOW CONSTRUCTION OF LARGE-SCALE ANALYT-ICAL QUERIES ON UN-STRUCTURED DATA.
9-5-12 ©2012 Scott Adams, Inc./Dist. by Universal Uclick
I'M A LITTLE TURNED ON BY THAT.
SETTLE DOWN. IT'S JUST A FRAMEWORK.

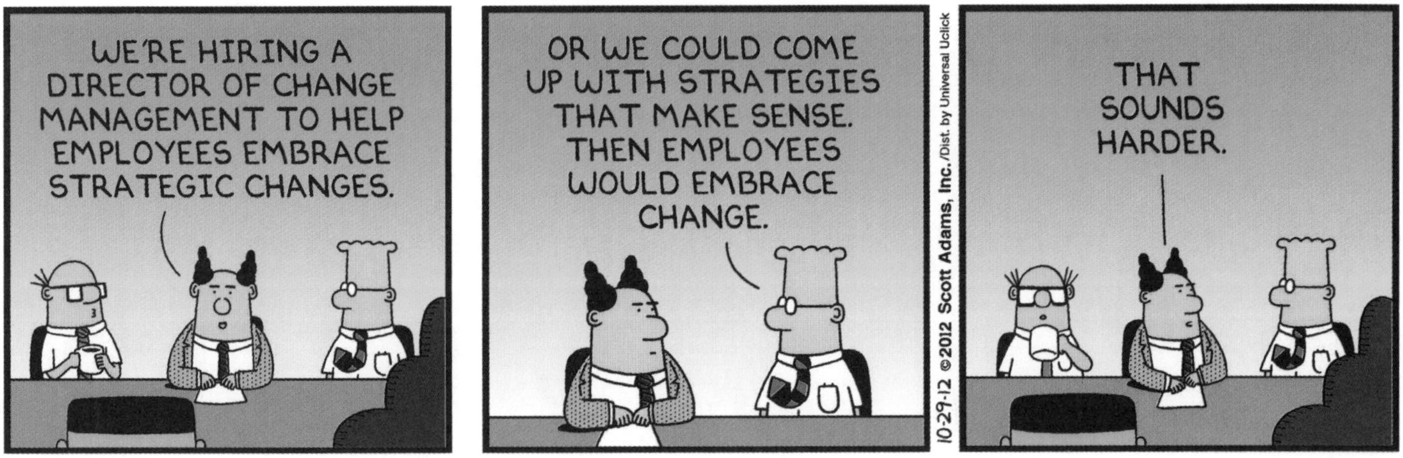
WE'RE HIRING A DIRECTOR OF CHANGE MANAGEMENT TO HELP EMPLOYEES EMBRACE STRATEGIC CHANGES.
OR WE COULD COME UP WITH STRATEGIES THAT MAKE SENSE. THEN EMPLOYEES WOULD EMBRACE CHANGE.
10-29-12 ©2012 Scott Adams, Inc./Dist. by Universal Uclick
THAT SOUNDS HARDER.

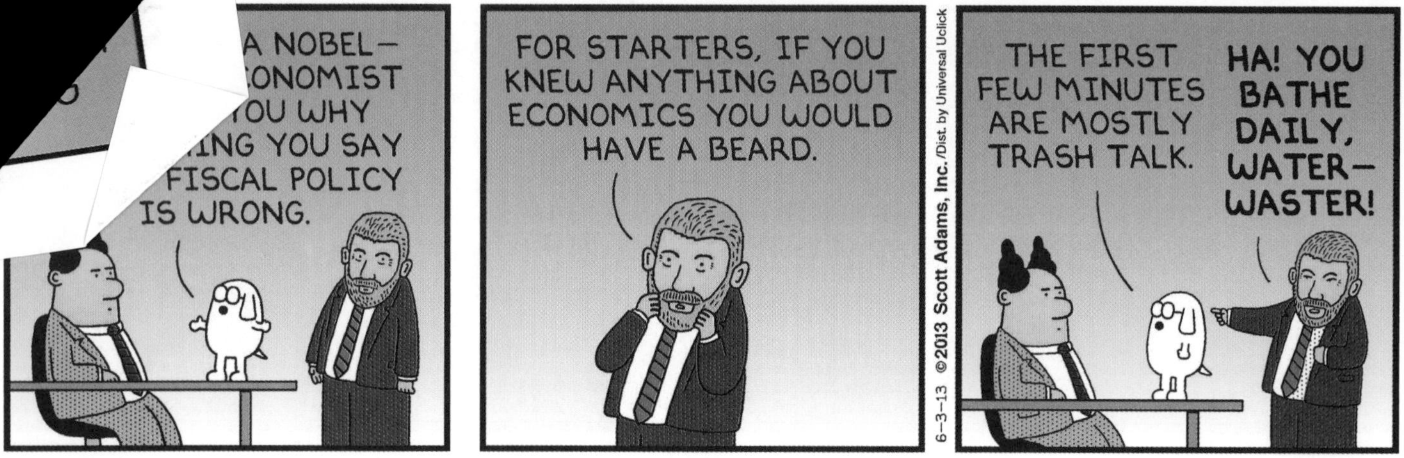
A NOBEL—
CONOMIST
YOU WHY
ING YOU SAY
FISCAL POLICY
IS WRONG.
FOR STARTERS, IF YOU KNEW ANYTHING ABOUT ECONOMICS YOU WOULD HAVE A BEARD.
6-3-13 ©2013 Scott Adams, Inc./Dist. by Universal Uclick
THE FIRST FEW MINUTES ARE MOSTLY TRASH TALK.
HA! YOU BATHE DAILY, WATER—WASTER!

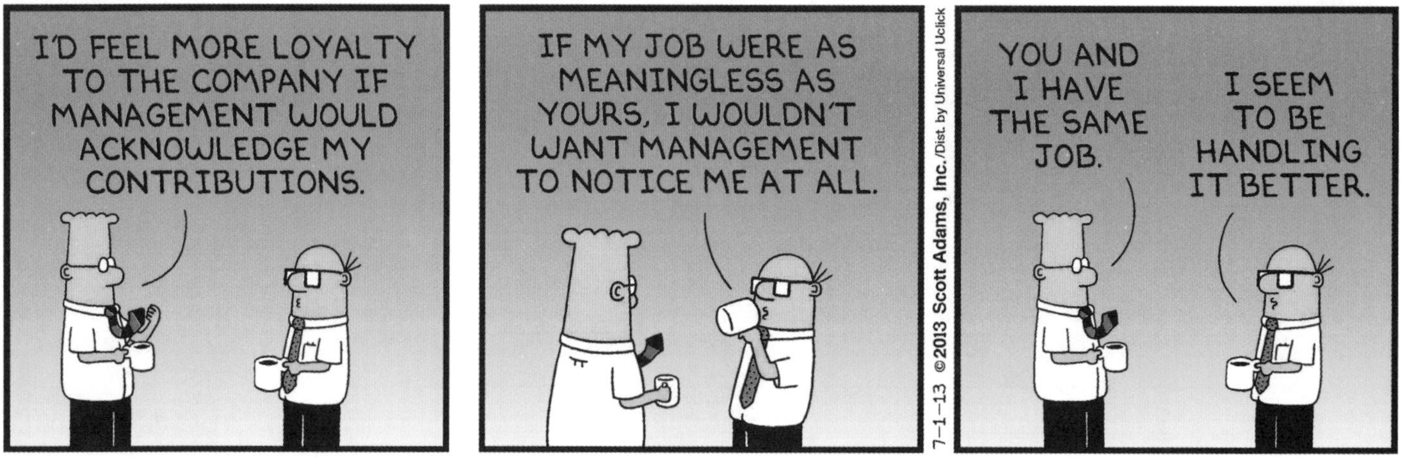
I'D FEEL MORE LOYALTY TO THE COMPANY IF MANAGEMENT WOULD ACKNOWLEDGE MY CONTRIBUTIONS.
IF MY JOB WERE AS MEANINGLESS AS YOURS, I WOULDN'T WANT MANAGEMENT TO NOTICE ME AT ALL.
7-1-13 ©2013 Scott Adams, Inc./Dist. by Universal Uclick
YOU AND I HAVE THE SAME JOB.
I SEEM TO BE HANDLING IT BETTER.

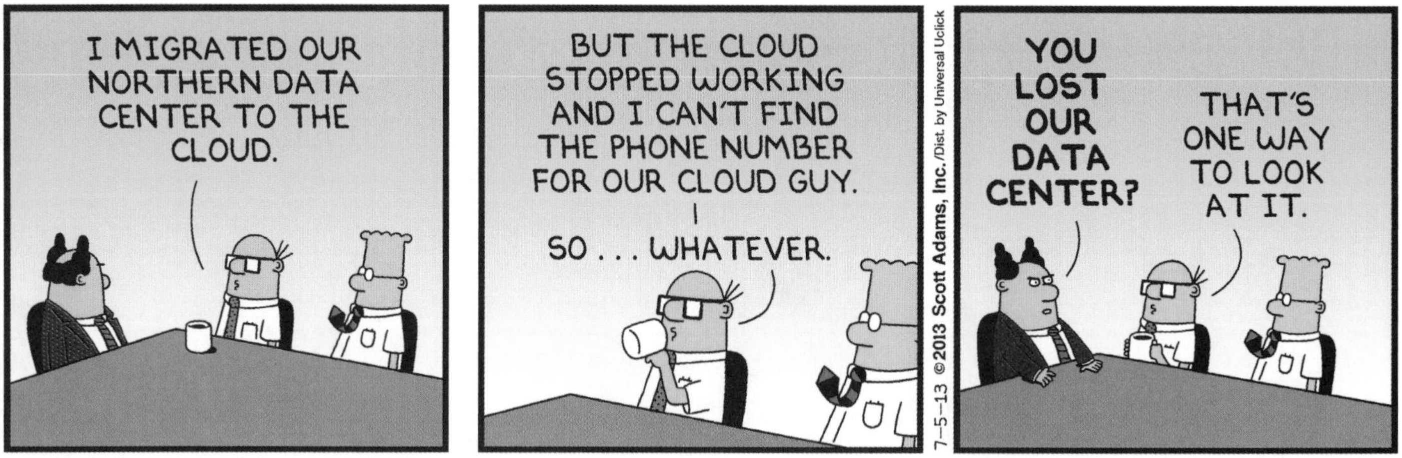
I MIGRATED OUR NORTHERN DATA CENTER TO THE CLOUD.
BUT THE CLOUD STOPPED WORKING AND I CAN'T FIND THE PHONE NUMBER FOR OUR CLOUD GUY.
SO . . . WHATEVER.
7-5-13 ©2013 Scott Adams, Inc./Dist. by Universal Uclick
YOU LOST OUR DATA CENTER?
THAT'S ONE WAY TO LOOK AT IT.

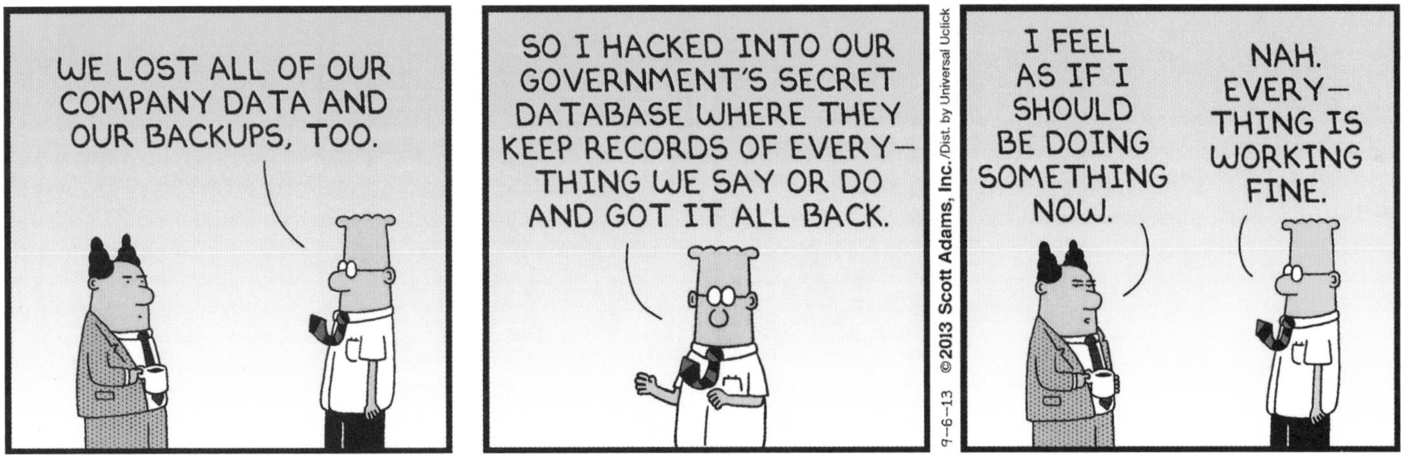
WE LOST ALL OF OUR COMPANY DATA AND OUR BACKUPS, TOO.
SO I HACKED INTO OUR GOVERNMENT'S SECRET DATABASE WHERE THEY KEEP RECORDS OF EVERY-THING WE SAY OR DO AND GOT IT ALL BACK.
9-6-13 ©2013 Scott Adams, Inc./Dist. by Universal Uclick
I FEEL AS IF I SHOULD BE DOING SOMETHING NOW.
NAH. EVERY-THING IS WORKING FINE.

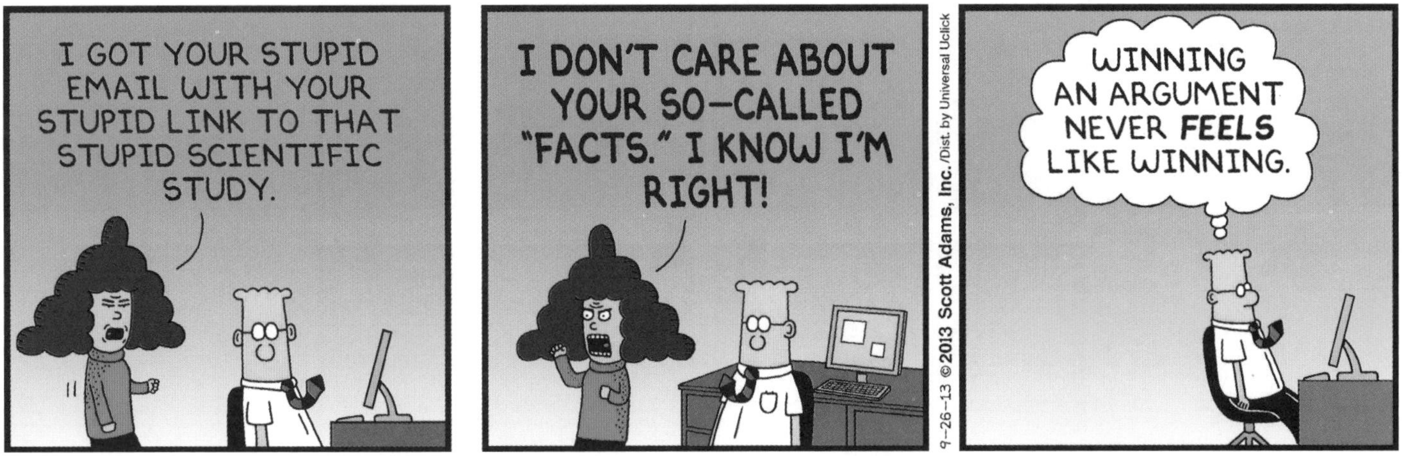
I GOT YOUR STUPID EMAIL WITH YOUR STUPID LINK TO THAT STUPID SCIENTIFIC STUDY.
I DON'T CARE ABOUT YOUR SO-CALLED "FACTS." I KNOW I'M RIGHT!
9-26-13 ©2013 Scott Adams, Inc./Dist. by Universal Uclick
WINNING AN ARGUMENT NEVER **FEELS** LIKE WINNING.

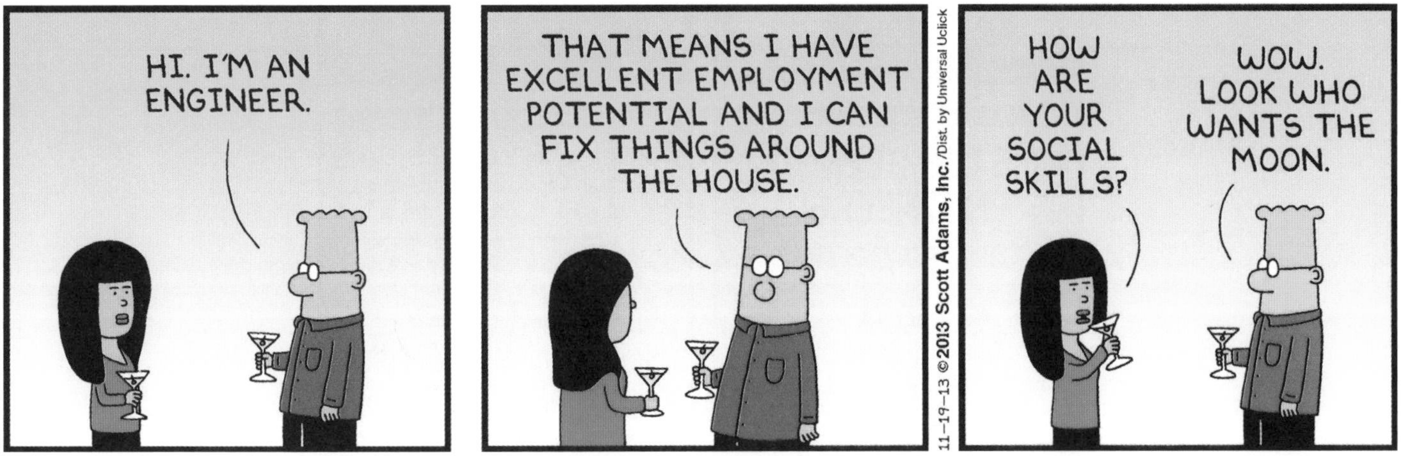
HI. I'M AN ENGINEER.
THAT MEANS I HAVE EXCELLENT EMPLOYMENT POTENTIAL AND I CAN FIX THINGS AROUND THE HOUSE.
11-19-13 ©2013 Scott Adams, Inc./Dist. by Universal Uclick
HOW ARE YOUR SOCIAL SKILLS?
WOW. LOOK WHO WANTS THE MOON.

WE'RE GOING TO USE THE JEFF BEZOS RULE OF MEETINGS.
BEZOS SAYS YOU SHOULD NEVER HAVE A MEETING THAT IS SO BIG YOU CAN'T FEED EVERYONE WITH TWO PIZZAS.
I CAN EAT TWO PIZZAS BY MYSELF.
HOW DO YOU COUNT THE PEOPLE WHO HAVE GLUTEN SENSITIVITY AND DON'T EAT PIZZA?
IF I APPLY ZENO'S PARADOX TO THE SLICE SIZE, CAN I HAVE INFINITE ATTENDEES?
AND WHAT DOES IT MEAN TO "FEED" EVERYONE? DO THEY NEED TO BE TOTALLY FULL?
STOP BEING ENGINEERS!
HOW DOES CHEESE BREAD FIT INTO THIS?
©2014 Scott Adams, Inc./Dist. by Universal Uclick
2-2-14

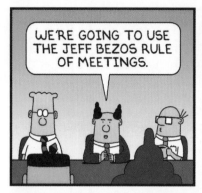

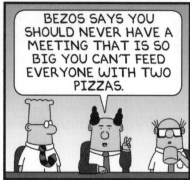

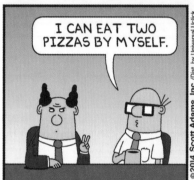

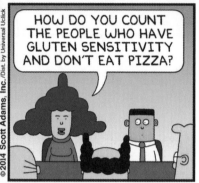

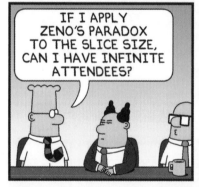

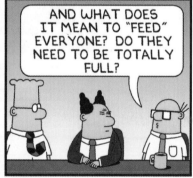

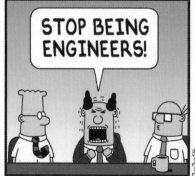

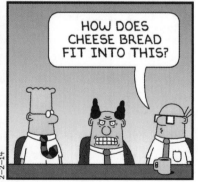

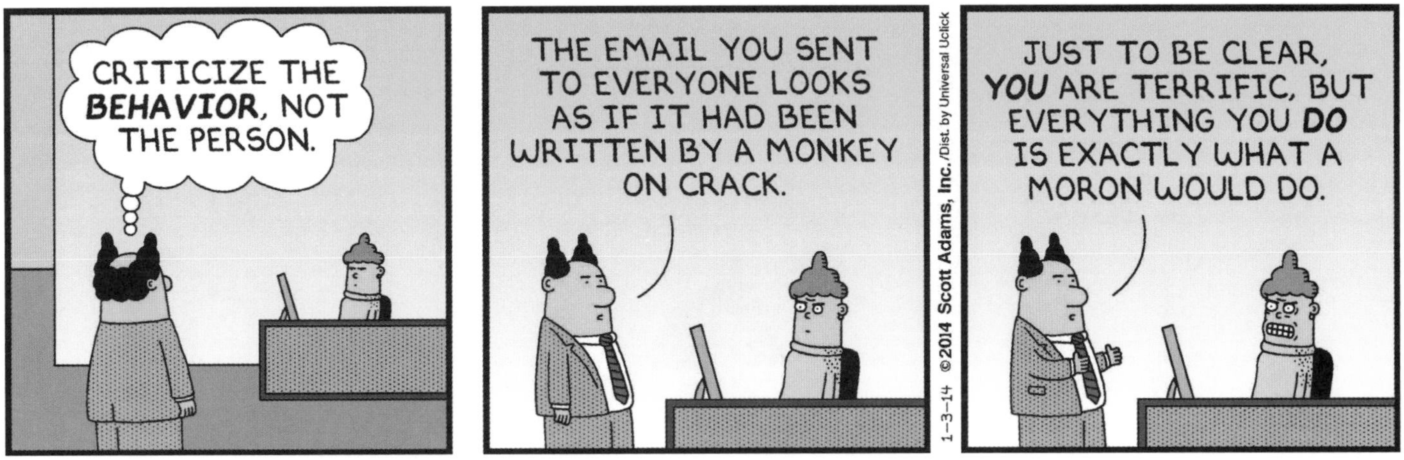
CRITICIZE THE **BEHAVIOR**, NOT THE PERSON.
THE EMAIL YOU SENT TO EVERYONE LOOKS AS IF IT HAD BEEN WRITTEN BY A MONKEY ON CRACK.
1-3-14 ©2014 Scott Adams, Inc./Dist. by Universal Uclick
JUST TO BE CLEAR, ***YOU*** ARE TERRIFIC, BUT EVERYTHING YOU **DO** IS EXACTLY WHAT A MORON WOULD DO.

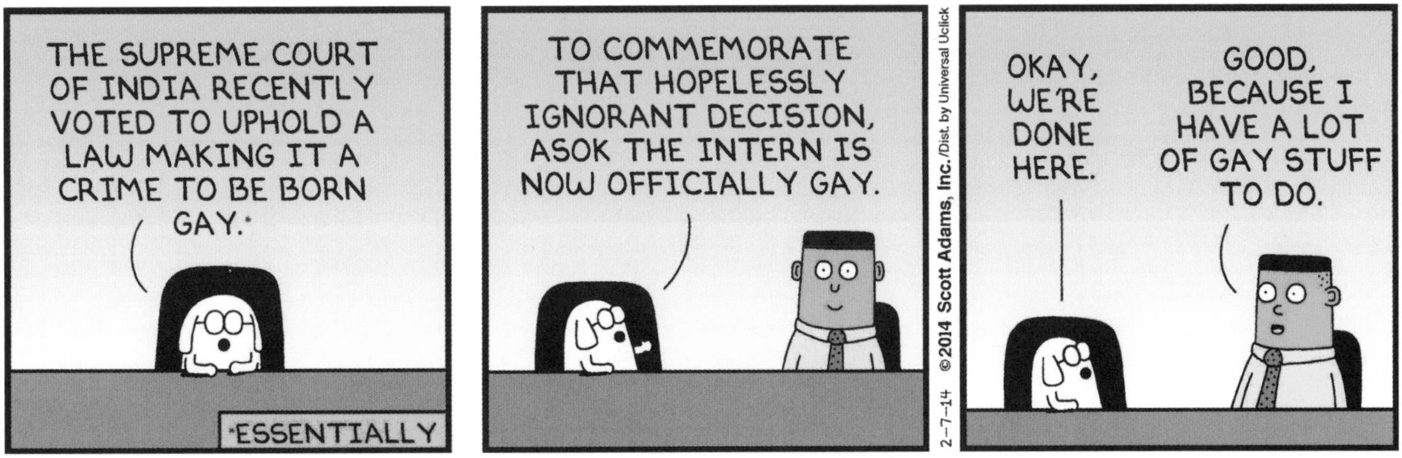
THE SUPREME COURT OF INDIA RECENTLY VOTED TO UPHOLD A LAW MAKING IT A CRIME TO BE BORN GAY.*
*ESSENTIALLY
TO COMMEMORATE THAT HOPELESSLY IGNORANT DECISION, ASOK THE INTERN IS NOW OFFICIALLY GAY.
2-7-14 ©2014 Scott Adams, Inc./Dist. by Universal Uclick
OKAY, WE'RE DONE HERE.
GOOD, BECAUSE I HAVE A LOT OF GAY STUFF TO DO.

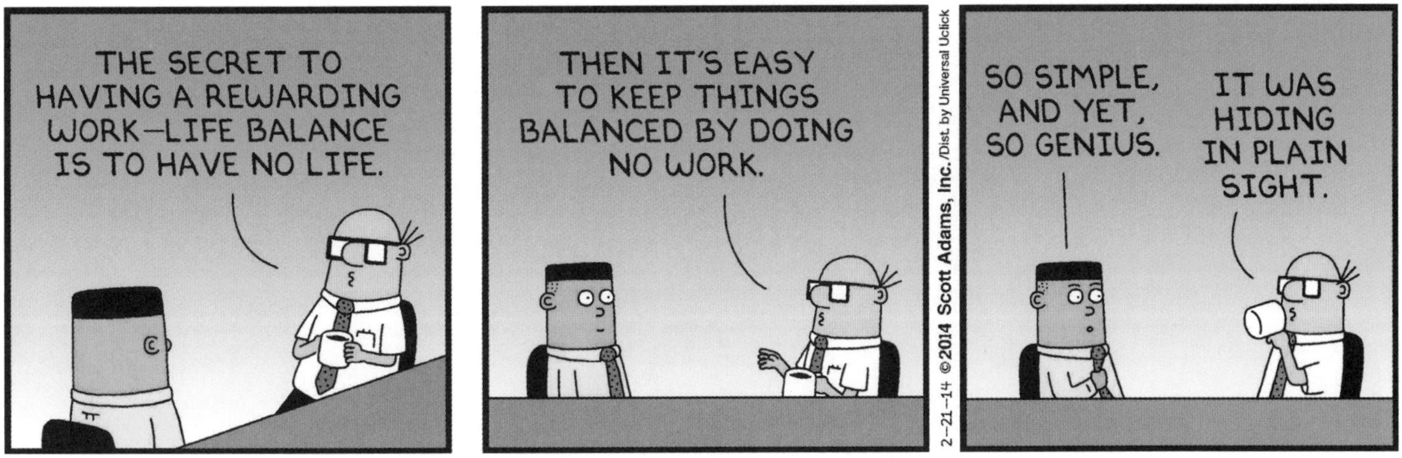
THE SECRET TO HAVING A REWARDING WORK-LIFE BALANCE IS TO HAVE NO LIFE.
THEN IT'S EASY TO KEEP THINGS BALANCED BY DOING NO WORK.
2-21-14 ©2014 Scott Adams, Inc./Dist. by Universal Uclick
SO SIMPLE, AND YET, SO GENIUS.
IT WAS HIDING IN PLAIN SIGHT.

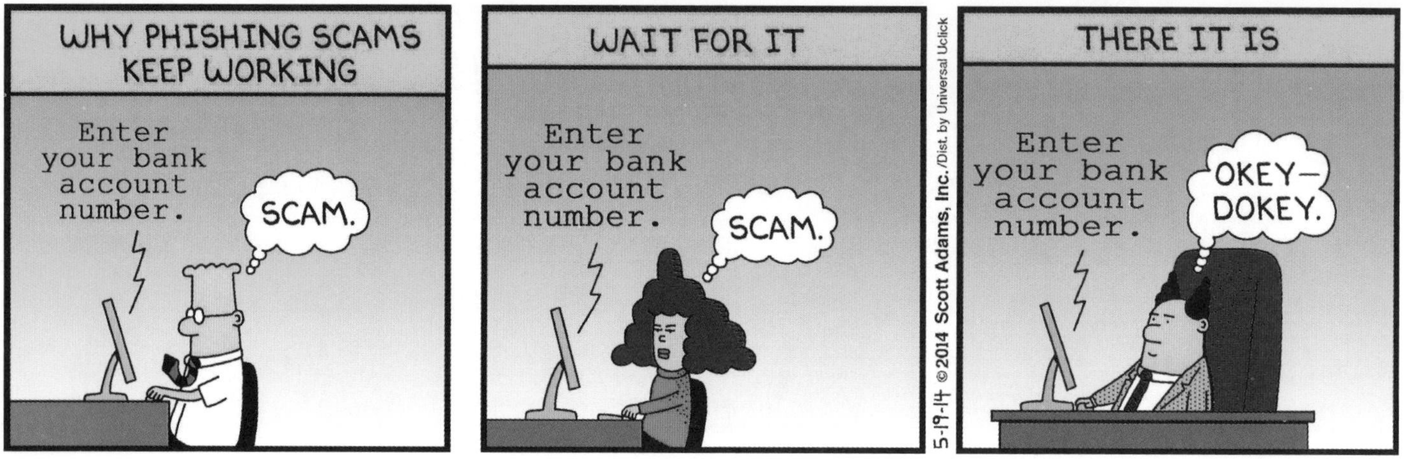
WHY PHISHING SCAMS KEEP WORKING
Enter your bank account number.
SCAM.
WAIT FOR IT
Enter your bank account number.
SCAM.
5-19-14 ©2014 Scott Adams, Inc./Dist. by Universal Uclick
THERE IT IS
Enter your bank account number.
OKEY-DOKEY.

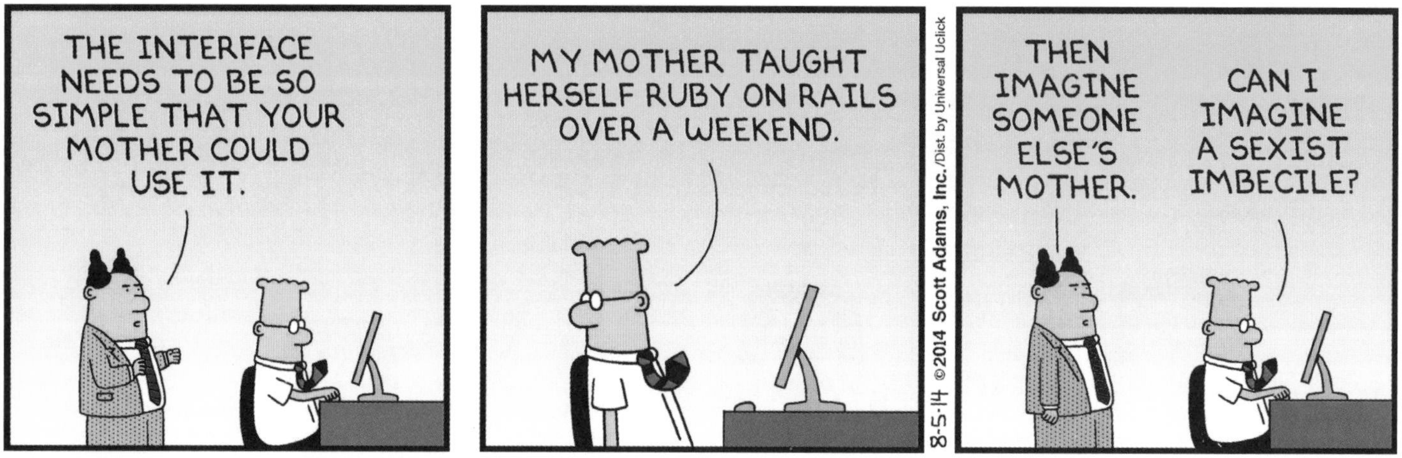
THE INTERFACE NEEDS TO BE SO SIMPLE THAT YOUR MOTHER COULD USE IT.
MY MOTHER TAUGHT HERSELF RUBY ON RAILS OVER A WEEKEND.
8-5-14 ©2014 Scott Adams, Inc./Dist. by Universal Uclick
THEN IMAGINE SOMEONE ELSE'S MOTHER.
CAN I IMAGINE A SEXIST IMBECILE?

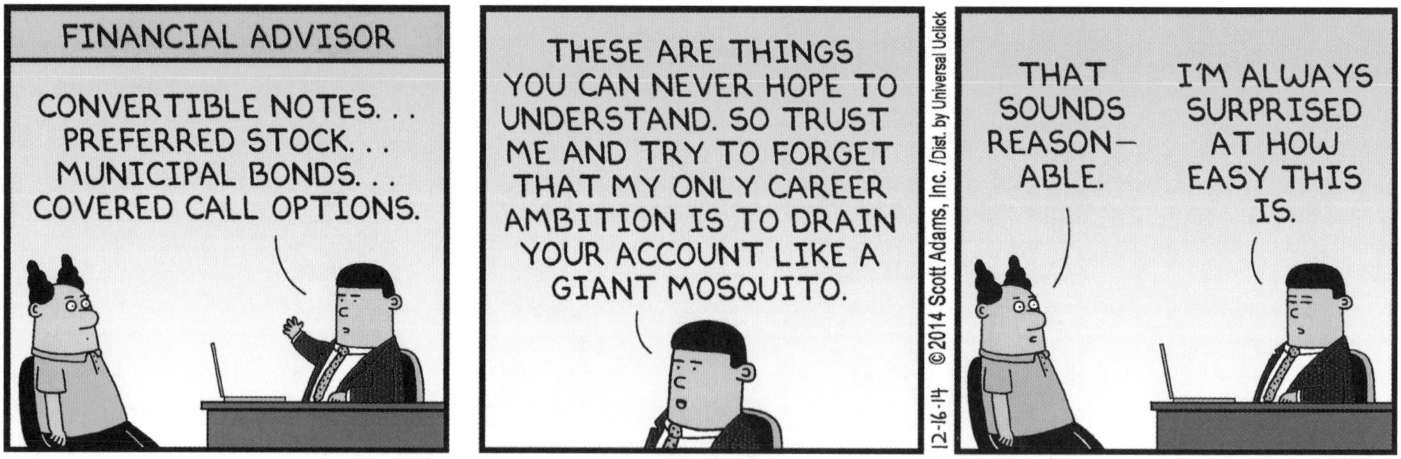
FINANCIAL ADVISOR
CONVERTIBLE NOTES... PREFERRED STOCK... MUNICIPAL BONDS... COVERED CALL OPTIONS.
THESE ARE THINGS YOU CAN NEVER HOPE TO UNDERSTAND. SO TRUST ME AND TRY TO FORGET THAT MY ONLY CAREER AMBITION IS TO DRAIN YOUR ACCOUNT LIKE A GIANT MOSQUITO.
12-16-14 ©2014 Scott Adams, Inc. /Dist. by Universal Uclick
THAT SOUNDS REASON-ABLE.
I'M ALWAYS SURPRISED AT HOW EASY THIS IS.

THAT DOESN'T SOUND LIKE A WORK CALL.
IT ISN'T.
I DON'T HAVE TIME TO DO MY PERSONAL STUFF ON MY OWN TIME. I HAVE TO DO IT ON WORK TIME.
I PAY YOU TO DO WORK STUFF, NOT PERSONAL STUFF.
© 2015 Scott Adams, Inc. /Dist. by Universal Uclick
THEN HOW WOULD I GET ALL OF MY PERSONAL STUFF DONE?
THAT'S NOT MY PROBLEM.
THEN WHY DID YOU BRING IT UP?
BECAUSE I NEED YOU TO DO WORK.
I TOLD YOU I CAN'T GET ALL OF MY PERSONAL STUFF DONE IF I DO YOUR WORK!
OKAY, OKAY.
1-4-15
I PROBABLY COULD HAVE HANDLED THAT BETTER.

HOW'S THE SOFTWARE COMING ALONG?
WE'RE IN THE ZENO'S PARADOX PHASE OF THE PROJECT.
THE WHAT?
© 2016 Scott Adams, Inc./Dist. by Universal Uclick
IT MEANS EVERY STEP WE TAKE GETS US HALFWAY CLOSER TO LAUNCH.
CAN YOU KEEP UP THAT PACE?
I'M HOPING IT WILL LOOK THAT WAY.
IS ZENO'S PARADOX A REAL THING?
YOU'LL FIND OUT.
1-31-16
NEXT WEEK
HOW'S YOUR PROJECT?
HALFWAY CLOSER THAN LAST WEEK!

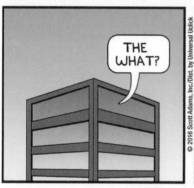

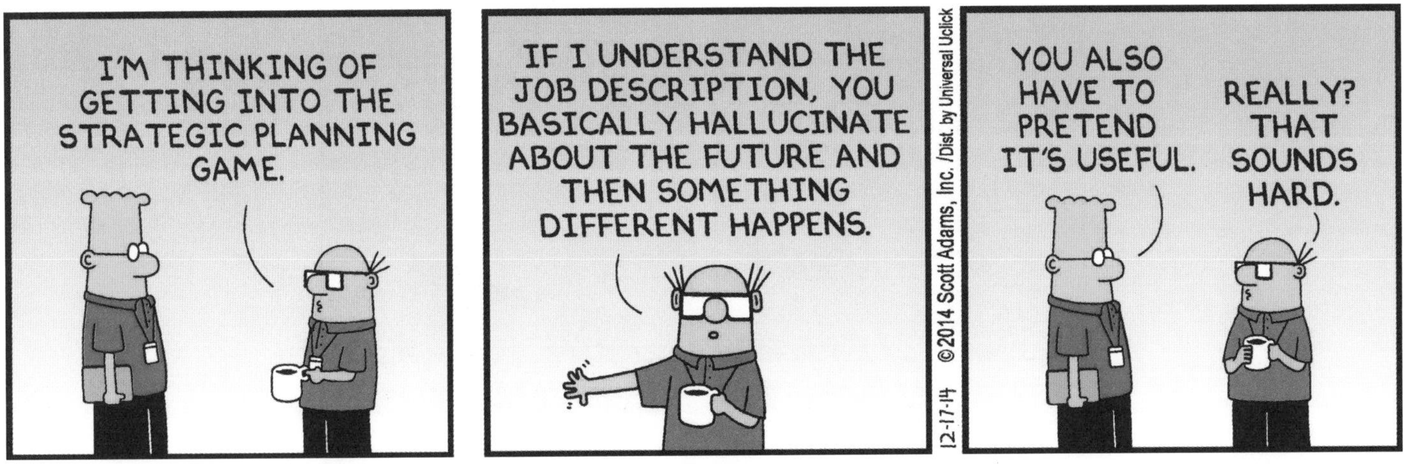
I'M THINKING OF GETTING INTO THE STRATEGIC PLANNING GAME.
IF I UNDERSTAND THE JOB DESCRIPTION, YOU BASICALLY HALLUCINATE ABOUT THE FUTURE AND THEN SOMETHING DIFFERENT HAPPENS.
12-17-14 ©2014 Scott Adams, Inc. /Dist. by Universal Uclick
YOU ALSO HAVE TO PRETEND IT'S USEFUL.
REALLY? THAT SOUNDS HARD.

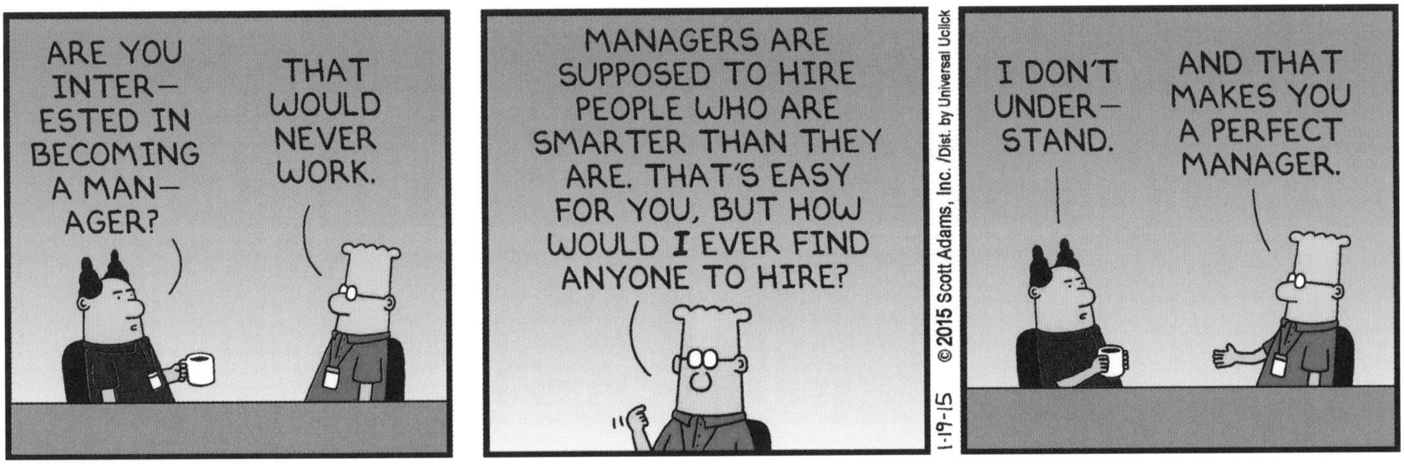
ARE YOU INTER-ESTED IN BECOMING A MAN-AGER?
THAT WOULD NEVER WORK.
MANAGERS ARE SUPPOSED TO HIRE PEOPLE WHO ARE SMARTER THAN THEY ARE. THAT'S EASY FOR YOU, BUT HOW WOULD I EVER FIND ANYONE TO HIRE?
1-19-15 © 2015 Scott Adams, Inc. /Dist. by Universal Uclick
I DON'T UNDER-STAND.
AND THAT MAKES YOU A PERFECT MANAGER.

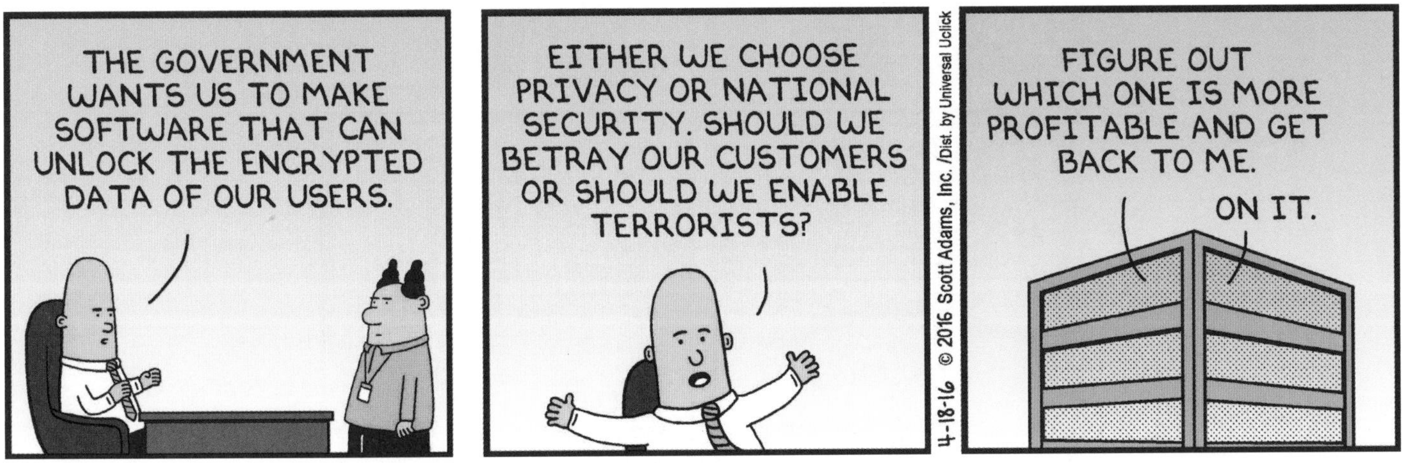
THE GOVERNMENT WANTS US TO MAKE SOFTWARE THAT CAN UNLOCK THE ENCRYPTED DATA OF OUR USERS.
EITHER WE CHOOSE PRIVACY OR NATIONAL SECURITY. SHOULD WE BETRAY OUR CUSTOMERS OR SHOULD WE ENABLE TERRORISTS?
4-18-16 © 2016 Scott Adams, Inc. /Dist. by Universal Uclick
FIGURE OUT WHICH ONE IS MORE PROFITABLE AND GET BACK TO ME.
ON IT.

I SIMPLIFIED THE USER INTERFACE AS YOU SUGGESTED.
YOU WANTED ONE BUTTON TO DO ELEVEN DIFFERENT FUNCTIONS.
IT WASN'T EASY, BUT I THINK YOU'LL BE PLEASED.
IF YOU WANT TO TURN UP THE VOLUME. . .
YOU HOLD THE BUTTON FOR EXACTLY FIVE SECONDS. . .
THEN DOUBLE–TAP, AND DOUBLE–TAP AGAIN. THEN HOLD FOR EXACTLY SIX SECONDS.
THEN PRESS IT ALL THE WAY DOWN, THEN HALFWAY UP, THEN 27% BACK DOWN. AND HOLD FOR NINE SECONDS.
OR YOU COULD ADMIT THAT YOU DON'T KNOW ANYTHING ABOUT INTERFACE DESIGN.
NEVER!
© 2016 Scott Adams, Inc./Dist. by Universal Uclick
6-12-16

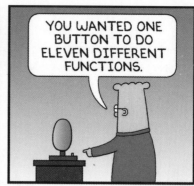

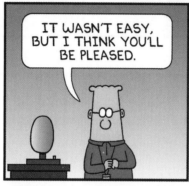

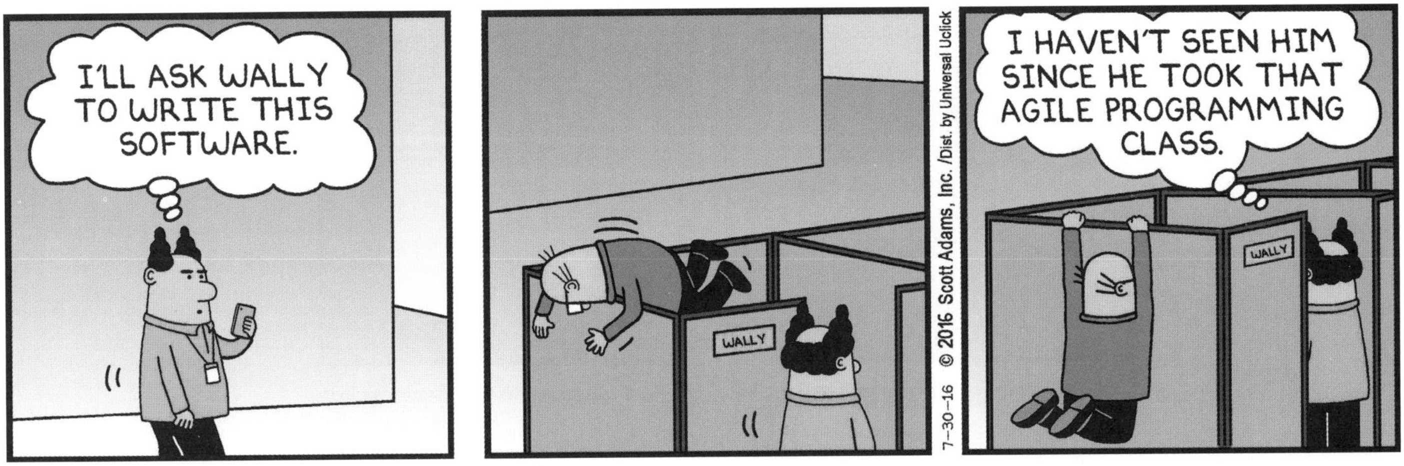
I'LL ASK WALLY TO WRITE THIS SOFTWARE.
WALLY
7-30-16 © 2016 Scott Adams, Inc. /Dist. by Universal Uclick
I HAVEN'T SEEN HIM SINCE HE TOOK THAT AGILE PROGRAMMING CLASS.
WALLY

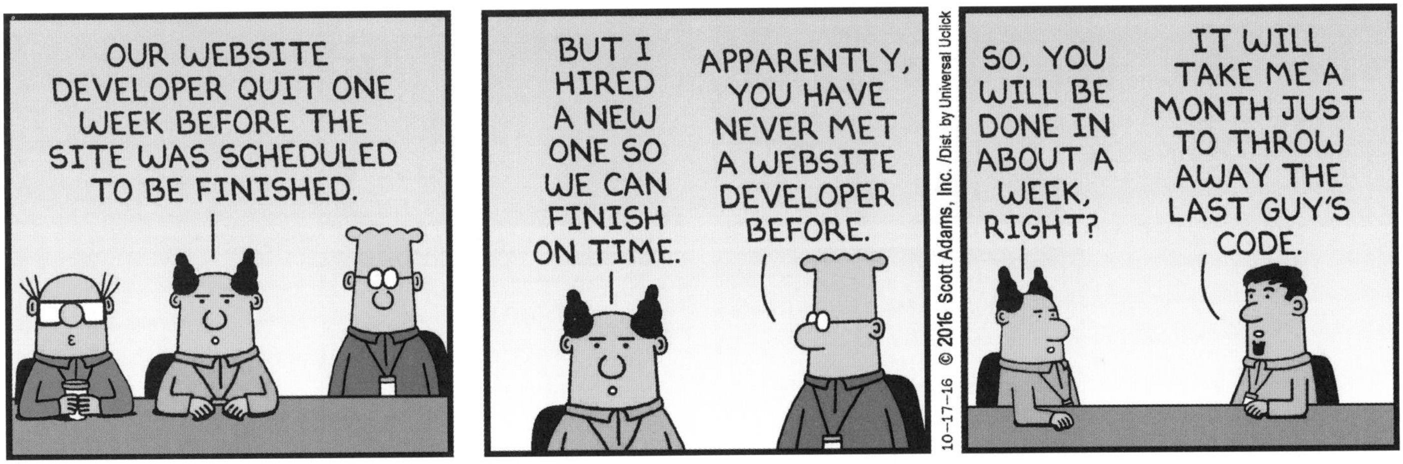
OUR WEBSITE DEVELOPER QUIT ONE WEEK BEFORE THE SITE WAS SCHEDULED TO BE FINISHED.
BUT I HIRED A NEW ONE SO WE CAN FINISH ON TIME.
APPARENTLY, YOU HAVE NEVER MET A WEBSITE DEVELOPER BEFORE.
10-17-16 © 2016 Scott Adams, Inc. /Dist. by Universal Uclick
SO, YOU WILL BE DONE IN ABOUT A WEEK, RIGHT?
IT WILL TAKE ME A MONTH JUST TO THROW AWAY THE LAST GUY'S CODE.

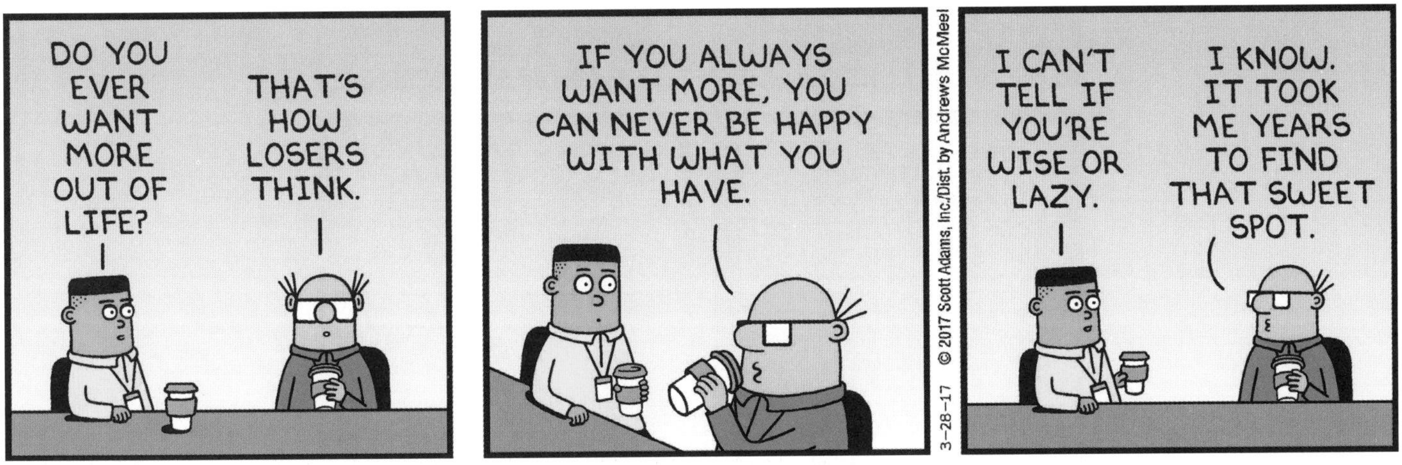
DO YOU EVER WANT MORE OUT OF LIFE?
THAT'S HOW LOSERS THINK.
IF YOU ALWAYS WANT MORE, YOU CAN NEVER BE HAPPY WITH WHAT YOU HAVE.
3-28-17 © 2017 Scott Adams, Inc./Dist. by Andrews McMeel
I CAN'T TELL IF YOU'RE WISE OR LAZY.
I KNOW. IT TOOK ME YEARS TO FIND THAT SWEET SPOT.

I INVITED A CLIMATE SCIENTIST TO EXPLAIN THE RISK OF CLIMATE CHANGE TO OUR COMPANY.
HUMAN ACTIVITY IS WARMING THE EARTH AND WILL LEAD TO A GLOBAL CATASTROPHE.
HOW DO SCIENTISTS KNOW THAT?
IT'S EASY. WE START WITH THE BASIC SCIENCE OF PHYSICS AND CHEMISTRY.
THEN WE MEASURE CHANGES IN TEMPER-ATURE AND CO2 OVER TIME.
WE PUT THAT DATA INTO DOZENS OF DIFFERENT CLIMATE MODELS AND IGNORE THE ONES THAT LOOK WRONG TO US.
THEN WE TAKE THAT OUTPUT AND RUN IT THROUGH LONG-TERM ECONOMIC MODELS OF THE SORT THAT HAVE NEVER BEEN RIGHT.
WHAT IF I DON'T TRUST THE ECONOMIC MODELS?
WHO HIRED THE SCIENCE DENIER?
© 2017 Scott Adams, Inc./Dist. by Andrews McMeel
5-14-17

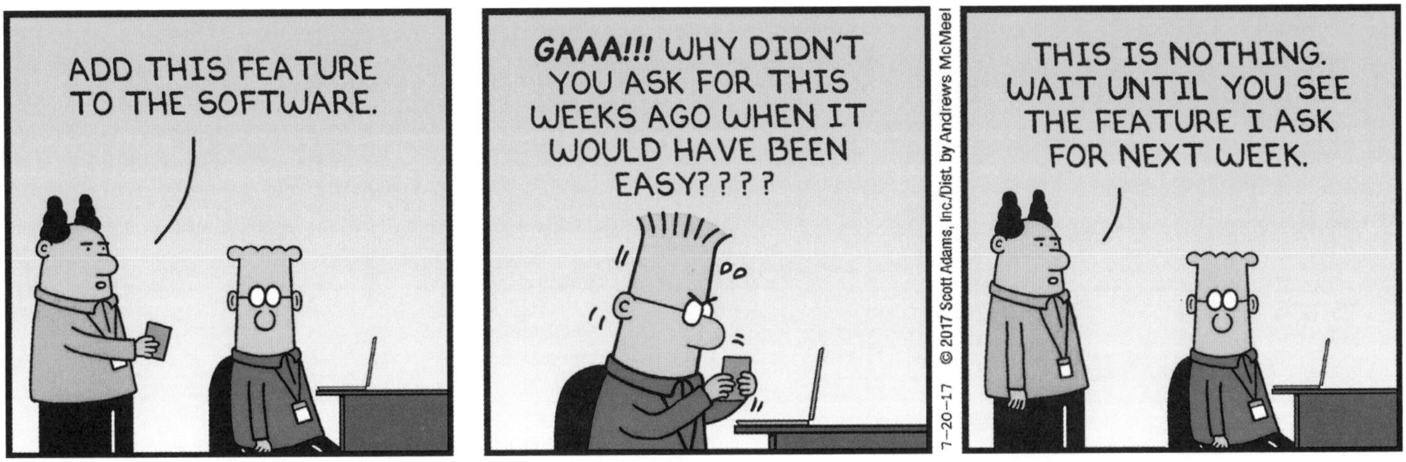
ADD THIS FEATURE TO THE SOFTWARE.
GAAA!!! WHY DIDN'T YOU ASK FOR THIS WEEKS AGO WHEN IT WOULD HAVE BEEN EASY????
7-20-17 © 2017 Scott Adams, Inc./Dist by Andrews McMeel
THIS IS NOTHING. WAIT UNTIL YOU SEE THE FEATURE I ASK FOR NEXT WEEK.

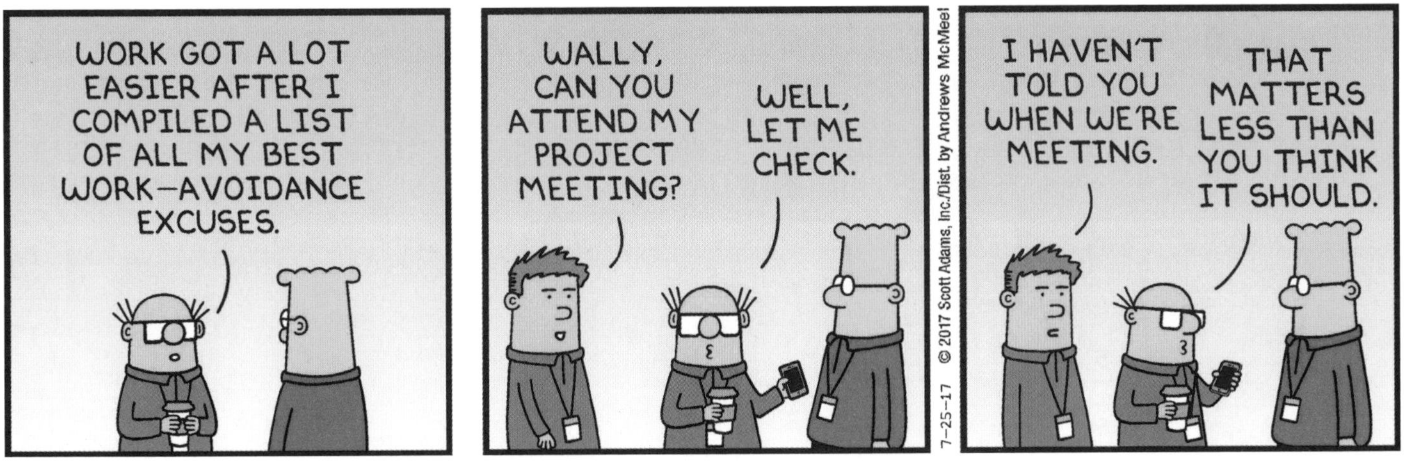
WORK GOT A LOT EASIER AFTER I COMPILED A LIST OF ALL MY BEST WORK-AVOIDANCE EXCUSES.
WALLY, CAN YOU ATTEND MY PROJECT MEETING?
WELL, LET ME CHECK.
7-25-17 © 2017 Scott Adams, Inc./Dist by Andrews McMeel
I HAVEN'T TOLD YOU WHEN WE'RE MEETING.
THAT MATTERS LESS THAN YOU THINK IT SHOULD.

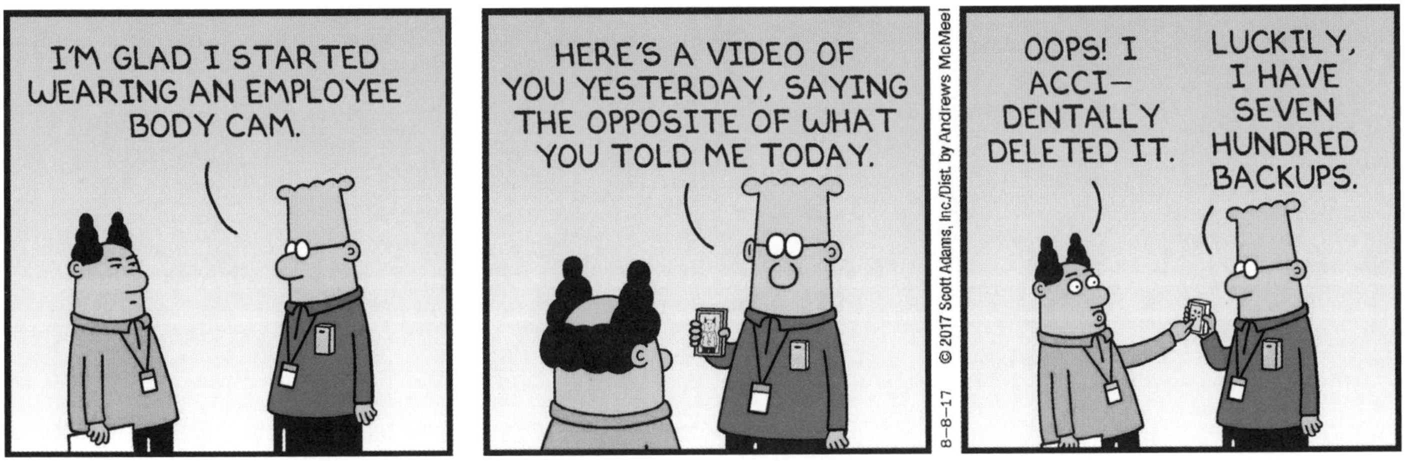
I'M GLAD I STARTED WEARING AN EMPLOYEE BODY CAM.
HERE'S A VIDEO OF YOU YESTERDAY, SAYING THE OPPOSITE OF WHAT YOU TOLD ME TODAY.
8-8-17 © 2017 Scott Adams, Inc./Dist by Andrews McMeel
OOPS! I ACCI-DENTALLY DELETED IT.
LUCKILY, I HAVE SEVEN HUNDRED BACKUPS.

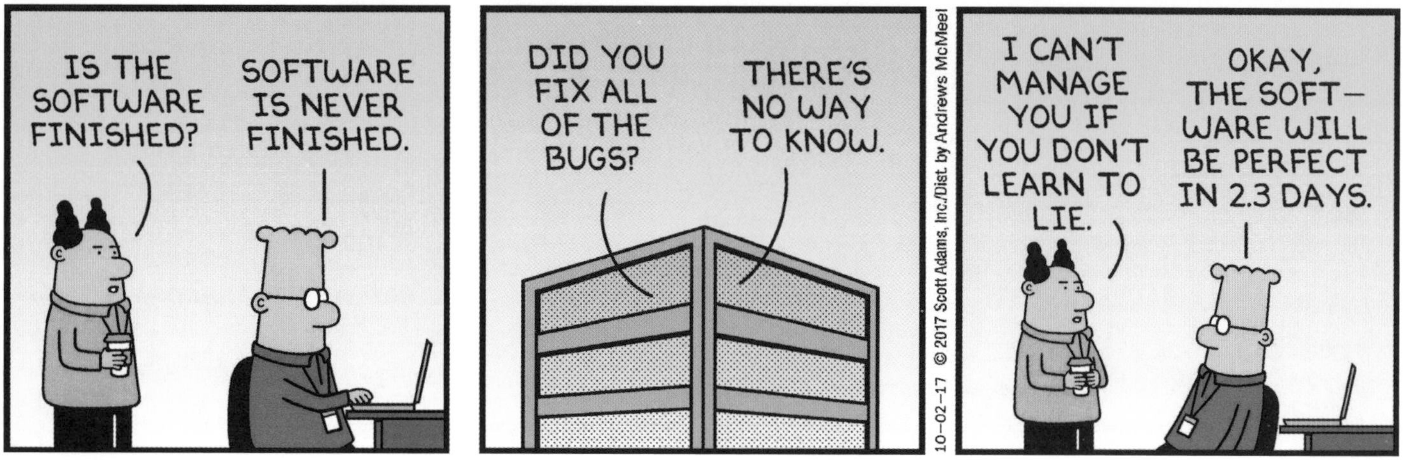
IS THE SOFTWARE FINISHED?
SOFTWARE IS NEVER FINISHED.
DID YOU FIX ALL OF THE BUGS?
THERE'S NO WAY TO KNOW.
10-02-17 © 2017 Scott Adams, Inc./Dist. by Andrews McMeel
I CAN'T MANAGE YOU IF YOU DON'T LEARN TO LIE.
OKAY, THE SOFT-WARE WILL BE PERFECT IN 2.3 DAYS.

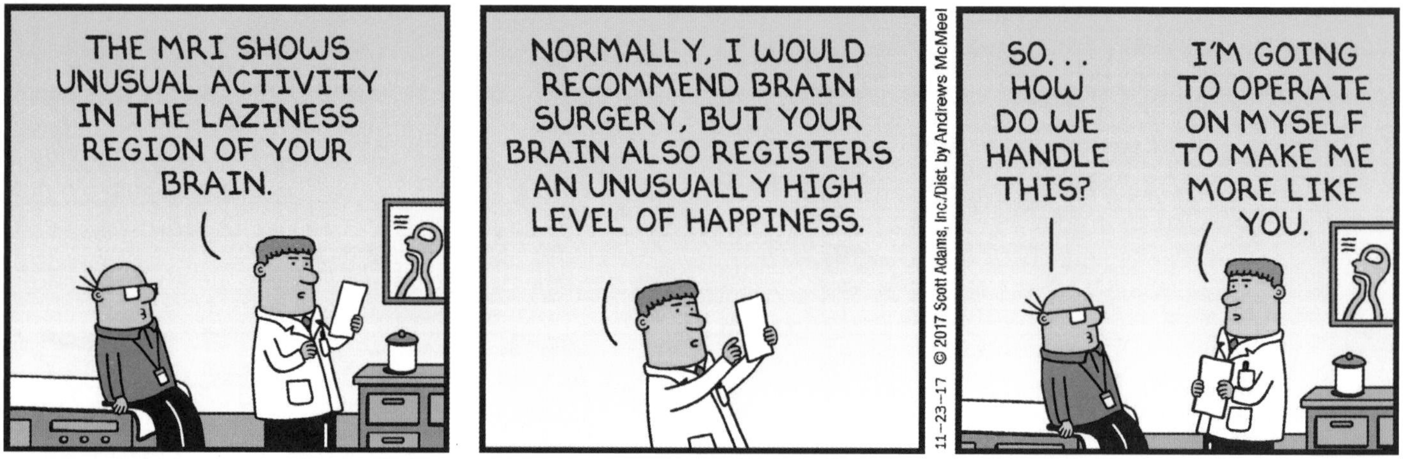
THE MRI SHOWS UNUSUAL ACTIVITY IN THE LAZINESS REGION OF YOUR BRAIN.
NORMALLY, I WOULD RECOMMEND BRAIN SURGERY, BUT YOUR BRAIN ALSO REGISTERS AN UNUSUALLY HIGH LEVEL OF HAPPINESS.
11-23-17 © 2017 Scott Adams, Inc./Dist. by Andrews McMeel
SO... HOW DO WE HANDLE THIS?
I'M GOING TO OPERATE ON MYSELF TO MAKE ME MORE LIKE YOU.

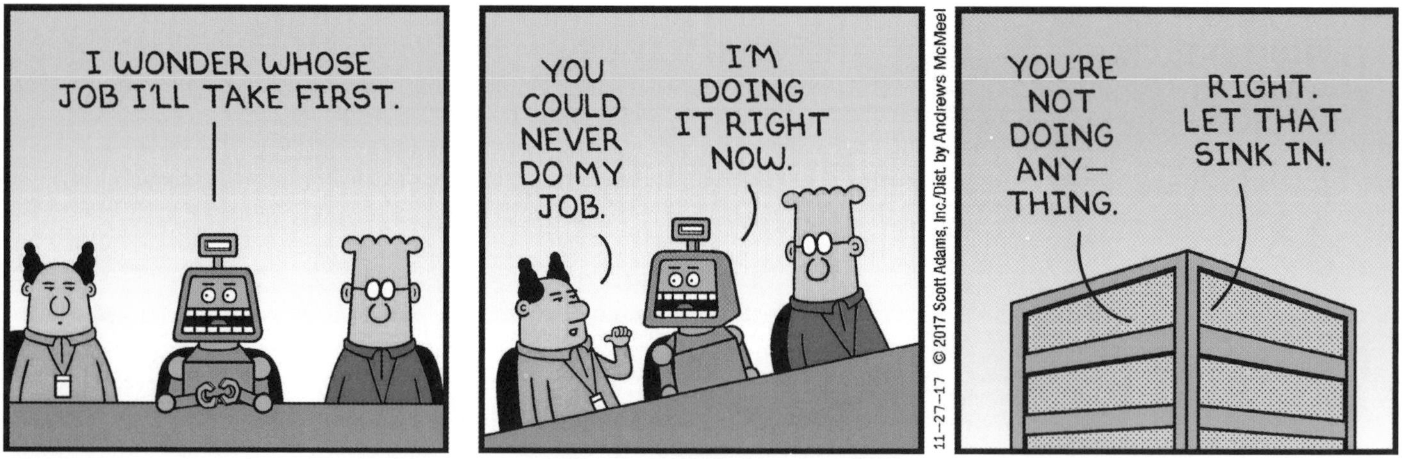
I WONDER WHOSE JOB I'LL TAKE FIRST.
YOU COULD NEVER DO MY JOB.
I'M DOING IT RIGHT NOW.
11-27-17 © 2017 Scott Adams, Inc./Dist. by Andrews McMeel
YOU'RE NOT DOING ANY-THING.
RIGHT. LET THAT SINK IN.

WHAT WOULD YOU SAY ARE YOUR BIGGEST WEAKNESSES?
I LIKE TO RIFLE THROUGH MY CO-WORKERS' DESKS WHEN THEY AREN'T LOOKING.
BUT I DON'T STEAL ANYTHING UNLESS I KNOW I CAN FRAME SOMEONE ELSE FOR THE CRIME.
I LEAVE FOR WORK AN HOUR LATE EVERY DAY AND BLAME TRAFFIC.
I AVOID ACCOM-PLISHING GOALS SO I WON'T FEEL LIKE A SELLOUT
SOMETIMES I'LL START A TRASH FIRE JUST TO GET OUT OF A MEETING.
AND I'VE GOTTEN EVERY ONE OF MY BOSSES FIRED FOR THINGS THEY DIDN'T SAY OR DO.
WOULD HE BE A GOOD FIT?
I LIKE WHAT HE HAS TO OFFER.
© 2018 Scott Adams, Inc./Dist. by Andrews McMeel
3-11-18

Andrews McMeel Publishing
a division of Andrews McMeel Universal
1130 Walnut Street, Kansas City, Missouri 64106
www.andrewsmcmeel.com

19 20 21 22 23 SDB 10 9 8 7 6 5 4 3 2 1

ISBN: 978-1-5248-5182-8

Library of Congress Control Number: 2019935463

www.dilbert.com

──── **ATTENTION: SCHOOLS AND BUSINESSES** ────

Andrews McMeel books are available at quantity discounts with bulk purchase for educational, business,
or sales promotional use. For information, please e-mail the Andrews McMeel Publishing
Special Sales Department: specialsales@amuniversal.com.